This splendid book offers a vivid analytical delineation of the multi-faceted PRC central authorities–Hong Kong SAR interactive dynamics under the "one country, two systems" formula. Illuminating this problematic center-region relationship with detailed case studies, Professor Lo's insightful work highlights the potentials as well as the limitations of this formula as actualized in Hong Kong to facilitate cross-Strait detente toward Beijing's much-cherished peaceful unification with Taiwan. Keen observers of Greater China development will benefit much from his masterful evaluation of the HKSAR experience's larger external strategic implications.
– *Ming K. Chan, Research Fellow, Hoover Institution, Stanford University*

This book by a distinguished political scientist is an in-depth study of the travail of two cities — absolutist Beijing and pluralist Hong Kong — during the crucial first decade of the HKSAR. Its incisive analysis of Hong Kong politics also provides a rich feast for thought on issues spanning the Taiwan Strait.   – *Bernard Luk, Professor, History Department, York University, Canada*

The most systemic analyses of the development of Hong Kong and its relationship with Beijing in the post-handover decade, with a thoughtful reference to Taiwan. Theoretically provocative and empirically rich, a must read for those concerned for the future of Hong Kong, Taiwan, and China.
– *Quansheng Zhao, Professor and Division Director, Comparative and Regional Studies, Director of Center for Asian Studies, American University, Washington, DC*

Sonny Lo's book is a remarkable *tour de force* of the "one country, two systems" actualization in Hong Kong. It presents a detailed overview of the interactions between the Beijing government and the HKSAR in the past decade as well as new political dynamics shaping Hong Kong's future. It is particularly interesting to read Lo's provocative exploration of the applicability of the Hong Kong model to Taiwan. A must read for anyone interested in the political dynamics of mainland China, Hong Kong, and Taiwan in the 21st century.
– *Suisheng Zhao, Professor of International Studies, University of Denver and Editor of the* Journal of Contemporary China

★ ★ ★ ★

This book critically assesses the implementation of the "one country, two systems" in the Hong Kong Special Administrative Region (HKSAR) from the political, judicial, legal, economic and societal dimensions.

The author contends that there has been a gradual process of mainlandization of the HKSAR, meaning that Hong Kong is increasingly economically dependent on the People's Republic of China (PRC), politically deferent to the central government on the scope and pace of democratic reforms, socially more patriotic toward the motherland and more prone to media self-censorship, and judicially more vulnerable to the interpretation of the Basic Law by the National People's Congress.

This book aims to achieve a breakthrough in relating the development of Hong Kong politics to the future of mainland China and Taiwan. By broadening the focus of the "one country, two systems" from governance to the process of Sino-British negotiations and their trust-building efforts, this book argues that the diplomats from mainland China and Taiwan can learn from the ways in which Hong Kong's political future was settled in 1982–1984. This is a book for students, researchers, scholars, diplomats and lay people.

★ ★ ★ ★

Sonny Shiu-Hing Lo is an Associate Professor in the Department of Political Science at the University of Waterloo, Ontario, Canada. He formerly taught Hong Kong politics at the Hong Kong University of Science and Technology (1993–1996) and at the University of Hong Kong (1996–2004). His single-authored books include *The Politics of Democratization in Hong Kong*, *Political Development in Macau* and *Governing Hong Kong: Legitimacy, Communication and Political Decay*. His new books are *The Politics of Cross-Border Crime in Greater China* and *Political Change in Macau*.

The Dynamics of Beijing–Hong Kong Relations

Hong Kong University Press thanks Xu Bing for writing the Press's name in his Square Word Calligraphy for the covers of its books. For further information, see p. iv.

The Dynamics of Beijing–Hong Kong Relations
A Model for Taiwan?

Sonny Shiu-Hing Lo

HONG KONG UNIVERSITY PRESS

Hong Kong University Press
14/F Hing Wai Centre
7 Tin Wan Praya Road
Aberdeen
Hong Kong

© Hong Kong University Press 2008

Hardback   ISBN 978-962-209-908-1
Paperback   ISBN 978-962-209-909-8

All rights reserved. No portion of this publication may be reproduced or transmitted in any form or by any means, electronic or mechanical, including photocopy, recording, or any information storage or retrieval system, without prior permission in writing from the publisher.

British Library Cataloguing-in-Publication Data
A catalogue record for this book is available from the British Library.

Secure On-line Ordering
http://www.hkupress.org

Printed and bound by Condor Production Ltd., Hong Kong, China.

Hong Kong University Press is honoured that Xu Bing, whose art explores the complex themes of language across cultures, has written the Press's name in his Square Word Calligraphy. This signals our commitment to cross-cultural thinking and the distinctive nature of our English-language books published in China.

"At first glance, Square Word Calligraphy appears to be nothing more unusual than Chinese characters, but in fact it is a new way of rendering English words in the format of a square so they resemble Chinese characters. Chinese viewers expect to be able to read Square Word Calligraphy but cannot. Western viewers, however are surprised to find they can read it. Delight erupts when meaning is unexpectedly revealed."

— Britta Erickson, *The Art of Xu Bing*

Contents

Acknowledgements		vii
Abbreviations		ix
Introduction		1
1.	Patron-Client Pluralism and Beijing's Relations with Hong Kong	7
2.	The Mainlandization of Hong Kong	39
3.	The Politics of Judicial Autonomy	81
4.	The Emergence of Constitutional Conventions	109
5.	The Implementation of the Basic Law	133
6.	Identity Change from the National Security Debate to Celebrations of the Tenth Anniversary	151
7.	The Election of the Hong Kong Deputies to the National People's Congress	185
8.	A Fusion of Mainland Chinese and Hong Kong Political Cultures in the 2007 Chief Executive Election	199
9.	Applying the Spirit of "One Country, Two Systems" to Taiwan's Political Future	227
10.	Conclusion	253
Notes		261
Bibliography		307
Index		323

List of Tables

Table 1.1	Patron-Client Relations between Beijing and Hong Kong's Political Actors	31
Table 2.1	Estimated Number of Participants on the July 1 Protests, 2003–2007	41
Table 2.2	The Evolving Self-Identity of the Hong Kong People, 1993–2007	64
Table 3.1	Events from the Court of Final Appeal's Ruling on January 29 to the NPC Interpretation of the Basic Law on June 26	84–85
Table 4.1	Distinguishing Conventions from Laws, Practices, Understandings, and Habits	110
Table 6.1	Timeline of the Development of the National Security Bill	152–153
Table 6.2	Some of the Local Groups Opposing Article 23 of the Basic Law	161–164
Table 7.1	The 54 Winners in the First Round of Voting	187
Table 7.2	Election Results of the Hong Kong Deputies to the Tenth National People's Congress	191–192
Table 8.1	The Support of Donald Tsang and Alan Leong in the Nomination Process	207–208
Table 8.2	Comparison of Tsang and Leong's Political Platforms	210
Table 8.3	Surveys Conducted by Lingnan University and the University of Hong Kong on the Performance of Candidates in the Chief Executive Election	220
Table 8.4	The Reasons Why Respondents Supported Tsang or Leong	221
Table 8.5	Public Support of Tsang and Leong	221

Acknowledgements

I express my gratitude to Colin Day of Hong Kong University Press for his support of my book project and to Dawn Lau for her editing work.

I must also thank Patrick Kwong and Joseph Cheng for granting me the copyright permission to use the revised version of my chapter on mainlandization in Professor Joseph Y. S. Cheng's edited book entitled *The Hong Kong Special Administrative Region in Its First Decade* (City University of Hong Kong Press, August 2007), Professor Rick Glofceski and Professor Albert Chen for giving me the authorization to reprint the updated version of my article entitled "The Emergence of Constitutional Conventions in the Hong Kong Special Administrative Region" in the *Hong Kong Law Journal* (Part 1, 2005, published by Sweet & Maxwell), and to Professor John Burns and Professor Ian Thynne for letting me adopt my essay on the 2007 chief executive election in *The Asia Pacific Journal of Public Administration* ("Symposium on the First Ten Years of the Hong Kong Special Administrative Region of the People's Republic of China," July 2007). These works have been revised and they are now appearing in this book as Chapter 2, Chapter 4, and Chapter 8 respectively.

Finally, I would like to dedicate this book to all those people who are yearning for a peaceful resolution of the political future of Taiwan.

Abbreviations

ATV	Asia Television
CCP	Chinese Communist Party
CCTC	China Central Television
CEPA	Closer Economic Partnership Arrangement
CFA	Court of Final Appeal
CPPCC	Chinese People's Political Consultative Conference
CPU	Central Policy Unit
DAB	Democratic Alliance for Betterment of Hong Kong
DP	Democratic Party
DPP	Democratic Progressive Party
ExCo	Executive Council
FTU	Federation of Trade Unions
HKMAO	Hong Kong Macao Affairs Office
HKSAR	Hong Kong Special Administrative Region
KMT	Kuomintang
LegCo	Legislative Council
LO	Liaison Office
LP	Liberal Party
MSAR	Macao Special Administrative Region
NCNA	New China News Agency
NGOs	Non-Governmental Organizations
NPC	National People's Congress
PLA	People's Liberation Army
POAS	Principal Officials Accountability System
PRC	People's Republic of China
PRD	Pearl River Delta
ROC	Republic of China
RTHK	Radio Television Hong Kong
SARS	Severe Acute Respiratory Syndrome
SCNPC	Standing Committee of the National People's Congress
SDC	Strategic Development Commission
TVB	Television Broadcasting
U.S.	United States

Introduction

The transfer of the sovereignty of Hong Kong from Britain to the People's Republic of China (PRC) on July 1, 1997 was a crucial experiment with the concept of "one country, two systems" designed and proposed by the late Chinese leader Deng Xiaoping. With Taiwan as the final target of reunification with China in mind, Deng hoped that the retrocession of the Hong Kong Special Administrative Region (HKSAR) would be as smooth as possible, laying the groundwork for his successors' attempt at wooing Taiwan back to the PRC orbit.

Nevertheless, as this book will argue, the governance of the HKSAR has proved to be superficially "successful" but substantially turbulent and conflict-ridden. The difficult years of governance in the HKSAR from July 1, 1997 to the sudden resignation of the former chief executive Tung Chee-hwa in March 2005 posed a tremendous obstacle for the PRC to demonstrate the success of "one country, two systems" to the world and to the Taiwan leaders. The popularity of Tung's successor, Donald Tsang, has made it easier for Beijing to sell the "one country, two systems" to the outside world, but not necessarily to Taiwan where the pro-independence elites and masses remain resistant to the Hong Kong model. Although civil liberties in the HKSAR have been by and large maintained since July 1997, the superficial phenomenon has hidden the fact that the "one country, two systems" has brought about tremendous tensions between the people of Hong Kong and Beijing, and between the Hongkongers and the C. H. Tung administration from July 1, 1997 to March 2005, when the chief executive stepped down for health reasons. Although the people of Hong Kong were in general satisfied with Beijing's political leadership, they were deeply dissatisfied with the fact that Beijing sided with Chief Executive C. H. Tung whose policies were out of touch with the public in the HKSAR. As this book will discuss, the debate over Article 23 of the Basic Law — the stipulation that outlaws subversion, sedition and treason — proved to be a disaster for the Tung administration in July 2003, compounded by the mismanagement of the Severe Acute Respiratory Syndrome (SARS) that broke out in the early half of the year. Although the Tung regime temporarily shelved the enactment of Article 23 of the Basic Law, the issue will sooner or later re-emerge as a sore point between some Hong Kong people and Beijing, and between the pro-democracy Hongkongers and the HKSAR government.

The tenth anniversary of the HKSAR on July 1, 2007 was punctuated by a glittering fireworks display on the Victoria Harbor, marked by a high-level visit by PRC President Hu Jintao, and characterized by a parade that celebrated the return of Hong Kong to the motherland. At the same time, the tenth anniversary demonstrated an official propaganda orchestrated by the pro-Beijing local and mainland mass media. While the mainland-backed media such as the China Central Television (CCTV) and Phoenix overwhelmingly portrayed the return of Hong Kong to mainland China as a triumph of the "one country, two systems," the local Chinese media displayed an increasingly politically correct line. What was alarming was the large number of mainland-born media professionals who worked for the CCTV and Phoenix. Naturally, their perception and description of the HKSAR developments were necessarily biased, excluding the views of most Hong Kong-born people who may not be fluent in Mandarin and who were not really interviewed by the CCTV and Phoenix, except for those pro-Beijing Hongkongers such as Jasper Tsang Yok-sing and Cheung Chi-kong.[1] Compounding the problem of biased television coverage of Hong Kong was the increasingly self-censored news of the local TVB and ATV whose ownership change in recent years has been accompanied by a silent revolution toward a tendency of reporting "good" rather than "bad" news on the HKSAR.

From an objective standpoint, Hong Kong remains alive rather than "dead," as the local mass media in the HKSAR have accurately stressed. It is ludicrous for any commentator to propound the imminent "death" of Hong Kong; the HKSAR will surely survive. But the crux of the question is whether it is going to retain its politico-economic and socio-cultural uniqueness as distinct from the rest of mainland China. The question of convergence between the HKSAR and the mainland, and the related issue of divergence, have so far not been seriously studied by Hong Kong commentators, journalists, observers, and scholars.

Chief Executive Donald Tsang has been maintaining a high degree of personal popularity, affecting the public acceptance of his policy to integrate Hong Kong with the motherland. The economy of the HKSAR has become prosperous after the mainland's economic measures in mid-2003, such as the implementation of the Closer Economic Partnership Arrangements (CEPA), the free individual visit scheme, and the relaxation of mainland enterprises and securities to float their shares and bonds in the Hong Kong stock market. Underlying the apparent "success" of "one country, two systems" are, as this book will argue, the twin processes of self-censorship on the part of the local mass media and the deeper penetration of the PRC politico-economic influence on the HKSAR. Hong Kong remains important in its functions for the PRC modernization; Hong Kong's clean government, assertive civil society and rule of law demonstrate the strengths of the Hong Kong model of governance to mainland China. Yet the dialectical process of mainland's politico-economic influence on the HKSAR has to be recognized simultaneously. Chapter One will delineate all the existing perspectives on Beijing's relations with the HKSAR. It will argue that patron-client politics are increasingly crucial to our understanding of the complex and dynamic Beijing–Hong Kong relationship.

Chapter Two of this book argues that the turbulent governance of the HKSAR from July 1997 to March 2005 was attributed to the policies of the Tung regime, which sought to converge with the PRC politically, and that Hong Kong's politico-economic convergence with the mainland has been deepened by Donald Tsang's policy of integration with the mainland. In the legal sphere, as Chapter Three will argue, the politicization of the legal system has become inevitable. The debate over the right of abode of the mainland Chinese in the HKSAR resulted in the decision of the HKSAR government to request that the National People's Congress should interpret provisions of the Basic Law. The entire debate was highly political to the extent that legal issues in Hong Kong have often become politicized, polarized, and perhaps distorted. On the other hand, constitutional conventions in the HKSAR, especially its relationships with Beijing, have gradually emerged since the transfer of sovereignty. Chapter Four will examine the birth of constitutional conventions in the HKSAR. The implementation of the Principal Officials Accountability System (POAS) since July 2002 has already propelled the government to become more accountable to the public. Ministerial resignations could be seen in the Tung administration, laying the groundwork for a silent process of political reform. However, such ministerial resignations in the event of scandals and blunders remain dependent on the personal factor in Hong Kong politics. Politically, the development of constitutional conventions in the HKSAR is a significant part of "one country, two systems," but it takes time for their further development and consolidation. Chapter Five will explore the overall implementation of the Basic Law and the difficulties of developing mainland Chinese conventions in dealing with Hong Kong.

An excellent example showing that legal issues are bound to be politicized was the debate over the national security bill in 2002 and 2003. Chapter Six shows that the entire debate was extremely political, leading to public outcry and the government's decision to postpone the enactment of the national security bill indefinitely. The whole debate illustrated the polarization of identity of the people of Hong Kong. Those who identified themselves as Chinese tended to support the bill, whereas those who identified themselves as Hong Kong people reacted to the bill fiercely and believed that its passage would sound a death knell to their civil liberties.

Due to the failure of Beijing's united front work in the HKSAR during the Tung era, it has changed its policy toward Hong Kong for the sake of winning the hearts and minds of the Hong Kong patriots since mid-2003. Chapter Seven uses the example of the election of the Hong Kong members to the National People's Congress to demonstrate how Beijing's officials attempted to control the election process. However, due to the pluralistic nature of Hong Kong's political actors, some Hong Kong NPC candidates leaked out issues that embarrassed the PRC officials. The elections showed that although mainland China's agents were keen to exert some degree of control over the selection of NPC members, the election results demonstrated some surprises to them. This phenomenon also illustrated the pluralistic setting of Hong Kong where PRC officials cannot have an absolute and easy control over even the pro-Beijing political elites.

Chapter Eight will show that the 2007 chief executive election represented an amalgamation of mainland Chinese and Hong Kong political cultures. The mainland cultures of emphasizing the use of *guanxi* and patrimonial practices have pervaded Hong Kong politics, especially at the top level of the political leadership involving the POAS and the appointment of the members of the top policy-making Executive Council. Yet the 2007 chief executive election opened up the mainland-style political process by allowing a party-affiliated candidate, Alan Leong of the Civic Party, to compete with Beijing-preferred Donald Tsang. The campaigns, as Chapter Eight will demonstrate, displayed a merging of the mainland and Hong Kong political cultures — a sign of convergence between the two places.

Chapter Nine adopts a comparative perspective to contend that although the problematic operation of the "one country, two systems" in Hong Kong cannot become a model for the PRC to reunify Taiwan in the long run, the formula's spirit can be applied to the Taiwan problem. Taiwan has developed a political system and unique identity very different from Hong Kong. Still, the spirit of the "one country, two systems" in Hong Kong and Macao, characterized by mutual compromise, concessions, trust, and perseverance during the Sino-British negotiations, can be applied to tackle Taiwan's political future.

1
Patron-Client Pluralism and Beijing's Relations with Hong Kong

The study of the political relationships between the HKSAR and its motherland, the PRC, has embraced at least several perspectives: Hong Kong's annexation of the mainland; the clash of civilizations; Beijing's political control over Hong Kong; bureaucratic politics; planning and coordination; and fiscal relations.[1] This chapter reviews these perspectives and will advance a modified form of patron-clientelism, which entails political patrons operating in a pluralistic environment where the support from clients and followers cannot be ensured and where non-clients are determined to oppose the clientelistic regime. The conventional wisdom on patron-client politics is that the relationships between a superior patron and an inferior client are asymmetrical as well as unequal.[2] Most of the literature on patron-clientelism has focused on the unequal interactions between the patron and clients, including wealth, status, influence, and exchange.[3] This chapter will explore how the central government in Beijing — the superior patron — deals with the non-clients in the Hong Kong political scene, namely the democratic elite and how it rewards the clients in the HKSAR. It will argue that patron-client pluralism, combined with the personnel control paradigm and other perspectives, provides us with a useful multiple framework to comprehend Beijing's complex politico-economic relationships with the HKSAR. Arguably, the mainland Chinese–style of "machine politics" will shape the political development of the HKSAR in the foreseeable future.[4] Under the umbrella of the "one country, two systems," Beijing is the powerful patron distributing political rewards to its clients, friends, and followers in Hong Kong.

The Annexation Perspective

The annexation theory argues that the HKSAR is like a tail that can wag the PRC "dog."[5] Proponents of the Hongkongization of the PRC maintain that Hong Kong's influence on the mainland can be felt not only culturally and economically but also politically. Since the transfer of Hong Kong's sovereignty from Britain to the PRC on July 1, 1997, politico-legal influences of the HKSAR on South China can be seen, including how the people of Hong Kong articulate their interest by protests, how they force local governments in South China to respond to their demands, and how some of the Hong Kong laws, particularly property law, have been selectively adopted in Shenzhen.[6] A recent issue of the *Yazhou Zhoukan* has argued that Hong Kong has tremendous socio-legal influence on the mainland, including non-governmental organizations (NGOs) that assist the mainlanders in dealing with poverty, schooling, and environmental protection, social workers who educate the mainlanders on how to develop social work as both a profession and an academic discipline, and Hong Kong leaders of the monetary and securities sectors that provide a legal framework for the mainland's stock market and financial reforms.[7]

These politico-legal and socio-economic impacts of Hong Kong on the whole of mainland China, however, cannot be overstated. Many Hongkongers' subjective perception of the HKSAR influence on the mainland is often much stronger than the objective reality. Objectively speaking, the PRC politico-legal development has its own momentum independent of Hong Kong's influence.[8] Although Hong Kong's NGOs do have an impact on the mainland society, the extent of influence is limited. Any mainland groups independent of the control and supervision of the Ministry of Civil Affairs are disallowed. Moreover, Hong Kong groups and individuals who have interactions with their mainland NGOs are always under the watchful eyes of PRC agents and informants. Indeed, Hong Kong's legal framework provides a useful reference for the mainland's financial system and stock markets. But the extensive use of *guanxi* in the mainland stock and financial markets remains vulnerable to bribery and corruption, unlike Hong Kong where the Independent Commission Against Corruption remains authoritative and powerful.

Socially, the interactions between mainland Chinese and the Hong Kong people have promoted the former's political consciousness. The annual candlelight vigil in commemoration of the dead victims in the 1989 Tiananmen incident did propel some mainland Chinese who visited the HKSAR to ponder the issue of political authoritarianism and repression in the mainland.⁹ True, the younger generation of the mainland has been under the influence of PRC socialization and propaganda; many of them publicly denied the Tiananmen tragedy when they first visited the HKSAR. Yet as time passed, and as they stay working and studying in Hong Kong, they have come to the realization that political propaganda cannot hide the military crackdown on the student demonstrators on Tiananmen Square. After all, the Hong Kong Alliance in Support of the Patriotic and Democratic Movement in China, which was founded in mid-1989, is playing an educative function of arousing the sensitivity of mainland visitors toward the Tiananmen tragedy. The HKSAR has invisible but tremendous educative impact on the seemingly politically apathetic visitors from the mainland.[10]

Culturally and socially, a certain degree of amalgamation between Hong Kong and the mainland can be seen. The Canto-pop culture of Hong Kong remains influential in South China, but many aspects of mainland culture and society, ranging from the extensive use of *guanxi* to mainland Chinese sports and arts, are now becoming far more prominent in the society of the HKSAR than ever before. The top level of the HKSAR leadership is filled with *guanxi* politics whereby the supporters of Donald Tsang, notably the Liberal Party leader James Tien who was appointed as the Chair of the Tourism Development Board at once after the 2007 chief executive election, have been rewarded with political positions. Mainland Chinese Olympics athletes have been regarded as heroes by the people of Hong Kong. Other mainland athletes have been "imported" into various sports in the HKSAR, notably table tennis, so as to help Hong Kong gain medals in international sports contests. Mainland Chinese art works and paintings as well as antiques have their prices fetched up to unprecedentedly high levels at public auctions in the HKSAR. Intermarriage between Hong Kong people and mainlanders has also increased significantly since the 1990s. While 518,000 mainland Chinese migrated to the HKSAR from July 1997 to June 2007, 35 percent of the marriages in Hong Kong in 2007 involved a spouse from mainland China.[11] The number of babies born to pregnant women from the PRC rose from 7,810 in 2001 to 26,132 in 2006.[12] More mainland professionals have emigrated to work in Hong Kong where the government is opening the door to talents from the motherland so as to maintain the capitalist enclave's economic competitiveness. The integration of the society and culture of both Hong Kong and its motherland is irresistible.

Yet one socio-cultural dimension of Hong Kong that cannot be easily transformed is the difficulty of translating the cultural identity of many Hongkongers into their blind political identification with the Chinese Communist Party (CCP) regime. It is common for Beijing elites, and their agents in the HKSAR such as the pro-Beijing political party Democratic Alliance for Betterment of Hong Kong (DAB), to assume that cultural identification of Hongkongers as Chinese can be easily transformed into their loyalty of the CCP. While more local Hong Kong people have joined the DAB than ever before, some out of political patriotism and others opportunism, many Hongkongers separate their identification with culturally Chinese from the political support of the CCP. This group of strong Hong Kong identifiers, especially those pro-democracy citizens, views the Hong Kong society as not only unique but also carrying values such as the rule of law and justice that cannot be easily attained in the socialist mainland.

From a critical perspective, however, the annexation paradigm has not yet distinguished the transformations within Hong Kong from those within the PRC, and from the changes that are the outcome of the interactions between the two places. Hong Kong's society has become more identified with the PRC than ever before, partly due to the changing identity of more Hong Kong people who see themselves as Chinese than the pre-1997 era, and partly due to the rapid and global rise of the PRC, which is no longer seen by many Hongkongers as an old-style and rigid communist regime. When the late Deng Xiaoping advanced the model of the "one country, two systems," he was referring to the different economic systems of capitalistic Hong Kong and the socialist mainland at that time. Post-Deng China has witnessed a deepened process of capitalist revolution, which is propelling the PRC toward an uncertain political destination, no matter whether it would be socialist authoritarianism, democratic socialism, or capitalist democracy.[13] It is beyond the scope of this book to examine the PRC politico-economic metamorphosis, but the argument concerning Hong Kong's annexation of the mainland has a major flaw: the sweeping generalization has failed to take into account the pervasive PRC political, social, and economic influence on the HKSAR. It can be argued that the mainlandization of the HKSAR, rather than the Hongkongization of mainland China, has become the phenomenon since the retrocession of Hong Kong began on July 1, 1997.

Politically, it must be admitted that Hong Kong's political influence on the entire PRC regime is limited. The former PRC president Jiang Zemin warned the people of Hong Kong that they should not intervene in the politics of the mainland, while promising that the PRC would not meddle in the HKSAR affairs. As it turned out, both PRC officials and Hong Kong people have been trying to influence each other. PRC officials in the HKSAR, notably the Liaison Office, have remained active in the local legislative and District Councils elections, playing the role of coordinating pro-Beijing candidates, mobilizing supporters to vote for "patriotic" political parties, clandestinely orchestrating electoral campaigns, and openly criticizing the pro-democracy elites in Hong Kong.[14] Some pro-democracy elites in Hong Kong, especially the leaders and members of the Hong Kong Alliance in Support of the Patriotic and Democratic Movement in China — a "subversive" organization formed during the Tiananmen incident in May–June 1989 — hoped that the PRC would undergo Western-style democratic reforms.[15] Their political expectation on mainland China's democratization, and their activities in support of the direct elections of the chief executive and the entire legislature in Hong Kong as soon as possible, are viewed by PRC authorities as extremely politically dangerous.[16] In the minds of PRC ruling elites, the Hong Kong democrats are attempting to implant a Western-style polity in the HKSAR, thus serving as an agent for the Western nation-states to contain mainland China and possibly "subvert" the regime led by the CCP. It is the clash of the mainland political culture, which views Western democracies as undesirable, and the Hong Kong democratic tradition, which dreams of a Western polity characterized by the rotation of party in power, that has made political disputes over democratization in the HKSAR conflict-ridden and deadlocked.

The HKSAR economic dependency on the PRC has arguably made more people, especially the business elites, far more politically conservative than ever before. From July 1993 to April 2007, a total of 98 mainland enterprises were listed in the H shares (main board) of the Hong Kong stock market, carrying a market capitalization of HK$3372.5 billion.[17] While the assets of all these listed companies increased significantly and benefited Hong Kong's investors, they also accumulated a huge amount of capital from the HKSAR — a process of interdependency that is deepening. The introduction of the Closer Economic Partnership Arrangement (CEPA) into the HKSAR by Beijing in the summer of 2003, and the ensuing free individual visits scheme, have already helped Hong Kong's economic rebound tremendously but also rendered it an economic appendage of Beijing.[18] With the PRC's rapid economic growth, the HKSAR ruling elites, including the former publicly ostracized chief executive Tung Chee-hwa and the current popular successor Donald Tsang, believe that Hong Kong has to adopt a dependent development strategy.[19] On the one hand, the HKSAR has to depend on the high growth rate of the motherland to boost its internal tourism. On the other hand, Hong Kong can continue to develop economically. This strategy has been working, but it has a number of detrimental impacts politically and economically. Economically, whenever the PRC sneezes, the HKSAR coughs. The best example is the recent mainland macro-level measures aimed at cooling down both the overheated economy and the Shanghai and Shenzhen stock markets, which immediately witnessed a slight decline in the Hong Kong stock index. What the Hong Kong authorities perhaps ignore is that the territory's heavy economic dependence on the mainland has actually weakened the foundation of the HKSAR economic survival and tenacity. The PRC economic performance cannot be assumed to be linear — a premise that has been turned into an official propaganda by the Hong Kong ruling elites. Any blind political patriotism of the Hong Kong governing elites would plunge the HKSAR into another economic chaos in the future. Such turbulence would perhaps be as serious as the aftermath of the 1997 Asian financial crisis due to ongoing official tendency of propagating "good news" — a situation perpetuated by the increasingly self-censored local Chinese print media.[20]

Politically, Hong Kong's economic reliance on Beijing means that more business elites are believing that there can be an artificial separation between the political and economics. The business tycoons, and many other elites leading the small and medium enterprises, firmly believe that without Western-style democracy, the HKSAR economy will survive and prosper with the back-up from Beijing. This view reinforces the anti-democratic orientations among the upper-middle classes. Many senior civil servants, who are imbued with a vested interest in dealing with less public complaints that are sometimes stirred up by the democrats, view democracy as administratively burdensome. In the words of the former secretary for security, Regina Ip, Singapore represented "a paradise for Hong Kong civil servants," meaning that Singapore's strong state and weak society facilitate the work of public servants who can easily ignore public opposition and resistance.[21] Many big businessmen regard democracy as "socialist" welfare states characterized by high tax and political mob rule — an ignorance of Western welfare states that remain pro-capitalist in their outlook and economic policies. Many other land developers believe that Western-style democracy in the HKSAR would institute severe checks and balances on their business negotiations with the currently strong executive branch. In short, the society of Hong Kong carries strong anti-democratic currents, which are probably stronger than the phenomenon that a majority of the respondents in surveys conducted since July 1997 have been constantly expressing their support of the direct elections of both the chief executive and the entire legislature. Yet in a survey conducted by the Hong Kong Transition Project on 800 respondents in May 2007, 45 percent disagreed with the statement that "Hong Kong people are mature enough to elect the chief executive by universal suffrage;" 50 percent agreed with it; and 5 percent did not know.²² It seemed that the people of Hong Kong are divided on whether the chief executive should be directly elected by universal suffrage. While a segment of mass conservatism is looming, the impact of Hong Kong's dependent development upon the cautious political mentality of the business elites will prolong the arrival of Western-style democracy in the HKSAR.

Socially and legally, the PRC Standing Committee of the National People's Congress (SCNPC) has never hesitated to interpret the Basic Law — the mini-constitution of the HKSAR. It interpreted the right of abode of the mainland Chinese in Hong Kong in June 1999, after the request made by the HKSAR government that there would be 1.67 million mainlanders flooding into the territory if the verdict of the Court of Final Appeal were followed. The SCNPC interpretation made the finality of the Court of Final Appeal void, as critics maintained. But supporters of the SCNPC interpretation argued that the move aimed at stabilizing Hong Kong's society and preventing any influx of a large amount of mainlanders who would have been qualified to reside in the HKSAR under the court decision. The second interpretation of the Basic Law took place in March 2004, shortly after the 500,000 protesters took to the streets on July 1, 2003 against the maladministration of the Tung regime. The SCNPC interpretation was a political move pre-empting any decision by the HKSAR government to yield to the demands of democrats for the direct elections of the chief executive and the entire legislature in 2007 and 2008 respectively. It must be noted that Beijing's hard-line interpretation of the Basic Law coincided with the re-election of the pro-independence Taiwan Democratic Progressive Party (DPP) President Chen Shui-bian. The fear of Beijing of the political Taiwanization of the HKSAR was real. The Taiwanization of Hong Kong means that the territory's chief executive would be not only directly elected by universal suffrage but also outside the control of Beijing. The third interpretation of the Basic Law by the SCNPC came in March 2005 shortly after Mr. Tung resigned for health reasons. The SCNPC aimed at pre-empting any legal challenge made by any democrats in the HKSAR on the tenure of office of the new chief executive. Although the Basic Law states that the chief executive's office lasts for five years, Beijing wanted to give the former British-trained Donald Tsang two years for observation so as to decide whether it would support him for a further five years of office. The interpretation on the office of the new chief executive was clearly political and pre-emptive.

The three interpretations of the SCNPC on the Basic Law had a number of features showing the clash of mainland Chinese and Western civilizations. It was marked by the request from the HKSAR government, despite the fact that in December 2003 the Tung regime consulted Beijing on the issue of political reform rather than submitting a formal request for the SCNPC interpretation. Arguably, however, such consultation with Beijing was tantamount to a hidden consent in the SCNPC interpretation, which is legal according to Article 158 of the Basic Law. Another characteristic of the three interpretations was that the SCNPC did not hesitate to impose its will on the HKSAR. Intervention, as the late Deng Xiaoping said in 1984, would be sometimes necessary and positive for Hong Kong. This interventionist tradition of the SCNPC in Hong Kong affairs regarding the relationships between the HKSAR and Beijing means that judicially, the Hong Kong system has been politicized or mainlandized to some extent. From the common law perspective, the local courts in the HKSAR should have the final adjudication. But their autonomy is actually granted by the central government from the perspective of the mainland politico-legal culture.

At the middle and lower levels of the Hong Kong judiciary, however, the local courts can deal with cases ranging from tort to family law, from criminal law to the law of inheritance in a highly autonomous manner. Yet in the area of constitutional law and those policy issues that involve Beijing's relations with the HKSAR, such as the right of abode, political reform, and the office of the new chief executive, the local courts including the Court of Final Appeal do not really have a "high" degree of judicial autonomy as promised in the Basic Law.

Finally, the three interpretations of the SCNPC on the Basic Law showed that each time the PRC side appeared to make progress in the process of explaining its action. The first interpretation in 1999 was more a top-down verdict delivered by the SCNPC and backed up by the pro-Beijing media in Hong Kong and the HKSAR ruling elite's justification. The second interpretation was arguably more unilateral, but the high officials of the SCNPC went to Shenzhen to consult the opinions of the Hong Kong elites prior to the interpretation. Such consultation appeared to be cosmetic, as top members of the SCNPC at that time had already publicly supported the need for the Basic Law interpretation. Still, the action of SCNPC members to consult the Hong Kong elites represented a small progressive step toward "democratic" procedures. The third interpretation in 2005 envisaged the disclosure of the voting result of all members of the SCNPC — an unprecedented move although all the 152 members voted for the interpretation. Arguably, each interpretation proceeded in a way that forced the PRC authorities to be more accountable for their decisions over Hong Kong. This accountable drift was an outcome of a vociferous civil society in the HKSAR. While the SCNPC impact on Hong Kong society was considerable in its three interpretations, its move toward transparency was a testimony to the impact of the HKSAR vocal opposition.

Theorists of the tail wagging the dog have failed to analyze the complex political, economic, social, cultural, and legal dynamics of Hong Kong's relations with the PRC. It is perhaps too early to say that Hong Kong is annexing the mainland politically, economically, culturally, socially, and legally. The transformations of the PRC have its own momentum separate from the influence of the geographically small HKSAR. Politically, the PRC influence on the HKSAR remains extensive, ranging from personnel control of the political leadership at the top to popular mobilization of supporters to vote in local elections at the bottom. On the contrary, Hong Kong's political influence on the mainland remains restricted to South China, particularly Guangdong and Fujian, where mainlanders are displaying a style of political protests parallel to the Hong Kong tradition combined with the use of mobile phones and information technology. Economically, Hong Kong is indisputably far more dependent on the mainland support, capital, and growth than ever before. The regular outflow of mainland capital to the Hong Kong stock market appears to benefit the HKSAR in the short run, but any drastic economic fluctuations in the mainland economy would predictably entail an immediate impact on the Hong Kong economy.

Most importantly, the economic dependence of Hong Kong on Beijing has strengthened the anti-democratic bias of the local capitalist class, which narrowly sees every policy associated with the welfare states in the West as negative and entailing high tax that would discourage foreign investment and local business.[23] As long as the local capitalist class in the HKSAR is an appendage of the PRC rapid economic growth, Hong Kong's democratization is by no means optimistic. Socially and culturally, Hong Kong has been merging with the mainland, but its distinct rational patriotism, as opposed to uncritical and blind political patriotism that stems from a very strong cultural identity in the PRC, remains very different.[24] It will take decades for the PRC, and its uncritical agents in Hong Kong, to transform the cultural identity of many Hongkongers into loyal political patriots.

The Clash of Civilization Perspective

Samuel Huntington has maintained that the Sinic or Chinese civilization is a far cry from the West. While the Chinese civilization emphasizes political harmony, hierarchy, authority, and collectivism, the Western civilization cherishes political representation, social pluralism, the rule of law, and individualism.[25] Despite the fact that the societies of Hong Kong and the PRC have been merging slowly, the clash of Western and mainland Chinese civilizations has been prominent in the incessant political disputes over the scope and the pace of political reform in the HKSAR.

From the perspective of Beijing, if a Western-style democracy were injected into Hong Kong, the political impacts on the mainland would be twofold. First and foremost, those "politically incorrect" democrats would be directly elected as the chief executive and they would occupy over half of the Legislative Council seats, thus presenting a huge security menace to the PRC authorities and sovereignty over the HKSAR. What Beijing fears is a democratically inclined chief executive and legislature defiant of the central government's instructions and policy intentions, creating a scenario of another Taiwan led by the pro-independence Democratic Progressive Party (DPP). Although very few, arguably none, of the Hong Kong people really dream of Hong Kong independence, Beijing's mentality is that democratization in the HKSAR would generate political separatism. The term "Hong Kong independence" does not refer to any Hong Kong people who want a *de facto* and *de jure* separation from the mainland, but to those pro-democracy local elites who are eager to seize political power, to implement a Western-style democracy in the capitalist enclave, and to augment the HKSAR autonomy to an extent unacceptable to Beijing. The second ramification that follows from the first consequence is that a democratic Hong Kong would generate more internal pressure on the PRC to democratize the provinces, thus creating havoc on the central-local relations. The separatists in Xinjiang province, and those pro-independence Tibet activists, would surely take advantage of Hong Kong's democratization to clamor for more autonomy, self-determination, and even separation from Beijing. This worst-case scenario would not be tolerated by Beijing as long as the CCP remains firmly in power. After all, Taiwan would also demand political separation from Beijing, thus rendering the late Deng Xiaoping's hope of using the Hong Kong and Macao model of "one country, two systems" to reunify Taiwan politically and practically impossible. In short, Western-style democracy in Hong Kong is, in the minds of Beijing, the worst-case scenario that would be tantamount to the end of the CCP, the collapse of its unitary system, and the disintegration of mainland China. Nevertheless, the Hong Kong democrats believe that democratization in the HKSAR would prove the validity of the creativity and innovative potential of the "one country, two systems," thus strengthening the formula's appeal to Taiwan. The two conflicting visions of the impact of Western-style democratization in the HKSAR have so far been neglected by observers, especially those who argue that Hong Kong is like a political tail that can wag the Chinese dog in the long run. The tail-wag-the-dog theory, however, is potentially "subversive" to Beijing authorities. Even if the PRC is undergoing gradual democratic reforms, including village elections at the grassroots level and reform of the National People's Congress at the top, democratization in the Chinese style means gradualism, continuous CCP dominance, and persistent central control over the personnel arrangement of the localities.[26]

The mainland Chinese legal culture is perhaps epitomized by the remarks made by the PRC experts on the Basic Law, such as Wang Zhenmin, Rao Geping, Xu Chongde and the late Xiao Weiyun. While Rao emphasized that "one country" must dominate the "two systems," Wang has stressed the persistence of the differences of the "two systems" as opposed to the "one country, one system" in ancient China's Qin dynasty.[27] All mainland legal experts of the Basic Law have been sharing common views: namely gradualism should be the norm of Hong Kong's political changes, the ultimate sovereignty and political veto power are possessed by the central government in Beijing, and the autonomy enjoyed by the HKSAR is more limited than what some Hong Kong people have been expecting. Wang Zhenmin also told the author that the Hong Kong mass media misunderstood him and misinterpreted his remarks when he stressed that consensus among the people of Hong Kong would be a must prior to Beijing's decision on the territory's political reform.[28] Although the Hong Kong media linked his remark with the need to enact Article 23 of the Basic Law before democratization in the HKSAR, he stressed that the two issues were not really related.[29] Yet the way in which the HKSAR media reported and described Wang's comment, which provoked immediate criticisms from the pro-democracy elite in Hong Kong, was a manifestation of a clash of Hong Kong media ethos and the mainland elite culture. While the Hong Kong media have frequently developed the proclivity of overstating one's comment through selective quotations, the mainland legal experts were not used to this misrepresentation approach.

The clash of civilizations between the mainland ruling elites and the Hong Kong political culture was vividly seen in the public outburst of the former PRC president Jiang Zemin over the aggressive questioning from a Hong Kong reporter, Sharon Cheung Po-wah, on whether Beijing had already crowned C. H. Tung as the second chief executive prior to the 2002 chief executive election, which saw Tung as the only candidate automatically elected. While the Hong Kong media viewed the event as an indication of Jiang's personal temper vented on the Hong Kong reporters, a careful study of the events showed that prior to Cheung's question that provoked Jiang, other Hong Kong reporters had kept on asking the president questions concerning the popularity of Tung.[30] Governing in a largely authoritarian political context without media scrutiny and aggressive public questioning, Jiang's strong reaction to Cheung's question was arguably understandable. His outburst was a testimony to the clash of mainland Chinese and Western civilizations. While the mainland ruling elites were not used to assertive and poignant questioning from the media, which were seen by the CCP elites more as the tool of political propaganda than as the fifth branch of government, the Hong Kong reporters adopted a Western style of political practices and asked embarrassing questions that could easily exceed the bottom line of tolerance of the ruling elite.

The Political Control Perspective

The PRC system of *nomenklatura* is an essential ingredient of its politico-personnel control over the HKSAR.[31] Since Hong Kong's return to its motherland, more Hong Kong people have been incorporated into the PRC *nomenklatura*, such as the top leaders of the Hong Kong Friendship Promotion Association, an organization listed as one of the major Hong Kong groups under the job description of the mainland United Front Department.[32] It was estimated that, in 1983, about two to three thousand underground CCP members existed in the HKSAR.[33] Twenty-four years later, it is perhaps not surprising that its membership might have increased by at least between ten and twenty times. With more mainland enterprises being listed in the HKSAR stock market, and with more mainland students visiting and staying in Hong Kong, the CCP *nomenklatura* system is encountering the difficulty of exerting effective control over them. How to renew the CCP control over the increasingly mobile members is a daunting task to the Liaison Office and its officials in the HKSAR. Yet with the global emergence of the PRC, more Hong Kong business people have joined the CCP, partly because of their recognition of the need to foster better *guanxi* in their business expansion in the mainland, and partly due to their patriotic fervor.

From the perspective of united front work on grassroots-level CCP supporters and members, and on top-level personnel control, the *nomenklatura* system has been operating smoothly. The two examples that illustrate the effectiveness of the *nomenklatura* system are the chief executive elections in

March 2007 and the mobilization of pro-Beijing voters to cast their ballots in the previous direct elections held for the Legislative Council and the eighteen District Councils.[34] Groups controlled by the *nomenklatura* mechanism, such as the Chinese Chamber of Commerce and the agricultural sector, envisaged candidates nominated without the need to compete in the election of the members of the Election Committee that would select the chief executive. Moreover, the local united front organizations, notably the New Territories Federation of Associations, the Kowloon Federation of Associations and the Fujianese Association, have been displaying an impressive degree of solidarity and efficiency in mobilizing members and residents in the District Council elections.

It is very unlikely that the *nomenklatura* system will break down in the near future. Yet the latent crisis is how to ensure the political loyalty of all CCP members in the HKSAR, especially those who are increasingly exposed to the values of independent thinking, personal autonomy, and political pluralism. Occasionally, a few CCP members would defect from Hong Kong, violating the party discipline and rules to disclose the party's inner operations.[35] Yet these political "renegades" appear to be a minority and they do not really affect the long-term development of the underground CCP in the HKSAR.

Still, in the event of a sudden political crisis in the PRC, such as the 1989 Tiananmen incident, the CCP *nomenklatura* system would predictably be plunged into uncertainties and ordeals. The cycle of defection of CCP members would perhaps reoccur — a scenario reminiscent of the departure of some members of the editorial board of the Hong Kong *Wen Wei Po* shortly after the June 1989 incident in the PRC.[36]

The *nomenklatura* in the HKSAR raises a sensitive but realistic issue of whether the HKSAR leadership is already filled by some underground CCP members who cannot reveal their identity in public. In the Executive Council, for example, it is widely rumored that Jasper Tsang, Cheng Yiu-tong, and C. Y. Leung are "members" of the underground CCP in the HKSAR.[37] Adding to this batch of loyal CCP "members" is Tsang Tak-sing, the younger brother of Jasper Tsang and the principal official responsible for home affairs starting from July 1, 2007.[38] Tsang Tak-sing was imprisoned for two years shortly after his 1967 protest against the Hong Kong education system and the Opium War, but his political "liability" in the colonial days is absolutely an asset in the HKSAR years.[39] Regardless of the number of underground CCP members at the top level of the HKSAR leadership, there is arguably a hidden CCP under the disguise of a political system without any ruling party. Donald Tsang is already viewed as a chief executive forming his own "party" by relying on his former colleagues in the civil service. While the extent of underground CCP membership at the top level of the senior civil service in the HKSAR is unknown, it can be safely said that Donald Tsang's apparent "civil service party" is actually accompanied by a more influential underground CCP at the highest echelon of the Hong Kong administration. In brief, *nomenklatura* has been playing a critical role in shaping the leadership of the HKSAR. After all, the Director of the State Council's Hong Kong and Macao Study Institute, Zhu Yucheng, has reiterated the late Deng Xiaoping's remark that the HKSAR leadership has to be led by a group of "patriotic Hong Kong people."[40] Patriotism is defined loosely here as those Hong Kong elites who staunchly support Beijing's policies toward the HKSAR and those who have already joined the CCP clandestinely without revealing their true political status. Those Hong Kong people who oppose Beijing's policies toward the territory, especially the central government's reluctance to envisage a rapid introduction of the direct election of the chief executive, are running the risk of being labeled as "unpatriotic." The ingredients of ambiguity and fluidity in the mainland Chinese concept of patriotism are intertwined with the ultimate arbitrariness of one-party rule, where the CCP upholds the power of interpreting who is patriotic and who is not.

An anonymous member of the underground CCP suggested that it should reveal the Party's operation in Hong Kong in a transparent way.[41] Nevertheless, none of the underground CCP members has tackled this demand frankly and boldly. From Beijing's perspective, the *nomenklatura* in the HKSAR has to be kept confidential. Nor is the disclosure of its underground branch operation in Hong Kong viewed as necessary. Consequently, Beijing's political penetration into the HKSAR remains secretive. Moreover, the pro-democracy call for Beijing and the HKSAR government to accept the introduction of a party government in Hong Kong is bound to be problematic, for the issue of the underground CCP remains unresolved in the first place. Therefore, while Beijing sees *nomenklatura* as indispensable for its politico-personnel control over the HKSAR, its confidentiality constitutes a hindrance to any proposal of party-izing the top level of the government leadership. Partyization means that the top-level political leaders of the HKSAR, including the chief executive and principal officials, are explicitly political party members. Even if the chief executive may be allowed to be a party member in the future when he or she is directly elected, an underground CCP will likely accompany some political appointees.

The Bureaucratic Politics Perspective

While the political control paradigm depicts a fairly homogeneous CCP exerting control over the politico-personnel developments in the HKSAR, the bureaucratic politics of mainland agencies have highlighted their inherent tensions and contradictions. The opinion differences between the Hong Kong Macao Affairs Office (HKMAO) and the former New China News Agency (NCNA) were well-documented.[42] Prior to the return of Hong Kong to the PRC, the HKMAO was reportedly supportive of chief executive candidate Tung Chee-hwa, while the NCNA tended to favor another candidate Yang Ti-Liang.[43] Institutional politics was also accompanied by personal differences. During the tenth anniversary of Hong Kong's return to the PRC, the former director of the New China News Agency, Zhou Nan, openly criticized his predecessor Xu Jiatun for being disloyal to his wife in 1989 when Xu left the mainland for the United States. In response to Zhou's criticism, Xu revealed that shortly after the Tiananmen incident in June 1989, when he reported to Beijing on a suggestion made by Hong Kong businessman Helmut Solmen that Hong Kong could be administratively rented to Britain, Lu Ping of the HKMAO criticized Xu for being "unpatriotic." The revelations on the personal differences between Zhou and Xu, and Lu and Xu, illustrated the complexities of mainland officials responsible for Hong Kong matters.

The most serious problem concerning the Liaison Office (formerly New China News Agency) in Hong Kong after July 1997 was its failure to report to Beijing accurately the massive discontent toward the Tung regime. The political correctness of the Liaison Office and its proclivity of reporting "good" news to the central government explained why it could not predict the unprecedented half a million protestors on July 1, 2003. As a result, the central government in Beijing removed and replaced a number of deputy directors of the Liaison Office in Hong Kong. The failure of the Liaison Office to assess Hong Kong's public opinion coincided with a spy scandal in which one of its officials was found to leak out confidential information to the British agents. The dual crises of internal management and external evaluation of Hong Kong's development throughout 2003 dealt a severe blow to the prestige of the Liaison Office. Since the central government's action to revamp the Liaison Office, its representatives have appeared to be more cautious in the handling of Hong Kong matters, especially public remarks and comments. Its tensions with the HKMAO have been suppressed, at least apparently. On the surface, it seems that the revamped Liaison Office is enjoying a honeymoon period with the HKMAO. Yet the personal rivalries between the officials of the Liaison Office and that of the HKMAO remain a mystery.

The relatively subdued public profile of the Liaison Office has been surprisingly accompanied by a more high-profile Commissioner of the PRC Foreign Ministry in Hong Kong, Lu Xinhua. Lu has made public remarks in support of Wu Bangguo, the general-secretary of the PRC National People's Congress, who stressed in June 2007 that the autonomy of Hong Kong has been granted by the central government in Beijing. Lu's high-profile remarks do not mean that the Foreign Ministry has taken any action to interfere in the HKSAR domestic affairs. The Foreign Ministry has since July 1, 1997 been playing an auxiliary role that facilitates Hong Kong's external relations with other nation-states. As a matter of fact, the former chief executive C. H. Tung revealed that the former PRC foreign minister Qian Qichen had given him "a high degree of autonomy" in visiting foreign countries and meeting foreign leaders without the company of officials from the PRC Foreign Ministry.[44]

The utility of the bureaucratic politics perspective is limited by the outside access to data on the hidden tensions and conflicts among the PRC agencies responsible for Hong Kong affairs. Above all, any political conflicts among the mainland organs have been heavily shaped by the personal factor. The personal relationships between the HKMAO director and the Liaison Office director will continue to be significant, in particular as rumors concerning the imminent departure of Zeng Qinghong, the protégé of the former PRC president Jiang Zemin, from the Standing Committee of the CCP Politburo were rife in mid-2007. Zeng reportedly headed a committee on Hong Kong, namely the Coordinating Leading Group on Hong Kong Affairs, immediately after the debacle of the legislation on Article 23 of the Basic Law in July 2003.[45] Under the circumstances in which the decline of the Shanghai faction or clique in Chinese politics was perhaps inevitable, the Hong Kong and Macao Work Committee headed by President Hu Jintao and the State Council's Hong Kong and Macao Study Research Centre led by the former Liaison Office deputy director Zhu Yucheng continue to play a crucial role in the formulation of the PRC policies toward the HKSAR. Zhu's personal *guanxi* with Zeng was rarely noted, but they had been former classmates in their secondary school years.[46]

In fact, the bureaucratic politics perspective is constantly accompanied by personnel changes. As mentioned before, in June 2007, it was rumored that Zeng Qinghong would step down from the Standing Committee of the Politburo.[47] While this rumor turned out to be accurate in the seventeenth CCP Congress in 2007, personnel instability in the PRC bodies responsible for Hong Kong matters created a political vacuum in which other mainland officials were voicing their remarks on the HKSAR in a far more profile manner than before. For instance, the secretary-general of the Standing Committee of the National People's Congress, Wu Bangguo, stressed in June 2007 that the autonomy enjoyed by the HKSAR is conferred upon by Beijing, and that it is much more limited than what many Hong Kong people expect. Wu's comment aroused the criticisms from some Hong Kong democrats, such as Margaret Ng and Martin Lee, who accused Wu of changing the original intent of the Basic Law. From an objective perspective, however, Wu reiterated the long-standing position of Beijing, but his remark came at a time when the Donald Tsang administration was preparing to put forward a consultative paper on political reform in the summer of 2007. Hence, Wu's remark could be interpreted as a sign that Beijing did not wish to envisage a soft-line stance adopted by the Tsang administration on democratization. It was also perhaps a reflection of the personnel instability surrounding Zeng's political future.

Another reason why Wu assumed a higher profile on Hong Kong affairs was that in the midst of top personnel changes in the PRC leadership, the officials responsible for Hong Kong matters underwent a transition period. Wu's comment on Hong Kong was accompanied by the remark of Qiao Xiaoyang, who said that the nomination of chief executive candidates in the HKSAR should consult Beijing's views beforehand — a view on "prior communication" that sparked immediate criticisms and concerns from the pro-democracy elites. Echoing the views of the NPC elites Wu and Qiao, Zhu Yucheng stressed on June 16, 2007 that any political reform in the HKSAR would have to meet the criteria of gradual and orderly process, balanced representation, and the need to take care of the interests of various classes.[48] Zhu's open comment could be seen as an indication that regardless of Zeng's future directions, PRC officials responsible for Hong Kong policies were dominated by a tripod composed of Wu, Qiao, and Zhu.

Interestingly, missing in the picture of PRC official remarks on Hong Kong matters was the top bureaucrats of the HKMAO. Director Liao Hui has remained as low profile as before, while his lieutenant and vice-director Chen Zuo'er merely revealed how Beijing fully supported the Tung administration during the Asian financial crisis, the SARS episode, and the CEPA arrangements.[49] Neither of the two revealed their views with regard to political reform. Of course, this did not mean that they had different opinions from Wu, Zhu, and Qiao. However, the phenomenon of Wu, Zhu, and Qiao voicing their views on Hong Kong's autonomy and democratization did illustrate the shift of the core elites responsible for Hong Kong matters from the HKMAO to both the NPC elites and the Hong Kong and Macao Study Institute after the July 1, 2003 protests. As mentioned before, officials of the Liaison Office (LO) in the HKSAR have turned to become more cautious in public, and the commentaries in *Ta Kung Pao* and *Wen Wei Po* under the LO control have become more rational and less emotionally charged — another proof of the LO's political adjustment after its failure to predict the July 1, 2003 earthquake. Coupled with the low-profile approach adopted by the HKMAO, the circumspect attitude of LO officials can be interpreted as another sign of their declining influence on Beijing's Hong Kong policies. As one mainland researcher who visited the HKSAR after the July 1, 2003 protest said, "I am merely responsible for reporting the views of the Hong Kong people to Beijing, but I do not really know the decisions of the top-level authorities on Hong Kong matters."[50] If palace politics remain a hallmark of mainland Chinese politics, its secrecy and personalism constitute the defining features of Beijing's policies toward the HKSAR. This phenomenon persists after Xi Jinping has replaced Zeng to head the central coordinating committee on Hong Kong and Macao since late 2007.

The Planning and Coordination Perspective

Since Hong Kong's retrocession to its motherland, planning and coordination have become increasingly crucial to the economic development of the HKSAR. Several major changes can be seen in terms of mutual planning and coordination. First and foremost, Hong Kong has joined the "9 plus 2" formula and has been cooperating with Macao, Fujian, Jiangxi, Hunan, Guangdong, Guangxi, Hainan, Sichuan, Guizhou, and Yunnan. The HKSAR government claims that

> With a population of about 450 million, Pan-Pearl River Delta (PRD) is roughly the size of North America Free Trade Agreement (NAFTA), or the expanded European Union, or Association for Southeast Asian Nations. The region's combined GDP was US$730 billion in 2004, accounting to about 40 percent of China's total output. Based on the "9+2" Regional Cooperation concept, a South China "common market" is being developed. However, the Pan-PRD Regional Cooperation is not intended to be a rigid and formal organization or agreement as the European Union or NAFTA. It aims to raise the overall regional competitiveness through better and closer cooperation.[51]

While it is too early to assess whether the 9 plus 2 formula can really enhance the overall regional competitiveness, it is now commonplace for the HKSAR to emphasize the need for regional cooperation, planning, and coordination.

The second prominent feature of Hong Kong's planning and coordination with the mainland is its stress on economic integration with the motherland and investment in the PRC northwest provinces. The policy of economic integration with the mainland was the centerpiece of the Tung administration and it has been accelerated and deepened by the Tsang government. In a sense, the 9 plus 2 formula was a manifestation of Hong Kong's closer economic integration with its motherland. Another important ingredient of economic integration was the introduction of the Closer Economic Partnership Arrangement (CEPA) in the HKSAR in July 2003. The CEPA was originally hailed by the HKSAR leadership and Beijing as advantageous to the Hong Kong businessmen, but later critics questioned whether the CEPA was really beneficial to the Hong Kong business community, partly because of the complexities of the mainland's red tape and partly because of the limited number of business people who are the beneficiaries of the scheme. The most conspicuous planning, yet without much coordination and consequences, was the idea of encouraging Hong Kong business people to invest in mainland China's northwest. The Tung administration led a delegation to visit northwest China, but it remains highly doubtful whether more Hong Kong businessmen are really far more interested in investing in Shannxi, Qinghai, Xinjiang, and Gansu provinces than ever before. The lack of common dialect and local culture makes northwest China far less attractive to the Hong Kong business people than Guangdong province, which remains the most convenient place for their strategic investment. The hiatus of encouraging Hong Kong people to invest in northwest China partly reflected the central government's deliberate policy of facilitating the economic development of the less developed inner regions and partly illustrated the "policy wind" from the centre that has to be followed by the localities, including the HKSAR.[52]

The third planning and coordination area that involves the HKSAR and its neighboring regions is the idea of constructing the Hong Kong–Zhuhai–Macao bridge. Investors who are keen to envisage the realization of the proposed bridge, such as Gordon Wu, put the blame of the delay on some of the former senior bureaucrats of the HKSAR government, implicitly the former chief secretary Anson Chan.[53] The bridge's idea was floated in 2003, but due to the differences of opinions among Hong Kong, Macao, and Zhuhai on the technical issues such as capitalization, ownership, and management, the central government in Beijing had to intervene in the bridge's proposed construction by acting as an impartial referee. Zhuhai and Macao did not really hope to subsidize tremendously the construction of the bridge, whereas Shenzhen cast a covetous eye on the bridge by proposing a double Y formula, which meant that one of the bridgeheads would reach Shenzhen. Indeed, Shenzhen's idea was to reap the economic benefits of the bridge, thus stimulating the region's tourism development. Zhuhai, however, saw Shenzhen as the competitor. Macao was often subdued in its demand. Its Chief Executive Edmund Ho revealed that during the early phase of the discussion, the HKSAR government under the Tung leadership was so eager to see its rapid construction that it rejected the idea of having a railway line on the bridge.[54] Moreover, the Macao government did not really wish to insist on Macao's name to be put earlier before either Hong Kong or Guangdong, thus unveiling the political sensitivities of naming the bridge. The central government's State Development Planning Commission has studied the bridge proposal and tried to come up with a consensus acceptable to Guangdong's provincial government and the local governments in Zhuhai, Hong Kong, and Macao.

Other policy areas of planning and coordination between the HKSAR and Beijing, and between the HKSAR and Guangdong province, are extensive. After the early retirement of the former chief secretary Anson Chan in April 2001, her successor Donald Tsang accelerated the processes of planning and coordination with the mainland. They included discussions between the HKSAR and Guangdong authorities in the Hong Kong/Guangdong Cooperation Joint Conference, the talks on 24-hour passenger clearance at Lok Ma Chau and Huangguang, the co-location of customs and immigration facilities, the cooperation at border control points, the integration of Hong Kong's developmental strategies into the PRC five-year plan, the development of logistics and the Nansha region, the collaboration in cross-border environmental protection, the supply of Dongjiang water to Hong Kong, and the promotion of information technology.[55] The eventual 24-hour opening of the border points in Lok Ma Chau and Huangguang, and the agreement between the HKSAR and Shenzhen on the co-location of border checkpoints for the new 5,545-meter-long Western Corridor represented a triumph of cross-border planning, cooperation, and coordination.[56] In particular, law enforcement agencies, particularly the police forces in Hong Kong, Macao, and Guangdong province, have been cooperating closely in the areas of "strike hard campaigns" that are conducted simultaneously in the three places and aim at drug abuse, cross-border prostitution, and trafficking of women.[57] Other disciplinary forces such as the customs and immigration are collaborating closely in the Pearl River Delta region, signifying the triumph of cross-border cooperation between Hong Kong, Macao, and Guangdong province.[58]

In spite of the smooth cross-border cooperation between the HKSAR and its neighboring regions on border security and crime control, infrastructure projects that involve economic benefits tend to be controversial and potentially conflict-ridden. Just like the hurdles to the finalization of the technical details concerning investment, ownership, and maintenance of the proposed Hong Kong–Zhuhai–Macao bridge, the five-party Airport Committee embracing Hong Kong, Macao, Guangzhou, Shenzhen, and Zhuhai encountered deadlock after the fourth meeting in June 2003. The five-party Airport Committee did not meet from June 2003 to June 2007 because of the competing economic interests of the five airports. The fifth meeting was scheduled to meet in Guangzhou, which said that it would have difficulties convening the conference due to the need for Baiyun airport to be relocated.[59] The economic tensions between the five airports were unveiled when the Zhuhai airport, which was traditionally under-utilized and possessed only four percent of the passenger capacity compared with the Shenzhen counterpart, eventually decided in 2007 to cooperate managerially with the Hong Kong international airport. The Zhuhai move aroused the concern of some Macao elites, who bemoaned that the Macao airport missed a golden opportunity to compete with other regions by forging a partnership with Zhuhai. However, given the fact that Zhuhai had resistance to the construction of Macao's airport as early as the 1990s,[60] the sour relations between the two were by no means conducive to further airport cooperation. In terms of the passenger capacities handled by the five airports in 2006, Hong Kong remained the strongest (44 million), followed by Guangzhou (26 million), Shenzhen's Baoan airport (18 million), Macao (4.9 million), and Zhuhai (800,000).[61] In terms of cargo capacities, Hong Kong topped the list (3.5 million tons), followed by Guangzhou (650,000 tons), Shenzhen (560,000 tons), Macao (220,000 tons), and Zhuhai (8,800 tons).[62] Although Macao and Zhuhai were at the lower end of both cargo and passenger capacities, the fact that they could not cooperate more closely demonstrated their mutual jealousies.

Beijing also intervened in the finalization of the Shenzhen Bay Bridge and Port, where the co-inspection border check point involving both Hong Kong and Shenzhen customs has been operating since July 1, 2007.[63] Originally, the Shenzhen NPC members opposed the idea of extending the bridge into Shenzhen, raising the fear of Hong Kong–style protests and anti-CCP slogans on the bridge. After the HKSAR government clarified that such protests and banners would be disallowed, and in the wake of Beijing's intervention, 150 of the 167 SCNPC members voted for the draft resolution on the co-inspection border point in October 2006.[64] Clearly,

Beijing played the role of a finalized actor in any deadlock between Shenzhen and Hong Kong regarding infrastructure development.

Amidst intense rivalry is cooperative management. The HKSAR secured the full support of both Beijing and Shenzhen to use the Shenzhen airport to handle cargoes from Hong Kong during the apex of the SARS crisis. After the HKSAR Airport Authority's participation, the Zhuhai airport has improved its management and cargo as well as passenger capacities. The dialectical processes of mutual competition and cooperation will shape the relationships between the airports in Hong Kong, Macao, Zhuhai, Shenzhen, and Guangzhou in the coming decades.

Fiscal Relations

It is important to note that Article 106 of the Basic Law stipulates that the HKSAR shall use its financial resources exclusively for its own purposes and that they shall not be handed over to the central government. In fact, the central government does not levy taxes in the HKSAR. Although Article 107 of the Basic Law also states that the HKSAR government should strive to maintain a fiscal balance, the former Financial Secretary Donald Tsang adopted a tight fiscal policy and implemented budget deficits — moves that were supported by the central government in Beijing after the Asian financial crisis. Obviously, the HKSAR has been enjoying a relatively high degree of fiscal autonomy *vis-à-vis* the central government.

Yet Beijing can extract resources from the HKSAR by floating the shares and bonds of mainland enterprises in Hong Kong — a phenomenon that has gained currency since mid-2003. Indeed, the central government's policy of allowing mainland enterprises to participate in the HKSAR stock market has yielded mutual benefits. The Chinese Securities Regulatory Commission said in June 2007 that eligible financial firms would get licenses as qualified domestic institutional investors (QDII) starting from July 5, 2007, thus allowing mainland securities and fund-management firms to invest in the HKSAR so as to cool down the overheated mainland stock market.[65] On the one hand, Beijing's enterprises can accumulate capital through Hong Kong. On the other hand, the assets of many Hong Kong stock buyers have increased significantly since 2003. In particular, prior to the tenth anniversary of Hong Kong's return to the PRC, the stock market and Heng Seng Index in the HKSAR were unprecedentedly buoyant arguably because of the politico-economic factor, namely Beijing's determination to ensure an international image of an extremely prosperous Hong Kong and a successful model of the "one country, two systems."

However, critics have warned that the mainland and many Hong Kong stock buyers have lacked a sense of crisis consciousness and the frenzied growth of the stock markets in both the PRC and the HKSAR might precipitate a sudden collapse. Business tycoons Li Ka-shing and Lee Shau-kei warned the people of Hong Kong in late May 2007 that they should be cautious in their stock investment. Yet Hong Kong and Macao tycoon Stanley Ho in early July 2007 dismissed the remarks made by Li and Lee, saying that optimism would prevail in the development of China's and Hong Kong's stock markets. Although Beijing adopted its macro-level measures to exert some control over the overheated economy in the mainland, the reality was that the mainland stock markets remained overheated. The situation reflected the vast amount of wealth possessed by the rapidly growing middle class in the PRC. To help the central government provide a channel for the overheated economy to cool down, Hong Kong's stock and property markets have become a critical channel. From the interdependency perspective, both the PRC and the HKSAR have been benefiting from the massive mainland investment in the latter's stock and property markets. From the perspective of dependency relations, however, the HKSAR is running the danger of being immersed deeper into the mainland Chinese economy, whose oscillations would produce unpredictable, chaotic, and perhaps disastrous reactions from the materialistically-minded and stock market–driven public. No wonder it was reported in June 2007 that the Hong Kong Monetary Authorities had begun to study a contingency plan in response to any possible collapse of the mainland A shares.

Patron-Client Politics in a Pluralistic Context

Arguably, most political scientists studying Hong Kong's relations with its motherland have neglected the relevance and significance of patron-clientelism.[66] James Scott elaborated on the asymmetrical relations between the patron and the clients, especially how the patron can induce the loyalties from their clients.[67] Alex Weingrod stressed the reciprocal process in which party politicians distributed public jobs and resources in exchange for various kinds of political support, especially voting.[68] J. D. Powell emphasized the unequal dynamics between the patron and clients in terms of their wealth, status, and influence.[69] The complex relationships between political patrons and their friends and followers were epitomized by Scott as "machine politics." He wrote:

> The machine is best characterized by the nature of the cement binding leaders and followers. Ties based on charisma, coercion, or ideology were occasionally minor chords of machine orchestration; the 'boss' might take on some heroic proportions, he might use hired toughs or the police now and again to discourage opposition, and a populist ideological aura might accompany his acts. Such bonds were, for the machine, definitely subsidiary to the concrete, particularistic rewards that represented its staple means of political coordination. It is the predominance of these reward networks — the special quality of the ties between leaders and followers — that distinguishes the machine party from the non-machine party.[70]

The machine politics in the HKSAR is characterized by a powerful patron — Beijing — whose clients in the post-colonial capitalist enclave are enjoying political legitimacy and power conferred upon by the central government. Table 1.1 illustrates the inducement used by the central government to elicit political loyalties from its clients in the HKSAR. The chief executive, as the most powerful patron in the Hong Kong polity, can offer various inducements to solicit and solidify the political support from other clients, ranging from the core to the peripheral ones. The core clients of both C. H. Tung and Donald Tsang, for example, were the leaders of the Democratic Alliance for Betterment of Hong Kong (DAB), the pro-Beijing Federation of Trade Unions, members of the policy-making Executive Council (ExCo), and the political appointees under the Principal Officials Accountability System (POAS) established since July 2002. Civil servants are the non-clients of the HKSAR polity and hence, to secure their political support, both Beijing and Tsang have to rely on some former senior bureaucrats to hold the positions of principal officials, especially the portfolio that manages civil service affairs. From Beijing's united front perspective, civil servants in Hong Kong have to be lured to the side of the chief executive, thus maintaining the "executive-led" system where the senior bureaucrats and political appointees assisting him remain the most powerful elite. The other elements of the non-clients, namely the pro-democracy elites, are destined to be politically excluded from participation in the influential policy-making bodies, notably ExCo. Meanwhile, both Beijing and the HKSAR government adopt the policy of divide and rule toward the pro-democracy elite, offering concrete economic and political benefits to those who are vulnerable to co-optation. A notable example is perhaps LegCo member Lau Chin-shek, whose moderate political stance since Beijing

Table 1.1 Patron-Client Relations between Beijing and Hong Kong's Political Actors

Political Actors	Nature of Loyalties	Inducements
Chief Executive (client of Beijing, patron in Hong Kong)	Political loyalty to Beijing	Explicit politico-economic support, economic policies helping Hong Kong
ExCo members (core clients)	Political loyalty to patrons Chief Executive and Beijing	Support of the Chief Executive, prestige, status, power
Principal Officials (core clients)	Loyalty to Beijing and the Chief Executive	Prestige, status, political influence, policy-making power
Leaders of the Democratic Alliance For Betterment of Hong Kong (core clients)	Loyalty to Beijing and the Chief Executive	Prestige, status, political influence, policy-making power, and the ability to nominate party members to the Chief Executive for political appointments to advisory bodies, the Central Policy Unit and to District Councils.
Leaders of the Liberal Party (core clients)	Loyalty to Beijing and the Chief Executive	Prestige, status, political influence, policy-making power, and the ability to nominate party members to the Chief Executive for political appointments to advisory bodies, and District Councils.
(Non-clients) Civil servants	Loyalty to the Chief Executive	Encourage them to unite behind the Chief Executive and select experienced bureaucrats to join the Principal Officials Accountability System
Pro-democracy Elite	Very weak loyalty to the Chief Executive	Adopt divide-and-rule policy to split the democrats, politically exclude them from participation in the top policy-making body ExCo, minimizing their influence on the eighteen local District Councils

allowed him to visit his ailing mother in Guangdong showed that the HKSAR government has acted as an essential intermediary. The Lau case also illustrates the effectiveness of co-optation. Indeed, some die-hard democrats cannot be politically co-opted; "radical" elements such as Leung Kwok-hung and Raymond Wong have been using You Tube to publicize their political views and platforms as they argue convincingly that the mainstream Chinese media in Hong Kong have already marginalized them.

The patron-client politics in Hong Kong is an extension of Beijing's united front policy toward the HKSAR. The united front tactic is built on a powerful patron dispensing material and non-material benefits to its clients. In the case of Hong Kong, Beijing dispenses non-material benefits to all its friends and followers, namely social status, economic influence, and political power. Materially, the benefits acquired by the Hong Kong business elites are tremendous but hidden, especially with regard to their investment and business ventures in the mainland. Yet the united front policy implemented by Beijing is a skillful one that does not entail explicit material benefits conferred upon the Hong Kong clients. Otherwise, not only can the Independent Commission Against Corruption pursue such cases involving explicit material benefits, but many Hongkongers would see such reciprocal exchanges as morally and legally improper. In short, non-material rather than material benefits are the *sine qua non* of Beijing's patronage umbrella in the HKSAR.

It must be noted that patron-client politics in the HKSAR have been operating in a pluralistic context. While patron-clientelism is a hallmark of CCP politics in the mainland whereby its friends and followers have been occupying key positions of the public, semi-public, and private sectors, the Hong Kong circumstances tend to be more politically heterogeneous. With a more vibrant mass media, which however have shown signs of self-censorship especially among the local Chinese print and electronic media, the Hong Kong polity is subject to more external checks and balances. Adding to this external constraint is the complexities of the co-opted clients. In particular, the Liberal Party led by James Tien has posed a problem of co-optation from Beijing's point of view. Tien quitted ExCo suddenly in early July 2003 after his meeting with Liao Hui and the United Front Department's deputy director Liu Yandong, thus plunging the whole Article 23 saga into political turmoil.[71] Tien's political loyalty to both Tung and Beijing was partial and conditional, but he succeeded in influencing Donald Tsang's re-election as the chief executive in March 2007. In exchange for Tien's political support, Tsang had little choice but to quickly appoint him as the head of the Tourism Development Board, which under the previous headship Liberal Party member Selina Chow had been criticized for failure to supervise the mismanagement of the former director Chong Ming-wah. The crux of the matter is that James Tien's Liberal Party remains the kingmaker in the Legislative Council where neither the underground CCP members nor the pro-Beijing DAB can command the majority of its seats. As a result of a politically fragmented system, Beijing and the chief executive have to look for coalitional support, especially from the Liberal Party, thus making the "executive-led" regime relatively weaker than what they had hoped.

Even the DAB occasionally demonstrates its conditional support of the chief executive, particularly Donald Tsang whom the pro-Beijing party once viewed as a "pro-British" bureaucrat. Shortly after Tsang was elected as the chief executive replacing C. H. Tung, the DAB projected an image of keeping a distance from the former senior civil servant. Yet as a pro-CCP political party perhaps led by underground CCP members in the HKSAR, the DAB had little room for maneuver. It had to provide full political support for Tsang, who after all has been governing the HKSAR under Deng Xiaoping's principle of a broad "patriotic" coalition.

Another difficulty of patron-clientelism that is operating in a pluralistic polity is how to buy the political support of civil servants. Traditionally, civil servants merged the role of both policy implementators and politicians in Hong Kong under the British rule. This dual role has been curbed to some extent by the injection of the Principal Officials Accountability System (POAS). In order to rescue the declining morale of the senior civil servants, especially the senior Administrative Officers who do not see any prospect of being promoted as the top policy secretaries, Beijing and C. H. Tung devised the POAS in such a way as to allow the transfer of senior bureaucrats from public service to the batch of political appointees temporarily or permanently. Donald Tsang's new batch of POAS starting from July 1, 2007 embraces a considerable portion of former civil servants, thus demonstrating the imperative of Beijing to buy their political support through the appointment power and finesse of the chief executive. Former civil servants who are now working for Tsang's POAS include Secretary for Education Michael Suen, Secretary for Civil Service Denise Yue, Secretary for Transport and Housing Eva Cheng, Secretary for Development Carrie Lam, Secretary for Labour and Welfare Mathew Cheung, and Chief Executive Office Director Chan Tak-lam.[72] This co-optative strategy, however, does not ensure absolute political loyalty of all civil servants. Their massive protests against the policies of Tung, including civil service reforms and salary cuts, were reminders of the fragile political support among public servants. Some Administrative Officers also privately expressed their mistrust of the POAS. In short, the POAS mechanism can perhaps buy off the political support of some, but certainly not all, senior bureaucrats.

Despite the fact that economic prosperity would minimize machine politics, as argued by James Scott,[73] the reality of the Hong Kong case is that the HKSAR economic prosperity is accompanied by extensive political patronage without violating the Prevention of Bribery Ordinance. Basically, political positions are rewarded to friends and supporters of the chief executive without any monetary benefits. The patron-clientelism without monetary forms of corruption remains the defining feature of the Hong Kong style of patronage politics.

Toward Multiple and Complementary Perspectives on "One Country, Two Systems"

Although the annexation perspective that portrays the coming rapid transformation of the CCP and the inevitable triumph of capitalism over socialism appears to be risky and premature in its conclusion, it will be increasingly prominent as the HKSAR proceeds into the year 2047, when the Basic Law will be perhaps renewed by another mini-constitution and when Hong Kong will likely merge with the mainland in a more comprehensive way.

In the short run, however, the political control perspective has its utility. The evolution of *nomenklatura* is connected with the PRC's long-term transformation, including the question whether Hong Kong would "annex" the mainland or vice versa. On the other hand, the political control perspective is intimately linked to the clash of civilization thesis. So long as the mainland Chinese civilization remains resistant to Western values such as individualism, pluralism, the rule of law, and internal as well as external checks and balances, the PRC will still use its *nomenklatura* to exert politico-personnel control over the HKSAR.

The bureaucratic politics perspective is equally relevant to the Hong Kong circumstances, especially if the PRC polity is characterized by fragmented authoritarianism. The varying agencies responsible for Hong Kong affairs, and their personnel changes, will largely condition the ways in which the center's policy toward the HKSAR is formulated. Factional politics in Beijing will also condition the chances of various candidates for the chief executive in the HKSAR. The unpredictable personal factor on the side of Beijing cannot be neglected in any analysis of elite strife in Hong Kong.

Yet the central government in Beijing is by no means a monolithic actor focusing on politico-personnel control over Hong Kong alone. Instead, it has been playing the role of a more impartial referee adjudicating in the disputes between Hong Kong and its neighboring Chinese regions on various issues, particularly infrastructural projects such as the Hong Kong–Zhuhai–Macao bridge. The multi-faceted roles of Beijing, ranging from a political controller to an economic coordinator, cannot be swept under the carpet in any analysis of its relationships with the HKSAR.

The fiscal relationships between Beijing and the HKSAR will not remain static. So long as Beijing fully supports the Hong Kong model of "one country, two systems," it must prop up the HKSAR economy by all means. On the other hand, the HKSAR provides a safety valve for Beijing to handle the overheated mainland economy and to allow domestic capital to flow into the Hong Kong economy. Yet this situation would unlikely be a permanent one. In the event of any drastic economic fluctuations in the PRC, the fiscal relations with the HKSAR will perhaps alter. In particular, as long as the HKSAR does not need to pay taxes to the central government, some mainland provinces may cast a covetous eye on the special privilege enjoyed by Hong Kong. It remains unclear whether this privileged economic status will be retained in the years beyond 2047, when Hong Kong will likely be integrated more fully into the orbit of the mainland Chinese politico-economic system, regardless of whether the PRC would remain socialist or capitalist.

In the short and medium terms, patron-client pluralism will remain the defining characteristic of the relationships between the HKSAR and Beijing. Beijing as the most powerful patron remains dominant over any political actor in the HKSAR. Beijing also as the ultimate patron must prop up the HKSAR regime by all means, including economic measures such as CEPA, individual free visits schemes, and allowing mainland enterprises to float their shares in Hong Kong's stock market. As the most influential client of Beijing and the most powerful patron in the Hong Kong polity, the chief executive is bound to be politically loyal to Beijing. Naturally, the chief executive is far more accountable to the central government than to the Hong Kong people. Indeed, public opinion in the HKSAR does matter especially if a large segment of the population is alienated, as with the case of C. H. Tung whose resignation for health reasons was a face-saving move orchestrated by Beijing. His resignation proved that Beijing did listen to public opinion in the HKSAR, but only at a very critical juncture. The ways in which Beijing handled Tung showed that it learnt politically how to manage the HKSAR. By listening to the strong public opinion against

Tung, Beijing's leadership had to slightly alter its paternalistic political culture. The clash of mainland Chinese and Western civilization did exist in the public discontent toward C. H. Tung. Beijing had to moderate its hardline stance on Hong Kong matters, realizing the failure of the Liaison Office to understand the real public opinion in the HKSAR from July 1997 to July 2003.

On the other hand, the pro-democracy elites in the HKSAR expect the chief executive to be more accountable to the people of Hong Kong and less so to the central government. This tug of war between the chief executive and the pro-democracy elites will lead to incessant disputes, political polarization, and endless struggle in the years to come. The ongoing political contention over the pace and scope of democratization in the HKSAR illustrates the deep political divide between the chief executive and his political clients on the one hand and the pro-democracy elites on the other. The pro-democracy elites hope for a democratic China where the official verdict on the 1989 Tiananmen incident will be reversed and which will allow more political space for Hong Kong's democratic reform. Their political ideals, however, remain "subversive" to the central government as long as the clash of mainland Chinese and Western civilizations persists. The HKSAR is a polity sandwiched between the PRC and the Western ideals. As a former British colony absorbing much of the Western values, such as the rule of law, pluralism, individualism, transparency, and checks and balances, Hong Kong remains a crucial test case for democratization in mainland China under the CCP leadership. The future development of the PRC, including the CCP transformation, its *nomenklatura*, political cultures, planning/coordination roles, and patron-clientelist practices will evolve and shape the politics of the HKSAR in the coming decades. In a nutshell, the relationships between Beijing and the HKSAR will be dynamic, reflecting the clash between Western and Chinese civilization, the internal metamorphosis of the mainland, and the adaptation of the most powerful patron to a pluralistic political setting in Hong Kong.

If these multiple perspectives are applied to solve the problem of Taiwan's political future, they would have to be revised or jettisoned so that the "one country, two systems" would become politically attractive to the ROC on Taiwan. First and foremost, Taiwan will surely find the PRC politico-legal control over the HKSAR unacceptable and counter-productive to any solutions on the island. Similarly, the *nomenklatura* system cannot be applied to the Taiwan problem, for it would be seen as clandestine political infiltration into the island. The rigid implantation of any patron-client model into Taiwan will be counter-productive to any breakthrough in Beijing-

Taipei relations, for those Taiwan people who are seen to be co-opted by the PRC would be vulnerable to political retaliation from the pro-independence Taiwanese. Playing any game of patron-client relations in Taiwan would not only have to be extremely cautious but would also backfire if anti-PRC sentiment were instigated by Taiwanese political demagogues. While it is unclear whether bureaucratic politics in the mainland will shape the PRC policies toward Taiwan, the fiscal autonomy enjoyed by the HKSAR *vis-à-vis* Beijing will be politically acceptable to the Taiwan side. Still, the Taiwan security apparatus views the mainland capital and investment in the island as a potentially dangerous or "subversive" step toward politico-economic integration. If Taiwan's political landscape is divided by the pro-integration Kuomintang (KMT) and the pro-independence Democratic Progressive Party (DPP), economic integration with the mainland is viewed as sinister by DPP supporters. Yet the integrationists in Taiwan see engagement with the mainland as a progressive step toward peaceful dialogue and settlement of Taiwan's political future.

The annexation perspective remains controversial when it is applied to the Beijing-Taipei relations. Both the KMT and DPP supporters hope that the capitalist revolution in the PRC would bring about Western-style democracy or lead to the eventual CCP collapse. This annexation scenario, or the Taiwanization of the PRC, is bound to be rejected and guarded against by the CCP. Beijing hopes that by allowing the investment of Taiwanese business people in the mainland, economic integration would trigger political reunification. Economic integration between Taiwan and the PRC would hopefully, from the CCP angle, facilitate Beijing's "annexation" of Taiwan. The controversy over the Taiwanization of the PRC, or the Sinification of Taiwan, will persist so long as the Taiwan polity and society are split into two camps, one being integrationists and the other separatists.

2

The Mainlandization of Hong Kong

Since Hong Kong's return of its sovereignty from Britain to the PRC on July 1, 1997, its political development has proved to be turbulent. This chapter aims at analyzing the dynamics contributing to Hong Kong's governing crisis. It will argue that the most significant factor leading to its governance crisis from July 1997 to March 2005 was the tension between convergence and divergence. While the concern of "one country" has been propelling Hong Kong toward a system more politically similar to the PRC than ever before, the demands of maintaining the "two systems" has become an obstacle to the policy intentions of both Beijing and its clientelist Hong Kong regime. The chapter will first examine the end of the Tung Chee-hwa administration. Then it will discuss the theory of convergence and explore how the two dimensions — political and economic — of convergence have been unfolding in Hong Kong since its retrocession. Finally, it will assess the strategy of mainlandization of the Donald Tsang administration, the problem of recolonizing the Hong Kong polity, and the political consequences of Hong Kong's increasing politico-economic convergence with mainland China.

The End of the Tung Chee-hwa Era

On March 10, 2005, the HKSAR Chief Executive Tung Chee-hwa tendered his formal resignation to the State Council of the PRC, terminating his seven years and eight months of turbulent governance. Tung used poor health as a justification for his resignation.[1] Yet the new PRC leadership under President Hu Jintao and Premier Wen Jiabao after 2003 viewed the Tung administration as having "inadequacies" in governance.[2] Hu publicly appealed to the Tung government to look into its "inadequacies" on

December 21, 2004, when he attended the fifth anniversary of the Macao Special Administrative Region.[3] After the mass protests of half a million Hong Kong people on the streets on July 1, 2003, Beijing set up a coordination committee led by Politburo member Zeng Qinghong to deal with the Hong Kong crisis, which stemmed from the public outcry over the proposed enactment of Article 23 of the Basic Law — a provision that outlaws treason, sedition, secession, and subversion in the HKSAR.[4] The protestors were dissatisfied with a whole range of government policies, including housing, social welfare cuts, civil service reform, and the crisis mismanagement of the SARS.[5] The mass protests shocked the PRC leaders who immediately decided to establish the coordination committee. It was composed of eighteen members including officials from the State Council's Hong Kong and Macao Affairs Office, the Liaison Office in Hong Kong, the Liaison Office in Macao, the Ministry of Public Security, the Ministry of National Security, the Party Central Committee's United Front Department, and the People's Liberation Army.[6]

Although Beijing propped up Tung after the political earthquake on July 1, 2003 by signing the Closer Economic Partnership Arrangement (CEPA) with the HKSAR government and by allowing more mainland tourists to visit the territory, the gradual economic rebound in Hong Kong could not prevent dissatisfied citizens from taking to the streets.[7] On July 1, 2004, about 500,000 people again protested against the Tung administration, ensuing reports that three popular radio hosts — Albert Cheng, Raymond Wong, and Allen Lee — quitted their radio phone-in programs mainly because of mysterious intimidation (see Table 2.1 for the estimated number of protestors).[8] The HKSAR's "one country, two systems" was designed by PRC leaders, including the late Deng Xiaoping, as a show window for mainland China to appeal to the ROC on Taiwan for reunification.[9] Nevertheless, the Tung regime's turbulent governance discredited the Hong Kong model and embarrassed the Beijing leadership. Understandably, Beijing's leaders such as Hu and Zeng publicly expressed their mild criticisms of the Hong Kong government. After all, Tung's patron, the former PRC President Jiang Zemin, transferred political power to the new PRC leaders and stepped down from his chairmanship of the Central Military Commission in March 2005. The withdrawal of Jiang from the PRC political arena, the displeasure of the new leaders over Tung's performance, and the gradual economic recovery of the HKSAR in 2004 and early 2005 presented a golden opportunity for the embattled and unpopular chief executive to offer his resignation.[10] Beijing's acceptance of his resignation ended the Tung era in the HKSAR.

Table 2.1 Estimated Number of Participants on the July 1 Protests, 2003–2007

Year	Number estimated by organizers	Police estimates	Number estimated by researchers at the University of Hong Kong
2003	500,000	350,000	429,000–502,000
2004	530,000	200,000	180,000–207,000
2005	21,000	17,000	20,000–24,000
2006	58,000	28,000	33,000–39,000
2007	68,000	20,000	29,000–35,000

Source: *Sing Tao Daily*, July 2, 2007; and *Ming Pao*, July 2, 2007.

Convergence and the Hong Kong Case

This chapter uses the case of the HKSAR to illuminate whether the territory has undergone a path of political, economic, social, and legal convergence with its motherland and overlord, the PRC. During the late 1960s and early 1970s, the theory of convergence emerged, predicting that the former Soviet Union's socio-political metamorphosis would be parallel to the American democratic development. The convergence theory's premise was that "all industrial societies do share certain salient features," such as a pluralistic society, a participatory and democratic polity, economic abundance, bureaucratization, and the use of merit to assess individual performance in public and private organizations.[11] Another assumption was a firm "belief in progress, expressed as theories of development and modernization based on economic determinism."[12] The eventual collapse of the former Soviet Union has appeared to prove the validity of the convergence theory, for democracy seemed to be the outcome of economic modernization; nonetheless, critics have pointed to the authoritarian nature of the new Russian regime.[13] It is premature to jump to the conclusion that the PRC's rapid socio-political development is corroborating the convergence theory; the CCP remains a politically preponderant force in the mainland although the Chinese economy is increasingly marketized and globalized. It is debatable whether marketization and economic liberation in the PRC will bring about Western-style democracy.[14]

Regardless of the predictions on mainland China's future development, Hong Kong can shed light on the dimensions of the HKSAR's convergence with the PRC during the Tung Chee-hwa era from 1997 to 2005.[15] Instead of having the PRC's authoritarian system converging politically with Hong Kong's semi-competitive system where the opposition can challenge the ruling political forces,[16] a reverse process of convergence diluting Hong

Kong's political and economic uniqueness could be seen. In a nutshell, the HKSAR's return to the motherland has propelled the former's polity and economy to move closer to the latter's than before. Although the HKSAR polity and economy have increasingly become dependent on and convergent with the PRC,[17] its legal system and society remain relatively diverged from the PRC's.[18] The legal system of Hong Kong retains its common law, although Beijing has increasingly interpreted the Hong Kong Basic Law. The society of Hong Kong remains relatively pluralistic and defiant of the government, unlike the relatively weaker society in the PRC.[19]

Convergence and Mainlandization Policy

The turbulent governance of the Tung era was an outcome of his mainlandization policy, which attempted to make Hong Kong politically and economically converge with the PRC. Tung's failures overshadowed his successes, although his regime's hallmark was to embark on policies that transformed the HKSAR into an entity more akin to the PRC than ever before. A subtle process of mainlandization, or Sinification, of Hong Kong could be witnessed; various aspects of the political, economic, and legal systems were converging with the PRC. The term "mainlandization" has been used by some Hong Kong people and observers to refer to the political and legal processes in which the HKSAR has demonstrated the practices of mainland China. Political scientists Anthony Cheung and Wilson Wong expressed their concerns about the trend of the "mainlandization" of the civil service in Hong Kong where the bureaucracy might become less Weberian and more vulnerable to political penetration.[20] The former Democratic Party chairman Martin Lee argued in 1999 that without democratic conventions, the PRC would weaken the rule of law in the HKSAR.[21] Journalists pointed to the likelihood that "mainlandization" of Hong Kong would lead to self-censorship in the mass media.[22] During the debate over the National Security (Legislative Provisions) Bill, some Hong Kong people expressed grave concerns that their civil liberties would be restricted or "mainlandized."[23] Cheung, Wong, Lee, and others have not clearly defined "mainlandization," which to them refers specifically to a trend that the HKSAR's uniqueness is diluted to some degree. Mainlandization does not carry any negative connotation; it here refers to the HKSAR government's policy of making Hong Kong politically more dependent on and similar to Beijing, economically more reliant on the mainland's support, socially more patriotic toward the motherland, and legally more reliant on the interpretation of the Basic Law by the Standing Committee of the National People's Congress. It is the dependency psyche of the HKSAR administration that has triggered Hong Kong's swift convergence with the motherland in multi-faceted aspects. Tung Chee-hwa's premise that the interest of "one country" must precede the interest of the "two systems" and that the motherland's development must be beneficial to Hong Kong laid the foundation for his dependent development policy toward Beijing.[24] His successor Donald Tsang, as will be discussed, has been maintaining the policy of dependent development — a strategy that brings about mainlandization of the HKSAR.

Ideologically, the ruling elites in the HKSAR firmly believe that political correctness along the line of the CCP leadership is a must, that *realpolitik* can ensure the continuous survival and prosperity of the HKSAR, and that the global rise of mainland China is advantageous to Hong Kong's socio-economic development. This pro-PRC ideology is bound to clash with the pro-Western ideology held by many liberal-minded Hong Kong intellectuals and professionals, who have a deep conviction that the emergent PRC remains relatively "underdeveloped" in the rule of law, the protection of civil liberties, the independence of mass media, and the existence of political opposition. Dependent development, in the eyes of the liberal-minded Hong Kong people, runs the risk of making the HKSAR convergent with the mainland politically, socially, economically, and legally. Huntington's clash of civilization thesis can be applied to our understanding of the dichotomy between convergence and divergence. While followers of the mainland Chinese civilization see any convergence between the HKSAR and the PRC as culturally positive, politically inevitable, and mutually beneficial, the Hong Kong supporters of Western civilization regard it as culturally, politically, economically, and legally retrogressive. In short, many liberal-minded and Western-educated Hongkongers see the divergence between the HKSAR and Beijing as a necessity that can retain Hong Kong's specificity. Those who identify themselves strongly as Hongkongers are likely to be more pro-Western, while those who identify themselves strongly as Chinese are likely to favor convergence. Ideologies, civilizations, and identities are closely intertwined in the dialectical struggle between convergence and divergence.

From the perspective of political convergence, the HKSAR under the Tung leadership became similar to the PRC's practices in two prominent aspects. First and foremost, Beijing's political intervention in the HKSAR affairs was deeper as the legitimacy crisis of the Tung administration became serious.[25] Such intervention took the forms of PRC leaders, such as Jiang

Zemin, voicing support of Tung and mobilizing the pro-Beijing trade unions, Fujianese associations, and other united front organizations to vote for like-minded candidates in both Legislative Council and District Councils elections.[26] The PRC officials' open support of the candidate of the chief executive election in 2005 and then 2007, former chief secretary Donald Tsang, was a testimony to Beijing's political intervention in the HKSAR polity.[27] Another feature of mainlandization of Hong Kong's political arena was the prominence of patronage in the Tung administration that appointed pro-Beijing elites into advisory committees and policymaking organs such as the top advisory Executive Council (ExCo).[28] At the same time, the democrats were excluded from participation in these bodies until Donald Tsang became the acting chief executive in March 2005, when he began to appoint some of them into bodies such as the Equal Opportunities Commission while removing a few pro-Beijing elites from advisory bodies.[29] However, Tsang's co-optation strategy immediately after his election as the third chief executive appeared to revert to Tung's exclusionist style; democrats such as Martin Lee, Kuan Hsin-chi, Christine Loh, Tik Chi-yuen, Wong Wai-yin, and Lo Chi-kin were not reappointed to the Strategic Development Commission (SDC) in June 2007.[30] Although many other conservatives and pro-Beijing elites were simultaneously not appointed to the SDC, the new batch of appointees has included mainly moderates and pro-establishment elites, such as Regina Ip, David Akers-Jones, Elsie Leung, Rosanna Wong Yick-ming, Eric Li Ka-cheung, and Tung Kin-shing. On balance, the new SDC is politically dominated by conservatives. If the PRC's united front strategy is marked by the political exclusion of critics, it can also be seen in Tsang's appointment of SDC members in June 2007.

Success and Failure of C. H. Tung from the Convergence Perspective

Tung Chee-hwa was a diligent chief executive whose moral integrity was widely recognized. He reportedly worked for long hours every day.[31] Tung succeeded in projecting an image of a persistent leader in face of public criticisms and condemnations. From the perspective of the PRC government, Tung succeeded in helping Hong Kong survive the Asian financial crisis of late 1997 and 1998. Beijing praised him for implementing the unprecedented concept of "Hong Kong people ruling Hong Kong" and the tenet of "one country, two systems," albeit the reality was his proclivity of tilting toward the concerns of Beijing, such as the labeling of the Falun Gong as a "cult" in the HKSAR.³² During the tenth anniversary of the HKSAR, President Hu publicly eulogized Tung for laying the foundation of "one country, two systems."³³ From the perspective of convergence, Tung had impressive achievements, including the emphasis on patriotism and the determination to make Hong Kong economically dependent on the mainland. His famous quotation — "Whenever the motherland is good, Hong Kong is good too" — illustrated the necessary political correctness demanded by the central government in Beijing.

Tung was free from either corrupt scandal or any event riddled with conflict of interest. When Tung announced his resignation to the people of Hong Kong on March 12, his last statement was that he would not return to his family shipping business. Tung was a generous leader in the eyes of the public; he seldom asked his principal officials to resign despite the fact that a number of them committed grave errors.³⁴ From the perspective of the tourist industry, Tung succeeded in not only finalizing an agreement with the Walt Disney to build the Disneyland theme park on the Lantau Island but also forging a closer economic relationship with the PRC. Tourism in Hong Kong has benefited tremendously from the visits of mainlanders to Hong Kong in July 2003. Apart from Tung's success in enlisting the support and trust from the central government, some commentators pointed to Tung's relative tolerance of the political opposition without using the police to suppress and arrest its members, although some democrats were constantly monitored by Beijing's agents and the local police.³⁵ It is fair to conclude that the Tung era allowed sufficient political space for the opposition to survive.

Yet Tung's failures overshadowed his successes. Critics have pointed to the failure of the first HKSAR government from July 1, 1997 to June 2001 in formulating and implementing a coherent set of policies for Hong Kong. In 1997, Tung and his advisers had the good intention of providing affordable housing to all the people of Hong Kong by building 85,000 units per year. However, due to the onset of the Asian financial crisis in late 1997 and 1998, his new housing policy was abandoned in 1998 without announcing its end to the public until the summer of 2000. Critics maintained that his regime's communication gap with the public was wide, a problem compounded by the implementation of other reforms without adequate consultation, such as civil service reform, education reform, and the reduction of government subsidies to social service agencies.³⁶

The Tung administration demonstrated inexperience in tackling abrupt crises, such as the outbreak of the bird flu in late 1997 and later the sudden emergence of SARS in March 2003.³⁷ The hesitancy of Tung was exacerbated by the fact that these health crises were completely new and unprecedented. It was the former chief secretary, Anson Chan Fang On-sang, who made the decision to slaughter the infected chickens, thus stopping the spread of the deadly disease. The outbreak of SARS originated from the PRC, but it fully exposed the poor coordination between not only the HKSAR's Health Department and the mainland's health authorities but also between the Health Department and the Hong Kong Hospital Authority.[38] Tung performed much better in the outbreak of SARS than the bird flu, for he urged the health officials to tackle the crisis in a more determined manner. However, the series of governing crises plunged his popularity to an all-time low prior to the mass protests on July 1, 2003.

Another failure of the Tung administration was its patronage strategy that excluded all his political foes, notably the democrats, from ExCo and many advisory bodies while awarding friends and supporters with appointed positions. The pro-Beijing elites were given preferential treatment in ExCo, District Councils, and public corporations. Yeung Kwong, a pro-Beijing working-class leader who instigated the 1967 riots in Hong Kong, was awarded with the Grand Bauhinia Medal in July 2001 amidst public outcry.[39] It was natural that the anti-British patriots have been accorded with special treatment and political rehabilitation since the post-colonial era. Unfortunately, the pro-Beijing elite's performance did not really measure up to public expectations. Some of them constantly made remarks offending the general public; others like the leaders of the pro-Beijing political party Democratic Alliance for Betterment of Hong Kong (DAB) were uncritical supporters of Tung and became increasingly detached from public sentiments. The Housing Authority headed by former ExCo member Rosanna Wong Yick-ming was engulfed in a short piling scandal in which housing units in the Home Ownership Scheme were found to have substandard foundation — a scandal leading to Wong's resignation. Prior to the massive protests against Article 23 of the Basic Law on July 1, 2003, Jasper Tsang of the DAB arrogantly said that the public opposition was "misled." After the mass protests, he quickly apologized to the public.[40] In May 2007, Ma Lik, the late DAB leader, went so far as to deny the human casualties during the 1989 Tiananmen tragedy and to claim that "even pigs run over by tanks would not be turned into mincemeat."[41] Student democrat Wang Dan referred to Ma as "utterly devoid of conscience."[42] Overall, the pro-Beijing and pro-government elites who have been dominating the political arena failed to demonstrate either their competence in assisting Tung to manage crises effectively or their political conscience in admitting the CCP errors in the 1989 Tiananmen tragedy. The exclusion of democrats from participation in an overwhelming majority of the policy-making and advisory bodies resulted in a one-sided view encircling the Tung leadership and perpetuating its communication gap with the public. The price of political patronage was high to C. H. Tung.

From the vantage point of convergence, Tung's patronage politics had much in common with the PRC. Beijing also backed Tung up for his decision to distribute political favors to supporters and clients, notably the DAB and many pro-Beijing elites. Yet from the perspective of many Hong Kong people, Tung's policy of mainlandization had the impact of political alienation. Most civil servants, for example, detested his reforms. During Tung's first term of office, his sour relationships with some civil servants sowed the seeds of discord and discoordination in the government. Tung's ExCo was dominated by the business people, who advocated civil service reform and who saw public servants as being overpaid and underworked. ExCo's approval of civil service reform antagonized many civil service unions that viewed the chief executive as being hostile to public servants. Tung's disagreement with the former chief secretary Anson Chan, who had been promoted by Christopher Patten as the first Chinese chief secretary before the handover and whose determination to defend the uniqueness of the "two systems" clashed with Tung's preference for the concerns of "one country," emerged as a thorny problem of governance, especially in the eyes of the pro-Beijing elites who were deeply distrustful of Chan's political loyalty.[43] The retirement of Chan from politics in 2000 cleared the way for Tung to install his own batch of political supporters into the new Principal Officials Accountability System (POAS) on July 1, 2002, when the chief executive began his second term after a non-competitive chief executive election in which he had become the only candidate endorsed by both Beijing and the majority of the members of the 800-member Election Committee.[44] Some former civil servants such as Donald Tsang and Michael Suen joined the POAS; nevertheless, Tung's civil service reform had already cultivated distrust and dissent among many civil servants.

The implementation of any mainlandization policy required political finesse on the part of Tung; nevertheless, his failure was his inability to balance various political actors. Tung was viewed as too pro-business, anti-civil servants, anti-democracy, indecisive, over-ambitious in his grandiose plans and policies, and protective of principal officials whose performance was questionable. The outcome was a relatively weak post-colonial state where the pro-Beijing elites were fragmented; even the pro-business Liberal Party and the middle-lower class DAB bickered over issues concerning livelihood and Article 23 of the Basic Law. The chairman of the Liberal

Party, James Tien, quitted ExCo on July 6, 2003, thus plunging the Tung regime into disarray and forcing him to announce the indefinite postponement of the legislation on Article 23.[45] Compounding the weak post-colonial government was Tung's lack of personal charisma and political authority. Tien presented Tung with an ultimatum that he would resign from ExCo if the National Security (Legislative Provisions) Bill were not postponed.[46] The PRC officials responsible for the HKSAR affairs turned a blind eye to the rapidly deteriorating governing environment before the mass protests on July 1, 2003, feeding the central government with over-optimistic and over-positive reports about the territory. Due to the total underestimation of the Hong Kong crisis by the PRC officials stationed in Hong Kong in late June 2003, when media reports predicted a large turnout of protestors on July 1, Beijing was alarmed and decided to send various work teams and researchers to understand the public sentiments in a more accurate manner.[47]

Tung's Convergence Crisis and Beijing

The crisis of governance in the Tung era actually reflected the dilemmas and difficulties of his convergence policy. If he adopted policies politically converging with the mainland, they were bound to alienate the majority of the Hong Kong people. Ironically, Beijing found such convergence policies politically acceptable. Adding fuel to the fire was the role of pro-Beijing elites, such as the DAB leaders and other die-hard conservatives, who regarded themselves as the most powerful political actors and who arrogantly denounced the pro-democracy elites as "unpatriotic." Waving the banner of patriotism, many members of the pro-Beijing Hong Kong elites became a political liability to C. H. Tung, who was increasingly seen by the public as having fallen under the influence of the politically correct but substantially mediocre "patriots." In reality, what was in Beijing's interest was not necessarily the interest of the people of Hong Kong — a position that was ignored and denied by Tung as he assumed the harmonization of interests between the Hong Kong people and the central government.

Beijing's high-profile and uncritical support of Tung for the second term of office was a strategy attributable to two major factors. First and foremost, Beijing found Tung a perfect ally in his policy of converging Hong Kong with mainland China. The Hong Kong people, in the minds of Beijing, lacked a strong sense of patriotism. Tung's vision of patriotism had much in common with Beijing's, for both equated nationalistic sentiment with political loyalty to the Chinese Communist Party.[48] Since Tung had been endorsed by the former president Jiang Zemin in late 1996 until 2003, when the elderly Chinese leader began to transfer his political power to the younger successor Hu Jintao, Tung's leadership problem became a political taboo constantly shunned by the uncritical pro-Beijing elites in Hong Kong. Although a minority of Hong Kong businessmen and some mainland Chinese entrepreneurs did express their dissatisfaction with Tung's performance to Beijing's leaders, PRC officials responsible for Hong Kong affairs swiftly conducted united front work to appease the tycoons' anger.[49] Some of the local business elites were alienated by the Tung regime's apparently preferential treatment offered to tycoon Li Ka-shing's son, Richard Li, in the development of the Cyberport without any public tender.[50] Still, Beijing and Jiang's high-profile support of Tung for the second term of office stifled the local elite's criticisms, not to mention any need for Beijing to truly understand the public discontent in Hong Kong before the political earthquake on July 1, 2003.

Second, compounding the problem of Beijing's insistence in propping up the unpopular chief executive was the political dominance of its agents and officials handling the Hong Kong affairs, notably the State Council's Hong Kong and Macao Affairs Office (HKMAO) led by Liao Hui and the Liaison Office (LO) in Hong Kong led by Jiang Enzhu and later Gao Siren. Liao and Gao were at loggerheads at the central government's Hong Kong and Macao Work Committee meeting in 2004.[51] Prior to the political tsunami on July 1, 2003, the LO was too close to the pro-Beijing Hong Kong elites and naturally provided over-positive reports on the HKSAR to Beijing. Yet the HKMAO kept a very low profile under Liao's leadership — a far cry from his predecessor Lu Ping who had confronted and argued with Christopher Patten over Hong Kong's political reform.[52] As Jiang Zemin was determined to support Tung for the second term and angrily accused the Hong Kong reporters of being "too simple, too naïve,"[53] both PRC officials and pro-Beijing elites quickly became loyal followers of Jiang without the political will to remove or unseat Tung. Yet once Beijing was determined to let Tung resign and designate Donald Tsang as the replacement chief executive, the uncritical pro-Beijing elites toed the official line.[54] In short, the supporters of Beijing in the HKSAR, notably the LO officials, favored Tung's convergence policy. When Tsang was the candidate favored by Beijing, the local hard-line leftists in the HKSAR had no choice but to support him, although they doubted whether Tsang would continue to make Hong Kong politically and economically converge with the mainland. If uncritical clientelist support of the patron is a hallmark of mainland Chinese politics, such mainlandization can be seen in the Tung era and in the current Tsang administration, where pro-Beijing elites are in practice self-serving opportunists bending easily with the political wind from the central government.

In an attempt to ameliorate the governing crisis resulting from the convergence policy, the second Tung administration altered its composition with Beijing's full backing. The introduction of the POAS on July 1, 2002 was a move designed to unify the advisers of Tung and consolidate his regime legitimacy.[55] Unfortunately, the newly appointed principal officials, who served the government on contractual terms and who were not civil servants, needed more time to accumulate their political experience and expertise. In March 2003, the former financial secretary Antony Leung was embroiled in a car purchasing scandal in which he bought a luxurious car when he knew that the vehicle license tax would increase.[56] From early to mid-2003, the former secretary for security, Regina Ip, alienated the public by trying to push through the passage of the National Security (Legislative Provisions) Bill that would outlaw sedition, treason, secession, and subversion.[57] The public widely regarded the bill as an infringement upon their much-cherished civil liberties, whereas an overwhelming majority of lawyers rose up against the attempt at legislating on Article 23.[58]

The legitimacy crisis of the second Tung administration was aggravated by the defiant Bishop (now Cardinal) Joseph Zen, whose relations with Beijing remained frosty, who publicly spoke against the government on its refusal to grant mainland Chinese the right of abode in the HKSAR in 1999, and who mobilized members of the Catholic Church to protest against Article 23 of the Basic Law. Zen's opposition provided the spiritual leadership in the society's confrontation with the post-colonial regime.[59] Due to the mobilization by the Catholic Church, radio hosts, lawyers, intellectuals, students, working-class employees, and middle-class homeowners who suffered from negative equity after the Asian economic crisis, half a million people went to the streets on July 1, 2003 to protest against the Tung regime's misrule.[60] At this juncture, the new Chinese leadership of President Hu and Premier Wen Jiabao (Wen left Hong Kong and stayed in Shenzhen on July 1, 2003) was shocked by the seriousness of public discontent in the HKSAR.[61] Wen reportedly told his subordinates that there must be something wrong in the HKSAR governance.[62] Liao Hui reportedly offered to resign but it was rejected by Beijing, whereas the LO leadership underwent a reshuffle.[63] Beijing's officials responsible for Hong Kong matters were forced by the circumstances to reassess their previous policy of steadfastly supporting Tung, to receive various delegations from Hong Kong, and to emphasize the importance of maintaining the stability of the HKSAR.

From the perspective of convergence, Cardinal Zen detested the HKSAR government policy of mainlandization and allied with the democrats to oppose the chief executive. Cardinal Zen's previous socialization as a priest working in Shanghai for ten years also nurtured his deep conviction on how the CCP controlled the Catholics in the mainland.[64] Beatrice Leung observes that Cardinal Zen is "equipped with divine and profane qualities" and "can be the Sign of the Time to speak the message of God in his struggle for the gospel value: justice, peace and the respect of human rights which are the expression of God's love in action."[65] Cardinal Zen tends to see the mainland Chinese civilization in a more critical manner, believing that the CCP had a long history of persecuting many believers of the Catholic Church and the mainland supporters of the Vatican. Ideologically, Cardinal Zen also believes that the HKSAR should have the direct elections of both the chief executive and the whole Legislative Council as soon as possible.[66]

Ideologically, Cardinal Zen has shared common views with the former chief secretary Anson Chan. While Anson Chan is widely viewed as a representative of the "Hong Kong conscience," Cardinal Zen identifies himself strongly with Hong Kong. Chan saw the POAS as a scheme that would curb the role and power of the senior Administrative Officers, thus triggering her early retirement from the HKSAR government in 2001. Zen, on the other hand, saw Tung's policy of mainlandization with great suspicions, a position similar to Chan's doubts on whether the idea of constructing the Hong Kong–Zhuhai–Macao bridge would really be beneficial to the HKSAR. Both Zen and Chan have such a strong Hong Kong identity that their distance from the values beholden by the CCP — political loyalty, harmony, and conformity — is constantly at odds with those Hong Kong people who strongly identify themselves with mainland China. The pro-Beijing identifiers in the HKSAR constantly criticize Cardinal Zen as "excessively" political and Anson Chan as "suddenly" supportive of Western-style democracy. Underlying the accusations are the ideological and identification differences between Cardinal Zen and Anson Chan on the one hand and the pro-Beijing supporters on the other. The high-profile action of both Cardinal Zen and Anson Chan in support of democracy in the HKSAR is also a symbol of the authoritative and charismatic societal elites *vis-à-vis* the political preponderance of Beijing and the HKSAR leadership.

On the PRC side, neither President Hu nor Premier Wen realized the devastating consequences of Tung's convergence policy until the abrupt political earthquake on July 1, 2003. Since then, Beijing has accepted a modified and gradual version of convergence in Hong Kong, making the

HKSAR economically dependent on the mainland while accepting some degree of political uniqueness on the part of Hong Kong. In August 2005, it was reported that PRC leaders accepted a political model of democratization for the HKSAR, where the legislature would have its directly elected members increased in proportion to the functional constituencies–produced members.[67] Overall, Beijing's leaders did not fully grasp the catastrophic consequences of Tung's full-scale mainlandization policy in the HKSAR.

Political divergence in the HKSAR in the form of confrontations between the Hong Kong people and Beijing's trusted chief executive was shocking to the central government. If mainland Chinese politics remain characterized by face, the massive protests against the Tung regime were counter-productive to any PRC attempt at promoting the "one country, two systems" to Taiwan. Although the coordination committee established by Beijing to tackle the Hong Kong crisis immediately after July 1, 2003 came up with a mix of economic and political measures to rescue Tung's legitimacy crisis, the capability of the second HKSAR government under Tung could not be enhanced significantly. The economic and political measures embraced the CEPA and the visits of mainland Chinese tourists from various provinces, boosting the economy of Hong Kong to such an extent that the enthusiasm of Hongkongers in public protests would be hopefully dampened. Nevertheless, the PRC united front work could not stop an estimated half a million protestors to take to the streets again on July 1, 2004.[68] The reasons why protestors continued their action on July 1, 2004 were mainly politico-legal; many of them found Beijing's interpretation of the Basic Law in April 2004 over Hong Kong's democratic progress as legally arbitrary while others saw the mysterious dismissal by the Commercial Radio of very popular phone-in program hosts such as Raymond Wong and Albert Cheng as politically conspiratorial, silently self-censored, and socially unacceptable.

In response to Hong Kong's unprecedented series of public outbursts, Beijing strengthened its united front work, such as arranging the visits of the PRC Olympic athletes and medalists to Hong Kong and sending United Front Work Department's director Liu Yandong to preside over the Buddha finger's exhibition in the HKSAR. All these moves were calculated to win the hearts and minds of the Hong Kong Chinese, to invoke their nationalistic sentiment and to emphasize the need for political harmony before the September 2004 Legislative Council elections.[69] The Tung regime's popularity rose gradually in the wake of Beijing's united front work. During the Legislative Council elections held on September 12, 2004, the pan-democratic camp merely captured twenty-five seats — eighteen from direct elections and seven from functional constituencies — in the sixty-member legislature.[70] The pro-Beijing and pro-government elites succeeded in grasping the majority of the seats in the Legislative Council, thus preventing the democratic forces from achieving a political breakthrough.

Yet in late 2004, the Tung administration was soon immersed in another governing crisis. It was in a hurry to privatize the shopping malls of public housing estates by encouraging members of the public to buy the Link Reit shares. Nonetheless, a shop owner, supported by a few democrats, protected her interest by filing a lawsuit, plunging the government's plan of enlisting the Link Reit into a political crisis. Critics of the Tung administration argued that the principal officials responsible for issuing the Link Reit shares did not have the crisis consciousness to anticipate a possible legal challenge from any ordinary citizen, leaving a burden to Tung's successor Donald Tsang.[71] Although the eventual court ruling was in favor of the Link Reit, the entire saga deepened the legitimacy crisis of the Tung regime. With the benefit of hindsight, the Link Reit controversy stemmed from the miscalculation of principal officials and senior civil servants working for Tung, for they assumed that the privatization of shopping malls of public housing estates would achieve economy, efficiency, and effectiveness — the three managerial values of public administration. As it turns out, although privatization does lead to better management of some shopping malls, many shopkeepers could not afford to pay for higher rents and had to close down their businesses. Tung's subordinates failed to anticipate the unintended consequence of their policy changes.

From the angle of convergence, Tung's maladministration exacerbated his governing crisis, alienated the masses, and undermined the public perception of Beijing's policy toward the HKSAR. Many members of the public saw Beijing as propping up an obviously unpopular chief executive, putting the blame on the central government and generating a political divide between Hong Kong and the PRC. If such divergence between the HKSAR and Beijing were not arrested, the "one country, two systems" would be endangered and become a political joke. Hence, Beijing was determined more than ever before to intervene in the governance of Hong Kong, triggering the inception of a smooth and orderly transition from the Tung era to the Tsang administration.

The hallmark of the Tung era from July 1, 1997 to March 2005 was his emphasis on the need to uphold the convergence policy with Beijing rather than the specialness of the "two systems." The image of the "one country, two systems," which is supposed to make the HKSAR a show window for

Beijing to reunify Taiwan, was certainly blemished, if not discredited, by Tung's turbulent and unskillful governance. The PRC had to change the HKSAR leadership for the sake of not simply improving the international image of the "one country, two systems," but also stabilizing the HKSAR in the long run. The "one country, two systems" concept originally aimed at making Hong Kong's economy separate from the PRC socialist system. It was never intended as a principle of allowing the HKSAR to develop a political system totally separate from the PRC. However, the Hong Kong democrats consistently interpret the "one country, two systems" as a justification for them to call for a faster pace and larger realm of democratic reform. They are determined to lessen the degree of the HKSAR's convergence with the PRC, but Beijing and the Tung regime were keen to keep the lid on Hong Kong's democratization or minimize its political divergence with the motherland. The ongoing tug of war between Beijing's convergence policy and the democrats' divergence tactics remains a bone of contention; it also reflects a clash of mainland Chinese and Hong Kong's Western-style civilizations. The mainland stress on the power of "one country" epitomizes the deep-rooted centralized tradition in ancient China, whereas the pull away from the centre toward more local autonomy in favor of the "two systems" symbolizes a Western desire for more freedom.

Since the 1980s the PRC's economic system has become far more "capitalist" than ever before by adopting the strategy of marketization.[72] Politically, Beijing's determination to maintain the political *status quo* in Hong Kong has remained constant. This assumption contradicted the premise of the last Hong Kong governor, Christopher Patten, who was determined to speed up the process and widen the scope of political reform in Hong Kong prior to the return of the enclave's sovereignty to the PRC.[73] Patten's premise had much in common with the democrats, who have insisted that the HKSAR's autonomy should be protected by an accelerated process of democratic reform. In his memoir, Patten openly praised the democrats, unveiling his political affinity with the pro-democracy activists.[74] Beijing and its supporters in Hong Kong, namely the "patriotic" elites embracing the pro-business Liberal Party and the middle-lower class DAB, had opposed a faster pace of political reform both before and after the retrocession. Prior to the Legislative Council elections in the HKSAR, the DAB must vow to support direct elections of the chief executive, but its timetable is constantly adaptable to the whims of Beijing. The DAB dilemma of attracting votes in elections and sticking to Beijing's political bottom line remains its hallmark in Hong Kong politics.

Mainlandization of the Hong Kong Polity

Beijing's distrust of the democrats and their political alliance with Patten led to the rolling back of democratic reforms shortly after the handover.[75] To prevent the democrats from capturing most of the seats in the post-colonial legislature, Beijing supported the Tung regime to take a number of measures. First, the proportional representation system was introduced into the direct elections held for the first HKSAR's legislative elections.[76] The idea of the proportional representation was to balance the political representation in direct elections. Apparently, this justification was strong. Yet a closer examination of the Legislative Council's composition proves that the injection of the proportional representation system was democratically unjustifiable. The Legislative Council in 1998 had sixty seats of which twenty were directly elected by citizens in geographical constituencies; ten elected from an Election Committee; and thirty elected from functional constituencies composed of occupational groups such as lawyers, teachers, accountants, engineers, and workers. As the legislature was not wholly directly elected, the use of the proportional representation system in direct election was biased in favor of the pro-Beijing candidates.[77] LegCo's electoral system was therefore designed in such a way as to maintain the political preponderance of the pro-government and pro-Beijing elites while at the same time having the unintended consequence of fragmenting the democrats, who bickered among themselves for party nomination to run in the legislative elections.[78] The end result was a distorted representation in the Tung era; he was surrounded by his mostly uncritical supporters. If cronyism marks the patrimonial politics of the mainland regime, it has also seeped into the political arena of the HKSAR, albeit the British colonizers also relied on the local comprador class as agents to maintain political stability. If colonization was characterized by patron-client politics in Hong Kong under British rule, recolonization has arguably become prominent in the HKSAR where the political loyalists of Beijing have been awarded with influential positions throughout the policy-making institutions.

Moreover, the HKSAR government rolled back democratic reform by abolishing the Urban Council and the Regional Council in 2000. Its justification was financial, asserting that the two Councils had drained the government's resources.[79] The hidden motive behind the abolition of the two Councils was political. Dismantling the two fully directly elected bodies, the Tung regime deprived the democrats of their stipends and exacerbated their internal bickering. Without sufficient participatory channels, the politically ambitious democrats eventually competed among themselves for nomination by pro-democracy parties in LegCo's direct elections. Financially and politically, the cessation of the two Councils weakened the democrats.

To prevent the HKSAR from becoming a base for the democrats to challenge both the local government and Beijing, the Standing Committee of the National People's Congress (SCNPC) interpreted the Basic Law in April 2004. After the political tsunami on July 1, 2003, the HKSAR government was shocked by the extent of public discontent. The democrats grasped the golden opportunity to demand a faster pace and larger scope of political reforms, called for the election of the chief executive by universal suffrage in 2007, and advocated the selection of all legislators by direct election by 2008. The HKSAR government was unprepared. Nor was it able to put forward any document on political reform. In December 2003, when Tung visited Beijing, PRC leaders asked him to consider firstly the central government's view on the pace and scope of political reform in the HKSAR. The message was clear: Beijing was reluctant to envisage the birth of a democratic Hong Kong similar to democratic consolidation in Taiwan where the presidential election was held in March 2004.[80] The timing of Beijing's decision to apply its brake on Hong Kong's democratization coincided with its assessment of the Hong Kong circumstances and its trepidation that the HKSAR would follow Taiwan's footstep. According to the PRC assessment of the mass protests in Hong Kong on July 1, 2003, the political earthquake plaguing the Tung administration was attributable to four types of "troublemakers": politicians, media professionals, academics, and foreigners.[81] Politicians referred to the pro-democracy activists; media professionals meant radio hosts such as Albert Cheng, Raymond Wong, and Allen Lee who were critical of the Tung regime; academics embraced the pro-democracy sympathizers, providing advice to the democrats and organizing the protests against Article 23 of the Basic Law; and foreigners referred to some British and American expatriates who joined the mass protests on July 1, 2003.[82]

Taiwan's presidential election held in March 2004 served as a serious menace to Beijing. The pro-Taiwan independence Democratic Progressive Party (DPP) led by Chen Shui-bian, who was eventually re-elected after a mysterious assassination attempt on him, was seen as detrimental to Beijing's sovereignty claim on the island. In the event that Beijing made any concession to the Hong Kong democrats prior to the Taiwan presidential election, it would send a "wrong" message to the Taiwanese on the renegade province. Understandably, Beijing's pressure on the Tung administration in December 2003 to decelerate Hong Kong's democratization was a pre-emptive strike against both the local democrats and the pro-Taiwan independence movement in Taiwan. In February 2004, the HKSAR government set up a task force on political reform, admitting in its first report that the central government in December 2003 had raised "serious concerns" about democratization in Hong Kong.[83] In April 2004, it prepared the second report claiming that the time would not be ripe to have direct elections on the grounds of the "immaturity" and "inexperience" of political parties.[84] It also argued that sectional interests would have to be maintained in the event of any political reform, implying that functional constituencies would have to be retained in the HKSAR for the sake of ensuring the representation of various groups. The HKSAR government's report paved the way for the SCNPC's interpretation of the Basic Law on April 26, 2004.[85] The SCNPC interpretation was as follows: "The election of the third Chief Executive of the HKSAR to be held in the year 2007 shall not be by means of universal suffrage. The election of the Legislative Council of the HKSAR in the fourth term in the year 2008 shall not be by means of an election of all the members by universal suffrage."[86] The collaboration between Beijing and the Tung government in exercising the joint veto over the direct election of the chief executive in 2007 and all legislators in 2008 became a *fait accompli*. The people of Hong Kong, especially the democrats, had no choice but to accept the political reality. The immediate price of the indefinite postponement of democratization was huge; the democrats became increasingly alienated and were determined to fully mobilize Hong Kong people to take to the streets on July 1, 2004.

Shocked by the pro-democracy tide on July 1, 2003, Beijing's agents, notably the Liaison Office and the national security apparatus, adopted a hard-line policy toward the democrats.[87] In February 2004, Xinhua said a "small number" of Hong Kong politicians were "unpatriotic" because they joined organizations subversive of the central government.[88] The campaign against "unpatriotic" Hong Kong people was targeted at the democrats, reminding the general public of Beijing's political criterion of singling out political "enemies."[89] In May, popular radio hosts like Albert Cheng, Raymond Wong, and Allen Lee were mysteriously intimidated. Cheng was frightened by political intimidation and decided to quit his radio phone-in program.[90] Wong's case was more complicated, for he had been reportedly involved in a huge debt. Lee received a mysterious call from a mainland official formerly affiliated with the State Council's Hong Kong and Macao Affairs Office.[91] One thing was clear: they were all politically intimidated to varying degrees. Their experience demonstrated the dominance of hard-line PRC policy toward the HKSAR. The public fiercely reacted to the fate of the three radio hosts and took to the streets again on July 1, 2004, demonstrating against the threats to their civil liberties reminiscent of the concern over Article 23 of the Basic Law a year ago.

At this juncture, Beijing began to sense the urgency of adopting a more soft-line policy toward the HKSAR. If not, the people of Hong Kong would most probably elect more democrats to the Legislative Council in September 2004, thus tipping the balance of the legislature in favor of the pro-democracy activists. Beijing's priority was to prevent the democrats from capturing half of the seats in the Legislative Council. Its strategy was to use economic enticement to woo the Hong Kong voters. As mentioned before, the visits to Hong Kong by the mainlanders, the Olympic medalists, the first Chinese astronaut Yang Liwei, and the Buddha finger were carefully calculated as pragmatic and soft-line measures winning the hearts and minds of the Hong Kong populace. The warm reception of the Olympic medalists in Hong Kong did not easily translate patriotism into an overwhelming political support for the pro-Beijing political forces. However, Beijing succeeded in exploiting the political pragmatism of Hong Kong people, believing that the improvement in the economy would not only reduce unemployment but also dampen the angry citizenry's demand for more democracy. The weakness of the Tung administration plunged Beijing deeper into the political arena of the HKSAR.

Beijing's involvement in the political landscape of Hong Kong became salient during the election campaign for the September 2004 Legislative Council elections. The strategy of Beijing was to blacken the image of the pro-democracy candidates and to polish that of the pro-Beijing counterparts. During the election campaign, two candidates of the Democratic Party — Alex Ho Wai-to and James To Kun-sun — were exposed by the mass media as having integrity problems.[92] The former was caught by the mainland Public Security Bureau (PSB) for soliciting a prostitute in Dongguan city, whereas the latter was found to have neglected the need to declare his business interest in a company. The PSB severely penalized Ho by throwing him into prison — a punishment viewed as abnormal and excessively severe as many Hong Kong men solicited prostitutes in the mainland. To's integrity problem was blown out of proportion by the mass media.

At the same time, the pro-Beijing DAB and Federation of Trade Unions (FTU) carefully shaped its political image by highlighting the cancer problem of its leader Ma Lik while shunning any sex scandal. The Liaison Office mobilized the members of the pro-Beijing interest groups and housing associations, including the Fujianese community, to support and vote for DAB and FTU candidates. As a result of this carefully orchestrated campaign, the alliance of the DAB and FTU succeeded in grasping nine of the thirty directly elected seats and four of the thirty functional constituency seats.[93] Together with some pro-establishment independents and combined with the eleven seats of the pro-business Liberal Party, which captured two directly elected seats and nine functional constituency ones, the pro-government coalition could prevent the pan-democratic camp from grasping half of the seats in the Legislative Council. Yet the agents of Beijing sank deeper into the electoral politics of the HKSAR, propping up the ramshackle Tung regime. Politically, Hong Kong witnessed obvious convergence with the PRC where political practices have been characterized by party intervention and limited democratic reforms.

The Legal Profession: Resistance to Mainlandization of the Legal System

While the polity of Hong Kong witnessed an obvious process of mainlandization, the legal community has been reacting strongly to any attempt by the HKSAR government and Beijing to dilute judicial autonomy of the HKSAR. The mainstream view of the legal community insists that the Court of Final Appeal (CFA) should be given the opportunity and the right to interpret the mini-constitution, the Basic Law. This premise, however, was challenged twice during the Tung era, and the third time shortly after the chief executive's resignation. The SCNPC interpreted the Basic Law three times: first in mid-1999 over the right of abode of the mainland Chinese in Hong Kong, the second in April 2004 concerning the direct elections of the chief executive and the entire Legislative Council, and the third in April 2005 over the question whether the successor to Tung would serve his remaining two years of office or a full five-year term.

The controversy over the right of abode issue focused on the question of procedural fairness. The legal community argued that the Basic Law conferred upon the mainland Chinese, whose father or mother had been born in Hong Kong, the right of abode in the HKSAR. This right was reaffirmed by the verdict of the CFA. Nevertheless, the CFA judgment was severely criticized by Beijing's legal experts and the members of the Basic Law Committee — a body that was composed of six Hong Kong people and six mainland Chinese and which makes recommendations to the SCNPC on the interpretation of the Basic Law.[94] Most controversially, the Tung government argued that the CFA judgment would open the floodgate to 1.67 million mainland Chinese who enjoyed the right of abode in the HKSAR.[95] It maintained that the HKSAR would be unable to absorb so many mainlanders, who would pose a tremendous burden on the housing, social welfare and education system in the enclave. Critics of the HKSAR government asserted that the 1.67 million figure was never scientifically proven. The crux of the problem was the HKSAR government's initiative to seek the SCNPC's interpretation of the Basic Law concerning the right of abode of the mainland Chinese in Hong Kong. The legal community became furious; its members believed that the finality of the CFA was overridden by the SCNPC. In response to the concerns of the legal profession, the HKSAR government promised that its request for the SCNPC to interpret the mini-constitution would be rare and kept to a minimum.

Although the SCNPC took the initiative to interpret the Basic Law in April 2004 over the pace and scope of democratic reform, the legal community saw it as Beijing's move to usurp the power of both the HKSAR government and the legislature to determine the prospects of democratization in Hong Kong. What infuriated the legal community most was the legislation on Article 23 of the Basic Law. The Article 23 Concern Group, which was composed of barristers and legal scholars, sprung up to express its deep concerns about the National Security Bill. Later it was transformed into the Article 45 Concern Group expressing its views on the direct elections of the chief executive and of the entire legislature. Members of the Article 45 Concern Group, such as Audrey Eu, Margaret Ng, Alan Leong, and Ronny Tong, were either re-elected or newly elected to the Legislative Council in September 2004.

The third SCNPC interpretation of the Basic Law in April 2005, a month after Tung's resignation, constituted another move from Beijing to erode the judicial autonomy of the HKSAR. Most members of the legal community argued that Article 46 of the Basic Law states clearly that the chief executive's term of office is five years, and that Tung's successor should serve five years. This argument was originally adopted but later rejected by the HKSAR government, which had drafted the Chief Executive Ordinance to embrace the five-year term of office. After the Secretary for Justice Elsie Leung visited Beijing to consult the views of the mainland legal experts, the HKSAR government changed its view, saying that Tung's successor would serve his remaining term.[96] Beijing's constitutional experts voiced their view in support of the HKSAR government's position. Xu Chongde, a mainland drafter of the Basic Law, remarked that the legislative intent of the drafters was to allow the successor of the chief executive, who may leave office suddenly, to serve the "residual" term.[97] Other mainland legal experts such as Wang Zhenmin maintained that the "residual" term was a convention not only in China but also in the United States. From the perspective of the majority of the Hong Kong lawyers, the SCNPC's interpretation of the term of office of the chief executive was more a political move than a legal one. About nine hundred legal experts protested against the SCNPC's move to interpret the Basic Law. Although the SCNPC's Legislative Affairs Commission sent its secretary-general Qiao Xiaoyang to Shenzhen to consult and listen to the views of the Hong Kong people, most members of the legal community were unconvinced and they insisted that Beijing should not deprive the opportunity of the CFA to interpret the Basic Law.

The clash between the Hong Kong legal community and Beijing's view of the Tung successor's term of office illustrated two different constitutional cultures. The former regards the CFA as the ultimate authority to interpret the Basic Law and sees the SCNPC's move as undesirable. Beijing and the HKSAR government led by Acting Chief Executive Donald Tsang viewed the SCNPC as a necessity to prevent a political vacuum in Hong Kong, especially after democrat Chan Wai-yip launched a legal challenge to the HKSAR government to change the interpretation from five to two years.[98] Another difference in their constitutional cultures is that while Beijing sees the SCNPC interpretation as a legal right empowered by the Basic Law, the Hong Kong legal community regards any top-down legal interpretation from Beijing as a political move.

Compounding the controversies surrounding the SCNPC interpretations of the Basic Law was the role of the Secretary for Justice Elsie Leung. The legal community was dissatisfied with her performance. In February 1999 Leung decided not to prosecute the chair of the Sing Tao Group, Sally Aw Sian, for falsification of the circulation figures of the *Hong Kong Standard* on the grounds of maintaining the jobs of the Sing Tao Group — making a remark regarded by the legal community as unjustifiable.[99] Leung's practice of consulting with the views of the mainland legal experts in 1999 and 2005 was seen as harmful to the interest of Hong Kong's judicial autonomy. In a sense, Leung's role was more a political officer than a purely legal authority, for she had to mediate between Beijing and the HKSAR regarding controversial constitutional and legal issues.

The clash between the HKSAR's legal community and the mainland's emphasis on the right of the SCNPC to interpret the Basic Law reflected the tensions between "two systems" and "one country." The Tung government was faced with the problem of how to reconcile Beijing's willingness to exercise the SCNPC interpretation with the Hong Kong concerns. Eventually, it sided with Beijing rather than the wish of the legal community in the HKSAR. Critics of the Tung regime accused it of surrendering the supremacy of the CFA in favor of the SCNPC and the same could be said of the third SCNPC interpretation in April 2004. From another angle, however, the three interpretations signaled a dialectical process in which the SCNPC right to interpret the Basic Law must clash with the values of the defenders of Hong Kong's common-law system.[100]

In defense of the separate identities of the "two systems," the mainstream legal community in Hong Kong became the critics of the Tung administration and acted as a bulwark against any possible encroachment upon civil liberties, as shown in the case of its opposition to Article 23 of the Basic Law. Furthermore, it serves as a deterrent to any post-colonial regime's attempt at requesting the SCNPC's interpretation of the Basic Law. Given the resilience of the legal community, which cherishes the finality of the CFA, Hong Kong's legal convergence with mainland China has been kept to a minimum.

Social Divergence and Economic Convergence with Mainland China

In the same vein, the society of Hong Kong has displayed a relatively high degree of independence from the post-colonial government. The relatively pluralistic society of Hong Kong is composed of interest groups financially and politically autonomous from governmental control. During the debate over Article 23 of the Basic Law, social groups critical of the legislation emerged, collaborated, and constituted a formidable force that propelled the government to shelve the National Security Bill. Secondary school students, intellectuals, radio hosts, the pro-democracy *Apple Daily*, human rights activists, working-class unionists, and religious priests and believers, notably the Catholic Church led by Bishop Joseph Zen, mobilized citizens fully in opposition to Article 23 of the Basic Law.[101] In a sense, they congealed and signaled the explosion of "an angry society" of Hong Kong, acting as the most powerful and heroic checks against any misrule of the Tung regime.[102] The National Security Bill served as a bone of contention that "crystallizes into a social movement when it taps embedded social networks . . . and produces collective action frames and supportive identities to sustain contention with powerful opponents."[103] Although the "powerful opponents" embraced both the Tung government and Beijing, social activists utilized e-mails, pagers, cell phones, internet chat rooms, radio programs, and personal networks with interest groups to mobilize Hongkongers to participate in the social movements on July 1, 2003 and 2004.[104] The maladministration of the Tung era ironically produced an unprecedented social movement strongly resistant to his government and policies.

The angry society of Hong Kong was the repercussion of the Tung government's policy of accelerating social convergence with the motherland.[105] The mother-tongue language education was implemented after the retrocession. Although a minority of parents opposed it for fear of the career prospects of their children, the policy was carried out at the secondary school level.[106] On the other hand, many formerly elite schools, notably the Catholic ones, had their status curbed by the emerging non-Catholic schools that have gained considerable government subsidies since the handover.[107] The previously pro-Beijing secondary schools, such as Fukien and Pui Kiu, have obtained considerable financial support from the government, which occasionally sends high-level officials to attend their graduation ceremonies. Patriotic education has been emphasized since the retrocession and characterized by a new curriculum reform that is inculcating a deeper knowledge of China's history and culture to the students. The national flags of the PRC are raised in more primary and secondary schools than the colonial era.[108] The pro-Beijing political party DAB advocated that national flags should be hoisted in the majority of schools and at all government offices. Yet patriotic education in the HKSAR is not an easy task, partly because of the relatively weak "patriotic" training of the teachers and partly because many students appear to have a weak nationalistic sentiment.[109] Although the anti-Japanese protests against the Diaoyu Island in 1997 and the Japanese attempt at revising the content of their textbooks in 2005 aroused the nationalistic fervor of the Hong Kong people, they are comparatively more rational and calm than the mainland Chinese. At the apex of the anti-Japanese riots in the PRC in April 2005, the Hong Kong people did not call for any boycott of Japanese goods as with the mainland Chinese. All in all, most Hong Kong people have increased their nationalistic sentiment since the retrocession, especially when they celebrated China's successful bid for hosting the 2008 Olympics, but patriotism in Hong Kong does not translate easily into their uncritical political support of the pro-Beijing forces in legislative and local elections. To many Hong Kong people, their cultural identity of being Chinese remains different from the uncritical political identification with the ruling party in the PRC.

In practice, the Hong Kong identity of the Hongkongers has remained strong since the handover. In June 1997, a survey showed that 44 percent of the respondents identified themselves as Hong Kong persons while 22 percent regarded themselves as Chinese; these figures remained the same in

November 2003.[110] Another longitudinal survey conducted by the Hong Kong Transition Project demonstrates that the Chinese identifiers only increased slightly from 25 percent in June 1997 to 29 percent in April 2007; the Hong Kong Chinese identifiers increased slightly from 24 percent from 1997 to 27 percent in 2007; the Hong Kong identifiers slightly decreased from 44 percent in 1997 to 37 percent in 2007; the Hong Kong British decreased from 4 percent in 1997 to 1 percent in 2007; and the overseas Chinese rose from 1 percent in 1997 to 4 percent in 2007 (see Table 2.2). It proves that the local Hong Kong identity remains much stronger than the national Chinese identity.[111] Although the Chinese identity has increased over the past decade, its strength remains weaker than the very strong Hong Kong identity which declined slightly in the first decade of the HKSAR.

Table 2.2 The Evolving Self-Identity of the Hong Kong People, 1993–2007

Year	Chinese	Hong Kong Chinese	Hongkong	Hong Kong British	Overseas Chinese	Others
			(Percent %)			
August 1993	20	34	35	10	–	1
August 1994	19	38	32	10	–	1
August 1995	22	32	36	8	–	1
August 1996	30	20	45	3	–	2
June 1997	25	24	44	4	2	1
December 1997	27	27	39	3	2	2
July 1998	22	27	44	4	1	1
July 1999	21	27	46	4	1	1
August 2000	22	27	45	4	2	1
July 2001	26	26	43	3	1	2
August 2002	28	24	44	2	1	1
November 2003	22	27	44	2	2	4
April 2004	26	27	41	2	1	2
July 2005	29	27	39	2	2	2
November 2006	21	30	44	2	1	2
April 2007	29	27	37	1	1	4

Source: Adapted from Table 13, in "Hong Kong, SAR: The first 10 years under China's rule," a report written by the Hong Kong Transition Project and commissioned by the National Democratic Institute for International Affairs, June 2007, p. 29.

On the other hand, the cultural Chinese identity of the Hong Kong people has traditionally been separated from their political identity, meaning that cultural identification does not necessarily bring about unquestionable and loyal attitude toward the Chinese government.[112] As a matter of fact, the local Hong Kong identity is so strong that it encompasses the citizens' perception of the rule of law, their freedoms and their well-being. As a former British official, Sir David Akers-Jones, remarked: "Our interpretation of the phrase 'one country, two systems' concentrated on the superiority of our system and its proud possession of the rule of law, our freedom, our administration, our simple tax structure and our economic well-being, so much so that we failed to evaluate the significance of what was happening north of the boundary in Shenzhen and of the changes taking place in the rest of Guangdong and throughout China."[113] Compared with the mainland Chinese and the Taiwanese, the people of Hong Kong also have "the strongest belief in political liberty."[114] The local identity was so tenacious that it resisted any attempt by the Tung government to implant the mainland system, either in the form of legislating on Article 23 of the Basic Law or requesting the SCNPC to interpret the Basic Law.

In the economic sphere, Hong Kong has transformed from "a core" shaping the development of peripheral China into a region more dependent on the mainland's economic support than ever before.[115] The HKSAR remains a vibrant financial center with an often buoyant stock market on which mainland enterprises are attempting to be listed. Nevertheless, the political earthquake on July 1, 2003 plunged the HKSAR into an economic dependency on the motherland. Beijing has been keen to pump into Hong Kong endless tourists and economic benefits so as to make the "one country, two systems" seemingly successful and to keep the formula superficially attractive to Taiwan for reunification. While the policy-makers of Taiwan are uninterested in the Hong Kong formula for reunification, Hong Kong's economic dependence on mainland China has been inevitable since the handover. The PRC's global emergence and its rapid economic growth have provided a huge and lucrative market for Hong Kong traders, businessmen, and professionals. Lawyers, accountants, engineers, business consultants, bankers, and even marriage consultants have utilized the lucrative China market to enhance their businesses in the mainland.[116] The new Disneyland in the HKSAR is financially relying on mainland tourists. Prior to the opening of the Disneyland in September 2005, the Trade Development Council visited China's provinces and promoted the special tour packages to mainland visitors. With many Hong Kong manufacturers operating their factories in South China and employing mainland Chinese workers, it can be said that economic relationships such as trade and investment between Hong Kong and the mainland are often interdependent.[117] Yet judging from the economic measures taken by Beijing to deal with the HKSAR's legitimacy crisis since July 1, 2003, Hong Kong's economy has undoubtedly become more dependent on China than before. The CEPA has provided more opportunities for Hong Kong businessmen to tap into the China market, while mainland tourists have stimulated the growth of the hotel, retail, and service sectors as well as the property market in the territory. Without the huge amount of mainland Chinese investment and tourists, the Hong Kong economy could not have achieved a swift rebound between July 2003 and July 2007.

The Tung regime's policy of economic integration with South China was propelled further in his second term of office by pushing ahead the plan of building the Hong Kong–Zhuhai–Macao bridge. Originally, the cross-border bridge was an idea floated by a few businessmen and policy advisors, notably engineer and businessman Gordon Wu and the pro-Beijing One Country Two Systems Economic Institute led by Shiu Sin-por. However, Tung during his first term of office did not push forward the plan of infrastructure coordination with the mainland until he was "re-elected" without opponent in March 2002. The policy deadlock was partly attributable to Tung's policy priorities, which focus on his reform agendas, and partly due to the resistance of the former chief secretary Anson Chan, who was at loggerheads with Tung and who had reservations about a closer integration with mainland China.[118] The plan of building the cross-border bridge was political; the Shenzhen Special Economic Zone attempted to get the bridge linked to Shenzhen. Its desire reflected a hidden regional rivalry with Zhuhai and a concern that both Zhuhai and Macao would reap the economic benefits from the bridge at the expense of Shenzhen. Beijing's final decision was that the bridge should be connected with only Zhuhai and Macao, thus sealing the fate of Shenzhen's ambition. After Tung's resignation, the HKSAR government has continued to negotiate with Zhuhai and Macao on the sites of the bridgeheads, capital accumulation, and other related issues such as toll fees and repair arrangements. The decision of constructing the Hong Kong–Zhuhai–Macao bridge signals the Tung government's determination to accelerate economic integration with South China.

Economic integration between Hong Kong and South China has accelerated and facilitated the process of social interactions. The border checkpoints between Hong Kong and mainland China, including Lok Ma Chau, are open twenty four hours per day so that Hong Kong people can visit the mainland and return to the HKSAR conveniently. The measure has greatly facilitated cross-border trade and the flow of goods. Yet the unintended social consequence of greater economic integration was that, in March 2003, the outbreak of SARS proved the porous nature of the borders and necessitated urgent measures in checking the body temperatures of travelers. While economic integration and infrastructure projects have enhanced bilateral trade and cross-border travels, they have simultaneously accelerated the detrimental impact of any infectious disease. The outbreak of widespread pig diseases in the PRC in 2006 and 2007 was under-reported in the Hong Kong media, resulting in the shortage of the supply of pork to the HKSAR.[119] Any social development in the PRC is bound to have an immediate impact on Hong Kong.

The political ramifications of Hong Kong's social divergence and economic integration with the mainland are obvious. Economic integration has promoted human interactions and minimized social divergence to a limited extent; more Hong Kong people have been visiting the mainland while more mainland Chinese who visit the HKSAR are silently appreciating the values of a pluralistic society.[120] Many mainland students are exposed to politically liberal print media, notably the *Apple Daily*.[121] It remains to be seen whether mainlanders who visit Hong Kong and who work in the territory will become more supportive of democratic values. A survey of 508 mainland visitors in the HKSAR showed that 39.2 percent of them thought that Hong Kong had the conditions for accepting the direct election of the chief executive, and that 57.9 percent felt that those pro-democracy Hongkongers are also "patriotic."[122] It seems that mainland visitors appear to be open-minded toward Hong Kong democratic development.

On the other hand, the pluralistic society of Hong Kong, where the legal profession is dedicated to the defense of judicial autonomy and civil liberties, remains the strongest colonial legacy that resists any attempt by both Beijing and the HKSAR government to mainlandize Hong Kong's legal system.[123] Conversely, the economic integration between Hong Kong and mainland China has strengthened the *realpolitik* sentiment of the local business community, which sees the motherland as a lucrative market and whose leaders see the democrats and defenders of the common law system as being "ignorant" of the mainland's economic progress and politico-legal cultures.[124] An overwhelming majority of the business leaders in the HKSAR are increasingly pro-Beijing in terms of their political orientations. During the tenth anniversary of Hong Kong's return to the PRC, Vincent Lo Hongsui, a Hong Kong business tycoon who has been investing in Shanghai since the 1990s, questioned why the people of Hong Kong kept on bickering over the issues of political reforms.[125] Being culturally and economically assimilated into the mainland, Lo obviously was socialized with a conservative political outlook. The anti-democratic, conservative, and anti-labor instincts of many Hong Kong business leaders have been consolidated by the rapid process of economic integration, for they realize that confrontations with the PRC would bring about detrimental effects on their businesses in mainland China and Hong Kong. Lo's political views are typical of the Hong Kong capitalist class, which is not only co-opted by the CCP but also regarding the PRC's authoritarian system as conducive to rapid economic development. The views of many pro-democracy Hongkongers are epitomized by the remarks made by the former Democratic Party leader Marin Lee, who has expressed his concern about the tendency of transforming "one country, two systems" to "one system," although both the PRC and the HKSAR are adopting a capitalistic style of economy.[126] Lee has gone so far as to assert that the HKSAR is now governed by Beijing authorities rather than the people of Hong Kong. He refers to the reality that in the area of political reform, the HKSAR ruling elites have to kowtow to the central government. The two conflicting visions of Hong Kong — one represented by the pragmatic and co-opted business elites and the other articulated by the pro-democracy idealists — will continue to shape the debates and issues surrounding convergence versus divergence in the coming decades.

Donald Tsang's and Beijing's Policies of Recolonizing the Polity and Mainlandizing the Economy

The departure of C. H. Tung from Hong Kong's political arena actually deepened Hong Kong's full-scale economic and political convergence with the PRC. Since 2005, Donald Tsang has been adopting the policy of making the political system akin to the colonial style of co-optation, selective exclusion, and postponed democratization. By co-opting supporters and some pro-democracy elites into the Strategic Development Commission (SDC), Donald Tsang was able to portray himself as the master of social and political harmony. The co-optation of pan-democracy elites into the SDC also served to legitimize the political discussions on a gradual process of democratic reforms. Still the democrats clashed with Tsang over his proposal of democratizing Hong Kong. On December 21, 2005, the HKSAR government's political reform blueprint, which proposed the Election Committee selecting the chief executive be widened from 800 to 1,600 members in 2007 and which empowered directly elected and appointed District Council members to elect six of the expanded 70-member Legislative Councilors in 2008, failed to gain the required two-thirds support of LegCo. LegCo rejected it by a 34 to 24 vote, with one abstention from Lau Chin-shek.[127] The Tsang supporters accused the democrats of being obstinate, while the latter argued that Tsang's reform blueprint was too conservative. Interestingly, after the political row, both sides calmed down and tried to hammer out a democratic blueprint in the SDC, which however has failed due to their deep ideological differences. Still, by co-opting some elements of the pan-democratic camp into the SDC, Tsang was seen as a political winner portraying himself as the master of political compromise and harmony. Realizing his liability as a former British-trained bureaucrat, and his asset as an experienced ex-civil servant, Tsang has been demonstrating his political loyalty to Beijing through the implementation of politico-economic policies favored by the central authorities, notably deeper economic integration and frequent political consultation with the center over democratic reforms in the HKSAR.

Another strategy of mainlandizing or recolonizing Hong Kong's political system is to exclude the political "troublemakers." Pan-democratic activists such as "Long Hair" Leung Kwok-hung and Emily Lau have been excluded from participation in the SDC to avoid any political impasse. On the other hand, these pan-democratic activists rejected the chief executive election in March 2007 as a "small circle election," thus perpetuating their own marginalization and exclusion in Hong Kong's increasingly narrow political space. The persistence of protest and boycott tactics by the pan-democratic "radicals" only served to discredit them in the long run, for the prevailing political atmosphere emphasizes social harmony, and these tactics make ordinary citizens feel that these "radicals" are unrealistic confrontationists. The continuous decline of popular support of Emily Lau in her direct elections of the Legislative Council in recent years has pointed to the increasingly limited political space that is surely unfavorable to the critical democrats in the HKSAR. Tsang's policy of political exclusion exacerbated the already hopeless predicament of the democratic radicals, who in Western democracies are viewed more as moderates than as "irrational" confrontationists.

Tsang's policy of postponing democratization forces the pan-democratic "radicals" into a political corner whereby they have little choice but to voice their grievances on the streets. Ironically, Leung Kwok-hung and Emily Lau are forced by the narrowing political space to participate in the Legislative Council's direct elections. The dialectical phenomenon of pan-democratic "radicals," who reject the "small circle [chief executive] elections" and who ironically have to compete in legislative direct elections, is a testimony to their tremendous difficulties in the HKSAR's truncated democratization. The mass media, which have increasingly covered Hong Kong's economic and political events positively since the citizen protests on July 1, 2003 and July 1, 2004, are under the severe threat of self-censorship that further erodes the political space for survival and development of the pan-democratic idealists. Apparently, the Hong Kong media are relatively free from governmental interference, but their subtle self-censorship and increasingly over-optimistic portrayal of Hong Kong's "one country, two systems" have deprived the pan-democratic "radicals" of any further springboard to launch and publicize their political platforms and ideas.[128]

The most prominent mainlandization strategy adopted by Donald Tsang is his determination to push ahead C. H. Tung's policy of economic convergence with the PRC. In an era when most Hong Kong people regard the rise of mainland China as a glorious development, and when more people in Hong Kong are identifying culturally and economically with the PRC, economic convergence between the HKSAR and the PRC has significant political implications. The HKSAR is increasingly tied to the economic fate of its motherland. Hong Kong is now marked by a prominent process of economic dependence on the PRC for trade opportunities, CEPA benefits, tourists' spending, and above all the mainland capital for prosperity in the Hong Kong stock and property markets. As a result, the economic bargaining power of the HKSAR *vis-à-vis* the mainland is losing ground very quickly. The HKSAR is simply a mainland Chinese city with the exception of possessing the rule of law, a more seemingly globalized population (which hides the fact that many Hong Kong youngsters are parochial in their social and political outlook), and a more pluralistic society and polity. In economic terms, Hong Kong's capitalist class is increasingly loyal to the PRC and sees any democratic reform blueprint initiated by the pan-democratic camp as potentially destabilizing. Businessmen who have vested interests in China's lucrative economic market dare not antagonize the PRC regime over any political and democratic reforms. In short, Hong Kong's economic dependence on the PRC is consolidating the ultra-conservatism of the business and capitalist class while simultaneously minimizing its economic leverage and bargaining power. If recolonization, which appears to be a politically "incorrect" term as Hong Kong is undisputedly a part of mainland China, is defined academically and theoretically as a process in which a powerful metropolis is exerting influence on its colonial enclave politically, economically, socially, and culturally, it does take place in the HKSAR's complicated relations with the mainland. Although Hong Kong is no longer a colony of Britain, it politically retains a semi-colonial system. Economically, the HKSAR is increasingly an appendage of Beijing. Socially, more Hong Kong people are identifying themselves with the rising and global China. Culturally, mainland China's "soft power" such as films, movie stars, culture, and sports is increasingly seeping into every corner of the Hong Kong society.[129] To argue that Hong Kong is still retaining a unique "two systems" is to ignore the harsh reality that the HKSAR has already become another PRC colony, regardless of whether the people of Hong Kong like the academic term or not after their retrocession to the motherland.

Indeed, recolonization has its dialectical process too. By integrating with the PRC, the HKSAR also has influence on the mainland's elite political culture, economic development, and social values. With a large number of Hong Kong people residing in South China, their activities of influencing government policies in Guangdong and the localities, as well as other provincial and municipal administrations, mean that the political culture of Hong Kong is also seeping into the mainland soil. Mainland officials are forced to be more responsive to the demands and criticisms of the Hong Kong people, both in the mainland and in the HKSAR. Guangdong's economic development would surely suffer in the event of any economic downturn in the HKSAR, and Macao as well. The soft power of Hong Kong, including their movie stars, cultural lifestyle, and social values, can be found in the PRC, notably Shanghai where Hong Kong businessmen have created Hong Kong–style leisure and entertainment places. Nevertheless, it is doubtful whether Hong Kong's soft power can really dominate China's soft power over the HKSAR. The first decade of the HKSAR experience has appeared to show that the mainlandization of Hong Kong, both politically and economically, has proceeded in a much faster pace and deeper scope than the process of Hongkongizing the PRC polity and economy. If this argument is valid, then Hong Kong's politico-economic convergence with the PRC is a destiny that can prolong, postpone, and procrastinate a blueprint of how to shape Hong Kong's political structure so that the previous vitality of "one country, two systems" can be enshrined.

Political scientist Joseph Nye has invented the concept of soft and hard power to trace the ways in which the foreign policies of the United States evolved, and to delineate how other countries in the world perceived the American military, economic, cultural, and political powers.[130] Hard power refers to the military and economic might a country possesses; nevertheless, they are by no means the only determinants of a nation-state's success in world politics. Instead, soft power that can co-opt others is an influential instrument through which foreign policy objectives are achieved without necessarily the need to resort to coercion. As Nye writes:

> Hard power can rest on inducements ("carrots") or threats ("sticks"). But sometimes you can get the outcomes you want without tangible threats or payoffs. The indirect way to get what you want has sometimes been called "the second face of power" . . . [I]t is also important to set the agenda and attract others in world politics, and not only to force them to change by threatening military force or economic sanctions. This soft power — getting others to want the outcomes you want — co-opts people rather than coerces them.[131]

Nye stresses that soft power is not simply the same as influence, and that it represents the ability to attract others through one's culture, values, and "the ability to manipulate the agenda of political choices."[132] Hard-power resources entail command behavior, including force, sanctions, payments, and bribes. However, soft-power resources tend to embrace culture, values, institutions, and policies.[133]

To borrow from Nye's terminology, the PRC attempt at recolonizing the HKSAR relies mainly on its soft power, which is increasingly effective in co-opting the Hongkongers, inducing political support from its friends and followers, and propelling the HKSAR regime to accelerate the policy of politico-economic convergence with the mainland. Underlying these transformations is the migration of more mainlanders than ever before — a process accelerated by the need for the HKSAR to import mainland talents so that Hong Kong's competitive edge would be retained. These mainland-born Hong Kong people will sooner or later play a crucial role in the governance of the HKSAR, integrating themselves into both the private and public sectors and perhaps displaying an outlook that will be far more culturally and politically patriotic than those Hong Kong–born colleagues. If this prediction is accurate, the metamorphosis of the HKSAR will perhaps undergo a silent revolution in terms of importation, socialization, recruitment, and promotion of the mainland-born Hongkongers in the run-up to 2047.

The Theory of Convergence and Implications for Taiwan

The processes of politico-economic convergence between the HKSAR and the PRC were initiated by the Tung regime and have been inherited as well as deepened by the Tsang administration. While political mainlandization has a dampening effect on the HKSAR's democratic prospects, the society of Hong Kong remains a pluralistic and vibrant one fighting against any attempts at making Hong Kong's legal system more akin to the mainland's. In particular, the legal profession has been constantly resistant to any erosion of the HKSAR's judicial autonomy through the SCNPC's interpretation of the Basic Law. At the same time, the relatively liberal society left by the British during the final years of their colonial rule had a deterrent effect on an attempt by the post-colonial regime to encroach upon civil liberties through the enactment of Article 23 of the Basic Law. The role of the Catholic Church, lawyers, intellectuals, human rights activists, outspoken radio hosts, and the democrats was critical to the Tung government's decision to shelve the legislation on Article 23. They provided a rallying point for the society to oppose the Tung regime. Beijing's leadership was given a rude awakening in the wake of the mass protests on July 1, 2003 and July 1, 2004, thus speeding up the "glorious" exit of Chief Executive Tung. Yet it remains to be seen whether the Hong Kong society will remain pluralistic enough to ward off any further process of mainlandization of the HKSAR's polity. As long as patriotic education proceeds at a snail pace, ironically the Hong Kong identity and values will constrain mainlandization. Yet if patriotic education proceeds rapidly and more Hong Kong people are identifying themselves with the rise of mainland China, societal resistance to any attempt of mainlandizing Hong Kong's polity will become weaker than the July 1, 2003 and July 1, 2004 protests against Article 23 of the Basic Law. As the PRC nationalism will gradually increase, especially during and shortly after the 2008 Olympics Games in Beijing, it will perhaps be a politically ripe time to resurrect and re-enact Article 23 of the Basic Law. After all, the HKSAR government has an obligation to legislate on Article 23 so that the national security of the central government will be fully protected. As Chinese nationalism grows stronger and the Hong Kong identity becomes relatively weaker, their narrowing gap will perhaps greatly facilitate the introduction of a new legislation on Article 23.

From the perspective of convergence, the traditional convergence theory cannot be applied to the Hong Kong case. Rather than having the PRC move closer to Hong Kong's polity, the HKSAR political system is under Beijing's control and shows features of mainlandization, notably the proliferation of clientelism, the reliance on politically correct but mediocre pro-CCP elites, the continuous co-optation of the business class, and the persistent view of pro-democracy activists as "pro-Western troublemakers." The PRC regime was supportive of Tung's policy of convergence, both politically and economically. Yet such convergence policy alienated the majority of the Hong Kong people, leading to an unprecedented crisis of governance. To defuse the crisis and to terminate the likelihood of Hong

Kong diverging from the political orbit of mainland China, Beijing had to intervene in the administration of the HKSAR more prominently after the massive protests on July 1, 2003. Tsang's skillful policy of recolonization has minimized the need for Beijing to explicitly interfere with Hong Kong's polity, although the remarks of PRC officials in support of Tsang as the chief executive election candidate in March 2007 stood out as a prominent hallmark of such intervention.

Tsang basically maintains Tung's policy of economic convergence with the PRC, but he has understood the need to temporarily slow down the process of political convergence for fear of any reoccurrence of the people's power on July 1, 2003. Yet soon after Tsang softened Tung's hard-line stance on the democrats from March to mid-December 2005, he has adopted the policy of mainlandization and convergence, propelling Hong Kong's polity back to the colonial era when co-optation was a rule rather than exception, and deepening the HKSAR economic dependence on the mainland. To put it succinctly, the HKSAR has become a new colonial appendage of the PRC, in terms of the power to control the polity and influence the economy. Socially, Tsang's subordinates have been adopting the previous policy of the Tung administration to enhance patriotism through educational reform. By doing so, both Tsang and his patron Beijing are moving the HKSAR socially much closer to the mainland than before. A decade later, when more Hong Kong people have stronger mainland Chinese cultural and political identity, the Hong Kong uniqueness will most probably be diluted further. Tsang's policies have much in common with his predecessor Tung, except for the fact that the former is far more publicly popular than the latter, and that the former realizes the temporary need to publicly distance himself from the leftwing/patriotic forces for fear of creating an image of the unholy triple alliance between the chief executive, the politically correct but aggressive leftwing forces, and the business elites. While this triple alliance was prominent in the Tung era, it has been persisting but has become more implicit in the Tsang administration. In fact, after the democrats rejected Tsang's political blueprint in December 2005, Tsang labeled them as the opposition faction and he has reverted to Tung's policy of politically excluding the "radical" democrats from the echelons of political power. Tsang has also showed his public alliance with the pro-Beijing and pro-business forces during his chief executive election campaign in early 2007. After the defeat of the pan-democrats in the 2007 District Council elections, all 102 appointed District Councillors were Tsang's clients, including 23 members of the Liberal Party and the DAB. None of the democrats was appointed, showing the seriousness of patron-clientelism.

Economically, Tung's convergence policies did not arouse public outcry, for the people of Hong Kong were pragmatic to envisage and receive the economic benefits from a closer economic partnership with the motherland. The patriotic think-tank of Tung and Tsang views economic convergence as not only a political expediency to rescue the HKSAR crisis of confidence, but also a necessary step toward political convergence between Hong Kong and mainland China in the long run. Tung's economic integration with the PRC topped his policy agenda during his second term of office, bringing about intensive social interactions between the Hong Kong people and mainlanders. While the political impact of enhanced social interactions on both Hong Kong and China remains to be unfolded, economic integration has already consolidated the anti-democratic and pro-Beijing political sentiments of local business leaders, who are determined to maintain friendly relations with their overlord China. The business sector is worried that any democratization in the HKSAR would unleash the "anti-business" and "anti-PRC" forces, notably the democrats, in support of more welfare policies to the detriment of the Hong Kong economy. As businessman Gordon Wu remarked in November 2005, the democrats who planned to protest against the Tsang administration's political reform blueprint were playing "mob politics."[134] The crux of the issue is that as long as the pro-business party, the Liberal Party, cannot grasp a majority of seats in the Legislative Council, other conservative-minded business elites must see democratization as anathema to their economic interests in both Hong Kong and the PRC. Politically, the conservative-minded business elites must ally with the politically patriotic forces to back up Beijing and the HKSAR government in the process of decelerating democratic reforms. In short, the triple alliance of the business elites, leftwing forces, and the HKSAR government must protect the interests of "one country" — their patron and overlord Beijing. On the contrary, the local democrats and those Hong Kong people who have strong local identity are determined to resist any move that may encroach upon their civil liberties. Political polarization in the HKSAR is destined to render the encounters between "one country" and "two systems" conflict-ridden.

Hong Kong under the leadership of Tung corroborated the multi-dimensional processes of convergence in which its polity was mainlandized and de-democratized to considerable extent. Every attempt was made by both Beijing and the HKSAR government to thwart the democrats from capturing a majority of the legislative seats. Nonetheless, the society was exhibiting strong reactions to mainlandization not only in the form of resisting the legislation on Article 23, but also opposing the SCNPC moves to interpret the Basic Law and to deprive the Court of Final Appeal of its opportunity to do so. In response to the strong societal backlash against Tung's policy of mainlandization, Beijing has been using economic enticements to enhance the political pragmatism of Hong Kong people. The closer economic integration between Hong Kong and mainland China has strengthened the political loyalty and conservatism of Hong Kong's business people. Undeniably the alliance between the Tung government, Beijing, leftwing forces, and the business elites stunted democratization, albeit the assertive and pluralistic society remains the strongest bulwark against any further move toward political convergence.

The relatively vibrant civil society will likely act as a deterrent to any further attempt at diluting Hong Kong's values of freedom, the rule of law, and group as well as individual liberties. The degree to which patriotic education proceeds, and the extent to which more Hong Kong people will develop their cultural identification with mainland China into a political identification with the CCP, are going to be the twin indicators of Hong Kong's social convergence with the PRC. If the "one country, two systems" formula is supposed to protect Hong Kong's social uniqueness and divergence, patriotic education is dialectically forging the social convergence between the HKSAR and the mainland.

The policy of mainlandization puts the priority of "one country" over the uniqueness of the "two systems," triggering public discontent and unleashing fierce opposition from society where the local Hong Kong identity remained relatively strong. Tung was a patriotic leader appreciative of the PRC economic progress, imbuing with the idea that the identity of the Hong Kong people could be transformed into a much stronger sense of Chineseness. Yet from July 1, 1997 to March 2005, the society of Hong Kong remained deeply divided between a resilient Hong Kong identity and an abortive governmental attempt to enhance the Hong Kong people's political identification with mainland China. That the Hong Kong people identified themselves as culturally Chinese could not be easily translated into their uncritical political support of the Chinese Communist Party. The resilience of the Hong Kong identity, which expressed itself saliently in the form of fighting for civil liberties and protecting the Court of Final Appeal's judicial autonomy *vis-à-vis* the SCNPC, clashed with the Tung government's policy of mainlandization or convergence. While the HKSAR has been propelled to converge with the PRC politically and economically, the strong Hong Kong identity in the society sustains the territory's social divergence with the motherland. The politico-economic convergence between Hong Kong and mainland China is inevitable, but the people of Hong Kong are determined to maintain some degree of socio-legal divergence between the two places. This coexistence of politico-economic convergence and socio-legal divergence will continue to mark the development of Hong Kong's integration with China in the years to come. If the conflict-ridden relations between Hong Kong people and the Tung administration were attributed to the policy of convergence, its lesson is that a diluted form of convergence policy could be implemented by Tung's successors and accepted by Beijing. Donald Tsang did dilute the convergence policy from March to December 2005, but since the democrats' rejection of his reform model, he has been keen to revert to the policy of politico-economic and social convergence. Enjoying a relatively high degree of popularity, Tsang's policy of politico-economic and gradual social convergence has become a silent revolution unnoticed by many outside and inside observers.

On the other hand, Tsang has embarked on a path of maintaining some degree of Hong Kong uniqueness by trying to introduce and accelerate democratic reforms, notably the increase in the number of directly elected legislators from thirty at present to thirty-five in 2007, and the corresponding increase in the number of indirectly elected legislators from thirty currently to also thirty-five in 2007, with the five new indirectly elected seats coming from the elections among District Council members.[135] Nevertheless, the local democrats opposed his reform blueprint. The crux of the problem was that the democrats who uphold political divergence of Hong Kong from China persisted in opposing the Tsang regime. Tsang was cautious in avoiding any transgression of the political boundary set by Beijing, while simultaneously using some political reforms to entice and split the internally divided and heterogeneous democrats. The implication is that tensions between "one country," whose interests are protected by the Tsang administration, and "two systems," which are upheld by local democrats, persist.

Arguably, the "one country, two systems" formula devised by Deng Xiaoping is inherently contradictory, displaying the dialectics of protecting the interests of Beijing while trying to preserve the uniqueness of the two systems. Yet in the process of political integration of Hong Kong into mainland China, this formula has proved to be controversial and conflict-ridden. Both the Tung and Tsang governments are keen to maintain the interests of "one country," albeit Tsang has learnt a bitter lesson from Tung to avoid antagonizing the majority of the people of Hong Kong. On the other hand, the local democrats are determined to fight for their civil liberties for the sake of preventing the HKSAR from drifting toward "mainlandization." The politics of the HKSAR will continue to display the ongoing tensions between the pull of convergence and the push of divergence. It is crystal clear that the concepts of divergence and convergence are pertinent but neglected in the study of the political, economic, and legal metamorphosis of post-colonial Hong Kong. The interests of "one country" certainly propel the HKSAR toward an irreversible path toward political, legal, and economic convergence. Yet the local demands of retaining the specialness of the "two systems" contribute to the push of divergence. The ongoing tug of war between convergence and divergence will continue to become the hallmark of Hong Kong's political, social, and legal transformations from now to 2047.

Tsang's policy of recolonization has significant bearings on Hong Kong's political development in the years to come. He recolonized the polity by strengthening the co-optative mechanism, marginalizing the "radical" democrats, postponing democratic reforms, and placating the anxiety of Beijing that Hong Kong's polity would be "Taiwanized" or democratized. Above all, the HKSAR's economic dependence on the PRC has already weakened its own bargaining power *vis-à-vis* the motherland. The silent process of recolonizing Hong Kong's polity and making its economy more dependent means that the HKSAR is increasingly losing its luster and uniqueness. When the PRC economy undergoes a sudden fluctuation, the HKSAR will surely suffer most, plunging the entire economy and society into turbulence and public panic. When China's polity experiences a sudden crackdown on any pro-democracy movement, the Hong Kong democrats will ironically enjoy a surge in their popularity.

Yet when mainland China steps into a gradual process of elite-led democratization,[136] Hong Kong's ultra-conservative capitalist class will surely fight against any public attempt at democratizing the Hong Kong polity. Ultimately, Hong Kong's polity and economy are by no means as optimistic as the local media portray. Mainlandization and colonization are dialectical processes impinging on Hong Kong, which also has influence on its motherland politically, economically, and socially. The past decade of developments in the HKSAR has already proved that mainlandization of Hong Kong is going to be deepened. Its colonization by the PRC means that many Hong Kong people retain a colonial dependent mentality, believing that Beijing must come to their economic rescues and that it is natural for sons and daughters to rely on their parent for politico-economic support. If the dependency relationships between Hong Kong and mainland China are deepened, the uniqueness of "one country, two systems" is going to be diluted inevitably even though both the HKSAR and PRC governments must point to the formula's "success" so as to lure Taiwan back into the mainland Chinese orbit. Regardless of whether Taiwan will accept the "one country, two systems" model, the reality is that the HKSAR has been politically recolonized and economically mainlandized. The specialness of Hong Kong has been undisputedly diluted since July 1, 1997; nevertheless, it is unclear whether the relatively strong civil society will be able to hold onto Hong Kong's identity and uniqueness until 2047, when Hong Kong will most likely be integrated more fully into mainland China's political, social, and economic spheres.

It is very unlikely that the majority of Taiwan people will accept the Hong Kong model of convergence with the PRC. Rather, they favor a political model that will really give a "high degree of autonomy" to the island. While the Kuomintang (KMT) favors a long-term reunification with the mainland, it is cautious in avoiding any public misperception that the party is advocating a convergence policy with the PRC. Convergence will surely become a negative phenomenon to the majority of Taiwanese, who do not want to envisage any attempt at diluting their extremely strong and assertive Taiwan identity. The local Taiwanese identity in the 1970s and 1980s has been gradually transforming into a strong national identity in the 2000s, so strong that there has been a process of de-Sinification of various public venues constructed and left by the KMT regime. If convergence has marked Hong Kong's gradual absorption into its motherland, divergence is characterizing the mentality of the ruling elites and masses in Taiwan *vis-à-vis* the PRC. In short, a negotiated settlement that will guarantee a significant degree of Taiwan's divergence, not convergence, with the PRC will be an ordeal for the diplomats from both sides in the years to come.

3
The Politics of Judicial Autonomy

The question of judicial autonomy of the HKSAR became heavily politicized from January 1999, when the Court of Final Appeal (CFA) made a controversial decision on the right of abode of the mainland Chinese, to June 1999 as the Standing Committee of the National People's Congress (SCNPC) of the PRC was requested by the HKSAR government to interpret the Basic Law — the mini-constitution of the HKSAR — concerning the right of abode issue.[1] For the CFA, the courts of the HKSAR have not only the final power of adjudication but also the power to review whether the legislative acts of the NPC conform to the Basic Law. This perception of judicial autonomy in the HKSAR, however, clashed with the PRC notion of a more restricted view of judicial autonomy. For the PRC, judicial autonomy in the HKSAR cannot override the SCNPC power of interpreting the Basic Law, nor does the CFA have the power to review its legislative acts. Although Article 19 of the Basic Law stipulates that the HKSAR enjoys judicial autonomy, one political scientist has contended that "there are many mechanisms already put in place through which the NPC and the Central People's Government, if not the Supreme People's Court, may interfere in the HKSAR affairs, including those of the judiciary."[2] The objective of this chapter is to use the debate over the right of abode in 1999 as a case study that can illuminate the problem of judicial autonomy in the HKSAR. It will argue that in order to maintain judicial autonomy in the HKSAR, various political actors will have to establish a constitutional convention or a habit of self-restraint.

The CFA Judgment and the SCNPC Interpretation of the Basic Law

The CFA judgment in January 1999 alienated legal experts in the PRC, for it claimed that the Hong Kong court could declare legislation by the NPC "invalid" if such legislation were inconsistent with the Basic Law.[3] From the perspective of mainland legal experts, parts of the CFA judgment usurped the NPC power. They launched an attack on the CFA judgment until the HKSAR government decided to ask the court to "clarify" its decision. On February 26, 1999, the CFA accepted an application by the HKSAR government to "clarify" its decision with regard to the right of abode of the mainland Chinese. The CFA clarified that its judgment on January 29 "did not question the authority of the NPC Standing Committee to make an interpretation under Article 158 which would have to be followed by the courts of the Region."[4] However, the CFA clarification was seen by some legal academics as "a political declaration."[5] Other commentators viewed the clarification as "a political show" that gave Beijing "face" or that could settle the controversy.[6]

After the CFA clarified the ruling, the HKSAR government became concerned about the social impact of the CFA judgment, namely an influx of Chinese migrants into the HKSAR. The government claimed that there would be 1.67 million Chinese eligible to enter Hong Kong under the CFA ruling, and that its expenditure would increase drastically in order to accommodate them. To cope with the "intolerable" social burden resulting from the CFA decision, the HKSAR government requested that the NPC should interpret relevant provisions of the Basic Law. The State Council passed on the HKSAR government's request to the SCNPC, which in June 1999 interpreted Article 22 and Article 24 of the Basic Law. The interpretation was as follows:

> [Article 22(4)] stipulates that "for entry into the HKSAR people from other parts of China must apply for approval. Among them, the number of persons who enter the region for the purpose of settlement shall be determined by the competent authorities of the Central People's Government after consulting the government of the region." This provision is based on the immigration management system that has been practised for a long time between the mainland and Hong Kong . . . [A]ll mainland residents have to submit their application to the concerned authorities on the mainland if they want to go to Hong Kong for whatever reason. After their applications are approved the mainland residents must carry valid

documents issued by the concerned authorities to enter Hong Kong . . . The legislative intent of Article 22(4) has affirmed this long-time established practice of the immigration management system . . . This legislative intent is to ensure that mainland residents would enter Hong Kong in an orderly manner which is in line with the interests of Hong Kong.[7]

On Article 24(2)(3), the SCNPC interpretation was as follows:

The first three subsections of Section 2 of Article 24 stipulate that "the permanent residents of the HKSAR shall be: (i) Chinese citizens born in Hong Kong before or after the establishment of the HKSAR; (ii) Chinese citizens who have ordinarily resided in Hong Kong for a continuous period of not less than seven years before or after the establishment of the HKSAR; (iii) persons of Chinese nationality born outside Hong Kong of those residents listed in categories (i) and (ii)." Of this, the stipulation of Subsection (iii), that "persons of Chinese nationality born outside Hong Kong of those residents listed in categories (i) and (ii)," refers to that when the person was born, either before or after the SAR was established, one of the person's parents must fall within the stipulation of Subsection (i) or (ii). The legislative intent of that is to prevent a mass influx of mainland emigrants into Hong Kong and to maintain the long-term prosperity and stability of Hong Kong . . . After the NPC Standing Committee has made its interpretation of the Basic Law's Article 22(4) and Article 24(2)(3), courts of the HKSAR shall uphold the interpretation made by the NPC Standing Committee when they handle cases with reference to the two articles.[8]

According to the SCNPC interpretation, mainland Chinese born before one of their parents became a permanent resident of Hong Kong do not have the right of abode.[9] The Chief Executive of the HKSAR, Tung Chee-hwa, said that he was "very, very pleased" that the SCNPC interpretation had "made a giant step towards solving a very difficult problem."[10]

Table 3.1 Events from the Court of Final Appeal's Ruling on January 29 to the NPC Interpretation of the Basic Law on June 26

January 29, 1999	The CFA ruled unanimously that Ordinance 3 of the immigration laws gazetted on 10 July 1999 could not be made retrospective.* It gave the HKSAR courts the power to interfere with the NPC decisions which might break the Basic Law. It also awarded the right of abode to children who had been born before a parent became a permanent resident of the HKSAR and to those illegitimate offspring.
February 10	Beijing officials said the CFA decision was mistaken and it violated the Basic Law.
February 26	The CFA clarified its ruling on the jurisdiction issue.
April 28	The HKSAR government claimed that the claimants of the right of abode could reach 1.67 million.
May 6	The HKSAR government said its spending would exceed HK$700 billion in ten years because of the influx of migrants.
May 19	The Executive Council endorsed a decision to seek the NPC interpretation on two provisions of the Basic Law governing the right of abode issue.
June 11	Beijing accepted the HKSAR government's request to review the CFA ruling. On the same day, the Court of Appeal ruled that mainland migrants who overstayed to claim the right of abode were detained unlawfully by the government and that they should not have been ordered to leave Hong Kong. The three Court of Appeal judges said the government had a duty to consider evidence submitted by the migrants to support their claim of having permanent residency. Justice Barry Mortimer said court judges must be "particularly vigilant" to ensure the right of abode of mainland migrants would not be limited or removed by domestic legislation or administrative arrangement. The government lawyer, Joseph Fok, warned the judgment might trigger an influx of migrants.
June 23	The SCNPC met in Beijing. Xinhua issued a despatch saying NPC members agreed that giving the "true legislative intent" of the Basic Law provisions would help uphold the authority of the PRC constitution, the Basic Law and Hong Kong's prosperity and stability. PRC official Qiao Xiaoyang said the CFA should have consulted Beijing before making its ruling in January 1999.
June 25	The Court of Appeal lifted restrictions on 17 mainland "overstayers" who claimed the right of abode in Hong Kong. The government lawyer, Geoffrey Ma, argued in the court that lifting restrictions would free the "overstayers" from the need to report regularly to the authorities and that it would encourage illegal immigration into Hong Kong. The Secretary for Justice Elsie Leung said the government's defeat proved that judicial independence had not been undermined.

Table 3.1 *(continued)*

	On the same day, the High Court ruled that children adopted from the mainland had the right of abode in Hong Kong. The government claimed that Article 24 (3) of the Basic Law conferred right of abode only on children born "naturally" of permanent residents. But Justice Brian Keith said the government's arguments against adopted mainland children having the right of abode would "result in the separation of the child from his adoptive parents" and adoptive siblings. In response to the High Court's ruling, mainland legal expert Wu Jianfan said that the ruling "violated" the legislative intent of the Basic Law, which during the drafting process had not considered the question of adopted children having the right of abode.
June 26	The NPC interpreted the Basic Law's Article 24 and overturned the CFA ruling.

Note: * The CFA refuted Ordinance 3 of the immigration law, which had been enacted by the Provisional Legislature and gazetted on July 10, 1999. This law required mainland migrants who were Hong Kong permanent residents to obtain one-way permits first. The CFA said the requirement was "unconstitutional" because the migrants already had the right of abode in Hong Kong.

Source: Constructed from *South China Morning Post*, June 12, 1999, p. 1; June 24, 1999, p. 1; June 27, 1999, p. 3 and June 26, 1999, p. 1. Also see *Hong Kong Standard*, June 26, 1999, p. 1 and June 27, 1999, p. 13. *Apple Daily*, June 26, 1999, p. A2.

The Authority of the CFA and Its Judges

In the controversy over the CFA decision, the authority of the CFA and of its five judges was undoubtedly undermined.[11] The Chief Justice Andrew Li Kwok-nang was criticized for his "ignorance" of the social impact of the court judgment. One commentator wrote:

> As the judiciary's chief, Li Kwok-nang cannot escape the responsibility that his judgment on January 29 brought about the central government's strong attack and thus endangering the foundation of Hong Kong's judicial independence. As a judge, he has no political responsibility. But as the judiciary's chief, he should shoulder the political responsibility of his mistake. His resignation could establish a model for the legal elite and successors to maintain judicial independence and to confront the central government's interference. If he does not resign, his fifteen years of office will have great difficulties.[12]

One Hong Kong member of the NPC, Victor Sit Fung-shuen, asked Li to resign because the chief justice had failed to consult the opinion of the NPC, to "probe the principles and spirit of the Basic Law," and look at the relevant provisions in the Macao Basic Law.[13]

Many members of the social elite criticized the CFA judges. The former solicitor-general, Daniel Fung Wah-kin, maintained that the CFA judges "should understand the societal operation" and that it was unnecessary to invite a foreign judge to the CFA in every case.[14] A former Basic Law Drafting Committee member, Louis Cha, accused Andrew Li of behaving like "a grandchild who beats up the grandfather [that is, the SCNPC]."[15] Cha even asked the CFA to "apologize" to the NPC.[16] Shiu Sin-por, the director of the One Country Two Systems Institute, criticized the CFA judges for adopting "a literal interpretation" of the Basic Law.[17] He suggested that Hong Kong's court judges should adapt to the "one country, two system" by considering the "general interest of the society" and the social consequences of their judgments."[18] Shiu also warned that "judicial activism" in the HKSAR would produce a lot of problems.[19] In a special House Committee meeting of the Legislative Council, Shiu made the following comments:

> The CFA said it had considered the long-term interests of Hong Kong but, in fact, it had not. The court did not understand that once mainlanders were entitled the right of abode, they should be allowed to come here very soon.[20]

However, when the CFA judges considered the right of abode of mainland migrants, they asked government lawyers to put forward arguments that would deal with the consequences of interpreting the immigration laws. As Justice Henry Litton said: "Overnight a thousand people can come in by *dai fei* (speedboat) and have access to legal advice the next day."[21] Similarly, Justice Charles Ching remarked that the CFA would not deliver a verdict "without being wholly aware of the social consequences on a matter as public as this."[22] He also said that Beijing would continue to control the number of mainland Chinese who would settle in the HKSAR, regardless of whether they had the right of abode. At one point, the CFA judges appeared to consider the consequences of their decision, although the CFA's final judgment did not specify the possible social consequences of its decision.

In response to the mounting criticism of the CFA ruling and its judges, a minority of court judges made an unprecedented move to defend the judiciary publicly. Justice Gerald Godfrey wrote:

> It has recently been suggested . . . that a "re-interpretation" of the Basic Law by the mainland SCNPC may serve to relieve the Government of the HKSAR from the inconvenience of implementing the "right of abode" decisions of the CFA, without doing any damage to the most important

difference, within our "one country," between the "two systems" it embraces, that is, the mainland's "system" and the SAR's "system." I refer to the rule of law, a concept perhaps less well understood on the mainland than in the SAR . . . It might make for more informed debate if those involved in it could be brought to understand that what is at stake here is a legal issue, not a political one.[23]

Later, Godfrey wrote another public letter and made the following comments:

There has been speculation that the invitation from the Government to the central authorities to "interpret" the Basic Law in a manner inconsistent with the CFA's interpretation of the Basic Law on the "right of abode" issue might prompt judges to resign. It should not do so . . . [T]here is no need for a judge to resign, even if this happens. If he finds that an interpretation of the Basic Law by the Standing Committee of the NPC has been properly obtained, he will do his duty and apply it. If he finds that it has not, he will do his duty and disregard it. The political fall-out, either way, will not be a matter for him.[24]

Apart from Godfrey's letters, one retired judge also made an unprecedented move to comment on the CFA's ruling. On his retirement from the Court of Appeal in May 1999, Justice Noel Power said:

That judges, as anyone, are as much servants of the society. They do not make the law, they administer it, and . . . they cannot be swayed by political considerations or expediency. The comments today seem to say that shouldn't be said.[25]

Other judges made their comments on the government's action to seek the SCNPC interpretation of the Basic Law anonymously. One judge said:

Any judge who wished to [comment publicly on current issues] should feel at liberty to defend the rule of law and the independence of the judiciary.[26]

Another judge who also did not want to be named thought most judges regarded the NPC's interpretation as "entirely a political matter and none of their business."[27]

From a political viewpoint, the CFA issued some provocative statements in its judgment regarding the "constitutional jurisdiction of the courts."[28] It said:

> What has been controversial is the jurisdiction of the courts of the Region to examine whether any legislative acts of the NPC or its Standing Committee are consistent with the Basic Law and to declare them to be invalid if found to be inconsistent. In our view, the courts of the Region do have this jurisdiction and indeed the duty to declare invalidity if inconsistency is found. It is right that we should take this opportunity of stating so unequivocally . . . As with other constitutions, laws which are inconsistent with the Basic Law are of no effect and are invalid. Under it, the courts of the Region have independent judicial power within the high degree of autonomy conferred on the Region. It is for the courts of the Region to determine questions of inconsistency and invalidity when they arise. It is therefore for the courts of the Region to determine whether an act of the NPC or its Standing Committee is inconsistent with the Basic Law, subject of course to the provisions of the Basic Law itself.[29]

It was this passage of the judgment that aroused the anger of the mainland legal experts, who regarded these wordings as an attempt by the CFA to usurp or override the NPC's power.

The Role of the Mainland Legal Experts

The PRC legal experts led the attack on the CFA decision. On January 6, 1999, the New China News Agency in Zhuhai published the remarks made by four mainland legal experts on the CFA ruling, criticizing the CFA for usurping the power of the NPC and "distorting the relationship between the central government and the HKSAR."[30] Xu Chongde, a professor of People's University of China, asserted that "no organization or department can challenge or deny NPC legislation and decisions."[31] He maintained that the entry into the HKSAR by any mainland Chinese belonged to the administrative relationship between the HKSAR and the PRC. To Xu, the CFA extended its power "promiscuously and it has to bear every historical responsibility so created."[32] He also believed that the CFA clarification of its decision was "one way to solve the problem," and that the PRC was "concerned about the inappropriate remarks that put the court above the NPC."[33] According to Xu, the CFA could "enhance its authority, not weaken it" by "correcting its mistakes."[34] He believed that the SCNPC interpretation of the Basic Law was the "best legal option" to resolve the crisis of a population influx into the HKSAR. As he said:

From the point of view of the urgency of resolving the crisis, the interpretation option is better than the amendment option because if the amendment option is chosen, Hong Kong will have to wait until the next annual NPC, which takes place in March [2000].[35]

Another mainland legal expert and a professor at Beijing University, the late Xiao Weiyun, asserted that although the CFA was empowered to make an interpretation under the Basic Law, it did not have the power to review or repeal legislation which might breach the mini-constitution.[36] He said:

> The NPC is the supreme state power organ according to the Chinese Constitution. Its legislation and decisions are not to be challenged or denied by any other organizations. That the CFA claims to have this power shows that the CFA believes it can override the NPC and its Standing Committee. This is totally unconstitutional and violates the principle of "One Country, Two Systems."[37]

Wu Jianfan, a professor of law at the Chinese Academy of Social Sciences, said that the Hong Kong courts "can only implement laws," that they "cannot doubt the laws," and that their power to interpret laws "is limited to aspects not concerning the central government's administration or the administrative relations between the central government and the HKSAR."[38] He concluded that "the ultimate solution" was for the CFA to "rectify" its decision.[39] To Wu, the central government would not take the initiative to interpret the Basic Law; the Hong Kong people themselves should reach a consensus on a solution to the right of abode problem.[40]

Shao Tianren, a professor at Beijing University, interpreted the CFA judgment as turning the HKSAR into "a political entity," for the court claimed that it had the power to declare legislation by the NPC as "invalid."[41] To Shao, if the CFA arguments were followed, the HKSAR courts would be able to scrap any existing law in Hong Kong. Clearly, the four mainland legal experts were alienated by the CFA's stand that it had the power to review and invalidate legislation by the NPC if such legislation were inconsistent with the Basic Law.

The Role of the Hong Kong Members of the Basic Law Committee: A Need for the Constitutional Convention of Self-Restraint?

During the entire debate over the CFA ruling, the Hong Kong members of the Basic Law Committee played a crucial role. They gave their views in public on how the NPC interpretation of the Basic Law could be backdated,[42] explained the significance of the NPC interpretation,[43] suggested the most effective way in which the HKSAR government could deal with the population influx,[44] and most importantly interpreted the Basic Law in public. To Maria Tam, the crux of the problem was not the ambiguities in the Basic Law "but that people cannot see how it should be interpreted."[45] She asserted that the CFA ruling did not have a legally binding effect on the mainland authorities, who could still regulate the number of migrants entering the HKSAR.[46]

The late Raymond Wu criticized Li Kwok-nang as "a child who does not understand matters" and he emphasized that "the SCNPC would not become another Li Hungzhang who had surrendered power [from the Qing dynasty to foreign countries] and humiliated the nation."[47] On February 26, when the CFA clarified its decision, Wu "appreciated" the court's action and said this would "dilute" the incident.[48] He also believed that the best solution to the right of abode dispute was an action by the CFA to "correct" or "rectify" its decision, but "unfortunately" there was no such mechanism in the HKSAR.[49] Wu called for the introduction of a rectification system.

> Judges are human, not superhuman. Such a rectification system should be in place. Without such a mechanism, how can we tell others we have rule of law here.[50]

In a public forum, Wu asked the Hong Kong people not to "superstitiously" see judges as "authorities who wear red robes and wigs."[51] The Hongkongers, to him, "should not believe in authorities superstitiously" and become "the slaves of law."[52] To Wu, those people who opposed the NPC interpretation of the Basic Law were like "patients" who were afraid of surgical operation. These "patients," Wu said, should receive psychotherapy.[53]

Yet the public remarks made by the Hong Kong members of the Basic Law Committee aroused the anger of some commentators, who believed that they should adopt a low-profile approach and an impartial attitude toward the CFA ruling. One editorial criticized their behaviour, saying that

People on the Committee for the Basic Law ought to examine what they have done. The Committee's main function is to advise Beijing professionally and arbitrate Hong Kong–mainland disputes arising from implementing the Basic Law. But some of them seem ignorant of their duty. They have done what arbitrators ought not to do.[54]

Albert Chen Hong-yi, a Hong Kong member of the Committee for the Basic Law, was criticized for his changing position on the right of abode issue. Chen wrote in February 1999 that the CFA judgment with regard to its right to review legislation by the SCNPC was only an *obiter dictum* without legally binding effect.[55] Originally, he advocated that the Basic Law should be amended.[56] Later Chen did not object to the SCNPC interpretation of Articles 22 and 24. When asked why he changed his view, Chen explained that "the most ideal solution" was to amend the Basic Law, and that he eventually accepted the SCNPC interpretation due to the "practical difficulty" of amending the mini-constitution.[57] Chen originally opposed the SCNPC to interpret Article 24, which to him belonged to the HKSAR internal affairs. But later he revised his view because Article 24 also dealt with the implementation by mainland organs such as the Public Security Bureau.[58] To Chen, the government's application to the CFA to clarify its ruling had precedents in common law countries such as Canada and India where there were "mechanisms" for the Canadian and Indian governments to apply to the Supreme Court for "authoritative interpretation on issues of constitutional importance."[59] Chen denied his changed views were due to any political pressure. He remarked that "one cannot stop at a certain stage in the process of academic exploration" and that adopting an open attitude to listen to others' views was "rational."[60] To Chen, the SCNPC interpretation of the Basic Law would amount to "a small degree of revising the constitution."[61]

Despite his changed views, one of Chen's constructive proposals to solve the dispute was the idea of establishing constitutional convention in the HKSAR. The Secretary for Justice Elsie Leung promised that the government would study mechanisms that would prevent it from abusing the request for the NPC to interpret the Basic Law. To Chen, this promise made by the government could set up a constitutional convention.[62] According to Chen, there should be unwritten principles restricting the HKSAR government's power to request the SCNPC interpretation of the Basic Law. These principles include (1) the approval of two-thirds of the members of the Legislative Council, (2) the endorsement of two-thirds of the Hong Kong members of the NPC, and (3) the issue concerned is related to the relationship between the mainland and the HKSAR. Chen elaborated that if the government applied to the CFA to seek interpretation of the Basic Law by the SCNPC on issues concerning central-local relations, and if the CFA rejected such application, then the government could strive for the support of half of the members of the legislature and half of the Hong Kong NPC members to seek the SCNPC interpretation.[63] Yet if the HKSAR government did not apply to the CFA to seek interpretation by the NPC, the government would be disallowed to seek the SCNPC help after the CFA ruling.[64] Chen's idea of setting up constitutional convention was supported by Maria Tam.[65]

However, Margaret Ng criticized Chen's idea as "horrifying."[66] Ng argued that constitutional convention relied on "self-restraint by the government," that it limited the government's exercise of constitutional rights, and that it "injected politics into the judicial process."[67] To Ng, the "injection of politics into the judicial process" is called "constitutional convention" rather than "interference."[68]

Objectively speaking, the interaction between the HKSAR's legal system and the PRC's is bound to be politicized. Such politicization, however, does not mean that the development of constitutional convention is unnecessary. Rather, the development of unwritten political habits is arguably an experiment with the concept of "one country, two systems" in which (1) the central government refrains from intervening in the HKSAR domestic affairs and (2) the HKSAR government also refrains from taking action that may induce Beijing's intervention. One mainland Chinese legal academic in Hong Kong, Liu Nanping, hoped that the SCNPC would develop a principle of no longer interpreting or revising the Basic Law after the right of abode issue in June 1999.[69] What Liu advocated was the need to establish a constitutional convention that the SCNPC would refrain from exercising its power to interpret the Basic Law. One democrat also advocated the idea of setting up "mechanisms" that would "limit procedures for seeking [the SCNPC] interpretation [of] the law."[70] Such mechanisms, if established, could constitute a constitutional convention.

Whether constitutional convention can be crystallized into law is a controversial issue.[71] But one legal academic suggested that a law should be passed to define the HKSAR government's power to seek the SCNPC interpretation of the Basic Law. Peter Wesley-Smith proposed the enactment of a law to restrict the HKSAR government's power to seek help from the SCNPC. He said that factors such as economic well-being could be used as one of the criteria, which could be subject to judicial review.[72]

Anyway, constitutional convention appeared to emerge when the Basic Law Committee had a meeting before the NPC Standing Committee discussed the HKSAR government's request for its interpretation of the Basic Law. In June, twelve members of the Basic Law Committee met in Beijing for three days.[73] They reached a consensus to endorse the HKSAR government's request for the SCNPC interpretation of the Basic Law. The Committee submitted its views, including dissenting ones, to the SCNPC for discussion.[74] It also suggested that the SCNPC should endorse the Certificate of Entitlement system to regulate migration from mainland China to the HKSAR.[75] The Committee proposed further that the Standing Committee could follow the resolution passed by the Preparatory Committee in 1996 with regard to Article 24(2)(3), which stated that a child would enjoy the right of abode in the HKSAR only if at birth one of the parents was already a permanent resident.[76]

As early as 1997, Yash Ghai called for the establishment of the constitutional convention of self-restraint. He wrote: "The development of some conventions as to how the SCNPC will exercise its powers would . . . be desirable. One might be that the Committee would not proceed to the interpretation of the Basic Law before the Hong Kong courts have given their decision giving the Committee the benefit of the courts' analysis. . . . Another might be that the Committee for the Basic Law should provide its reasons if it disagrees with a Hong Kong court's interpretation on a point on which it is consulted by the SCNPC. In such circumstances, a third convention might usefully be adopted — that the SCNPC as a rule would follow the recommendations of the Basic Law Committee."[77] In the right of abode controversy in 1999, none of the three conventions advocated by Ghai could be realized. Instead, some individual Hong Kong members of the Basic Law Committee were critical of the CFA judgments, thus politicizing Article 158 of the Basic Law.

The Role of Hong Kong NPC Members

When the Hong Kong NPC members signed a declaration supportive of the Basic Law on May 17, it was clear that there would be no realistic possibility of amending the Basic Law. Twenty-seven members signed their names on the declaration, saying that

> [t]he drafting process of the Basic Law did not have any mistake or loophole. It was the CFA which did not fully consider the legislative

intent [of the relevant provisions of the Basic Law.] The Basic Law is a constitutional document and it cannot be amended because of the CFA's interpretation . . . The Basic Law is a national law which gives the NPC Standing Committee the right of legislative interpretation. The interpretation by the NPC Standing Committee to clarify the legislative intent . . . is more suitable than amending the Basic Law.[78]

According to the Basic Law, the requirements of amending the Basic Law were the approval of the chief executive, the endorsement of two-thirds of the Hong Kong NPC members and the support of two-thirds of the members of the Legislative Council. Without the support of 24 of the 36 Hong Kong NPC members, there was no hope of revising the Basic Law.[79]

Before the NPC members made such a declaration, twenty of them signed a joint letter to the SCNPC, calling for the participation of the HKSAR government to check the requirements of those mainland migrants who applied to reside in Hong Kong. Ma Lik initiated the joint letter.[80] He said that the HKSAR government in the past had not participated in checking the requirements of mainland applicants who entered Hong Kong by using the one-way permits.[81] Ma and nineteen NPC members, including Allen Lee, believed that the HKSAR government should have a say in increasing the number of mainland professionals and technical experts who were eligible to enter Hong Kong. Allen Lee thought that the participation of the HKSAR government could tackle the problem of corruption in the process of granting 150 one-way permits for mainland Chinese every day.[82]

Some Hong Kong NPC members criticized the CFA for not consulting the SCNPC for formal guidelines on how the Basic Law should be interpreted. Ma Lik said that such consultation was "a serious matter [and] so a strict mechanism similar to amending the Basic Law is needed."[83] Echoing Ma's view, another Hong Kong NPC member Victor Sit Fung-shuen said the CFA should ask for the establishment of such mechanism and that any interpretation should receive the support of the Legislative Council and local NPC members.[84] Sit argued that every Hong Kong person could make a request for the SCNPC to interpret the Basic Law, although it might not be entertained by the SCNPC.[85] He questioned the correctness of the government's action to seek the SCNPC interpretation, for the CFA was the most suitable party to do so. Sit maintained that such an action by the CFA should have been done before the verdict on January 29. He suggested that since the CFA did not consult the SCNPC, the Hong Kong NPC deputies should make the request. Sit claimed that the government had asked the Hong Kong NPC members not to interfere with the matter, and that the Basic Law Committee members failed to take the initiative to resolve the dispute. Ma Lik supported Sit's call for a formal mechanism, for this would avoid an impression of the HKSAR government's "interference with the work of the judiciary."[86]

Other NPC members hoped that the CFA would "rectify" its decision. Tsang Hin-chi, the Hong Kong member of the SCNPC, maintained that the CFA should take measures to solve its own problem.[87] As early as February, he hoped that the Hong Kong delegation to the NPC would initiate a motion to request the NPC to study the CFA ruling.[88] One NPC member even went so far to suggest that Tung Chee-hwa should discuss with Andrew Li whether there would be a solution.[89]

When the SCNPC had a preliminary meeting to prepare for its interpretation of the Basic Law, three convenors of the NPC's Hong Kong delegation attended the meeting as observers, namely Ng Ching-fai, Maria Tam Wai-chu, and Yuen Mo. Another convenor, Ng Hong-mun, was invited but he could not attend the meeting.[90] They were all invited to attend the meeting as non-voting members and could express their views during the NPC's group discussions.[91] Allen Lee Peng-fei, however, complained that the majority of the Hong Kong NPC members were excluded from participation in the Standing Committee's preliminary meeting.

Lee, a local NPC member, also openly opposed the SCNPC interpretation of the Basic Law. He said that any interpretation would amount to "abolishing our CFA" and that the Basic Law should be amended.[92] Lee maintained that the Basic Law did not say that the HKSAR government could seek the SCNPC interpretation of the Basic Law.[93] However, other NPC members challenged Lee's views. For example, Maria Tam, also a Hong Kong member of the NPC, accused Lee in a forum of "forgetting what he had done" as a member of the Preparatory Committee and the Provisional Legislature, which in 1996 defined those who should have the right of abode in the HKSAR.[94]

A minority of NPC members toyed with the idea of asking the SCNPC to amend the Basic Law in order to stop the influx of migrants. Ma Lik originally raised the issue of requesting the SCNPC to amend the Basic Law. But he was cautious in making his remark, adding that

> I will take the lead of the call for amendments is very strong and the Government believes it can't stand [the migrant influx] any more.[95]

Later, Ma no longer voiced his idea of amending the Basic Law, especially when the government decided to ask for the SCNPC interpretation.

There were criticisms levelled at the Hong Kong NPC members, saying that they attempted to demonstrate "a real role to play in the constitutional crisis" triggered by the CFA ruling in January.[96] In practice, the NPC members encountered a dilemma. One commentator said that the NPC members were constrained by three factors: (1) the central government's request that they should not intervene in the HKSAR internal affairs, (2) the leadership of the New China News Agency (NCNA), and (3) the lack of resources which made it difficult for them to serve the Hong Kong people.[97] The activeness of the Hong Kong NPC members in the right of abode dispute could be interpreted as their attempt to assert their "autonomy."[98] On the one hand, "they cannot act on local affairs, but [on the other hand] they still have to face their constituency and the public here."[99]

The Position of the HKSAR Government

When the CFA considered the right of abode issue in January 1999, the HKSAR government did not seek to have the case referred to the SCNPC. Rather, the government believed that the CFA itself should consider whether such a step would be necessary. As Senior Counsel for the Director of Immigration Geoffrey Ma said in the court:

> It is not the Government's position that we are applying or wishing the CFA to refer [the case to the SCNPC]. The Government has no interest of its own in whether it is referred or not. But what is important as a matter of law is for this court to consider whether a referral has to be made.[100]

With the benefit of hindsight, the HKSAR government could have pre-empted the entire crisis by applying to the CFA to refer the case to the SCNPC in the first case. In the event that the government made such an application, the controversy over the CFA's decision could have been depoliticized. Indeed, if the government made such application, it could be criticized as surrendering the autonomy of the HKSAR.

Immediately after the CFA delivered its verdict on the right of abode issue in January 1999, the HKSAR government seemed to accept the court's decision. As the Director of Immigration Ambrose Lee Siu-kwong said:

> Both the Immigration Department and mainland officials agree to follow the CFA ruling. My visit to Beijing is to consolidate the implementation of granting the right of abode system.[101]

Similarly, the Secretary for Security Regina Ip asserted that the government would discuss with mainland authorities "on possible ways and means to facilitate the early entry into Hong Kong of those eligible persons."[102] A taskforce was later led by the Secretary for Administration Anson Chan Fang On-sang to examine the issue of how to manage mainland migrants coming to the HKSAR — a move praised by the mass media.[103]

Yet when the Secretary for Security Regina Ip remarked that the HKSAR government would discuss with the PRC authorities "the orderly entry of such children and the number [Hong Kong] can cope with each year," her remark aroused the concern of some critics of the government.[104] Legislative Councillor Margaret Ng accused Ip of misunderstanding the court judgment. She argued:

> The Government cannot afford to give the world the impression the SAR is inviting the mainland to devise ways to halt exit because the SAR is bound not to stop entry. The mainland is bound by the Basic Law just as much as the SAR is . . . [A]uthorities in the whole of China have the duty to give effect to it. To put down impediments must contravene the Basic Law.[105]

After the mainland legal experts criticized the CFA judgment, Tung Chee-hwa remained cautious and he understood the complexities of the issue. In response to reporters' question about the government's reaction to the criticisms of the mainland legal experts, Tung emphasized that the controversy over the right of abode issue stemmed from "an unprecedented historic undertaking" in the implementation of the "one country, two systems" concept.[106]

One day before the HKSAR government applied to the CFA for a clarification of its ruling, the Secretary for Justice Elsie Leung Oi-see made a controversial move to "inform" or "forewarn" the Chief Justice Andrew Li of the government's application.[107] Leung's action aroused the anger of her critics, who said that she made an "inappropriate" move and that her discussion with Li might include issues other than just informing the chief justice of the government's application.[108] Leung, however, made it clear that the PRC officials were unhappy about the CFA's provocative statement concerning the constitutional jurisdiction of the courts. She acknowledged that

> [t]he CFA had stated that the courts of the Region have the jurisdiction to examine whether legislative acts of the NPC or its Standing Committee are consistent with the Basic Law and to declare them to be invalid if

found to be inconsistent. Some commentators, both here and in Beijing, regarded those statements to mean that the CFA had put itself above the NPC, and that it had given itself the right to scrutinize and oversee each legislative act of the NPC.[109]

In late April, Tung Chee-hwa paid a visit to China and met with the PRC leader Jiang Zemin. It was speculated that Tung had already discussed the solution of making a request to the NPC to interpret the Basic Law.[110] On May 4, 1999, Anson Chan visited Beijing to discuss the right of abode issue with PRC officials such as Zhu Rongji and Qian Qichen.[111] Chan quoted Liao Hui, director of the State Council's Hong Kong and Macao Affairs Office, as saying that the HKSAR should settle the right of abode issue.[112] Chan met with Qiao Xiaoyang, the vice-chairman of the NPC's Legislative Affairs Commission, informing him of the three options considered by the HKSAR government: (1) "rectification" by the CFA, (2) seeking interpretation by the NPC, and (3) revising the Basic Law.[113] Although she said the HKSAR government had not decided the option, in the same month the government reportedly intended to abandon the solution of amending the Basic Law, for it would take ten months until the NPC would meet in March 2000.[114] For the government, these ten months would provide a "vacuum period" in which illegal immigrants would try to sneak into the HKSAR.[115]

Before the government asked the SCNPC to interpret the Basic Law, it emphasized the impossibility of the HKSAR to absorb 1.67 million migrants. According to the Tung administration, there would be a population growth of 25 percent over the next decade and a capital expenditure of HK$710 billion.[116] Moreover, the expenditure of various services would amount to HK$33 billion annually — "a burden beyond the HKSAR's ability to bear."[117] The HKSAR government presented the data in such a way as to legitimize the social and political necessity of requesting the SCNPC interpretation of the Basic Law's relevant provisions. In her answer to questions from Legislative Councillors, Regina Ip even said that such a large number of migrants would probably generate the possibility of "riots" in the HKSAR.[118] However, the statistical data concerning the 1.67 million mainlanders eligible to enter the HKSAR were severely criticized by some academics and critics, who accused the government of adopting a scaremongering tactic, exaggerating the negative impact of the migrants, and creating divisive sentiments in the society.

Then the HKSAR government initiated a motion in the Legislative Council (LegCo), seeking the support of the legislature for its request of the SCNPC interpretation of the Basic Law. The motion was endorsed with 35 votes supporting it, two votes against and one abstained.[119] Nineteen members of the democratic faction in LegCo staged a walkout of the chamber, expressing their opposition to the government.[120] Following the endorsement of the motion by LegCo, Elsie Leung and Regina Ip visited Beijing on June 2, discussing with officials of the State Council the content of the chief executive's report that would be submitted to the NPC Standing Committee.[121]

The chief executive's report to the State Council used the statistical data of 1.67 million to justify the incapability of the HKSAR government to handle "the demands of such a large number of new arrivals for education, housing, medical and health services, social welfare and other needs."[122] The HKSAR government emphasized that the decision to ask for the SCNPC interpretation of the Basic Law was "a decision which we have been compelled to take in the face of exceptional circumstances."[123] Some critics, however, said that once this exception was made, the HKSAR government might request the SCNPC help again in the future.[124]

The HKSAR government stressed the legality of the NPC to interpret the Basic Law. Anson Chan maintained that the government "has to decide on a course of action that is legal, constitutional, and which will offer an effective solution to the serious social and economic problems facing us as a result of the CFA ruling."[125] Elsie Leung remarked that

> I do understand that, to some lawyers trained in the common law, the exercise of a power of interpretation by a non-judicial body is an alien concept. However, I hope that they will appreciate that, under our new constitutional order, such a power may legitimately be exercised in respect of the Basic Law.[126]

Furthermore, Leung argued that the government's request for the SCNPC interpretation

> has full legal basis and does not seek to overturn the CFA decision. It is apparent that the majority of people, including members of the legal profession, have not queried legislative interpretation as an acceptable and established practice under the Civil Law system. There is in fact such a constitutional provision in Greece and Belgium.[127]

Echoing the views of Chan and Leung, Tung Chee-hwa asserted that the "mainstream community opinion" supported the government's action to ask for the SCNPC interpretation of the Basic Law.[128] Overall, the Tung leadership tried hard to convince the people of Hong Kong that it was legitimate, legal, and constitutional to ask for the SCNPC help to tackle the social and economic consequences of the CFA ruling.

It must be noted that Anson Chan's view on the SCNPC interpretation of the Basic Law was slightly different from Elsie Leung's. Before her visit to Beijing in May, Chan expressed her view in public that she did not favour the solution of asking the CFA to "rectify" its ruling, for there was no such mechanism in Hong Kong.[129] When the government opted for the alternative of asking the NPC to interpret the Basic Law, Chan said she did not want to envisage another similar situation in the future.[130] She also asserted that the maintenance of the "one country, two systems" would need to take into consideration the reaction and the feelings of the international society.[131] Her emphasis on the importance of "two systems" ran counter to the PRC officials' stress on the significance of "one country."[132] However, Leung refused to promise in public that the HKSAR government would no longer seek the SCNPC interpretation of the Basic Law.[133] It looked as if while Chan was a staunch supporter of judicial autonomy of the HKSAR, Leung tended to be much softer on the issue of judicial autonomy.

Supporters of the HKSAR Government

Members of the top policy-making body, the Executive Council (ExCo), supported the government in public. One ExCo member, Yang Ti-liang, made a controversial remark that the HKSAR government should set up a special group to review the Basic Law's content and that it should ask the SCNPC to interpret once and for all those contentious and ambiguous provisions of the Basic Law.[134] Later, he admitted in public that his idea had not been well thought. On the other hand, Yang disagreed with the idea of asking the CFA to "rectify" its decision, for there was no such mechanism in the HKSAR.[135] He believed that the best solution was the SCNPC interpretation of the Basic Law, and that the NPC would not exercise its power of interpretation arbitrarily.[136]

Many ExCo members publicly defended the government's action to seek the SCNPC interpretation. Leung Chun-ying said that the SCNPC would "very cautiously" interpret the provisions in the Basic Law.[137] Charles Lee Yeh-kwong maintained that the rule of law would remain "intact" even though the SCNPC interpreted the Basic Law.[138] Tam Yiu-chung argued the Basic Law was written "clearly" and it could not be amended, because the problem is [that] the CFA has interpreted it in another way. Even if the HKSAR government agrees to amend the Basic Law, the central government may not agree. Furthermore, the central government would need to convince all NPC deputies to accept such a method.[139]

Apart from ExCo members, one former member of the Basic Law Drafting Committee, Louis Cha, defended the position of the HKSAR government. Cha was dissatisfied with the CFA clarification. He contended that the CFA should have consulted the SCNPC before it made decisions on the right of abode issue on January 29, 1999.[140] He wrote a ten-thousand-word essay criticizing the CFA ruling.

The Law Society was another supporter of the government's action to request the NPC to interpret the Basic Law, but some of its members accused the Society of not consulting solicitors. Yolanda Fan Pui-lan, who led a signature campaign of some 280 solicitors, criticized the Law Society for always working in a "black box."[141]

Prior to the SCNPC interpretation of the Basic Law, the pro-Beijing groups in the HKSAR mobilized political support for the government. They advertised in various newspapers expressing their support of the government to seek the SCNPC interpretation, for Hong Kong would not be able to accommodate a large number of mainland migrants.

The Position of PRC Officials

The State Council was the first mainland government organ that supported and then criticized the CFA ruling. On February 2, officials of the State Council reportedly said that the central government respected and supported the CFA ruling.[142] However, on February 8, the State Council accused the CFA judgment of "violating the Basic Law."[143] In March 1999, the PRC leader Jiang Zemin told the Hong Kong NPC members that the CFA ruling would create tremendous pressure on the HKSAR, but he did not give any concrete solution to deal with the problem.[144] Premier Zhu Rongji told Anson Chan that in the end the HKSAR government would have to look for a solution on the right of abode issue.[145]

However, officials of the Hong Kong NCNA emphasized that the central government did not want to intervene in the right of abode controversy. The deputy director of the NCNA, Wang Fengchao, said that the HKSAR government should consider the ways to solve the problem of mainland migrants and that Beijing would not interfere.[146] Jiang Enzhu, the director of the NCNA, said that as far as he knew, amending the Basic Law would arouse the "opposition of many experts and scholars."[147] However, Jiang did not express his own view.

PRC officials were the staunch supporters of the HKSAR government's action to request the SCNPC interpretation of the Basic Law. The NPC deputy Wang Jiafu said the NPC Standing Committee's interpretation aimed "to reiterate the true legislative intent of the relevant provisions and to avoid the serious social consequences brought about by the judgment."[148] Other mainland deputies emphasized that it was lawful for the HKSAR government to seek the SCNPC interpretation if it encountered difficulties in implementing the Basic Law.

In a preliminary meeting of the chairman and vice-chairmen of the SCNPC, PRC officials legitimized the action of the HKSAR government to seek the SCNPC help. Qiao Xiaoyang, the deputy director of the NPC Legislative Affairs Commission, said that the CFA should have sought an interpretation from the NPC before making its final judgment, that the SCNPC interpretation would be "necessary and appropriate" to guarantee the "correct" implementation of the Basic Law, and that Tung Chee-hwa had made a proper request for SCNPC interpretation in accordance with the powers granted him by articles 43 and 48 (2) of the Basic Law.[149]

Qiao also remarked the right of abode issue illustrated that "one country" was more important than "two systems."[150] As early as January 29, the Legislative Affairs Commission held a meeting to discuss the CFA ruling.[151] It was unclear about the position of the Commission at that time. In May, Qiao said that the option of amending the Basic Law was not ruled out.[152] Qiao appeared to reveal the Commission's position on June 22, when he criticized the CFA for not seeking the interpretation by the SCNPC before its ruling on January 29.[153] He also accused the CFA ruling as a deviation from the legislative intent of the Basic Law.[154]

Critics of the HKSAR Government

Critics of the government defended the authority of the CFA, opposed the government's application to the court to clarify its ruling, and vehemently opposed the SCNPC to interpret the Basic Law. One lawyer who wrote a letter anonymously to the newspaper editor asserted that parts of the January judgment of the CFA were "misinterpreted" by the mainland legal academics, and that Elsie Leung should "not just go [to Beijing] to listen to more opera-singing."¹⁵⁵ The Bar Association denied that the CFA had attempted to usurp the SCNPC power. The Bar Association declared that

> if the legislative act of the NPC or its Standing Committee is inadvertently inconsistent with the Basic Law, then it must be right for the SAR courts to investigate the acts of the NPC or its Standing Committee insofar as they purport to have effect in the SAR on matters within the limits of autonomy . . . We firmly believe this is the effect of the judgment of the CFA. It does not intend to usurp the functions of the NPC or its Standing Committee or to act contrary to the [mainland] constitution . . .¹⁵⁶

The Bar Association suggested that any amendment of the Basic Law should receive the support of the legislature and the Hong Kong members of the NPC. Moreover, the proposed amendment should be subject to confirmation by a referendum or plebiscite.¹⁵⁷

Critics believed that the CFA clarification of its judgment was unnecessary. The International Commission of Jurists accused the HKSAR government of putting political pressure on the court and showing "scant respect for the independence of the judiciary."¹⁵⁸ The government's application to the CFA to clarify its ruling, to critics, undermined the "rule of law."¹⁵⁹ Yash Ghai wrote:

> Law no longer seemed important to the resolution of the matter. Our own Department of Justice weighed in by trying to turn these politically motivated attacks into a challenge cast in the medium of the law . . . [I]t asked the court to "clarify" its decision. It was, and was widely seen, as an invitation to "recant," an occasion for "self-criticism," to appease the political forces that were so disdainful of its view of legality.¹⁶⁰

Other critics of the government's application to the CFA pointed to its submissive attitude toward political pressure. One editorial said,

> [The CFA's] statement that the court cannot question any act of the NPC which accords with the Basic Law is merely a more tactful way of reiterating that it has the right to determine whether such actions comply with the mini-constitution . . . If such a change of phraseology provides a face-saving formula for local leftists and mainland legal scholars to withdraw their previous objections to the judgment, Hong Kong will breathe a collective sigh of relief. Some may even accept reluctantly the damage done to the rule of law by the Government's behaviour as a price worth paying to forestall a greater controversy . . . [T]he time is long overdue for the administration to come unequivocally to the court's defence.¹⁶¹

To the critics, the rule of law was undermined when the HKSAR government sought the SCNPC interpretation of the Basic Law. Martin Lee said:

> The message to the whole world is very clear. If the CFA's ruling is in favour of the Government, then it is final; however, if the CFA's ruling is against the Government, then it is only semi-final.[162]

Similarly, barrister Denis Chang Khen-lee questioned whether the CFA "has to ask [the SCNPC] for [the Basic Law's] legislative intent for every case . . . ? If that's the case, why should we have the court to interpret the law?"[163] A petition letter signed by 500 lawyers was submitted to the Executive Council by Margaret Ng to express their opposition to the government's request for the NPC to interpret the Basic Law.[164] For many lawyers, this government action would undermine and politicize the rule of law in the HKSAR.

Critics of the government organized themselves to oppose the SCNPC interpretation of the Basic Law. A group of university lecturers led by Yash Ghai launched a signature campaign among academics and placed an advertisement that accused the government of disrespecting the rule of law. Twenty-three lecturers and staff members at the Faculty of Law at the University of Hong Kong issued a declaration saying that the HKSAR government undermined the autonomy of Hong Kong by seeking the intervention from Beijing, and that even Zhu Rongji had asked the HKSAR to solve the right of abode problem by itself.[165] Kam Wong, a lecturer at the Chinese University of Hong Kong, suggested in public that the Legislative Council should impeach the chief executive for inviting the interference from the central government and refusing to implement the CFA ruling.[166]

The Mass Media and Public Opinion

The mass media was split into those who supported the government and those who opposed it. The *Hong Kong Standard*, *Wen Wei Po*, *Ta Kung Pao*, and *Oriental Daily* supported the government. The *Hong Kong Standard* often criticized the court, saying that its judgments would encourage illegal immigration into Hong Kong.[167] It also labelled those critics of the government as "people . . . who cannot accept that we now live and work under the Basic Law, a national law of the PRC."[168] The *Oriental Daily* appealed to the Hong Kong people for support of the "reality" that public opinion was against the influx of mainlanders.[169]

On the other hand, the *South China Morning Post* opposed the government's action to ask the CFA to clarify its ruling and to request the SCNPC to interpret the Basic Law. The rule of law was frequently emphasized in its editorials.[170] Similarly, the *Apple Daily* was critical of the government's move to request the SCNPC interpretation of the Basic Law, asserting that this would amount to the "death" of the rule of law.

The entire controversy over the right of abode of mainlanders divided the society of Hong Kong into those who were sympathetic toward them and those who despised them. As one commentator observed: "The fierce attack among some quarters in the community against the CFA ruling stemmed from longstanding bias towards people from the mainland and fears that their arrival would cause more economic and social hardship."[171]

A minority of Hong Kong people believed that the CFA should "rectify" its ruling rather than ask the SCNPC to interpret the Basic Law. One citizen wrote:

> As the judges of the CFA are not infallible, I suggest that it would have been preferable to ask them to rectify the matter, because their previous verdict was not in the public interest. Asking the Standing Committee of the NPC to re-interpret . . . the Basic Law will affect the independence of the judiciary and the principle of Hong Kong people ruling Hong Kong will be undermined.[172]

Another citizen believed that the CFA should seek the SCNPC interpretation before it ruled on the right of abode issue.

> The movement of a large number of individuals to Hong Kong from other parts of China, is surely a matter which affects not only Hong Kong but also the rest of China and it seems a pity therefore that the CFA in Hong Kong did not seek an interpretation from the NPC before handing down a judgment on the right of abode.[173]

In fact, some Hong Kong people were critical of the lawyers and democratic legislators who opposed the government's action to seek the SCNPC interpretation, for they believed that the HKSAR would not be able to absorb the mainland migrants. One angry citizen wrote:

> The attitude of so many Hong Kong lawyers towards the right of abode issue is extremely disappointing. While no-one disputes the significance

of the "rule of law" and an "independent judiciary," how can anyone argue that such concepts are more important than the wishes and welfare of the people they are meant to serve? . . . Any average Hong Kong resident can tell you that well before the Government issued its "scaremongering" figure of 1.67 million, the same vast majority of Hong Kong citizens were already adamantly against the influx.[174]

Interestingly, some Hong Kong people were critical of the drafters of the Basic Law, believing that the drafters should shoulder the responsibility for the ambiguities in Articles 22 and 24. One commentator asked the Basic Law drafters to "apologize" to the Hong Kong people for their failure in plugging the loopholes in Article 24.[175] One citizen angrily labelled the drafters as "criminals for thousand years."[176]

Public opinion surveys showed that most Hong Kong people did not understand the technical issues concerning the options of revising the Basic Law and asking the NPC to interpret the Basic Law. In a survey of 506 people conducted by the University of Hong Kong's Social Science Research Centre, 70.5 percent of the respondents said they were not clear toward the option of revising the Basic Law; only 29.5 percent said they were clear about it.[177] Similarly, 73 percent of them said they were unclear about the alternative of SCNPC interpretation of the Basic Law; only 27 percent said they were clear about it. Another survey of 911 people conducted by the Chinese University of Hong Kong showed more than 65 percent of the respondents disagreed that the government had exaggerated the number of eligible migrants at 1.67 million; and 73 percent of them rated societal interest above legal opinion and human rights on whether mainlanders should be allowed to enter Hong Kong.[178] A poll conducted by the Hong Kong Policy Institute showed that 60 percent of the respondents supported the SCNPC interpretation of the Basic Law to deal with the population influx, and 40 percent supported the option of revising the Basic Law.[179] It appeared that although most Hong Kong people were not sure about the technical procedures regarding the alternatives of amending the Basic Law and seeking the SCNPC interpretation, the majority were pragmatists who tended to support the idea of asking the NPC to interpret the Basic Law. Given that most Hong Kong people put the societal interest above legal opinion and human rights, it was natural that they accepted the fastest solution to prevent an influx of migrants from China.

Conclusion: The Need to Develop the Constitutional Convention of Self-Restraint and Implications for Taiwan

With the benefit of hindsight, the HKSAR government could have pre-empted the entire crisis if it had applied to the CFA to seek the SCNPC interpretation of the Basic Law prior to the court's ruling on January 29. Later, this "mistake" was admitted by an official of the Department of Justice, Ian Wingfield.[180] However, the crux of the problem was not the lack of foresight on the part of the HKSAR government. Arguably, the entire right of abode issue was over-politicized from the beginning of the CFA judgment to the HKSAR government's decision to seek the SCNPC interpretation of the Basic Law. Even if the HKSAR government could have made a move to apply to the CFA to seek the SCNPC interpretation of the Basic Law, its action might still be criticized as infringing upon the power of the CFA.

Objectively speaking, the CFA judgment made politically provocative remarks that alienated the PRC legal experts. The claim that the CFA had the right to review legislation by the NPC was politically unacceptable to the mainland legal experts, who led the attack on the court's ruling until the HKSAR government came up with the solution of applying the CFA to clarify its ruling. Clarifying its ruling, the CFA intentionally or unintentionally made a political gesture that would hopefully settle the right of abode issue.

However, the HKSAR government itself viewed the CFA ruling as socially and economically unbearable. The HKSAR government regarded the SCNPC interpretation of the Basic Law as the most effective and fastest way to defuse the crisis of a population influx. Although the HKSAR government argued that this was done in an exceptional circumstance, whether it would establish a constitutional convention of refraining from seeking the SCNPC help remained doubtful.[181]

In the entire right of abode debate, the role of the Basic Law Committee members and the Hong Kong NPC members was influential. In the event that the Hong Kong members of the Basic Law Committee could establish a constitutional convention of refraining from making their interpretation of the Basic Law in public, the whole right of abode issue might have been depoliticized. On the other hand, the Hong Kong NPC members appeared to be a group with divided views. Although most NPC members acted collectively to declare their position, some of their individual remarks in public have raised the issue whether they should adopt a much lower profile and more impartial stance in the future than the 1999 constitutional crisis.

In the event that they fail to establish their own constitutional convention, the hyper-politicization of the process of interpreting the Basic Law will be inevitable.

Similarly, whether the PRC legal experts would establish a constitutional convention of refraining from attacking the CFA judgment remains to be seen. In the event that they fail to adopt a much lower profile in the future, over-politicization of the process of interpreting the Basic Law will also be unavoidable. Overall, the constitutional convention of self-restraint needs to be developed by (1) the members of the Basic Law Committee, (2) the mainland legal experts, (3) the Hong Kong NPC members and (4) the HKSAR government. Since constitutional conventions are political habits that can change over time, some degree of uncertainty will not only characterize the politics of interpreting the Basic Law, but also shape the HKSAR judicial autonomy in the foreseeable future.

The politics of judicial autonomy in the HKSAR has tremendous implications for any negotiated settlement between the PRC and Taiwan. Taiwan will unlikely accept any model that will empower the SCNPC to interpret the Taiwan constitution, except for perhaps a very few provisions that would be necessary to maintain the ties between the two places. Any action of the SCNPC to interpret the Taiwan constitution would be seen as politically and legally unacceptable. Therefore, the resolution of Taiwan's political future demands a more creative and innovative model that will avoid the occurrence of the SCNPC interpretation of the Hong Kong Basic Law.

4

The Emergence of Constitutional Conventions[1]

The origin of the concept of conventions can be traced back to British scholars who wrote on the relationships between law and politics. A. V. Dicey referred to conventions as customs, practices, maxims, or precepts that embraced a group of constitutional or political ethics.[2] Sir Ivor Jennings distinguished conventions from non-obligatory usages or practices.[3] To Jennings, conventions are supported by constitutional reason or principle, but usages are not. He treats conventions as a homogeneous group of rules, whereas John Mackintosh in *The British Cabinet* identified different orders of constitutional conventions.[4] Mackintosh remarked that some conventions are fundamental, meaning that breaking them would overturn the basic principles of the constitution. Some conventions are less important because they can be altered without changing the nature of the constitution.[5]

Mere usages without obligatory force are not of much interest to constitutional lawyers. According to Hilaire Barnett,

> The idea of obligation is of prime importance here, for if a person is under an obligation which is recognized by observers of the constitution and that person fails to act in accordance with the obligation, then that failure will give rise to legitimate criticism which will invariably be phrased in terms of "constitutionality." To reiterate, the obligation imposes a standard of conduct which is expected to be followed. The obligation is "normative": by that is meant that the rule is "prescriptive" — that it dictates the appropriate form of action in a particular situation.[6]

Peter Hogg also emphasizes that "a convention is a rule which is regarded as obligatory by the officials to whom it applies, [whereas] a usage is not a rule, but merely a governmental practice which is ordinarily followed."[7] Hogg maintains that a usage may develop into a convention.

If a practice is invariably followed over a long period of time, it may come to be generally regarded as obligatory and thereby cease to be merely a usage. The resulting convention may be called a custom. This process of evolution from usage to convention (or custom) is the way in which most conventions have been established. It should be noticed, however, that very little turns on the question whether a practice is as unenforceable as a usage. The most that can be said is that there is a stronger moral obligation to follow a convention than a usage, and that departure from convention may be criticized more severely than departure from usage.[8]

While Hogg distinguishes conventions from usages in terms of the degree of public criticisms, Barnett distinguishes conventions from laws, practices, understandings, and habits by using the criteria of (1) the regularity of conduct, (2) reflectiveness, (3) the degree of obligation imposed, and (4) the sanction following the breach (see Table 4.1). He views the "absolute" degree of obligation as the hallmark of conventions. Moreover, any breach of conventions leads to the charge of unconstitutional conduct, whereas any violation of laws constitutes an unlawful conduct.

Table 4.1 Distinguishing Conventions from Laws, Practices, Understandings, and Habits

	Habits	*Understandings*	*Practices*	*Conventions*	*Laws*
Regularity of Conduct	Yes	Not necessarily	Yes	Yes	Yes
Reflectiveness	No	Yes	Yes	Yes	Yes
Degree of obligation imposed	None	Weak	Strong	Absolute	Absolute
Sanction attending breach	None	Justification required	Justification required	Charge of unconstitutional conduct	Unlawful conduct

Source: Hilaire Barnett, *Constitutional and Administrative Law* (London: Cavendish, 1995), p. 33.

As a matter of fact, Hogg and Barnett have developed Jennings's criteria of conventions. Jennings believed that mere practice was by no means a convention. He raised three defining characteristics of conventions in the following way:

> We have to ask ourselves three questions: first, what are the precedents; secondly, did the actors in the precedents believe that they were bound by a rule; and thirdly, is there a reason for the rule? A single precedent with a good reason may be enough to establish the rule. A whole string of precedents without such a reason will be of no avail, unless it is perfectly certain that the persons concerned regarded them as bound by it.[9]

This chapter will adopt Jennings's criteria of conventions to analyze the development of constitutional conventions in the HKSAR.

In Britain, conventions could hardly develop except over time. Cabinet ministers, who are accountable to the parliament through the question period, may resign in the case of personal scandals.[10] Other conventions that exist in Britain include the practice that the government must resign when the Parliament passes a vote of no-confidence. The concepts of collective responsibility and individual responsibility have been deeply entrenched in the British parliamentary system.[11] This chapter uses the case of Hong Kong to study the evolution of constitutional conventions from the British rule to the Chinese governance, with special emphasis on the resignations of principal officials in the HKSAR.

Constitutional Conventions in Hong Kong from the British Rule to the Post-Colonial Era

In the case of Hong Kong, before the transfer of sovereignty on July 1, 1997 from Britain to the PRC, very few academics had discussed conventions, not to mention politicians. Political scientist Norman Miners argued that one of the most significant conventions in Hong Kong under British rule was that Britain adopted a relatively non-interventionist policy toward Hong Kong. However, constitutional expert Yash Ghai tended to disagree with the way in which Miners used the notion of conventions. While Miners emphasized the importance of conventions in Hong Kong under British rule, Ghai believed that conventions "have not played a significant role."[12] Ghai also wrote:

> Not all the examples Miners cites of the divergence between the legal provisions and practices are really instances of conventions properly understood, that is, treated as binding (as is evidenced from increased Whitehall intervention in policy and administration in Hong Kong in the last few years before the transfer of sovereignty). Such as they were, they operated within an overarching framework in which the Governor's

position remained dominant and membership of key institutions was through his nomination. In any event, conventions may register shifts of power within the colony, but they do not alter the nature of the powers themselves. Changes in Hong Kong's constitution came about less through conventions or formal amendments, than through legislative measures within the framework of the Letters Patent, principally through the provision for local advisory bodies.[13]

Ghai's definition of conventions appears to be different from Miners's. While the former implicitly defines the concept as obligatory practices, the latter views conventions as simply political habits that are by no means legally binding. Just like Miners, other Hong Kong political scientists define conventions as political habits. Stephen Davies and Elfed Roberts wrote:

> [C]onstitutional conventions [are] those rules covering the exercise of constitutional powers which arise from custom, agreement, and expediency. Strict and precise constitutional laws covering all aspects of the exercise of government power would be a major obstacle to the administration of a modern state . . . Constitutional conventions arise in practice and have no formal, written status as law. They are sustained by custom and habit. In consequence they allow for flexibility. But insofar as they have constitutional standing as rules, conventions prevent arbitrariness. Thus a breach of a convention is not an illegal act, but it is a conspicuous breach of constitutional propriety. The sanction on a breach of a constitutional convention is therefore not due process of law before a court and consequent punishment. Rather, breach of a convention results in a loss of political expediency expressed through such means as a vote of no confidence by the legislature.[14]

Davies and Roberts, as with Miners, argued that there were "many conventions" in Hong Kong under British rule. They remarked:

> Hong Kong is no exception, though there are few clear political sanctions for breaching convention. There are many conventions of this sort in Hong Kong ranging from the way in which government officials exercise their powers, to the way in which the Governor consults the Executive Council, and from the way in which the legal system is structured and operates, to the practices of [Office of Members of Executive and Legislative Council]. One emerging convention is that government officials are now expected to consult affected groups on all intended major policy changes. The most important is the convention that the British Government does not exercise its right to dictate how Hong Kong should be run.[15]

While Miners, Davies and Roberts chose to adopt the definition of conventions as advanced by Dicey, Ghai appeared to use a relatively narrower definition of conventions as articulated by Jennings.

The concept of conventions emerged in the HKSAR in June 1999, when the Hong Kong people debated over whether the SCNPC should interpret provisions of the Basic Law concerning the right of abode of the mainland Chinese in Hong Kong. Some observers believed that the SCNPC's interpretation of the Basic Law in June 1999 challenged the HKSAR's judicial autonomy. Ghai contributed to the debate by articulating the concept of conventions. He argued that Article 158 of the Basic Law, which empowers the SCNPC to interpret the Basic Law, should be "judicialized."

> This means that all decisions should be based on legal arguments presented to any body which makes the decision or recommendations. Lawyers should be allowed at each stage, right up to the Standing Committee. The deciding body must give reasons for its decisions, which would also help towards the development of precedents in this area. And the members of the Committee for the Basic Law (CBL) should avoid entering into public controversies on the interpretation of the Basic Law and commenting on cases pending before the courts. Such restraint would avoid any appearance of bias having made up their mind before they are consulted by the SCNPC before making an interpretation. The development of some conventions as to how the SCNPC will exercise its powers would also be desirable. One might be that the Committee would not proceed to the interpretation of the Basic Law before the Hong Kong courts have given their decision giving the Committee the benefit of the courts' analysis (which may involve points of common law). Another might be that the Committee for the Basic Law should provide its reasons if it disagrees with a Hong Kong court's interpretation on a point on which it is consulted by the SCNPC. In such circumstances, a third convention might usefully be adopted — that the SCNPC as a rule would follow the recommendations of the Basic Law Committee.[16]

Since some Hong Kong members of the CBL — a body that is expected to arbitrate in any dispute between Beijing and the HKSAR on the Basic Law's provisions — criticized the judges of the Court of Final Appeal during the right of abode issue, a constitutional convention of self-restraint on the part of CBL members should arguably be developed.[17] After the SCNPC's interpretation of the Basic Law in June 1999, the pro-Beijing elites take it for granted that Beijing has been trying to develop a convention of refraining from interpreting the HKSAR's Basic Law.

Nevertheless, the SCNPC exercised its right of interpreting the Basic Law again in April 2004, nine months after the street protests by half a million Hong Kong people on July 1, 2003.[18] The SCNPC ruled out the possibility of having a chief executive directly elected by universal suffrage in 2007 and a wholly directly elected Legislative Council in 2008. As the decision of the SCNPC said:

> The election of the third Chief Executive of the HKSAR to be held in the year 2007 shall not be by means of an election of all the members by universal suffrage. The election of the Legislative Council of the HKSAR in the fourth term in the year 2008 shall not be by means of an election of all the members by universal suffrage. The ratio between members returned by functional constituencies and members returned by geographical constituencies through direct elections, who shall respectively occupy half of the seats, is to remain unchanged. The procedures for voting on bills and motions in the Legislative Council are to remain unchanged.[19]

The SCNPC's action of interpreting the Basic Law was a swift response to the demand on the part of many Hong Kong people for a faster pace of political reform. In the wake of the massive protests on July 1, 2003, Beijing was deeply concerned about the likelihood that the HKSAR government made concessions to public demands for political reform without sufficiently consulting the central government. In December 2003, when Chief Executive Tung Chee-hwa visited Beijing, the PRC leaders urged him to consider Beijing's views with regard to the pace and scope of Hong Kong's political reforms. In January 2004, the HKSAR government set up the Constitutional Task Force led by Chief Secretary Donald Tsang, Secretary for Justice Elsie Leung, and Secretary for Constitutional Affairs Stephen Lam. In February, the Task Force visited Beijing and discussed Hong Kong's political reforms with the State Council's Hong Kong and Macao Affairs Office and the Legislative Affairs Commission of the National People's Congress. In April, the SCNPC interpreted the Basic Law's provisions on political reforms in the following ways:

> The HKSAR must pay heed to the views of the Central Authorities; any proposed amendment must comply with the provisions of the Basic Law. Amendments to the design and principle of the political structure prescribed in the Basic Law must not be lightly contemplated; no proposed amendments shall affect the substantive power of the appointment of the Chief Executive by the Central Authorities; any proposed amendments must aim at consolidating the executive-led system headed by the Chief

Executive and must not deviate from this principle of design; development towards the ultimate aim of universal suffrage must progress in a gradual and orderly manner step by step. The pace should not be too fast . . . [A]ny proposed amendments must enable different sectors of society to be represented in the political structure, and to participate in politics through various channels.[20]

From the perspective of Beijing, the HKSAR government should establish a convention of heeding its views with regard to the pace and scope of political reform in Hong Kong. This practice was arguably established in Hong Kong under the British administration, which yielded to the pressure from the PRC with regard to the pace and scope of electoral reform introduced to the Legislative Council in 1988.[21] In the eyes of Beijing, this British practice of consulting with the PRC over the territory's political reform should be maintained. However, from Beijing's perspective, Governor Christopher Patten violated the practice or "convention" of consulting with the PRC over his political reform blueprint in 1992 and 1993, thus leading to its unilateral decision of setting up another "stove," the Provisional Legislative Council, in January 1997 to counter Patten's last legislature.[22] The SCNPC's interpretation of the Basic Law in April 2004 can be seen as a continuity of the PRC's policy toward Hong Kong's political reforms, for Beijing is consistently afraid of the danger that democratization in the HKSAR would produce a chief executive and a legislature outside its sphere of political influence. Therefore, the principles of maintaining an executive-led system, retaining functional constituencies in the Legislative Council, and preserving the separate voting mechanism in the legislature have to be upheld from the PRC's vantage point.

Constitutional Conventions and the "Accountability System" in the HKSAR

In 2000, Chief Executive Tung Chee-hwa announced that his government would study how to implement the "accountability system" for senior officials. On July 1, 2002, the Principal Officials Accountability System (POAS), as it is called by the government, was formally introduced.[23] There were fourteen principal officials under the new system comprising three Secretaries of Department and eleven Directors of Bureau.[24] While the POAS appeared to try to achieve the objective of enhancing the accountability of the HKSAR government,[25] it was widely believed that the "system" attempts at consolidating the Tung administration and improving the chief executive's leadership. Since the chief executive has been criticized as having weak political leadership, the PRC government hopes that the POAS can hopefully buttress Tung's rule, increase his popularity, and groom a group of politicians for the future leadership of the HKSAR. Critics, however, doubted whether the POAS would really bring about accountability, for the principal officials are responsible to the chief executive who is not elected by all the people of Hong Kong.[26]

Apart from Andrew Wong, a former member of LegCo who wrote a paper on how to develop both accountability and conventions in the HKSAR, other analysts also articulated the concept of conventions.[27] However, they did not really distinguish between the concept of conventions and that of practices. Nor did they mention any timeframe in which practices may develop into conventions. In a sense, they have tended to adopt a loose definition of conventions as articulated by Miners, Davies, and Roberts. In 2002, when LegCo held a series of meetings to discuss the "accountability system" proposed by the HKSAR government, its agenda embraced the topic of conventions. While some legislators believed that the politically appointed principal officials "should" resign in case of scandals or policy mistakes, other LegCo members argued that the political appointees "must" do so. Their consensus, however, is that conventions need to be developed in the HKSAR so as to consolidate the government's accountability to the public. Again, none of the LegCo members appeared to distinguish between conventions and practices.

There are at least four main factors explaining why conventions are suddenly gaining currency in the HKSAR. First and foremost, the Basic Law remains ambiguous in many areas. Coincidentally, conventions belong to the gray areas between law and politics. The element of ambiguity in both the Basic Law and conventions means that they can be merged in the discussion of the development of the "accountability system." Second, conventions can evolve over time, just like the meaning of the provisions of the Basic Law. Given the difficulty of revising the Basic Law at least in the short run, the development of conventions has the advantages of buying time and allowing the HKSAR's political system to transform gradually. Third, conventions have been seen as necessary so as to realize the objective of achieving "a high degree of autonomy" for the HKSAR, as what Ghai did when he argued for the judicialization of the process of interpreting the Basic Law in 1999. Fourth, for those politicians and academics who adopt a loose definition of conventions, they believe that conventions can either develop the accountability of the HKSAR government or restrain Beijing from intervening in Hong Kong affairs. To the advocates of conventions, the concept is by no means new to Hong Kong. As argued by Miners, Davies, and Roberts, some of the conventions tended to be more "fundamental," such as the British non-interventionist policy toward Hong Kong and the Hong Kong government's consultation with affected interest groups. Critics such as Ghai have questioned whether conventions really existed in Hong Kong under British rule, for breaching these conventions would not necessarily bring about public condemnation and criticisms.

Strictly speaking, Ghai's view appears to be more convincing. Neither the colonial officials nor the local politicians articulated the concept of conventions. Nor did they demonstrate a consistent behavior showing the three criteria of conventions as discussed by Jennings — precedents, actors' beliefs, and reasons to observe the rules. In particular, the colonial administrators did not really have a firm belief in such conventions as consultative governance. As mentioned above, the British colonial administration could also ignore public opinion arbitrarily. For example, the British administration consulted public views cosmetically over the future of Hong Kong not before but after the Sino-British Joint Declaration was initialized in September 1984. The people of Hong Kong had no choice but to accept the Sino-British Joint Declaration over Hong Kong's future. Moreover, despite the fact that opinion surveys showed the majority of Hong Kong people favored the introduction of direct elections to LegCo in 1988, the British administration yielded to the PRC's pressure and interpreted public opinion as favoring a delay over the injection of direct elections into LegCo from 1988 to 1991.[28] If we adopt Jennings's criteria of conventions, it can be said that the practice of consulting public opinion was by no means firmly entrenched in Hong Kong under British rule. The reason is that the administration of Governor Edward Youde and Governor David Wilson could choose to turn a blind eye to public opinion, and to interpret it in a way that maintained Sino-British harmony. To borrow from Jennings, the political actors or the colonial rulers did not believe in the need to consult and respect public opinion over the future of Hong Kong and the introduction of direct election to LegCo in 1988.

The so-called conventions as discussed by Miners, Davies, and Roberts appeared to be practices that were not really obligatory. In general, as Miners discussed, the British government seldom intervened in Hong Kong affairs before the Sino-British agreement was reached in 1984. Yet when the British intervened more visibly in the transitional affairs of Hong Kong from 1984 to June 1997,[29] very few Hong Kong people raised any objections and pointed to any unconstitutional conduct on the part of the British. Nor did the majority of the Hong Kong people find such British intervention constitutionally unacceptable.

Nevertheless, political actors in the HKSAR have inherited some relatively "older" practices that were adopted for some period of time in Hong Kong under British rule. First, the chief executive refrains from exercising his power to veto bills concerning government policy and government expenditure. He delegates this veto power to the LegCo President. The existing LegCo President, Rita Fan, is following the convention of her predecessor, Andrew Wong, who must explain in writing why he refused to allow a private member's bill to be tabled in LegCo.[30] Second, so far the chief executive must sign the bills passed by LegCo, although Article 49 of the Basic Law stipulates that he can return the bill back to LegCo for reconsideration. Third, the chief executive has actually been following the practice of Patten to visit LegCo regularly for the sake of answering questions from legislators during the chief executive's question session.

Yet Patten's practice was different from Tung's. The former was far more aggressive than the latter in terms of communication with ordinary citizens, going to town halls to answer questions from the public regarding his political reform blueprint, attending televised debates with his opponents such as the Chairman of the DAB Jasper Tsang Yok-sing, and meeting with legislators in LegCo's question and answer sessions.[31] Shortly after July 1, 1997, Tung no longer went to LegCo to answer questions from legislators, thus arousing some criticisms from legislators. Yet the degree of public criticisms was very limited; most citizens did not really feel that Tung's practice was constitutionally improper. Since mid-1998, however, Tung began the practice of attending question and answer sessions in LegCo — perhaps a positive practice in the long-term development of a constitutional convention. In the event that the third and fourth chief executive follow the practice of attending question and answer sessions in LegCo, this practice will develop into a constitutional convention.

Some previous practices have been slightly modified. First, the chief executive has been regularly meeting with the leaders of political parties since the middle of 1998. Practices, like conventions, can change over time. Tung developed a practice of meeting with pro-government party leaders like the DAB, the Liberal Party, and the Hong Kong Progressive Alliance more often than with opposition parties such as the Democratic Party and the Frontier. At one point in 1998 and 1999, some high-ranking government officials even appeared in the annual meetings of political parties, such as the DAB. In late 1999 and 2000, high-ranking officials became less prominent in attending annual party meetings — a sign that they might sense the necessity of maintaining an appearance of political "neutrality." Such "neutrality" of senior civil servants was ironically more strictly observed in the colonial era when Governor Wilson and Governor Patten did not attend any annual party meeting. However, in July 2002, when the DAB celebrated its tenth anniversary, the chief executive and his principal officials, such as Secretary for Justice Elsie Leung and Financial Secretary Antony Leung, resumed their practice of attending the pro-government political party's celebration — a sign that the "political neutrality" of principal officials has become a myth since the POAS was introduced on July 1, 2002.[32] In reality, with the introduction of the POAS, and after the appointment of the senior members of the Liberal Party and DAB into the top policy-making Executive Council, principal officials have been relying on the support of the two parties to ensure that government bills and policies can be approved by LegCo. Due to the inevitability of politicization since the establishment of the POAS, "political neutrality" of principal officials is a myth. After all, they are a far cry from the civil servants, who are supposed to remain politically neutral in the sense that they need to implement the policy decisions of whoever become the principal officials of the HKSAR government.[33]

After the political earthquake in July 2003, when the government shelved the National Security (Legislative Provisions) Bill in view of widespread public discontent, Chief Executive Tung resumed the practice of regularly meeting with the leaders of opposition parties, such as the Frontier, the Democratic Party, and the Association for Democracy and People's Livelihood. It remains to be seen whether this practice will develop into a convention during the office of the third and fourth chief executive. However, preliminary observations show that Donald Tsang does not regularly meet with the leaders of various opposition parties, thus shifting his practice to the pre-July 2003 phase of the Tung administration.

Second, prior to the introduction of the POAS, chief executive Tung had occasionally attended the party conventions of the DAB and the Liberal Party — a departure from the practice of Patten. The last Governor usually maintained a policy of political "neutrality" toward party conventions, although his political reform agenda and beliefs tended to have much in common with the democrats like LegCo members Martin Lee and Emily Lau. Following the implementation of the POAS, the chief executive is the same as other principal officials he has appointed, siding with the Liberal Party and DAB in order to build up his political support in the legislature.

Third, the executive-legislative relationships have become much more tense and rocky than the situation in the final years of the British rule. Governor Patten constantly required civil servants to lobby for the support of LegCo members for government bills and policies, especially his political reform blueprint which was narrowly passed by the legislature. The aggressive lobbying style of senior civil servants has appeared to weaken since the handover. At the same time, LegCo members in the HKSAR have complained that the government did not respect them. Former legislators such as Ronald Arculli, Christine Loh, and Leong Chi-hung voiced their concern about the deteriorating executive-legislative relations in the HKSAR. In short, the practice of assertive lobbying on the part of civil servants in LegCo has changed since the retrocession, while the confrontational relationships between the executive and the legislature have been exacerbated. How to develop the practices of managing executive-legislative relations remains a difficult task for the HKSAR government in the years to come.

An important precedent that has the potential to establish a convention in the future was the resignation of Rosanna Wong Yick-ming, the former head of the Housing Authority, over the scandal of substandard piling in the home ownership scheme. She had decided to resign even shortly before LegCo passed a vote of no-confidence on her and Tony Miller, an official of the Housing Department. Public criticisms were severe because the piling scandal raised a moral issue of whether at least some leaders of the Housing Authority had to shoulder the political responsibility of resignation over public mismanagement. Editorials in most Chinese newspapers were critical of the governmental role in the piling scandal. One LegCo member, Margaret Ng, said:

> Though LegCo has no power to require officials to resign, there is no reason why the Chief Executive should not, by convention, seriously consider asking an official to resign when the Council has passed a vote of no-confidence. The decision would still remain with the Chief Executive whether to actually ask the official to resign. It would depend on the circumstances of each case, but would greatly strengthen accountability if it is implicitly accepted once a no-confidence vote is passed, resignation has to be seriously considered.[34]

Clearly, a minority of legislators called for Miller's resignation in order to establish a constitutional convention of requiring officials to take their responsibility for making mistakes. However, after the short piling case, Miller remained a government official although Wong had the political will to resign from the Housing Authority.

The resignation of Wong was arguably a precedent because the piling scandal raised a public outcry. Even LegCo members across the political spectrum from left to right reached a rare consensus that either Wong or Miller would have to shoulder the political responsibility for the piling scandal. However, in April 2001 Wong was appointed by the government to head the Education Commission — a move that demonstrated the government's insufficient knowledge of the importance of conventions. The appointment also showed the lack of pro-government elites who are capable of leading semi-official agencies or public bodies.

Some new conventions appear to take shape in the HKSAR without violating the Basic Law while at the same time enhancing the accountability of the government. First, the members of ExCo who are principal officials are now attending LegCo's weekly meetings, answering questions from legislators, explaining government policies, defending government action, and lobbying for political support. They have already replaced the senior civil servants to play a more proactive and political role in dealing with executive-legislative relations. Sometimes ExCo members, including those without ministerial portfolios, have lunches with LegCo members so as to establish regular communication channels between the executive branch and the legislature. Whether this practice of communicating with legislators will turn into a more durable and obligatory form of convention remains to be observed.

In a sense, the conventions of the relationships between principal officials and LegCo have been codified. According to Chapter Two of the "Code for Principal Officials under the Accountability System," principal officials

> will be designated under Article 62(6) of the Basic Law to attend meetings of the Basic Law to attend meetings of the Legislative Council, its committees, subcommittees and panels and to speak on behalf of the Government . . . Principal officials have a duty to represent the Government and to transact business at meetings of the Legislative Council, and as necessary its committees, subcommittees and panels, e.g. to introduce bills or motions, address the Legislative Council, present papers, make statements, answer questions and take part in debates in respect of matters relating to their respective portfolios. Principal officials shall endeavor to ensure that they would be available to attend meetings of the Legislative Council when matters relating to their respective portfolios are discussed. Principal officials shall give accurate and truthful information to the Legislative Council and correct any error at the earliest opportunity.[35]

Under the HKSAR government's POAS, the role of ExCo members who are also principal officials is transformed from amateur politicians to full-time professional politicians. They help the chief executive bolster or enhance his legitimacy. ExCo members who are simultaneously principal officials, such as Henry Tang and Elsie Leung, are full-time political appointees working for the chief executive. Other ExCo members who are not principal officials or who do not have any portfolios, such as Leung Chun-ying and Cheng Yiu-tong, are part-time politicians with their full-time jobs outside the government. As a matter of fact, the mouthpieces of the government, such as *Ta Kung Pao* and *Wen Wei Po*, interpreted the most significant contribution of the "accountability system" as improving the Tung administration's governance.[36] It appears that the patriotic or pro-Beijing media portrayed the "accountability system" as a panacea to the relatively weak governance of the HKSAR from July 1, 1997 to 2001. However, the pro-Beijing elites have elevated the importance of consolidating governance to the extent that the question of how to achieve accountability has been relatively neglected, including the critical issue of developing various constitutional conventions.

Another new practice, if not a convention, is that the politically appointed principal officials have to go to the eighteen districts to lobby for the support of local politicians — a requirement that is not specified in their Code of Conduct. Understandably, according to the government's POAS, the Secretary for Home Affairs (Ho Chi-ping) was retained in 2002 without being merged with any other portfolios. In fact, Ho played a crucial role in assisting other politically appointed principal officials to visit various districts and in garnering the political support from District Councilors as well as district residents. Ho also led other principal officials to visit various districts in March and April 2003 when the HKSAR was affected by the outbreak of SARS. Other principal officials occasionally visited the districts so as to collect public opinion on various government policies. While Antony Leung went to the Eastern District in February 2003 to gather public views on the government's financial policy, former secretary for security Regina Ip went to different districts in late 2002 to promote the government's proposals on Article 23 of the Basic Law that outlaws treason, sedition, and subversion. In general, principal officials were expected to act like elected politicians touring various districts even though the people of Hong Kong had not elected them. The practice of "ministerial" visits to eighteen districts serves the function of enhancing their legitimacy and mandate in the eyes of the ordinary citizens. Again, it remains to be seen whether this new practice of the principal officials will turn into a convention over time.

Third, LegCo slightly adjusts its role *vis-à-vis* the HKSAR government by regularly interacting with the principal officials and by trying to pass a vote of no-confidence on any "minister" who performs poorly, who has behaved scandalously, or who commits policy blunders. So far, LegCo has not reached a consensus in these two aspects. Ideally, LegCo's sub-committees can be restructured in such a way as to match various "ministerial" portfolios. In other words, different "principal officials" can attend corresponding LegCo's subcommittees. Since the Tsang administration began, the legislators have gradually reached a consensus on this matter.

From the perspective of some mainland constitutional experts, such as Xiao Weiyun, the practice of LegCo in initiating a motion of no-confidence on any principal official actually violated the Basic Law. From the PRC perspective, the principle of executive-led system has to be maintained and so logically no-confidence motion initiated by any legislator is seen as constitutionally improper. In a sense, there is a clash of views between some pro-democracy legislators and the PRC's constitutional experts. The former view no-confidence motions as a necessary practice that can be translated into a convention of checking the power of the executive, but the latter regard it as constitutionally undesirable.

On the other hand, while pro-democracy legislators tried their best to pass a vote of no-confidence on those principal officials who performed unsatisfactorily, pro-establishment legislators were determined to block their move to force any principal official to resign. An illustration was Financial Secretary Antony Leung's car purchasing scandal in March 2003. Leung purchased a luxurious Lexus 430 shortly before he raised the registration tax for vehicles in his budget on March 5, 2003. He failed to declare his purchase of the car to ExCo, while his colleague Yeoh Eng-kiong declared that he had bought a car in the same ExCo meeting. Some pro-democracy legislators called for Leung's resignation. He survived a non-binding motion which was initiated by Margaret Ng to ask him to step down, and which was eventually defeated by a vote of 31 to 22, with four abstentions.[37] The pro-government DAB and Liberal Party protected Leung, insisting that he had been negligent.

Fourth, the central government in Beijing appeared to adopt a relatively non-interventionist attitude toward the development of the POAS in the HKSAR. At the very least, few Chinese officials publicly voiced their views on the direction of POAS — a positive step in enhancing the HKSAR's autonomy at least apparently. The relatively low profile adopted by the Chinese officials regarding the "accountability system" was a far cry from their high profile during the Sino-British debate over Chris Patten's political reform plans. Although there were unsubstantiated reports saying that the HKSAR's accountability proposal was submitted to Beijing and was slightly revised by the Hong Kong and Macao Affairs Office, Beijing's self-restrained attitude toward the local political reform was apparently conducive to the development of "a high degree of autonomy" in the HKSAR. Unfortunately, the protests by half a million people on July 1, 2003 forced Beijing to become more interventionist in propping up the Tung administration by setting up a special coordination committee on Hong Kong affairs.[38] As mentioned in Chapter Two, the committee was under the leadership of the Vice-Premier Zeng Qinghong and it was composed of eighteen members, including representatives from the People's Liberation Army, the Ministry of National Security, the Liaison Office in Hong Kong, the Liaison Office in Macao, the United Front Department, and the Ministry of Public Security.[39] Nonetheless, from the PRC's perspective, the POAS not only protected the Tung administration but it also can serve as a useful device that will groom the HKSAR leadership in the long run. Hence, it seems that while the PRC self-restrained attitude appeared to establish a convention of not intervening in Hong Kong's POAS, such an attitude was attributable to its political calculation and consideration. In brief, while the central government refrains from intervening explicitly in the development of the POAS in the HKSAR, it has not hesitated to interfere with the need to bolster the weak administration of Tung Chee-hwa shortly after the debacle over the legislation on Article 23 of the Basic Law in July 2003.

Establishing a New Constitutional Convention of "Ministerial" Resignation

As mentioned before, after the establishment of the POAS, the scandal involving Financial Secretary Antony Leung erupted in March 2003. The Leung scandal tested whether Chief Executive Tung had the political will to accept his "ministerial" resignation. The immediate result was a negative one, for Tung did not believe that Leung had made a blunder that justified his voluntary resignation. The entire scandal illustrated some practical difficulties in establishing the constitutional convention of "ministerial resignation" in the HKSAR.

On March 10, 2003, Leung wrote a letter to Chief Executive Tung, offering his resignation; nevertheless, the chief executive "requested [Leung] to withdraw [his] resignation on March 15."[40] Leung's letter said:

> I write to tender my resignation from the office of the Financial Secretary of the HKSAR with immediate effect . . . Although I have no intention whatsoever to lessen my tax liability through making the purchase shortly before the announced increase in Vehicle First Registration Tax on 5 March 2003, I should not have made the purchase so as to avoid any perceived conflict of interest. I accept that I was not in full compliance with the Code of Principal Officials under the Accountability System, particularly section 5.1 which stipulated that principal officials shall avoid putting themselves in a position where they might arouse any suspicion of dishonesty, unfairness or conflict of interest. I am deeply sorry about the negative image this has caused to the Administration. I accept responsibility for the mistake I made, and I believe that resignation is the proper cause of action for me in the circumstances.[41]

In public, Chief Executive Tung stepped up his defense of Leung, insisting that the latter had made "an honest mistake" in failing to disclose his car purchase ahead of tax increases.[42] Tung also said: "I have considered everything thoroughly and the practical situation at that time. I think he had no intention to hide the truth, nor to avoid tax."[43]

Despite the fact that the mass media and members of the public called for Leung's resignation,[44] the chief executive formed an alliance with the Liberal Party and DAB to block the attempt by pro-democracy activists to remove Leung. First and foremost, Chief Executive Tung did not believe that Leung's car purchase represented an unforgivable blunder that deserved his resignation. As a paternalistic Chinese leader in the HKSAR, Tung had a track record of retaining subordinates whose performance was problematic, including Chief Executive Office's special assistant Andrew Lo who had been involved in the alleged interference with academic Robert Chung's surveys of the chief executive's popularity in the summer of 2000. Similarly, in 1999, when LegCo moved a no-confidence motion to call for the Secretary for Justice Elsie Leung to resign, the Liberal Party and DAB again formed a coalition to defeat the motion. While the chief executive remains a paternalistic leader protective of his subordinates, the pro-government parties also see any no-confidence motion on senior and principal officials as a zero sum game beneficial to the democrats but detrimental to the executive-led administration in the HKSAR.

In the Leung scandal, the HKSAR government adopted the policy of reprimanding him in public. This move established a new convention of having three levels of managing "ministerial" scandals or mistakes.[45] The first level is marked by public apology, such as Secretary for Financial Services and the Treasury Frederick Ma who publicly apologized for his handling of the penny-stock incident.[46] The second level is to reprimand the principal official in public, as with the case of the government's and the chief executive's initial handling of the Leung scandal. Unless the principal official makes a blunder or has a scandal that seriously undermines the government's image and credibility, neither the chief executive nor Beijing is reluctant to envisage an erosion of the power of the executive-led administration in the HKSAR.[47] The case of Leung in March 2003 proved that neither the chief executive nor Beijing was prepared to experiment with the constitutional convention of "ministerial" resignation.

The third level — resignation of the principal official concerned — has been implemented since the resignation of Antony Leung shortly after the debacle over Article 23 of the Basic Law in July 2003. Following the decision of Regina Ip who resigned for "personal" reasons, Leung offered his resignation on July 16, a day after the Independent Commission Against Corruption (ICAC) handled its report into the car purchase incident to the Department of Justice.[48] Leung's resignation was a sign that he eventually accepted the responsibility of his scandal, thus establishing a convention of ministerial resignation in the view of a public outcry. Regina Ip's resignation used personal reasons, showing her reluctance to bow to public criticisms for her defiant attitude toward the legislation on Article 23 of the Basic Law.[49] She had actually tendered her resignation to Tung on June 25, six days before the mass protests on July 1, 2003. Strictly speaking, Ip's resignation did not really demonstrate a convention of ministerial accountability to the public for her policy "mistake." After all, she insisted that the legislation on Article 23 was a necessary step in accordance with the Basic Law. If so, Antony Leung's departure was arguably far more significant than Ip's move in establishing the constitutional convention of ministerial resignation.

Another significant event that eventually established the constitutional convention of ministerial resignation was the decision of the Secretary for Health, Welfare and Food, Dr. Yeoh Eng-kiong, to resign on July 7, 2004 for his role in the SARS tragedy. Although SARS cost the lives of 299 people in the HKSAR out of 1,755 infected citizens, Yeoh initially refused to resign. He apologized to the public four times on July 5, 2004 for the government's handling of the SARS crisis.[50] However, LegCo's report on SARS criticized Yeoh and the Director of Health Margaret Chan for mishandling the SARS crisis. For one thing, Yeoh made a misleading statement on March 14, 2004 by saying that there was no pneumonia outbreak in the community.[51] Moreover, Chan refused to quarantine residents of the Block E in Amoy Garden, where 329 residents were infected with the SARS virus and 42 of them died. The poor communication between the Department of Health and the Hospital Authority was also a target of LegCo's criticisms.[52] In March 2003, Yeoh was resistant to any idea of his resignation and he made the following remarks:

> I accepted fully the responsibility for the inadequacies on our health care system during the SARS outbreak . . . I explained that the overall total responsibility in terms of the impact on the total community and the other social systems was the Chief Executive's. I reiterated that the ultimate responsibility for health work remains with me and that I continued to carry my political responsibility. The Director of Health is the public health adviser to the government and responsible for public health in Hong Kong. The statutory powers concerning the prevention of infectious diseases are vested with the Director of Health. But in implementing and performing this role, the Director is accountable to me in how he or she carries this out. I am accountable for any decision, professional or administrative, made by the Director.[53]

Critics of Yeoh said that he tried to shift the political responsibility to the chief executive and the director of health.[54]

Some members of the public continued to call for his resignation.[55] Eventually, on July 6, 2003, one day after LegCo published its report on SARS, the mass media highlighted the remarks made by Kwok Sin-hung, whose wife died of SARS in Amoy Garden. Kwok asserted that "many Hong Kong people are dissatisfied with both the LegCo report and the fact that no official is responsible" for the SARS tragedy.[56] He even described Yeoh's reluctance to resign as a "shameful" and "unscrupulous" action.[57] On July 7, Yeoh tendered his resignation to Chief Executive Tung, who accepted it. The next day, the chief of the Hospital Authority Leong Chi-hung also resigned in the name of realizing the principle of accountability.[58] Yeoh's sudden resignation appeared to show that the constitutional convention of ministerial resignation due to public outcry was further entrenched in the HKSAR.

The resignation of Antony Leung provided a precedent for Yeoh to follow, to borrow from Jennings's criteria. Furthermore, while Antony Leung as a political actor believed in the need to establish a precedent of resignation, he fully understood the reason behind his move — conflict of interest on the part of the principal official. Although Tung in March 2003 asked him to stay on, the mass protests against the government on July 1 triggered his decision to quit his position and to rescue the government's serious legitimacy crisis.[59] Similarly, although Yeoh was originally resistant to any public pressure upon him to resign, he eventually bowed to public criticisms. Perhaps the remarks made by Kwok were decisive in bringing about Yeoh's resignation even though Yeoh and Leong Chi-hung had both insisted that they had accumulated much experience in dealing with SARS. Strictly speaking, Yeoh did not appear to cherish the principle of ministerial resignation. He simply did not really believe that he had made any policy mistake, for other actors such as the chief executive and the director of health had to shoulder the collective responsibilities. Nonetheless, public criticisms became so severe that he had no choice but to resign in order to rescue the legitimacy crisis of the Tung administration. To borrow from Hogg, the majority of Hong Kong people believed that Yeoh had the "moral obligation" to resign for the government's unsatisfactory handling of the SARS crisis.

Ministerial resignation also affected the administration of Chief Executive Donald Tsang in June 2007. The Commissioner of the Independent Commission Against Corruption (ICAC), Fanny Law Fan Chiu-fun, resigned in June 2007 after a commission of inquiry that looked into allegations of official interference with academic freedom at the Hong Kong Institute of Education (HKIE) found her behavior as a former permanent secretary for education improper. The Commission heard the testimony of witnesses and concluded that Law attempted "to silence critics by addressing them personally or through their superiors, irrespective of the motive."[60] Two academics at the HKIE publicly criticized the government's education policies, incurring the wrath of Law who then expressed privately to her staff that one of them should be dismissed or denied promotion. Law, however, asserted that she had not interfered with academic freedom and that she was actually a victim of the "unhealthy political situation in Hong Kong."[61] In fact, some senior civil servants of the HKSAR government have appeared to look down upon critical academics, treating their public criticisms as politically undesirable. Law's resignation perhaps reflected the problematic training of some senior civil servants, who have been socialized to accept Western scientific management without the need to be more openminded toward public criticisms. Moreover, the Commission of Inquiry did not find any improper behavior on the part of the Secretary for Education and Manpower Arthur Li Kwok-cheung, who had been accused by a high-level academic of the HKIE, Bernard Luk, of making verbal threats — a claim without concrete evidence to the Commission. The academic freedom debate demonstrated the need for both senior civil servants and principal officials to tolerate opposing views in the society.[62]

The impact of the resignation of Lam Woon-kwong, the director of the Chief Executive's Office, on the practice of principal officials affected by any sex scandal remains to be observed. Lam resigned on January 7, 2005 immediately after a magazine, *Sudden Weekly*, published a story not only showing photographs of Lam with a woman outside a hotel in Tokyo but also interviewing Lam's wife.[63] Lam said that "in view of the media report on my private affairs, I tendered my resignation to the Chief Executive."[64] One report claimed that Lam resigned "in fact because he and Chief Executive Tung did not meet eye to eye on some issues."[65] Apparently, Lam's resignation was due to his displeasure with the mass media's handling of his private affairs. It remains to be seen whether Lam's practice would be followed by any future principal official whose extra-marital affair is exposed by the mass media. As a matter of fact, Lam's extra-marital affair had been covered by the mass media long before the report of *Sudden Weekly*, but the public did not appear to react to it negatively. On the surface, Lam's resignation was a personal decision rather than an outcome of any public pressure, unlike the cases of Leung and Yeoh. In any event, it remains to be seen whether any future principal official whose extra-marital affair is unveiled by the mass media would follow Lam's footstep.

In July 2007, the chief of the Radio Television Hong Kong (RTHK) and the Director of Broadcasting Chu Pui-hing announced his decision to retire earlier shortly after he had been photographed by reporters hiding behind a mainland woman who was found to work in several karaoke bars.[66] Although Chu was not a political appointee under the POAS, he was a senior civil servant held accountable to his superior, the Secretary for Commerce and Economic Development Frederick Ma Si-hang. According to the Chief Executive's Office, Chu would have to report his incident and submit his retirement application to the Commerce and Economic Development Bureau and the Civil Service Bureau.[67] While Chu maintained that his incident was a private affair and that it did not involve any improper wrongdoings such as the acceptance of money and offerings, the suspected sex scandal highlighted the fact that, under the POAS, senior civil servants whose behavior is questioned by the mass media and the public would remain vulnerable to resignation.[68]

The resignation of Chief Executive Tung Chee-hwa in March 2005 reveals a number of important practices on how Beijing handled the chief executive's sudden departure. Whether these practices would become constitutional conventions remains to be observed. First, Tung submitted his resignation formally to the PRC government's State Council on March 10 after he had verbally informed Beijing of his intention to resign in January 2005.[69] Whether any future chief executive who suddenly resigns would follow Tung's practice remains to be seen. Second, Tung had informed the

Executive Council members of his decision to resign on March 7 prior to his formal resignation tendered to the central government on March 10. It remains to be seen whether any future chief executive who suddenly resigns would also follow Tung's practice, for the Executive Council is a close advisory body of the chief executive. Third, the PRC government adopted the practice of nominating Tung to the Chinese People's Political Consultative Conference (CPPCC), and then electing him as one of its vice-presidents. The PRC's moves were not only a sign of political reward to Tung but also a recognition of his "achievements" implementing the "one country, two systems" in Hong Kong. Whether the future chief executive of the HKSAR who steps down will receive the same official status conferred upon Tung by the central government remains to be seen. Fourth, the caretaker government led by Donald Tsang immediately retained all the principal officials and the members of the Executive Council, thus stabilizing the personnel dimension of the HKSAR leadership at least in the short run.[70] Clearly, the central government hopes that this will become a practice or perhaps even a convention in case of any sudden resignation of the chief executive. Fourth, and most controversially, Beijing is keen to establish a practice that, in the event of the sudden resignation of the chief executive, the new chief executive elected within 180 days will have a shorter term of office rather than the normal five years term.[71] Some legal experts in Hong Kong and Legislative Council members questioned whether Beijing's interpretation of the Basic Law might violate the literal interpretation of the office of the chief executive.[72] Obviously, there was a huge discrepancy between the two interpretations of the Basic Law.

Fifth, and perhaps most importantly, with regard to the controversy over the new chief executive's term of office after the predecessor's resignation, the HKSAR government established a practice of consulting the views of the mainland legal experts on the Basic Law. The former secretary for justice Elsie Leung admitted that she consulted the views of the mainland legal experts, such as Xu Chongde, after Tung had suggested her to do so.[73] In fact, during the SCNPC's interpretation of the Basic Law concerning the right of abode of mainland Chinese in June 1999, the HKSAR government also consulted the views of the mainland legal experts. It appears that this practice will sooner or later become a crucial convention in the relationship between the HKSAR and the central government in Beijing.

Conclusion and Implications for Taiwan

While constitutional conventions were relatively insignificant in Hong Kong under British rule, they are undoubtedly shaping the post-colonial political system. Some relatively "older" practices have continued to be adopted by the HKSAR's political actors since July 1997. A few practices have been slightly revised. Whether these practices can develop into conventions remains to be observed in the years to come. More significantly, Rosanna Wong's resignation served as the precedent that had the potential to be turned into a convention. The case of Antony Leung corroborates that originally neither the chief executive nor Beijing was prepared to accept "ministerial" resignation for the sake of developing the practice into a constitutional convention in the HKSAR. However, the debacle over Article 23 of the Basic Law and the mass protests on July 1, 2003 constituted a political earthquake that necessitated political transformations. Eventually, both the chief executive and Beijing had to accept Leung's and Ip's resignations. Leung's resignation was a turning point in the development of the constitutional convention in the HKSAR, for it followed the precedent of Rosanna Wong's resignation and demonstrated a belief on the part of the principal official that resignation was morally obligatory and constitutionally justifiable. Public criticisms of Yeoh's handling of the SARS also became a crucial factor leading to his eventual resignation, thus entrenching the constitutional convention of ministerial resignation. Although the impact of Lam's resignation remains to be observed, the resignation of Tung Chee-hwa in March 2005 appeared to establish a number of important practices shaping the relationships between Beijing and the HKSAR.

Other new or old practices have the potential to be developed further into constitutional conventions, thus entrenching accountability into the HKSAR polity in a silent manner. At the same time, the responsibilities of principal officials have already been enshrined in their Code of Conduct, thus codifying some aspects of constitutional conventions in the HKSAR. Regarding the government's handling of any problematic behavior of principal officials, a three-tier level of management — involving public apology, public rebuke, and resignation — appears to gradually take shape.

Indeed, the personal factor is continuing to have a bearing on the development of constitutional conventions in post-colonial Hong Kong. If the chief executive and the politically appointed officials do not recognize the need for conventions, the accountability system for principal officials may run the risk of turning into a pseudo-accountability one in which the "principal officials" will remain accountable mainly to the chief executive rather than to the public. However, the ruling elites are increasingly aware of the importance of conventions. In April 2002, the Chief Secretary Donald Tsang and the Secretary for Constitutional Affairs Michael Suen publicly admitted that conventions would need to be developed in the future. Their remarks could be interpreted as a progressive step in the evolution of constitutional conventions in the HKSAR.

Perhaps even more importantly, the public is increasingly aware of the need for constitutional conventions. Opinion surveys conducted by the mass media in March 2003 concerning the Antony Leung scandal showed that public opinion was split on whether Leung should resign. This survey result can be seen as an encouraging sign that, apart from more LegCo members calling for the adoption of constitutional conventions, the mass media and the public have already improved the quality of their political discourse to such an extent that accountability — "ministerial" resignation in case of making serious mistakes or having scandals — is gradually emerging as a normative value.

The introduction of the POAS has already opened the door for ministerial resignations since July 2002. The crux of the problem is whether the political actors — the chief executive, the politically appointed principal officials, LegCo, the mass media, and the public — will continue to have the political will to consolidate and entrench the spirit of holding the principal officials accountable for their own behavior and performance. The prospects remain cautiously optimistic. Although the HKSAR is not a Western-style democracy in which the chief executive is directly elected through universal suffrage, ministerial resignation is an influential convention shaping the future development of democratization in Hong Kong.

The development of constitutional conventions in the relationships between Beijing and the HKSAR can have a significant demonstration effect on Taiwan's political future. In the event that the constitutional convention of self-restraint on the part of Beijing can be established, the Hong Kong model of "one country, two systems" would be more attractive to the ROC on Taiwan. Indeed, the Taiwanese may not appreciate the importance of developing constitutional conventions in Beijing's relations with the HKSAR, for Taiwan's legal system is more akin to the mainland counterpart than parallel to the Hong Kong common-law tradition. Yet if Taiwan policy-makers, think-tanks, and academics realize the political significance of constitutional conventions within the HKSAR and between the capitalist enclave and Beijing, they would perhaps adopt a new perspective on the likelihood of allowing any cross-Strait agreement on Taiwan's future to be developed further in the long run.

5
The Implementation of the Basic Law

While the previous chapter has explored the evolutions of constitutional conventions in the HKSAR, this chapter is going to explore the emergent conventions governing the Beijing-HKSAR relations. By reviewing the content of the Basic Law and how it has been implemented in reality since Hong Kong's retrocession to the PRC, we will delineate the new practices and conventions in Beijing's relations with the HKSAR. Finally, the difficulties of making constitutional conventions absolutely obligatory in the evolving relationships between Beijing and the HKSAR will be discussed.

Chapter 1 of the Basic Law

Constitutional practices and conventions develop through the implementation of the HKSAR mini-constitution, the Basic Law. Chapter 1 of the Basic Law contains eleven Articles that delineate the general principles of Beijing's policy toward the HKSAR.[1] Article 1, which states that the HKSAR is "an inalienable part of the PRC," appears to be neglected by most observers whenever disputes over political reforms in the HKSAR erupt.[2] In the minds of the pro-democracy Hong Kong elites, democratic reform would not affect Beijing's sovereignty over the HKSAR.[3] In reality, from the perspective of mainland Chinese legal experts and officials, democratic reforms in the HKSAR cannot bring about any drift toward political separatism. Indeed, an overwhelming majority, arguably all, Hongkongers regard the HKSAR as "an inalienable part" of the PRC. Unfortunately, a serious perception gap exists between the pro-democracy supporters in Hong Kong on the one hand and the mainland Chinese legal experts and officials on the other. The former is eager to envisage the direct elections of both the chief executive and the entire LegCo. But the latter views such rapid democratization as not only an implantation of Western-style democracy into the HKSAR but also a risk of augmenting foreign influence upon Hong Kong, thus endangering the PRC sovereignty and threatening its national security. Article 1 of Chapter 1 is arguably downplayed in the ongoing disputes over political reform, but it is the central tenet that underlies the divergent perceptions of Beijing and the HKSAR. To use Barnett's terminology, both sides have fundamental differences over the impact of rapid democratic reform on whether the HKSAR would continue to be "an inalienable part of the PRC."

Article 2 of Chapter 1 stipulates that the National People's Congress (NPC) authorizes the HKSAR to "exercise a high degree of autonomy and enjoy executive, legislative and independent judicial power, including that of final adjudication."[4] It seems that many people of Hong Kong have forgotten that it is the NPC that authorizes Hong Kong to enjoy "a high degree of autonomy." The Standing Committee of the NPC interpreted the Basic Law in June 1999 on the right of abode issue of mainland Chinese, in April 2004 on the impossibility of having a chief executive directly elected by universal suffrage in 2007 and a wholly directly-elected LegCo in 2008, and in April 2005 over the shorter term of the new chief executive who would replace Tung Chee-hwa. Many people of Hong Kong reacted to the three interpretations made by the SCNPC strongly. This was understandable given the fact that most Hongkongers, especially the pro-democracy elites, tend to have a maximalist view of autonomy. However, the understanding of Article 2 from the PRC legal experts and officials is a far cry from most Hong Kong people. From the mainland perspective, the SCNPC is the supreme legal body authorizing Hong Kong to enjoy "a high degree of autonomy." Therefore, its interpretation of the Basic Law conforms not only to Article 158 of the Basic Law — which empowers the NPC to interpret the mini-constitution — but also a realization of the PRC sovereignty over the HKSAR. An Executive Council member of the HKSAR government, Leung Chun-ying, put it succinctly when he asserted that while the people of Hong Kong expected "an absolute degree of autonomy," Beijing actually conferred upon the HKSAR "a high degree of autonomy."[5]

Article 5 of Chapter 1 is perhaps an illuminating stipulation that highlights the practical transformations of mainland China rather than the HKSAR. It says that "the socialist system and policies shall not be practiced in the HKSAR, and the previous capitalist system and way of life shall remain unchanged for 50 years." While the HKSAR's capitalist way of life has been maintained, the PRC has been experiencing an unprecedented process of capitalist revolution, whose final destination remains unknown and unclear. However, the late Chinese architect of the "one country, two systems", Deng Xiaoping, had already remarked in June 1984:

> "One country, two systems" . . . means that within the PRC, the mainland with its one billion people will maintain the socialist system, while Hong Kong and Taiwan continue under the capitalist system . . . Our policy towards Hong Kong will remain unchanged for a long time to come, but this will not affect socialism on the mainland. The main part of China must maintain socialism, but a capitalist system will be allowed to exist in certain areas, such as Hong Kong and Taiwan.[6]

While there is no misunderstanding on both sides of Hong Kong and Beijing on the persistence of capitalist practices in the HKSAR, it is doubtful whether the PRC can and will maintain a socialist system even for an additional forty years due to the rapid and deepening capitalist metamorphosis in every mainland province.[7] It can be argued that, with the enactment of the property rights law by the NPC in 2007, the mainland economic system is converging with the protection of private property as stipulated in Article 6 of the Hong Kong Basic Law.

Chapter 2 of the Basic Law: Relationships between the Central Authorities and the HKSAR

Article 12 of Chapter 2 emphasizes that the HKSAR shall be a local administrative region which enjoys a high degree of autonomy and which comes directly under the central government. On the surface, this stipulation is not controversial. Yet from Beijing's perspective, the HKSAR enjoys local autonomy and is under the central government — a line repeated by mainland legal experts and the members of the Basic Law Committee such as Rao Geping and Wang Zhenmin.[8]

Article 14 states that the military forces stationed by the central government in the HKSAR shall not interfere in the local affairs of the HKSAR. Moreover, the HKSAR government may ask the central government for assistance from the garrison in the maintenance of public order and in disaster relief. By convention, the People's Liberation Army (PLA) has been refraining from interfering with the affairs of the HKSAR. Nor does any PLA commander voice their views on Hong Kong affairs in public. In actual practice, the PLA presence in the HKSAR is a symbol of Beijing's realization of its sovereignty over Hong Kong. It has also been playing the public relations functions of opening its camp to the people of Hong Kong, mobilizing officers to donate their blood in public, and cooperating with the local police force in joint exercises. In May 2007, the HKSAR Commissioner of the Police, Tang King-shing, invited the PLA Garrison Commander Lieutenant General Wang Jitang to inspect a passing-out parade at the Hong Kong Police College, signaling the improved cooperation between the two forces.[9] During the tenth anniversary of the HKSAR, Wang Jitang revealed that it also plays the role of protecting the HKSAR from any possible terrorist attack and that it collected information from the police force with regard to the anti-World Trade Organization protests in the HKSAR.[10]

According to Article 17, if the SCNPC considers that any law enacted by the HKSAR LegCo is not in conformity with the provisions of the Basic Law, it may return the law in question and the law would be invalidated. So far, the NPC Standing Committee has refrained from taking such action, although it did interpret the Basic Law three times, namely in 1999, 2004, and 2005. Hence, it can be argued that the NPC Standing Committee is developing a convention of self-restraint, attempting not to invalidate any law passed by the Hong Kong legislature. Doing so would be tantamount to an explicit erosion of legislative autonomy in the HKSAR and it would trigger a public outcry as well as resistance.

Article 18 empowers the SCNPC to declare a state of emergency in the HKSAR, by reason of turmoil that may endanger national security or unity. At the apex of the protests by half a million Hong Kong people against the maladministration of the Tung Chee-hwa government on July 1, 2003, the SCNPC adopted a relatively self-restrained attitude and did not declare any state of emergency in the HKSAR, although there were reports saying that a member of the Hong Kong Executive Council raised the idea that the PLA would have to be deployed to deal with any turbulence resulting from the series of citizen protests.[11]

Article 15, which allows the central government to appoint the chief executive and the principal officials of the executive authorities of the HKSAR, symbolizes the realization of Beijing's sovereignty over Hong Kong. When the pro-democracy candidate for the chief executive election, Alan Leong Kah-kit, challenged the authority of Beijing during his campaign in March 2007 that Beijing's power to appoint the principal officials should perhaps be revoked, his suggestion aroused the anger of the pro-Beijing media, politicians, and commentators. From the viewpoint of the central government, Article 15 is not simply symbolic but also substantial in that the formal appointment of both the chief executive and the principal officials represents the concrete powers and authority enjoyed by "one country" over the local administration. Article 15 has also been interpreted strictly by some pro-Beijing legal experts, who said that any election of the chief executive by universal suffrage in the future would have to be preceded by a nomination process in which those candidates going through direct election would first require the vote of all the members of the Election Committee.[12] Sources close to Beijing even claimed that the central government would prefer to have communication with the Election Committee before the nomination process so that any politically undesirable or unacceptable candidates would be screened out.[13] Hence, Article 15 is increasingly interpreted in a way linking to the direct election of the chief executive by universal suffrage. According to Queen's Counsel Alan Hoo, any "prior communication" would belong to politics and it requires the building up of "constitutional conventions."[14] But a Hong Kong member of the Basic Law Committee believes that any specified mechanism on top of the "democratic procedures" designated in Article 45 of the Basic Law would be "an empty and ambiguous idea" and that it would be "a political decision" to choose a particular nomination model at the end.[15] Due to the fact that the Basic Law has many areas open to interpretation, its content remains controversial.

Article 21 empowers the Chinese citizens among the residents of the HKSAR to elect locally the deputies of the region to the NPC. In practice, this stipulation has been observed, but the crux of the question is whether the method of selecting the Hong Kong members of the NPC would be democratized further, including the composition of the Election Committee that would return the Hong Kong representatives.

The most controversial provision in Chapter 2 is arguably Article 22, which states that "no department of the Central People's Government and no province, autonomous region, or municipality directly under the Central Government may interfere in the affairs which the HKSAR administers on its own in accordance with this Law."[16] While there is no evidence to prove that any mainland province, autonomous region, or municipality under the central government intervenes in the affairs of the HKSAR, the Liaison Office in the HKSAR as a representative of Beijing has been conducting campaign activities and coordinating work for the pro-Beijing candidates in both the LegCo direct elections and District Councils elections.[17] If the Liaison Office has developed a practice of reaching compromise among candidates of the patriotic front and conducting electioneering for them, its hidden and informal participation in Hong Kong's elections is arguably becoming a constitutional convention.

The attempt by the HKSAR government to legislate on Article 23 of the Basic Law became abortive in July 2003. Article 23 states that the HKSAR government "shall enact laws on its own to prohibit any act of treason, secession, sedition, subversion against the Central People's Government, or theft of state secrets, to prohibit foreign political organizations or bodies from conducting political activities in the Region, and to prohibit political organizations or bodies of the Region from establishing ties with foreign political organizations or bodies."[18] Given the complexities of legislating on Article 23, the HKSAR government and Beijing are buying time and waiting for the apex of Chinese nationalism in Hong Kong, where more people would find the national security legislation politically acceptable. In December 2007, PRC officials said that Macao would legislate on Article 23 — an indication that the Article 23 debated will be re-ignited in Hong Kong.

Chapter 3: Fundamental Rights and Duties of the Residents

Apparently, a majority of the rights mentioned in Chapter 3 have been respected.[19] They include the rights of permanent residents (Article 24); equality before the law (Article 25), the right to vote and stand in elections (Article 26); freedom of speech, assembly, demonstrations as well as press (Article 27); freedom from arbitrary arrest and detention (Article 28); freedom from arbitrary intrusion into a resident's home and premises (Article 29); freedom and privacy of communication of residents (Article 30); freedom of emigration (Article 31); freedom of conscience and religious belief (Article 32); freedom of choice of occupation (Article 33); freedom to engage in academic research and artistic creation (Article 34); the right to confidential legal advice (Article 35); the right to social welfare (Article 36); the freedom of marriage (Article 37); and the rights and interests of the indigenous inhabitants of the New Territories (Article 40). Indeed, critics of Chapter 3 have argued that the local mass media, particularly the Chinese print media, are exercising self-censorship and marginalizing the political opposition, particularly the more "radical" League of Social Democrats.[20]

The most problematic provision in Chapter 3 that governs the relationship between Beijing and the HKSAR is actually Article 30. It remains unknown whether the national security agents of the central government have conducted surveillance on the political activists of the HKSAR, especially their communications and private discussions. Given the fact that the HKSAR has been viewed by some mainlanders as a place where foreign agents may "collaborate" with the local human rights and political activists, it is possible that many Hong Kong political activists, particularly those in the pro-democracy camp, are under constant surveillance.[21] But the extent to which they are under the watchful eyes of the agents from Beijing is difficult to be assessed. If "political policing" was a tradition in Hong Kong under British rule, it has perhaps developed into either a practice or a hidden convention in the HKSAR.[22]

In August 2006, LegCo passed a bill regulating the use of interceptions of communications and covert surveillance by Hong Kong authorities. Although many forms of electronic surveillance require authorization from a member of a three-judge panel created to review such request, both foreign and mainland Chinese entities were left untouched by the law.[23] Thomas Kellogg observes accurately: "While activities of the PRC state security forces in Hong Kong are a sensitive issue; nonetheless, they need to be addressed. That would let all Hong Kong citizens know they are fully protected from unlawful foreign intrusion into their privacy from any and all sources."[24]

Political Structure and Beijing

Chapter 4 focuses on the political structure whose evolutions have displayed close and dynamic interactions with the central government. Article 43, which provides that the chief executive shall be "accountable to the Central People's Government and the HKSAR," is easier said than done. Both Tung Chee-hwa and Donald Tsang have been accountable to the central government since the formation of the HKSAR. Arguably, Tung was accountable to Beijing to such an extent that his accountability to the people of Hong Kong was neglected. The blind loyalty to the legislation on Article 23 was a case in point. Mr. Tung became so unpopular that even the central government had to allow him to resign for health reasons. The way in which Beijing handled the sudden departure of Mr. Tung proved that a new practice was emerging in the relationship between the central government and the HKSAR. If the chief executive, as with Mr. Tung, were deeply unpopular as to arouse constant public protests, as with the massive demonstrations on both July 1, 2003 and July 1, 2004, the central government would have little choice but to let the unpopular leader step down earlier so as to appease public anger. If this political practice is gradually developing into a constitutional convention, the position of the chief executive is going to demand more political finesse and wisdom, balancing the interests of Beijing with that of the people of Hong Kong.

Article 45 is the most contentious provision shaping democratic development. Although it states that the ultimate aim "is the selection of the Chief Executive by universal suffrage," the real practice is that Beijing is reluctant to envisage an early direct election of the chief executive through universal suffrage. Such rapid democratization would, in the eyes of Beijing, turn the HKSAR into another Taiwan under the leadership of the separatist Democratic Progressive Party (DPP). The crux of the problem is the lack of trust on the part of Beijing toward the people of Hong Kong. As mainland legal expert Xu Chongde said, "If you can guarantee me that those who are direct elected can be patriots, then I must support the selection of the Chief Executive by universal suffrage today."[25] Indeed, the definition of patriots remains unclear. While the former director of the Hong Kong and Macao Office Lu Ping insisted that the term patriots could be extended to not simply business tycoons but also middle-lower classes,[26] the late Deng Xiaoping defined patriotism ambiguously as "loving the motherland and Hong Kong."[27] If patriotism has been defined loosely, it refers to the patriots as those people who support the PRC resumption of its sovereignty over Hong Kong and, most importantly, those who support the policies of the Chinese Communist Party. Albert Ho, the chairman of the Hong Kong Democratic Party, pointed out clearly that the democrats are facing the risks of being easily labeled as "unpatriotic" because they may have "connections" and communications with foreigners, oppose the enactment of Article 23 of the Basic Law in the HKSAR, are sympathetic with the DPP in Taiwan, and constitute "a subversive threat" to the central government in Beijing.[28]

Article 46 states that the term of office of the chief executive shall be five years and that he or she may serve for not more than two consecutive terms. As a matter of fact, Beijing has appeared to develop a practice that it prefers a chief executive to serve two terms consecutively, thus giving a certain degree of stability to the Special Administrative Region. Mr. Tung Chee-hwa was originally designated to serve two terms, but his deep unpopularity appeared to alter the decision of Beijing to let him stay until the end of his second term of office. Beijing's attitude toward Donald Tsang again is a testimony that it prefers to have a chief executive serving much longer than the rest of the term vacated by Mr. Tung until mid-2007. A similar preference of Beijing for a consecutive two terms of office can be seen in the case of the Macao Special Administrative Region where the

Chief Executive Edmund Ho Hau-wah is securing the support of the central government until his term will expire in 2009. Hence, it can be said that Beijing's practice, if not necessarily convention, is to prefer a chief executive in both Hong Kong and Macao to serve for two terms, thus bringing about a certain degree of political stability and continuity to the two Special Administrative Regions.

By convention, Beijing has refrained from giving instructions or directions to the chief executive to dissolve LegCo. Article 50 says that if the chief executive refuses to sign a bill passed the second time by LegCo, and if consensus cannot be reached after consultation, he or she may dissolve LegCo. In the case of Macao under Portuguese rule, the Governor did dissolve the Legislative Assembly in 1984 during a row with the local Macanese legislators.[29] In the Hong Kong case, when LegCo rejected Donald Tsang's political reform blueprint in December 2005, a mainland legal expert Xu Chongde openly suggested that Tsang should dissolve LegCo, forcing the assembly to hold new elections, and then submitting the political reform package to the new legislature again.[30] Although Xu's view did not represent the central government's position and was rejected by other mainland legal experts, the idea of dissolving LegCo proposed by the PRC side was unprecedented. Still, Beijing has been refraining from asking the chief executive to dissolve LegCo, both in the cases of LegCo's rejection of Tsang's political reform proposals in December 2005 and the climax of LegCo and public protests against the legislation on Article 23 in July 2003. This practice of Beijing's self-restraint is arguably a hallmark of Article 50.

Article 68 mentions that the "ultimate aim is the election of all the members of the LegCo by universal suffrage." Due to Beijing's perception that the selection of all legislators by universal suffrage would open the door to a majority of pro-democracy elites dominating the legislature, this scenario is clearly politically unacceptable. In particular, some members of the pro-democracy legislators had participated in the Hong Kong Alliance in Support of the Democratic and Patriotic Movement in China in May and June 1989. They are still viewed as "subversive elements" by the central government, as Albert Ho remarked. On paper, Article 68 provides for universal suffrage of the entire legislature. In practice, however, it remains a distant goal that is extremely difficult to be achieved as long as the Hong Kong democrats are viewed as "subversive" elements by the CCP.

One crucial convention that is not really stated in the Basic Law is that the underground CCP remains active in the HKSAR. It has been playing a critical role in Hong Kong's local elections, mobilizing party members to vote for like-minded candidates, assisting local groups to submit their views to the government and LegCo on various issues that range from the national security bill to political reform, and forming an alliance across district groups so that the pro-Beijing DAB would have a better chance of getting its candidates directly elected to both LegCo and District Councils. It is important to note that by convention, while the DAB is led by possibly some underground CCP members in the HKSAR, its ranks-and-file members are the people of Hong Kong without necessarily being the hidden agents of the CCP. The DAB represents a united front organization spearheaded by the CCP and staffed by the local members of the Hong Kong public. It functions as a check against the pro-democracy parties, preventing them from easily grasping the directly elected seats in both the District Councils and Legislative Council, playing the role of a loyalist party supportive of governmental bills in the legislative chamber, occasionally criticizing the government so as to woo the support of the ordinary voters, and claiming to support the direct elections of the chief executive and the entire LegCo in the distant future. Ordinary citizens who are not highly knowledgeable on Hong Kong politics can be easily misled by the DAB's frequent pronouncement on its direct elections platforms, albeit it must bend with the political line adopted by the central government in Beijing.[31]

Chapter 5 and the Economic Relations between the HKSAR and Beijing

On the surface, all the provisions of Chapter 5 (Articles 105 to 135) demonstrate a high degree of economic autonomy enjoyed by the HKSAR. In particular, Beijing allowed the HKSAR government to implement Article 107 flexibly, i.e. the HKSAR "shall follow the principle of keeping expenditure within the limits of revenues in drawing up its budget, and strive to achieve a fiscal balance, avoid balance, and keep the budget commensurate with the growth rate of its gross domestic product."[32] When the former financial secretary Antony Leung prepared a deficit budget, the HKSAR government appeared to interpret Article 107 flexibly, with the approval of the central government in Beijing.

In practice, Article 112 has appeared to undergo a silent revolution or transformation. It says that the HKSAR government "shall safeguard the free flow of capital within, into and out of the Region."[33] Since mid-2003, in the wake of the implementation of the Closer Economic Partnership Arrangement and particularly the mainlanders' visit scheme to the HKSAR, and recently the relaxation of mainland capital flowing into the stock market of Hong Kong, Beijing has already been playing a crucial role in shaping "the free flow of capital" into the HKSAR. In the eyes of Beijing, the HKSAR is playing a critical function of absorbing the surplus capital from the overheated mainland economy.

Another unique relationship between the HKSAR and Beijing, which has not been mentioned by any provision of the Basic Law, is that the central government is playing the role of an arbitrator in Hong Kong's competitive interactions with Guangdong, Shenzhen, Zhuhai, and Macao. As mentioned in Chapter One, the idea of constructing the Hong Kong–Zhuhai–Macao bridge has been floated but not yet finalized. The major problem of the ambitious infrastructural plan was the rivalry among the regional governments in South China. The HKSAR was keen to develop the bridge with Macao and Zhuhai, but Shenzhen was once jealous of the plan and tried to lobby for a so-called "double Y proposal," which meant that the bridge would reach Shenzhen. As Shenzhen's competitor, Zhuhai was keen to envisage a "single Y model" in which Shenzhen would be excluded. In view of regional strife and delay, Beijing's State Planning and Development Commission has been studying both the feasibility and implementation of the proposed Hong Kong–Zhuhai–Macao bridge, acting as an impartial referee to adjudicate on the conflict-ridden relationships between Hong Kong, Zhuhai, and Macao.

Chapter 7: External Affairs

The HKSAR has been enjoying its autonomy in conducting external affairs upon the approval of the central government in Beijing. All the provisions in Chapter 7 appear to operate smoothly, including the participation of the HKSAR in international organizations by using the name "Hong Kong, China" (Articles 151 and 152); its arrangements in international agreements (Article 153); the issuance of passports and travel documents to those eligible residents (Article 154); the conclusion of visa agreements with other states upon the authorization of Beijing (Article 155); the establishment of Hong Kong's trade missions in foreign countries (Article 156); and the establishment of foreign consular and other official and semi-official missions in the HKSAR (Article 157). During the first decade of the HKSAR, its administration reached 134 visa agreements with foreign countries.[34] In 2007, Mr. Tung Chee-hwa publicly revealed that the Chinese Foreign Ministry allowed him to interact with foreign diplomats even without the presence of ministry officials. Overall, the HKSAR has been retaining a relatively high degree of autonomy in conducting its foreign relations with other states, with the full support of the central government in Beijing.

The Need to Harmonize Two Different Legal Systems and Cultures

Yet autonomy in Hong Kong's external affairs is contrary to the ways in which the NPC Standing Committee decided to interpret the Basic Law three times — in 1999, 2004, and 2005 — during the first decade of the HKSAR. These interpretations have displayed a pattern that arguably establishes a constitutional convention of the action of the SCNPC vis-à-vis the HKSAR. Two years before the first interpretation of the Basic Law by the SCNPC in 1999, constitutional expert Yash Ghai suggested that Article 158 should be "judicialized" in this way: "One might be that the Committee would not proceed to the interpretation of the Basic Law before the Hong Kong courts have given their decision giving the Committee the benefit of the courts' analysis . . . . Another might be that the Committee for the Basic Law should provide its reasons if it disagrees with a Hong Kong court's interpretation on a point on which it is consulted by the SCNPC . . . . [A] third convention might usefully be adopted — that the SCNPC as a rule would follow the recommendations of the Basic Law Committee."[35]

Although Ghai's proposals of setting up constitutional conventions were innovative and constructive, they would be difficult to be accepted by Beijing because of different legal cultures and values. From Beijing's perspective, allowing lawyers to be represented in each stage up to the SCNPC would perhaps be a transplant of the common law system into the mainland — an adversarial approach not favored by the mainland officials and legal experts who regard harmony as a virtue. Furthermore, members of the Basic Law Committee find it difficult to avoid giving their views on cases concerning Hong Kong, especially if the Hong Kong media aggressively look for their expert opinions. After all, the Basic Law Committee, from the mainland perspective, remains a consultative body.

However, two of the last three conventions suggested by Ghai appear to develop gradually. First, the SCNPC does refrain from usurping the power of adjudication of the Hong Kong courts, including the CFA. Instead, as mentioned before, it has been the HKSAR government rather than the local courts seeking the interpretation of the Basic Law by the SCNPC. Second, as a rule the SCNPC has been following the recommendations of the Basic Law Committee. There was no report or evidence to show that their views differed in the three interpretations in 1999, 2004, and 2005. However, the area that needs further development is the explanations of the interpretations by the SCNPC. The three interpretations published formally by the SCNPC were brief and lacked detailed explanations, thus making some Hong Kong people dissatisfied with the absence of legal justifications. To harmonize the two different legal systems and cultures, the SCNPC will have to provide its justifications in a more detailed way in the future.

Indeed, the harmonization of the two legal systems and cultures would be difficult if the people of Hong Kong remain defiant in their belief that the mainland Chinese concepts of power and autonomy are the same as their conventional understandings.[36] Mainland China's constitutional system developed from the Qing dynasty and the Nationalist era, when a mix of German, French, Japanese, and British laws was adopted.[37] The British legal influence waned as the Nationalist Party rose to power and looked to the Japanese law, which was shaped by Germany and could be seen as a branch of the Roman law.[38] After 1949, the CCP adopted the judicial principles of Marxism, Leninism, and Maoism, whose assumption was that laws "have deep-rooted class nature and cannot be passed from one political power to another."[39] The class-oriented and highly political nature of legal assumptions is arguably at odds with the common-law tradition in Hong Kong, where precedents and the supremacy of the local courts are perceived as of paramount importance. To many Hong Kong people, the power and autonomy enjoyed by the HKSAR must be maximal and at their utmost limits. Yet in the mainland Chinese political culture, autonomy arguably refers to a process in which a locality enjoys the freedom that is conferred upon by the central authorities, and the center often possesses the right to intervene in the locality. Above all, due to political necessity, the center does not hesitate to intervene in the affairs of the locality — the most important constitutional convention in Beijing–Hong Kong relations since July 1, 1997. However, this mainland constitutional convention has apparently been neglected by many pro-democracy Hongkongers. Intervention, as the late Deng Xiaoping argued, is not necessarily negative:

> Other people are afraid of intervention. Again, we should not fear all interventions; intervention in some cases may be necessary. The question is whether it is good or bad for the interests of the people of Hong Kong and for the prosperity and stability there.[40]

If political necessity provides the *raison d'être* for Beijing to interpret the Basic Law and to intervene in the HKSAR affairs, this constitutional convention is bound to clash with the Hong Kong politico-legal tradition in the years to come. Many Hong Kong people, especially the pro-democracy elites and the legal professionals, see any interpretation by the SCNPC on political grounds as legally unacceptable. After all, constitutional interpretations are a highly political and controversial process in which the SCNPC would be expected by the Hong Kong people to explain why it interprets the Basic Law, how it interprets the mini-constitution and when it exercises the interpretative power. In the short and medium terms, the conflicts between the two legal cultures will persist.[41]

Difficulties of Developing Constitutional Conventions

The British concept of constitutional conventions, when applied to the dynamic interactions between the HKSAR and the PRC, displays some difficulties. First and foremost, Barnett and Jennings have argued that conventions are obligatory, and that any violation would entail the charge of unconstitutional conduct. In the case of the HKSAR-Beijing relations, the political ingredient overshadows the legal and constitutional principles as well as reasons. The three SCNPC interpretations of the Basic Law appeared to lack clear constitutional principles or reasons at least in the sense of the British tradition. In fact, the interpretations were all pre-emptive and followed at least a report or request by the HKSAR government. This highly top-down nature of the SCNPC action means that Beijing's intervention in Hong Kong matters appeared to be arbitrary. Any SCNPC interpretation of the Basic Law, in the eyes of Beijing, is by no means an "unconstitutional conduct," a position contrary to the defenders of Hong Kong's judicial autonomy. In the very first place, the SCNPC interpretation lacked constitutional reasons or justifications, thus leading to the charge of "unconstitutional" conduct by Hong Kong's legal profession and critics. This deadlock reflected the clash of legal and constitutional values from both the HKSAR and the SCNPC. Harmonizing the two legal systems and cultures is a gigantic task, for the two sides do not really speak the same language or share the same assumptions in the first place.

Indeed, if the SCNPC elaborates on its constitutional reasons and principles whenever it interprets the Basic Law, such a move would ideally establish a constitutional convention in the British common-law sense. Otherwise, whenever the SCNPC takes any action to interpret the Basic Law, its action would be bound to be criticized as violating the Basic Law's spirit, which from the PRC perspective is actually empowering the SCNPC to do so. Due to different legal traditions, the conflicts between the members of the HKSAR legal community and the members of the SCNPC will persist.

The three cases of interpretations in 1999, 2005, and 2006 also illustrated difficulties of tracing a consistent pattern that can help us delineate any constitutional principles or reasons. All of them were pre-emptive moves made by Beijing to tackle any social and political crisis in the HKSAR. Moreover, it was the HKSAR government that made the request of such intervention. If Beijing and the HKSAR dominated the moves rather than giving the local courts the right and autonomy to refer the cases concerning HKSAR-Beijing relations to the SCNPC, their actions have already changed the Basic Law operation, which says in Article 158 that the local courts may refer the controversial cases to the NPC for interpretation. If constitutional conventions in the British sense have to be developed in the HKSAR-Beijing relations, both Beijing and the HKSAR government should delineate some basic principles governing the need for the SCNPC to interpret the Basic Law. Otherwise the whole process will remain highly politicized and titled in favor of the Beijing's interpretation with the uncritical support of the HKSAR government. Perhaps the highly political and unpredictable elements in the SCNPC interpretation of the Basic Law are making the transformation from "practices" to "durable conventions" in Beijing-HKSAR relations difficult, lengthy and conflict-ridden.

Summary

Some new constitutional practices have been emerging in Hong Kong's relations with Beijing since July 1, 1997. They include notably the action taken by the SCNPC to interpret provisions of the Basic Law, with or without the request of the HKSAR government, on the grounds of pre-emptive necessity, in 1999, 2004, and 2005. From the perspective of legal cultures, the HKSAR is very different from Beijing and their harmonization will be necessary so as to minimize the conflict-ridden process of legal and constitutional development. Yet such harmonization is easier said than done because of the vast differences on the two sides over the finality of the Court of Final Appeal. The democrats in the HKSAR see the CFA as a final adjudication body, and they view any intervention from the SCNPC as rendering the CFA a body of "semi-final court of appeal."[42]

By convention, Beijing has allowed the HKSAR to exercise a relatively high degree of autonomy in administering its economic affairs and external relations. This phenomenon is perhaps a mirror of the ongoing process of how the PRC is embracing global capitalism, making the mainland economic system more similar to the Hong Kong counterpart than ever before. At the same time, the rights and civil liberties of the people of Hong Kong have been maintained, perhaps with the notable exception of the surveillance on the HKSAR political activists by mainland security agents — a grey area in the Basic Law.

Another convention is that Beijing's representative, the Liaison Office, has established the firm practice of participating in local elections through various means, such as coordinating the candidates of the patriotic front, mobilizing pro-Beijing Hongkongers to support them in elections, and orchestrating the united front work on local groups, community leaders as well as politicians. On the surface, the role of political parties is not mentioned in the Basic Law. In practice, local political parties are tolerated to operate, and the underground Chinese Communist Party remains active.

Politically, the HKSAR autonomy is necessarily restricted. Mutual distrust between Beijing and the pro-democracy elites means that rapid democratization along the line of having the chief executive elected by universal suffrage and the direct elections of the entire Legislative Council is bound to be politically unacceptable to the central government. As a result, the objective of achieving "double direct elections" remains a distant one, waiting for the gradual democratic change or sudden political transformation in the mainland. The distrustful attitude of Beijing and the mainland legal authorities toward the pro-democracy elites in Hong Kong is understandable, given the long history of political separation, tense confrontation during the 1989 Tiananmen incident, and the mainland's concern about whether a fully Westernized Hong Kong would become a base for foreign nation-states to politically contain, undermine, and transform the PRC regime.

Many other practices, such as Beijing's preference to have a chief executive serving for two terms rather than one shorter term, remain to be developed into new constitutional conventions in the future. Similarly, the procedures in which the SCNPC interpreted the Basic Law remain to be codified into more enduring practices or constitutional conventions. The further development of constitutional conventions in Hong Kong's relations with Beijing will continue to unfold, shaping the perception of how the "one country, two systems" is implemented in the HKSAR and whether its model can, as the late Deng hoped, be used by the PRC to appeal to Taiwan for possible reunification in the long run.

The most useful part of the Hong Kong model that can be applied to solve Taiwan's political future is perhaps the external relations of the HKSAR.

Using the name "Hong Kong, China," the HKSAR can conduct international relations with the approval of the central government. Taiwan is already a *de facto*, albeit not *de jure*, nation-state. It does have some degree of international space and foreign diplomatic recognition, which will have to be at least retained by any Beijing-Taipei agreement on the political future of Taiwan.

6

Identity Change from the National Security Debate to Celebrations of the Tenth Anniversary

Bismark's famous remark that "politics is the art of the possible" can surely be applied to the HKSAR, where the public opposition to the National Security (Legislative Provisions) Bill in 2003 gradually transformed into celebration of the tenth anniversary of the HKSAR on July 1, 2007. Indeed, the nature of the two issues was different — one posing a threat to civil liberties and the other representing the motherland's glorious recovery of its sovereignty over Hong Kong. Nevertheless, amidst the changes was arguably a gradual transformation of political identity from being anti-national security legislation to strong pro-reunification sentiments. While the anti-national security thrust was spearheaded by civil society groups, the overwhelmingly pro-reunification atmosphere and the tenth anniversary celebration were led by an increasingly politically correct mass media. This chapter is going to analyze the subtle processes of identity transformation in the HKSAR. Although, as argued in earlier chapters, many Hongkongers who identity themselves as culturally Chinese do not necessarily equate their identification with the ruling party in the PRC, the societal sector most vulnerable to the mix between cultural and political identification is the mass media. The media self-censorship during the celebration of the tenth anniversary of the HKSAR demonstrated the resurgence and eventual victory of the national Chinese patriotism over the local Hong Kong identity.

Identity Politics, Policy Failure and Patron-Clientelist Exclusionism

In September 2002, the PRC officials suddenly raised the issue that the HKSAR government should enact Article 23 of the Basic Law.[1] Rumors were rife that when the former PRC president Jiang Zemin visited the

HKSAR in July 2002, he had to confront a group of Falun Gong protestors. Displeased by this, Jiang demanded that the Tung government speed up the process of legislating on Article 23. Once Jiang made such a decision, the mainland security apparatuses had a vested interest to envisage the Hong Kong government fulfilling the historical mission. This demand from the PRC did not grasp the realities of the Hong Kong politics, where pluralistic and oppositional forces mean that any legislation needs considerable politicking and difficult lobbying activities. The Tung administration appeared to reach a consensus with Beijing that Article 23 should be passed by LegCo and enacted by July 2003. As a result, a timetable was decided between the PRC and the HKSAR with the public being ignorant of the entire under-table dealings. Judging from the hurry in which the HKSAR government made a series of amendments to the draft Bill within June 2003 (see Table 6.1), a deadline of legislating on Article 23 did exist. But due to

Table 6.1 Timeline of the Development of the National Security Bill

Date	Developments
24/9/2002	The government released the "proposals to implement Article 23 of the Basic Law" consultative document.
26/9/2002	The Secretary for Security Regina Ip argued in LegCo that restaurant waiters, McDonald workers, and taxi drivers would not argue with her on every provision of the proposed legislation.
28/10/2002	Ip said in a forum at the City University of Hong Kong that most public views received by the government were in favor of the implementation of Article 23, but many of the 300 students who attended the forum found her remark unacceptable.
11/11/2002	Ip said in a forum at the Chinese University of Hong Kong that the audience should "lengthen their eyes" to see how the legislation on Article 23 would develop. She received a flag from the forum organizers saying that Ip was a very loyal official.
15/12/2002	60,000 people protested against the legislation.
22/12/2002	Pro-Beijing groups mobilized 40,000 people in support of the legislation.
24/12/2002	The end of the three-month public consultation period and the government received 97,097 local submissions.
28/1/2003	The government clarified the legislative proposals to implement Article 23 and released a compendium of submissions.
11/2/2003	ExCo endorsed the Bill to implement Article 23.
14/2/2003	The National Security (Legislative Provisions) Bill was gazetted.
26/2/2003	The Bill was introduced to LegCo for first and second readings.
6/3/2003	The First Bills Committee meeting was held.
3/6/2003	The government made draft amendments to the Bill.
7/6/2003	The government proposed the first draft Committee stage amendments to the Bill.

Table 6.1 (continued)

Date	Developments
16/6/2003	The government proposed the second draft Committee stage amendments to the Bill.
17/6/2003	Ip complained to the LegCo president for the remark made by legislator Mak Kwok-fung, who said she was a "cheater."
24/6/2003	Ip refused to answer James To's question in LegCo because she felt that he was "impolite."
25/6/2003	The government proposed the third draft Committee stage amendments to the Bill. The Secretary for Security Regina Ip tendered her resignation on personal grounds, but it was not revealed to the public until July 16, 2003.
27/6/2003	The House Committee of LegCo agreed to the resumption of the second reading debate.
28/6/2003	The government proposed the fourth draft of the proposed Committee stage amendments to the Bill. Ip said that the government had already made 51 amendments on the Bill and that those people who would participate in the July 1 protests would do so because of the holiday activities.
1/7/2003	Premier Wen Jiabao visited the HKSAR and said the legislation would not affect societal freedom. Then he went to Shenzhen. 500,000 people protested against the Tung regime.
2/7/2003	James Tien said that the business sector was very concerned about the protests and that the government had to appease public anger.
3/7/2003	Tien bypassed Tung to visit Liao Hui in Beijing.
4/7/2003	Tien remarked that Beijing had no timetable of legislating on Article 23 and that the government should postpone the legislation's discussion until December 2003. Tung for the first time responded to the protests on July 1 and said that the government had not yet made a decision.
5/7/2003	The government introduced three major amendments to the Bill: namely the defense on the grounds of public interest; the withdrawal of the proposal to give the police the power to make emergency investigative entry and arrest without any judicial warrant; and the removal of the mechanism whereby Hong Kong organizations subordinate to a mainland body could be banned on national security grounds. Tien did not say publicly that he would continue to support the government, although he lined up with other ExCo members behind Tung in public when the major amendments were announced by the chief executive.
6/7/2003	The Liberal Party announced that it hoped the government would postpone the legislation, which would be tabled to LegCo on July 9. Tien resigned from ExCo.
7/7/2003	Tung held a special ExCo meeting and then announced the decision to delay the second reading of the Bill.
9/7/2003	Pro-democracy citizens and groups held a vigil outside LegCo.
16/7/2003	Tung accepted Regina Ip's resignation.
17/7/2003	Tung announced to reopen consultation on the Article 23 legislation.
5/9/2003	Tung announced that the Bill be withdrawn.

Sources: http://www.article23.org.hk; *Apple Daily*, July 7 and 8, 2003; and *Sing Pao*, July 7 and 8, 2003.

the fierce public opposition in July 2003, the Tung administration eventually had to shelve the legislation indefinitely.

The HKSAR government mishandled the Article 23 legislation in several aspects. First, the fact that the Secretary for Justice Elsie Leung shied away from selling the proposed legislation in public, together with Chief Secretary Donald Tsang, pointed to an inevitable political disaster. Unlike a task force on political reform set up after the debacle on Article 23 and led by Tsang, Leung, and the Secretary for Constitutional Affairs Stephen Lam, the need for the Secretary for Security Regina Ip and her Permanent Secretary Timothy Tong Hin-ming to shoulder the responsibility of promoting Article 23 alone was a recipe for chaos. Ip had been a popular appointed official prior to her job of promoting Article 23 of the Basic Law. Nevertheless, her hard-line and determined attitude was incoherent with the need for a marketing-type official who should ideally have the political finesse to sell the National Security Bill to the public in a much softer manner. Perhaps Ip was a victim in the entire debate, although her obstinate attitude in public, especially her claim in October 2002 that Hitler's Germany proved that universal suffrage could produce dictators, added much fuel to the fire.[2] During the tenth anniversary of the HKSAR, Regina Ip publicly told the mass media that she was left alone to promote Article 23 of the Basic Law, and that even Elsie Leung later let her explain the legislation to the public without active involvement. It seemed that the majority of principal officials under the Tung administration did not really want to shoulder the burden of justifying the national security legislation to the public. The fact that Ip was a lonely political saleswoman illustrated Beijing's top-down pressure on the HKSAR government. Yet top-down policy implementation without realizing the pluralistic setting of Hong Kong's political arena sowed the seeds of public outcry — a problem that had to be shouldered by Beijing's policy-makers and think-tanks on the HKSAR. They simply did not fully understand the complex political configurations in Hong Kong.

Second, as Ip and Tong explained the content of the legislation to the public, none of the principal officials offered a helping hand, except for the pro-Beijing but politically haughty DAB. The pro-Beijing party was actually the most politically loyal force supportive of Article 23 from the beginning of the legislation to the political earthquake on July 1, 2003, when half a million Hong Kong people protested against the Tung regime. However, the DAB is often a blind political loyalist without the rational and open-minded acumen to accept different views. Jasper Tsang, for example, arrogantly referred to the half a million protestors as being "misled" by some democrats. Such irresponsible and arrogant remark led to his public apology on July 5, 2003.³ In short, leaving the task of promoting the National Security Bill to Beijing's trusted but arrogant client, DAB, was definitely a strategic error.

After all, Ip herself was an unskillful bureaucrat who knew how to implement government policies effectively but who was defiant of public opinion. Being a British-trained colonial official without any conception of the need to respond to public opinion, Ip herself committed grave errors in the process of explaining the Article 23 legislation to the public. Her hardline attitude toward a few legislators days before the July 1 protests (see Table 6.1) and her uncompromising as well as elitist approach to the national security bill was inimical to the public acceptance of Article 23 of the Basic Law. From the perspective of Hong Kong identity, Ip appeared to struggle between being a Hongkonger and a loyal civil servant implementing the policy decision from Beijing. The fact that she tendered her resignation on June 25 but it was not unveiled until July 16 proved her dilemma. Personal reasons such as the need to visit her daughter and her determination to study at Stanford University appeared to be strong justifications for abandoning the most difficult task of selling the National Security Bill to the people of Hong Kong before the deadline on July 9, 2003.

Furthermore, Chief Executive Tung himself failed to balance the competing interests between the DAB led by Jasper Tsang and the pro-business Liberal Party (LP) led by James Tien. Tung's lack of personal charisma had already been severely criticized by the public. His sluggish response to the July 1 protests until July 4, when he commented that the government had not yet made up its mind, was by no means conducive to the attempts at defusing the political time-bomb. Tung himself was also a weak leader under the spell of both Jasper Tsang and Cheng Yiu-tong, the two pro-Beijing hardliners in ExCo. On July 2, Tsang insisted that the Bill could be amended but that it would still be tabled to LegCo on July 9.⁴ Such a grave error demonstrated his overconfidence and defiance. Similarly, after James Tien of the Liberal Party bypassed Tung and visited the HKMAO Director Liao Hui in Beijing, Cheng Yiu-tong of the Federation of Trade Unions (FTU) said the remark of Tien, who said Beijing had no timetable to legislate on Article 23, was merely "a personal opinion."⁵ During the apex of citizen protests against Article 23 and the mobilization of the Civil Human Rights Front to appeal to supporters to surround LegCo on the night of July 9, it was rumored that Cheng might toy with the idea of summoning the help of the People's Liberation Army. In the minds of Tien, both the DAB and FTU were blind political followers of Tung and

Beijing, which actually underestimated the strong reactions of the people of Hong Kong to Article 23.

The change of political stance of James Tien reflected his dilemma of how to strike a balance between his Hong Kong identity and the mainland Chinese identity. He originally fully supported the implementation Article 23 of the Basic Law. Tien also seldom attended LegCo's sub-committee on Article 23, leaving the task of scrutinizing the Bill to other party members, notably Miriam Lau Kin-yee and Selina Chow.[6] On the eve of July 1, 2003, Tien even appealed to the people of Hong Kong not to protest on the streets.[7] However, after the massive protests on July 1, Chief Executive Tung held emergency meetings of ExCo in which he failed to balance the interests of the DAB and the LP. While the DAB was keen to see the bill concerning Article 23 rammed through LegCo on July 9, the LP had grave reservations.

As a businessman, Tien himself was shaken by the protests. He was afraid of the likelihood of a violent and bloody confrontation between protestors and police outside LegCo on July 9.[8] Influenced by the party elder Allen Lee and other LP heavyweights like Chow and Lau, Tien decided to become a rebel in ExCo and disobey Tung's decision of making minor concessions on the content of the bill. Tung and his advisers did not understand the complex character of Tien. In the mind of Tien, the national security bill should be shelved so as to defuse a political crisis in the HKSAR. Therefore, on July 6, when ExCo presided over by Tung decided that the national security bill would be slightly amended but would still be tabled to LegCo for consideration and approval on July 9, Tien himself felt that the LP position was still ignored. Although he came out with Tung and other ExCo members to meet the press with regard to the "united" stance on the three amendments to the Bill, he actually did not support the government's move.

Seeing the DAB as the lackey of Beijing and puppet of Tung, Tien was determined to demonstrate that the LP could play the role of kingmaker in Hong Kong politics. On July 6, soon after Tung made the decision that the amended bill would still be discussed in LegCo, Tien publicly announced that he resigned from ExCo. His action was supported by political mentor Allen Lee and LP core members Miriam Lau and Selina Chow. Tien's resignation plunged the Tung regime into a deeper crisis of governance. C. H. Tung was suddenly isolated, lacking sufficient LegCo votes to have the national security bill passed in the legislature. Nor did Tung's advisors dare mobilize any LP member to ignore the party line and vote for the government. Calculating the inevitable defeat in LegCo where 31 members would vote against the Bill, including eight LP members, the Tung regime held a special ExCo meeting on July 7 and decided to delay the enactment of the national security bill at once.

Two interpretations regarding Tien's move persist. The first was that when he visited Liao in Beijing on July 3, he got the message from the HKMAO director that Beijing hoped that the legislation would be passed as soon as possible, but that "the concrete details of when it would be legislated belong to the autonomy realm of the HKSAR, and Beijing has no specific timetable."[9] The crux of the issue was that Tien chose to stress Liao's remark on the absence of timetable, not on Beijing's desire to see an earlier enactment of Article 23 of the Basic Law. Hence, by selectively interpreting from what Liao said, Tien ran the risk of offending the Beijing authorities. The second interpretation was that Tien knew that the Liaison Office had failed to report the situation of public anger against the Tung regime to the central government in Beijing, and that his decision to go against both Tung and Beijing demonstrated that the LP was a political force to be reckoned with. After all, Tien actually helped Tung and Beijing defuse a political crisis in the HKSAR, a crisis that was unintentionally exacerbated by the die-hard loyalists such as Jasper Tsang and Cheng Yiu-tong. These two interpretations are by no means mutually exclusive. A former aide to Tien said that he was very "nervous" shortly after his decision to quit ExCo.[10] With the benefit of hindsight, Tien might have selectively quoted from Liao's unclear and cryptic remarks. Yet Tien also later felt that his "rebellious" action actually saved the Tung government from having to encounter a possible violent bloodshed between the protestors and the police on the night of July 9. The mass media in the HKSAR, particularly the *Apple Daily*, hailed Tien as the political hero who could defuse a political time-bomb and avoid further escalation of the citizens' determined confrontation with the pro-government LegCo members on July 9.[11] Democrats such as Chan Wai-yip, Martin Lee, and Emily Lau also praised the action of Tien to withdraw from ExCo.[12] Tien's political move perhaps had the unintended consequence of portraying himself as the champion of Hong Kong interests — a situation compatible with the unprecedented show of strong Hong Kong identity among all those who opposed the National Security Bill.

Shortly after half a million people protested on July 1, Liao tried to tender his resignation — an action implying that he himself understood his own responsibilities of either failing to tap the real public opinion in the HKSAR or miscommunicating with Tien. Whatever the error made by Liao, the HKMAO, Liaison Office, and the United Front Department all failed to handle the national security legislation in the HKSAR skillfully. The HKMAO director gave partial or unclear messages to Tien. The Liaison Office kept on reporting overly good news to Beijing rather than accurately understanding the depth and breadth of public discontent in Hong Kong. When Tien returned to Hong Kong from Beijing, it was reported that the Liaison Office sent officials to meet him and said that the central government hoped for the smooth passage of the Bill on July 9.[13] Clearly, the Liaison Office was totally out of touch with the political reality of Hong Kong, blindly following whatever misguided decision from the political center. The United Front Department also failed to win the hearts and minds of all Hongkongers, letting the clients of Beijing such as the DAB and other die-hard elites spread the messages of Beijing arbitrarily and yet seemingly authoritatively. The entire pro-Beijing circle surrounding C. H. Tung perpetuated the policy of excluding all the critics of the HKSAR regime from participation in consultative and policy-making bodies, and listening to the one-sided opinions of their own friends and supporters in Hong Kong. Tung prior to the political earthquake on July 1, 2003 had been surrounded by all his Hong Kong clients, thus failing to understand the genuine public opinions in the capitalist enclave. Beijing accepted all the wrong advices from its trusted clients in the HKSAR. The entire patron-client network linking Beijing with the HKSAR, and connecting Tung with his cronies was so secluded that the Tung-Beijing nexus created a huge gap with the people of Hong Kong. Patron-client exclusionism in the case of Article 23 legislation failed abysmally, generating total policy failure and tremendous public outcry.[14] Identity politics, policy failure, and patron-client exclusionism were intertwined here. Policy failure was a reflection of both identity concerns about the erosion of Hong Kong values and the failure of patron-clientelist politics where the feedback loop from the public did not work until the time-bomb exploded in the form of massive protests on July 1, 2003.

The Tung administration totally failed because arguably it could still attempt at trying to win the support of other independents and also a few pro-government LP members, such as Lau Wong-fat and Howard Young. That the government failed to secure enough votes in LegCo despite the LP's "sell-out" was a reflection of the weakness of the Tung regime, whose ability to secure votes in the legislature was no match for the last Governor Chris Patten. While Patten demanded that senior civil servants should lobby for the vote of each legislator to support his political reform blueprint in 1993, the Tung administration was weak in mobilizing senior bureaucrats to garner sufficient support of legislators. Tien's apparent heroism was an outcome of his ability to exploit the weak post-colonial Hong Kong leadership.

Nor did the Tung regime make a genuine effort to explain to the public confidently and forcefully the significance of the three amendments made on the National Security Bill. The public simply did not understand the technicalities and the importance of the three policy concessions. Furthermore, in terms of policy content and failure, the detailed amendments with regard to public interest defense, police power, and the proscription of organizations on July 5 were arguably too late. In the first place, many educated members of the public had already been frightened by the proposed police power to enter premises and arrest suspects without warrants. The public interest defense also failed to pacify the fear of many members of the public, including librarians who expressed their deep concerns in LegCo that books deemed to be "subversive" would perhaps be under the threat of being confiscated and censored.[15] The withdrawal of the provision on the proscription of organizations with linkages to mainland bodies was already scary to many existing Hong Kong groups, including the Catholics and Christian activists who had close interactions with their mainland counterparts, the Hong Kong members of the Falun Gong, and all other non-governmental groups that maintain connections with both mainland dissidents and activists as well as foreign human rights and labor organizations. The entire discussion on the policy content of the National Security Bill was simply too disturbing to many members of the public, which had already suffered psychologically and emotionally from the SARS crisis. In short, the content of some of the controversial provisions of the National Security Bill ran counter to the much-cherished values of the rule of law and the protection of civil liberties in the HKSAR. The policy proposals appeared to mainlandize the HKSAR to such an extent that the identity of Hong Kong would be eroded, if not totally annihilated.

Due to the public outbursts on Article 23 and the misrule of the Tung regime, two of its principal officials decided to resign in order to rescue the fragile legitimacy of the government. Regina Ip decided to quit the government on personal grounds. Once she decided to step down, the pro-Beijing media and the mainland officials heaped praise on her — a sign that the central government viewed her as being a loyal servant of Beijing's original policy intent, namely having the National Security Bill passed in early July 2003. On the other hand, Financial Secretary Antony Leung, who was embarrassed by his car scandal, opted for departure from the government. Although both Ip and Leung left the administration, their move could not fundamentally solve the crisis because it was the entire Tung administration that had been severely discredited for its controversial policies since the handover, such as civil service reform, the mother-tongue language education, the cyberport development in favor of some rich business tycoons, and the government's poor handling of such crises as bird flu and the SARS.[16]

From the perspective of identity, both Regina Ip and James Tien encountered a difficult choice. Ip privately sensed that she was a Hong Kong belonger, but the bureaucratic demand for her to adhere to the policy line of Beijing meant that she was bound to be unpopular and that she was forced to take on a politically impossible task. Her tendered resignation as early as June 25 implied that she was keen to leave the political scene, thus regaining her Hong Kong identity rather than being torn between the local identity that she held and the mainland Chinese identity that Article 23 demanded. The fact that she studied in the United States and then returned to Hong Kong as a more pro-democracy activist was a reflection of her innate desire for a more open, transparent, and accountable HKSAR. Yet her role as a loyal bureaucrat in 2002 and 2003 was destined to render the promotion of Article 23 problematic. Similar to Ip, Tien had a strong Hong Kong identity, but he was politically torn between the need to uphold mainland Chinese identity and support the bill on the one hand, and the tendency to stick to his Hong Kong identity that demanded him to reject the legislation. Torn between the two choices, Tien eventually opted for the defense of his Hong Kong identity. While Tung, Beijing's puppets such as the DAB and the FTU, and the mainland Chinese officials obviously opted for the interests of "one country," this mainland Chinese identity was at loggerheads with the strong Hong Kong identity, which was eventually shown in the resignation of both Ip and Tien.

Identity Politics in the Public Opposition to Article 23

The entire debate over the content of the national security bill was an indication of a serious clash between the Hong Kong identity and the mainland Chinese identity. The concern about civil liberties and the rule of law brought about an unprecedented cohesion of social groups to oppose the National Security Bill. In Table 6.2, the groups in opposition to the Article 23 legislation displayed several characteristics. First and foremost, they were ideologically liberal. While the Civil Human Rights Front was an umbrella flagship composed of many groups that opposed the National Security Bill, all of them had one thing in common: a very strong Hong Kong identity that cherished the rule of law, civil liberties, human rights,

Table 6.2 Some of the Local Groups Opposing Article 23 of the Basic Law

Group	Platform
Civil Human Rights Front	Formed in 2004 to oppose the SCNPC interpretation of the Basic Law and it mobilized many other like-minded groups to oppose Article 23 of the Basic Law.
7.1 United Front	A group of youth formed shortly after the mass protests on July 1, 2003, and it promotes the development of democracy in the HKSAR.
People's Demo	Established by a group of artists, media professionals, teachers, and lawyers to call for direct democracy, to oppose capitalist privatization, to express concerns about the listing of Link Reit, to supervise the operation of public estates' shopping malls, to fight for workers' rights, to oppose unfair trade practices and monopolies, and to advocate the development of community culture and public spaces.
Human Rights in China (Hong Kong Branch)	Founded by Chinese students and scholars in March 1989, the group is an international and Chinese non-governmental organization to promote human rights in mainland China. Its staff members include Chinese, North Americans, and Europeans who are determined to foster greater political space for democratic reform and social justice in both mainland China and Hong Kong.
China Labor Bulletin	Led by Director Han Dongfang, the group is concerned about the rights of workers in mainland China. It also conducts research on child labor, workers' rights, the status of women workers and labor. The group has a case intervention program and helps victims in mainland China hire lawyers to fight for their working-class interests.
Chinese Christian Church (Shum Oi Tong)	Active as early as 1982 over the Sino-British agreement on Hong Kong's future and the local administrative reform. The group also expresses concern about China's social and religious development, and Hong Kong's democratic progress, including the legislation on Article 23.
The Civic Party	Founded in March 2006 to promote democratic changes, to protect the rule of law, to improve the quality of life, to defend constitutionalism, and to participate in elections.
Article 23 Concern Group	Formed by a group of legislators and lawyers to express concerns about the content of the legislation on Article 23, and to publish a series of pamphlets on treason, subversion, secession, the prohibition of organizations, sedition, comparisons with foreign laws and state secrets.
Power for Democracy	Founded by legislators and intellectuals with the aims of promoting democracy, the rule of law and civil society.

Table 6.2 *(continued)*

Group	Platform
April Fifth Action	Struggling for universal suffrage in Hong Kong, opposing unemployment and poverty, eliminating pro-government parties, terminating one-party dictatorship in China, setting up unemployment benefits and minimum wage, and striving for the right to hold plebiscites in Hong Kong.
Democratic Power for Rescuing Hong Kong	Formed by a group of mainland political dissidents in Hong Kong, together with some Hong Kong political activists such as Tsang Kin-shing.
Asia Monitor Resources	An independent non-governmental organization focusing on Asian labor concerns, workers' rights, labor movement, specifically on the freedom of association, the right to collective bargaining, the elimination of forced and child labor, and the abolition of discrimination at work.
Civil Rights for Sexual Diversities	An independent non-governmental organization working for the rights of those people who are disadvantaged by laws, policies, and social prejudices because of sexual orientations, gender identity, and sexual expression.
League of Social Democrats	Founded by a few existing and former legislators, such as Leung Kwok-hung, Mak Kwok-fung, and Lo Wing-lok, and social activists such as Raymond Wong. It vows to fight against social inequality and government-business collusion, and advocates wealth redistribution in Hong Kong.
People's Radio Hong Kong	Formed in May 2004 to express its deep concern about the freedom of speech after the reports on mysterious intimidation of a few radio hosts, and it terminated operation in May 2007.
Women Coalition	Established on July 1, 2003 to defend the human rights of sexual minorities facing discrimination due to their sexual orientations and gender identity.
Human Rights Commission	An independent non-governmental organization that protects human rights, monitors public education, advocates legal reforms, and improves complaints channels.
Justice and Peace Commission of the Hong Kong Catholic Diocese	Returned power to the people, opposed Article 23 of the Basic Law, and it expresses concern about religious freedom in China.
Democratic Development Network	Formed by professors, medical doctors, lawyers, social workers and religious activists in July 2002 to promote contact networks among those who push for democracy in Hong Kong, to conduct study on democratization, and to urge for the government to review the progress of political reforms.

Table 6.2 *(continued)*

Group	Platform
Catholic Commission For Labor Affairs	Expresses concerns about occupational safety, social protection, unemployment, job creation, human rights, social inequality, political democratization, and the role of multi-national corporations in the process of globalization.
Social Workers' General Union	Formed in 1980 after a group of social workers fought for the interests of fishermen who were relocated. It vows to protect human rights, improve social services, unify social workers, and support social justice.
Christian Institute	A religious action and concern group that often expresses its view in support of social justice, political democratization, minimum wage for workers, poverty alleviation programs, and anti-globalization movement.
Christian Industrial Committee	Support of industrial and occupational safety in both Hong Kong and China, and opposed the legislation on Article 23 of the Basic Law.
Federation of Students	Formed in 1958 to promote student participation in social and political affairs, and to support democratic development.
Professional Teachers' Union	Fights for the interests of teachers, such as status and welfare, salaries and benefits, and promotes education as well as unionism.
Unison	Set up in March 2001 to promote policies and services in favor of the interests of ethnic minorities in Hong Kong.
Confederation of Trade Unions	Fights for the interests of workers, allies democratic and independent unions, and advocates the implementation of minimum wage for workers.
Christian for Hong Kong Society	Formed in 1987 to advocate direct elections and express concern about social justice, to educate the public, and to study Hong Kong's economy, politics, and human rights.
Rainbow Action	Set up in December 2000 to express its concern about human rights and to promote civic awareness of the rule of law.
Shumshuipo Community Association	Serves the interests of the community in Shumshuipo, including the interests of the youth, women, and elderly, as well as social welfare and family harmony.
Zi Teng	Formed by social workers, researchers, and labor activists who are concerned about the rights of women, including sex workers.
Neighborhood and Worker's Service Center	Set up in 1975 to help the unemployed and semi-employed people, including their job training. It is based in Kwai Chung district.

164 *The Dynamics of Beijing–Hong Kong Relations*

Table 6.2 *(continued)*

Group	Platform
Association for the Advancement of Feminism	Promotes women's welfare, eliminates discrimination against women, and advances feminism in Hong Kong.
San Po Kong Workers' Group	Promotes workers' interests and encourages members' participation in social affairs.
Hong Kong Journalists Association	Set up in 1968 to promote the work environment of media professionals, remove barriers to news gathering, and to protect press freedom in Hong Kong.
Women Christian Council	Established in 1988 to fight for the interests of women, promote social justice and feminist theology, and to renew the Church as well as improve Hong Kong's socio-political development.

Sources: See http://www.civilhrfront.org which contains all the links to the websites of these social groups.

and democratic development. Second, they cut across different social strata and occupations, including middle and working classes. Occupationally, the group members embraced intellectuals, professionals, students, workers, and religious activists. The 7.1 United Front was representative of young people who rose up voluntarily against Article 23 of the Basic Law. Third, the debate over the National Security Bill became a rallying point for many other social groups, either active or relatively dormant, that had the political will to oppose the legislation. Those active groups included the Civic Party, Article 23 Concern Group, Power for Democracy, League of Social Democrats, the Democracy Development Network, Social Workers' General Union, Professional Teacher's Union, the Confederation of Trade Unions, and the Hong Kong Journalists Association. Those which had become relatively dormant or neglected by the media but suddenly emerged as active embraced the April Fifth Action, Asia Monitor Resources, and Christian Industrial Committee. Fourth, many new groups emerged, such as People's Demo, Democratic Power for Rescuing Hong Kong, Power for Democracy, and the Democracy Development Network. Although their membership was small, their networks and linkages did provide the glue for other groups to be mobilized. Fifth, many religious groups were stimulated in the societal opposition to Article 23, including the Justice and Peace Commission, Catholic Commission for Labor Affairs, Christian Institute, Chinese Christian Church, and the Women Christian Council. Sixth, a few political groups promoting democracy in the PRC became active, such as Human Rights in China and the China Labor Bulletin. Seventh, a number of district-based groups also joined the Civil Human Rights Front, including the Shumshuipo Community Association and the Neighborhood Worker's Service Centre. Finally, some interest groups protecting the concerns of minorities were also involved, such as Zi Teng, Unison, and the Rainbow Action. Combined with student groups, women concern associations, all these groups formed a political alliance that could mobilize lots of protestors through their networks.

Apart from these groups, the mass media and individual citizens underwent an unprecedented process of political mobilization. While the *Apple Daily* appealed to the ordinary citizens to take to the streets, preparing pages that could be converted into protest banners easily, popular radio hosts such as Raymond Wong and Albert Cheng did the same. Individual citizens used emails, mobile phones, and text messages to remind their friends and relatives to join the protests. Many other middle-class citizens affected by negative equity also took to the streets. Social workers and civil servants whose salaries and benefits were curtailed by the Tung regime grasped the golden opportunities to protest against the government. Citizens dissatisfied with governmental performance over the SARS management and many other policy issues also felt that, as Hongkongers, they had to express their anger by joining the demonstrations. Religious believers were stimulated by the high-profile opposition of Bishop Zen to the Article 23 legislation. The anti-Tung protests on July 1, 2003 were the combined outcome of socio-media-religious mobilization, public fears, citizenry frustrations, governmental failure to promote the national security legislation, the chief executive's unpopularity, patron-clientelist failure, the pro-Beijing elite's arrogance, and the central government's miscalculations. The entire angry society of the HKSAR rose up to defend their cherished civil liberties — a testimony of the solidification of Hong Kong identity *vis-à-vis* the perceived threat of the imposition of mainland Chinese political identity. Arguably, although the local Hong Kong identity can coexist with the national Chinese identity, both of them could not comfortably do so in the entire controversy over the National Security Bill because it aroused the Hong Kong people's fear of losing their civil liberties.

The PRC Response: From Fragmentation to Assertiveness

The legitimacy failure of the Tung regime became a rude awakening to the new Beijing leadership led by President Hu Jintao and Premier Wen Jiabao, who were surely shocked by the political earthquake in the HKSAR. When

Premier Wen visited Hong Kong in late June 2003, he appealed to the Tung administration to listen to the views of the Hong Kong people and to improve his governance — a sign that the new Chinese leader adopted a more open-minded attitude toward public criticisms of Tung. At least, Wen did not fully support Tung to the extent of the former president Jiang, who had handpicked Tung to be the first HKSAR chief executive and who supported him for another term in 2002. Premier Wen returned to Shenzhen on June 30; nevertheless, he was annoyed by the extent of protests as he watched the mainland television news about Hong Kong. In particular, he was surprised by the number of protestors, for the Liaison Office, the HKMAO, and the HKSAR government's Central Policy Unit totally underestimated this number. During the tenth anniversary of the HKSAR, the head of the Central Policy Unit, Lau Siu-kai, publicly admitted that he had underestimated the number of protestors prior to July 1, 2003. The crux of the problem was that the new Beijing leadership realized the severity of public frustrations in the HKSAR, whose demonstration effect could be undermined by the inept Tung regime.

The massive protests in the HKSAR forced the entire mainland policymaking apparatus dealing with Hong Kong affairs to reassess its previous attitudes and approaches. For one thing, the Liaison Office was under fire in both Hong Kong and Beijing for misunderstanding the HKSAR circumstances and reporting all the good news on Hong Kong to Beijing. In April 2002, one LegCo member who was also a Hong Kong deputy to the National People's Congress had already written to Beijing to complain about the HKSAR problems, which were not accurately reported by the Liaison Office.[17] In reality, although the head of the Liaison Office Gao Siren was new to HKSAR affairs, his subordinates were too close to the HKSAR government's ruling elites, Beijing's loyal clients such as the DAB, and even the Central Policy Unit that failed to gauge the political temperature of Hong Kong prior to July 1, 2003. The Liaison Office was so preoccupied with justifying all its positive views on Hong Kong that it became blind to the objective reality, namely that the Tung administration was deeply unpopular and the public grievances became a time-bomb that could explode. Although the central government reshuffled the leadership of the Liaison Office by replacing a number of deputy directors, it remains to be seen whether it will avoid repeating the mistake of being politically correct to Beijing without any independent ability to analyze any weaknesses of the HKSAR leadership. The Liaison Office's failure during the July 1 protests perhaps also reflected the problem of its officials who developed a rigid view and vested interest in developing socio-political bonds with their cronies and clients, especially as they were not rotated frequently and their performance appraisal from Beijing, and the "newcomer" Gao Siren, appeared to lack vigor.

Another PRC agency under severe criticisms was the State Council's HKMAO led by Liao Hui. Liao's low-profile attitude toward Hong Kong policies was a far cry from his predecessor Lu Ping and it dealt a severe blow to the HKMAO image during the critical juncture in early July 2003, for it did not seek to clarify Liao's remarks during the meeting with James Tien. As a result, some Hong Kong people interpreted Liao's silence as a gesture endorsing what Tien said, while the Liaison Office led by Gao Siren was keen to see the national security bill passed by the legislature. Liao's low-key attitude was certainly a blemish in the PRC policy toward the HKSAR.

Most importantly, once the Hong Kong situation was out of Beijing's control, the central government set up a committee led by Zeng Qinghong, a protégé of the former president Jiang Zemin, who was responsible for hammering out Beijing's policy toward Hong Kong. Members of this committee included representatives from the Liaison Office (Gao Siren), the People's Liberation Army, the HKMAO, the Ministry of National Security, and the external and foreign trade departments. Judging from the internal composition of the committee, Beijing was keen to apply politico-economic measures, such as the CEPA and the relaxation of mainland Chinese visits to Hong Kong, to rescue the deeply unpopular Tung administration. When the HKSAR government made its decisions to amend the bill and later to postpone tabling the National Security Bill to LegCo, they were all communicated to the central government for approval. Beijing's policies toward the HKSAR were centralized by Zeng's committee that produced a more unified stance and more effective response to the Hong Kong political crisis. The degree of concerns shown from Beijing proved that the Hong Kong model of "one country, two systems" was in crisis; if the Tung regime was de-legitimized, the formula would have grave danger of being promoted to Taiwan in the long run.

Yet due to the fact that Zeng remained a protégé of Jiang in 2002, the former could not implement a drastically new approach to remove Tung from office, particularly as President Hu and Premier Wen were new to their positions. On July 4, 2003, Premier Wen publicly said that he hoped the HKSAR government would create an environment "favorable to foreign investment" — an indication that he could do little except hope that the Tung regime would respond promptly to the demands and wishes of the Hong Kong public.[18] In the short run, the coordination committee led by

Zeng was destined to have a greater say on Beijing's policy toward Hong Kong. Given that the conservatives from the Liaison Office and HKMAO, like Gao and Liao, were appointed to Zeng's committee on the HKSAR, the overall CCP policy toward the HKSAR was bound to be remedial and piecemeal. Yet, as Gao and especially Liao had to shoulder at least some responsibilities for their failure to tap the public opinion in the HKSAR, and as the new Hu-Wen leadership was embarrassed by the Tung regime's legitimacy crisis, the Zeng committee did not really exclude the possibility of removing C. H. Tung from office in the medium term. Hence, the politically ripe time for Tung to step down gloriously and with face would be March 2005, when the National People's Congress and the Chinese People's Political Consultative Conference (CPPCC) traditionally hold their meetings to hammer out crucial policies of the central government. By appointing Tung to the vice-directorship of the CPPCC, he would be able to retire from the HKSAR political arena with face and dignity — a mainland Chinese approach to politics. With the benefit of hindsight, Beijing skillfully orchestrated the "glorious" exit of Tung, buying time firstly to delay the speed and pace of democratization in Hong Kong throughout 2004 and secondly to allow Hong Kong's economy rebound to a level politically suitable for Tung's announcement that he would resign for personal reasons in March 2005.

This in-built conservatism turned Beijing's policy toward Hong Kong from political fragmentation between July and November 2003 to assertiveness from December 2003 onwards. The fragmentation of Beijing's policy toward Hong Kong was punctuated by numerous agencies whose voices on Hong Kong were different, and whose activities of collecting intelligence on the HKSAR were so diverse that they entailed the dangers of heterogeneity and hidden rivalries as well as comparisons. Perhaps understanding the inherently structural weaknesses of PRC agencies responsible for Hong Kong matters, Zeng's committee took a swift step to listen to the views of the Hong Kong elites while at the same time despatching researchers from Beijing to tap the public opinions of the HKSAR. A political feedback loop was resurrected at once. From July to November 2003, various delegations from the mainland were sent to the HKSAR at both the central and various provincial levels, discussing with the Hong Kong democrats, business elites, and Beijing's clients on the ways forward. The overall atmosphere was that Beijing appeared to be more liberal or open-minded in terms of listening to the views of the Hong Kong people.

However, as it turned out, Beijing's policy appeared to be more conservative and more hard-line than conventional wisdom would assume immediately after July 1, 2003. Beijing began to assert its influence on Hong Kong affairs when C. H. Tung went to Beijing to discuss the issue of political reform with the president. President Hu, obviously after being briefed by the Zeng committee on Hong Kong affairs, took a more hard-line position, saying that any move toward political reform would have to conform to the Basic Law, and that the central government was very concerned about it. In the minds of Hu and Zeng, Tung's weak leadership could open the door to sudden democratization, which would entail the dual risks of allowing the Hong Kong democrats to overturn the executive-led polity and transmitting wrong messages to Taiwan, where the pro-Taiwan independence DPP President Chen Shui-bian would compete for the second term in the March 2004 presidential election. It seemed that Beijing's leadership had Taiwan in mind when considering Hong Kong's public pressure for the direct elections of the chief executive and the entire LegCo. The new Hu-Wen-Zeng leadership obviously wanted to maintain the political *status quo* in the HKSAR, to pave the way for a silent change of Tung's leadership in March 2004, and to avoid a scenario in the HKSAR which would help the anti-CCP democrats grasp political power. In short, political stability was the principle of Beijing in dealing with the complicated Hong Kong circumstances. Listening to President Hu's view on Hong Kong's political reform, Tung as Beijing's client undoubtedly protected the interest of the "one country" over that of the "two systems." After consulting with his advisers, Tung decided to set up the task force led by Donald Tsang, Elsie Leung, and Stephen Lam to cope with the public demand for democratic reforms. Critics said that Stephen Lam as the Secretary for Constitutional Affairs was ill-prepared for Tung's visit to Beijing in December 2003, for the former had at least six months to draw out a blueprint on the principles of political reform in Hong Kong after July 1, 2003. Lam was perhaps a political newcomer unfamiliar with the intricacies of Hong Kong–Beijing relations. The mass media in the HKSAR were dissatisfied with the evasive manner in which he constantly tackled media questions. Yet Lam's cautious attitude toward media questions was exactly the type of ministerial quality that could help Tung, and later Chief Executive Donald Tsang, to adopt a go-slow approach in Hong Kong's democratization.

Beijing's New United Front Tactics in the HKSAR

Beijing's united front tactics were quickly re-adjusted after the political debacle on July 1, 2003. A well-orchestrated propaganda on Hong Kong was adopted, coinciding with the Taiwan presidential elections in March 2004. The strategies of Beijing's policy toward Hong Kong were (1) to use semi-government officials as a mouthpiece to voice Beijing's perspectives, (2) to mobilize the official Chinese mass media to emphasize the need for Hong Kong people to attach importance to patriotism, (3) to listen to the opinions of the Hong Kong people from various social strata, and (4) to isolate a few pro-democracy elites in the HKSAR for criticisms so that the local voters would hopefully refrain from supporting the democrats in the September 2004 Legislative Council elections. As the late Chairman Mao Zedong, a key architect of the CCP united front tactic, said, "We must not close our doors for fear of enemy agents, our set policy being boldly to expand our Party . . . We shall make mistakes if we only pay attention to the one side and forget the other. The only correct policy is: 'Expand the Party boldly but do not let a single undesirable in.'"[19] While patron-clientelist exclusionism committed the exact mistake mentioned by Mao, the post-July 2003 PRC policy was forced to change to the dual principles of expanding the CCP tentacles while preventing the Hong Kong democrats from grasping political power in the HKSAR.

The arrival of Beijing's legal expert, the late Xiao Weiyun, at the HKSAR in January 2004 marked the beginning of the PRC crusade against the Hong Kong democrats, who organized the mainland democrats to escape from China after the Tiananmen incident in 1989 and who played a crucial role in mobilizing the public to protest on July 1, 2003. Xiao's arguments were blunt, hard-line, and direct: the people of Hong Kong did not understand the Basic Law and their behavior after the handover remained problematic, including the action of some legislators to initiate a vote of no-confidence on the principal officials.[20] Xiao also reminded the Hong Kong people of the need to understand that "one country" is often far more important than the "two systems," that the Basic Law drafters had not really thought about direct elections of the chief executive in 2007 and of the entire legislature in 2008, that political reform in the HKSAR did not necessitate the revisions to the entire Basic Law, except for its appendices. Xiao's comments were a political bombshell to the democrats who believed that democratization in the HKSAR would have a rosy future immediately after July 1, 2003. In fact, Xiao's hard-line approach reflected the thinking and strategies of the Zeng committee.

Furthermore, Xiao's comments highlighted the different political cultures between the Hong Kong democrats and the PRC. While the democrats opt for a Western style of political system where the chief executive is directly elected by citizens through universal suffrage, Beijing actually supports a more moderate system of political change. After all, Beijing does not trust that universal suffrage would be able to produce patriots who can govern Hong Kong with Beijing's interest in mind. While the democrats identify themselves as Hongkongers, they do not identity themselves with the ruling CCP in the mainland. However, as Xiao was a CCP member, his views and stance were clear. From the PRC vantage point, identification with China culturally entails identification with the CCP politically — a point unacceptable to many Hong Kong democrats. Xiao's arguments, however, represented a blend between the cultural identification with mainland China and the political identification with the CCP. While mainland political culture mixes cultural-politico identification into a melting pot, the Hong Kong democratic sub-culture tends to separate the cultural from the political dimensions.

Xiao's remarks were echoed by Hong Kong's pro-Beijing elites such as Hong Kong NPC member Tsang Hin-chi and Basic Law Committee members Raymond Wu and Maria Tam. Tsang and Wu blasted the democrats for being "unpatriotic," whereas Tam reminded the people of Hong Kong that the HKSAR source of political power came from Beijing, not the Hongkongers. The message was clear: Beijing would have the final say or veto power over the direction of Hong Kong's political reform. Xiao's united front work that was accompanied by the consensus from Beijing's political clients marked the inception of a wave of public discourse on patriotism.

From February to March 2004, the official Chinese mass media began to launch a campaign directed against the democrats in the HKSAR. The official Xinhua news agency, together with the *People's Daily*, emphasized that the HKSAR political reform would have to proceed in a gradual and orderly process, and that the late Chinese leader Deng Xiaoping stressed the need for Hong Kong to be governed by patriots.[21] In March 2004, Beijing's legal expert and former drafter of the Basic Law, Xu Chongde, explicitly outlined three criteria of unpatriotic Hong Kong people, namely (1) those who forged a close linkage with foreign countries like the United States (implying the former Democratic Party chairman Martin Lee), (2) those who organized the Hong Kong Alliance for the Promotion of Democracy in China (led by Democratic Party member Szeto Wah), and (3) those democrats who appeared to support Taiwan's independence movement (implying Frontier leader Emily Lau Wai-hing, although Lau insisted that she merely supported the right of the Taiwanese to decide their future, and that such a stance was not necessarily equivalent to supporting Taiwan independence).[22] Obviously, Xiao and Xu's remarks, together with official PRC mouthpieces, aimed at isolating a few democrats in the HKSAR.

Two major factors explained the PRC united front against the democrats in the HKSAR from January to March 2004. First and foremost, Zeng's committee adopted a hard-line position not only on the Hong Kong organizers of the July 2003 protests and the pro-democracy Alliance back in 1989, but also on the transmission of a political message to Taiwan, namely, any political leader directly elected by universal suffrage might not be patriotic in the eyes of Beijing. Even if Chen Shui-bian of the DPP might be re-elected — which he was in March 2004 — Beijing did not see him as "patriotic." In other words, Zeng's committee on HKSAR affairs adopted a double-edged sword that targeted both the Hong Kong democrats and the Taiwan pro-independence movement. As a protégé of Jiang, Zeng clearly regarded the Alliance led by Hong Kong Democratic Party member Szeto Wah as "unpatriotic." Szeto Wah, however, argued that patriotism could coexist with the demand for political democratization.[23] Martin Lee's high-profile visit to the American Congress in early March 2004 unintentionally provided more ammunition to the advocates of Chinese patriotism. He was criticized as being politically unwise, "unpatriotic", and as presenting a golden opportunity for the United States to attack the PRC policy toward Taiwan and to exert pressure on Beijing for democratic changes in the HKSAR.[24] The clash on the definitions of patriotism was vividly shown in the tug of war between the Hong Kong democrats and their critics from the PRC and the HKSAR.

In fact, the hard-line position of Zeng's committee on the democrats and the July 2003 protests was by no means surprising, for Beijing's mouthpiece *Ta Kung Pao* in July 2003 carried a number of commentaries designating the protests as a plot orchestrated by "political, academic, media and foreign troublemakers" who mobilized Hong Kong people on the streets of Hong Kong. Very few observers took the commentaries of *Ta Kung Pao* seriously at that time, but the arguments perhaps reflected the mentality of the Liaison Office and also the Zeng committee, whose hard-line position was corroborated and solidified from February and March 2004.

Second, the campaign against the democrats aimed at consolidating the pro-Beijing votes for the DAB and its allies, such as the Hong Kong Progressive Alliance, in the September 2004 elections held for the Legislative Council. Usually those Hong Kong people who identify themselves as Chinese are more likely to vote for the DAB, whereas those who identify themselves as Hong Kong people tend to vote for the Democratic Party.[25] If so, Beijing's united front campaign against the democrats would hopefully affect their supporters, whose voting behavior could be shaped by any scandals that the democrats might have. Shortly before the 2004 Legislative Council elections, a minority of pro-democracy activists were careless in their personal conduct. A case in point was the scandal involving DP member Alex Ho, who was caught by the Dongguan Public Security Bureau for soliciting mainland prostitutes in China. Ho's activities had been monitored by the mainland police for some time, especially after the defeat of DAB member Kwok Pit-chun during the 2003 District Council elections. Kwok was a political foe of Ho, and the former suffered from a sex scandal prior to the District Council elections.[26] There was no evidence to prove any linkage between Kwok's defeat and Ho's scandal, but it was possible that the PRC agents in the HKSAR might retaliate against the democrats for revealing the Kwok scandal. After all, the DP performed impressively during the 2003 District Council elections, whereas its political foe DAB suffered a severe blow. Alex Ho's sex scandal in the 2004 Legislative Council elections plunged the DP into chaos, especially the candidates participating in the Kowloon East constituency. Fred Li Wah-ming and his teammate Wu Chi-wai had to adopt a defensive position during the campaign. Not surprisingly, Wu failed to be elected.[27] Overall, the Alex Ho scandal tarnished the overall image of the pan-democratic camp — a reflection of the success of the PRC united front campaign.

Finally, the PRC united front campaign against the democrats also sends a message to foreign states like the U.S. that democratization in the HKSAR remains Beijing's internal affairs. Any attempt by foreign states to shape the process and scope of democratic reform in Hong Kong would fail. The dichotomy between "patriots" and "traitors" was illustrative of the way in which Beijing views the question of democratic development in the HKSAR. For those who cooperate with foreigners to push for democracy in Hong Kong, such as Martin Lee who in the past visited foreign states to "badmouth" the HKSAR, according to Beijing's view, they are treated as "traitors."

Identity Clashes, Anti-Foreignism, Hong Kong's Democratization, and China's Political Modernization

The whole debate over Article 23 of the Basic Law and the row over patriotism and identity had long-term repercussions on the HKSAR democratic development and mainland China's long path to political modernization. First and foremost, Hong Kong's democratization has become a battleground and a tug of war between the PRC and the Western powers, notably the United States. As long as the PRC ruling elites believe that mainland China can modernize by borrowing from Western technology but not the Western values such as democracy, democratization in Hong Kong remains a tortuous path that is destined to be torn between the Chinese civilization and Western civilization. Samuel Huntington has correctly argued that the Sinic or Chinese civilization is characterized by hierarchy, political authoritarianism, the subordination to authority, and conformity. This characterization remains enduring in the PRC where the ruling elites are clinging to these Chinese traditional values for the sake of maintaining political power. The Western-style democracy, or the Taiwan-style universal suffrage, remains a threat to the ruling elites in the PRC. Yet the HKSAR is a cosmopolitan city where many citizens and intellectuals accept the Western values of pluralism, individualism, autonomy, and equality. Martin Lee, Emily Lau, Ronny Tong, Audrey Eu, Alan Leong, Margaret Ng, and other democrats who orchestrated the July 2003 protests are typical of these liberal-minded and pro-Western activists. Their identity lies with Hong Kong, but their Hong Kong identity has strong Western legacies and influence. Yet these pro-Western intellectuals and elites have cultural clash with the PRC ruling elites and their supporters in the HKSAR.

While Hong Kong's democratization is fraught with tremendous difficulties and it encounters opposition from the PRC, Beijing's political change will face far more cultural obstacles than modernization theorists might have assumed. The PRC ruling elites remain wedded to the idea that mainland China can have its own unique path of modernization, that economic modernization does not entail total Westernization, that the Taiwan-style of democracy is unacceptable to the mainland, that Western democracies have their own problems, and that the Western powers would like to envisage Taiwan's persistent separation from the mainland. If anti-foreignism is deep-rooted in mainland China, it is resistant to the implementation of Western-style democracy, including Taiwan's democracy. Given that the PRC united front work has gained considerable inroad on the HKSAR since July 1, 1997, especially after the political earthquake on July 1, 2003, the surge of cultural-politico Chinese identity in the HKSAR is representing a strong ingredient of xenophobic sentiment that rejects Western-style democratization and democracy. Compounding the difficulty of democratization in Hong Kong is that foreign states such as the United States and Britain have been involved in varying degrees of politico-moral support of the local democrats. Yet the PRC ruling elites, and all their friends and followers in the HKSAR, remain inherently xenophobic, believing that the Western powers cannot and should not impose a political model on not simply Hong Kong but also mainland China.

Identity Change and the Mass Media Coverage of the Tenth Anniversary of the HKSAR

After the success of the PRC united front campaign prior to the 2004 Legislative Council elections in which the democrats captured only 27 of the 60 seats, it continued to deepen in the HKSAR up to the tenth anniversary of its return to the motherland on July 1, 2007. The way in which the mass media, both print and electronic, covered the tenth anniversary showed that the HKSAR has already become a place where the mix of cultural-politico identity is gaining significant breakthrough in the media profession. Self-censorship is arguably a disturbing political trend in the HKSAR, which points to a deepening process of mainlandization and Sinification.[28]

In terms of electronic media, the local television and radio stations have already displayed an obvious trend toward self-censorship. The TVB and ATV news on the HKSAR since July 1, 2003 have been constantly emphasizing the positive economic development of the territory, with the catch phrase "economic recovery" appearing repeatedly to the extent of becoming a persistent propaganda.[29] Although it was true that Hong Kong's economic rebound was obvious, the news reports tended to emphasize the spending power of mainland visitors, who according to the television news reports did spend lavishly in the HKSAR every day. While it was again true that many rich mainland visitors are big spenders and consumers in the HKSAR, those who are living in the low-cost apartments and rooms in the territory were not really covered in the news — a reflection of editorial bias and selective reporting. On the tenth anniversary of the HKSAR, the two television programs focused on why some Hong Kong people, who emigrated to overseas countries such as Canada, decided to return to the HKSAR. This was partially accurate; the crux of the problem was that there was virtually no in-depth report on why many overseas Hong Kong people do not opt for a return to the HKSAR. The stress on the economic prosperity of the HKSAR, coupled with the returnees, was a politically correct move that could please the patron Beijing. After all, the ownership of both TVB and ATV is now pro-Beijing and pro-establishment. Except for the Cable Television whose news and programs tend to be more diversified and factually accurate, both the TVB and ATV news displayed a more obvious trend of self-censorship.[30] On the night of July 1, 2007, after the democrats mobilized citizens to join the protests, the TVB (Chinese channel) covered the story very briefly while its English channel tended to spend more time on the footage on the protests.[31] Comparatively, the ATV spent less time than the TVB covering the protests on July 1, 2007, focusing instead on all the celebrations and the official governmental functions. Only the Cable TV news spent more time covering the citizens' protests and interviewed the participants on why they did so, with one saying that although the economy improved, there were lots of problems such as the huge income gap between the rich and the poor that had to be resolved by the government.[32] Objectively speaking, the Cable Television news was far more factually accurate and balanced than both the TVB and ATV opposite numbers.

Judging from the political affairs program of the TVB and ATV during the tenth anniversary, TVB's Sunday File tended to be more objective and balanced than ATV's Hong Kong Current Affairs. On June 30, 2007, ATV's program Hong Kong Current Affairs broadcasted its interviews with the former HKMAO director Lu Ping and the former director of the New China News Agency Zhou Nan.[33] Lu revealed that the late Deng Xiaoping was concerned about whether the British would use up all the public coffer of Hong Kong before July 1, 1997, and that the British administration had the problems of making the land prices high, salaries high, and welfare expenditure high. Chen Zuo'er, the current deputy director of the HKMAO, said in the program that the British administration's budget, if allowed before 1997, would be used up by 2000. Hard-liner Zhou Nan stressed that Hong Kong's politics and economy would require stability, that universal suffrage to the late Deng would not necessarily choose those patriotic Hongkongers, and that democratization in the HKSAR would have to be gradual and orderly. The entire thrust of the ATV program was to lay down the PRC official perspectives — a politically safe approach. The TVB Sunday File, however, tended to be more titled toward the Hong Kong identity. It interviewed two citizens: forty-four-year-old Yu Wai-kin who identified himself as both a Hongkonger and a Chinese, and Professor Edward Chen who stressed that the young people of Hong Kong should be proud to be Chinese, and that the patriotic education in the HKSAR should not entail "hard" promotion."[34] While Yu remarked that the Hongkongers are different from the mainlanders, he felt there must be "political restrictions" in the HKSAR. Chen, on the other hand, believed that there is no contradiction between being a Hongkonger and a Chinese, and that loving the country does not necessarily mean loving the motherland.

Overall, the views of Yu and Chen are complimentary, demonstrating a certain degree of Hong Kong identity that can coexist with the Chinese identity. But both share the assumption that loving the motherland does not mean loving the ruling party in the PRC. The TVB Sunday File was more objective than its daily news program and more pro-Hong Kong than the ATV program shown on June 30.

Interestingly, the English channels of both TVB and ATV were more independent than their Chinese news coverage of the tenth anniversary. The TVB (Pearl) invited academic Michael DeGolyer to analyze the survey results of the Hong Kong Transition Project on July 1, 2007, whereas the Newsline program of the ATV invited Robert Chung and Francis Moriarty to share their views on Hong Kong's public opinion on the night of July 1.[35] Moriarty raised the issue of self-censorship among the Hong Kong journalists and the question of the future of the Radio Television Hong Kong (RTHK), which represents an indispensable part of the Hong Kong identity. Robert Chung, on the other hand, echoed Moriarty's view, saying that members of the public might not be able to identify the tendency toward media self-censorship, and that the intellectuals like journalists and academics would have the conscience to raise public awareness on such problem. Since the analysts were independent and gave their own views without any constraint from political correctness, the English channels of both TVB and ATV performed far more credibly than their Chinese channels.

The way in which the mainland-owned media reported the HKSAR during the tenth anniversary illustrated a fundamental problem: the mainland media had obvious political prejudice in reporting all the positive aspects of Hong Kong's development. The official China Central Television (CCTV Channel 9), for example, interviewed all those pro-Beijing elites and a few mainlanders who worked and resided in Hong Kong.[36] It interviewed Wu Changqi, a scholar at Beijing University who formerly taught at the Hong Kong University of Science and Technology. Wu said that Hong Kong would still retain and attract foreign talents and mainland students, and that Hong Kong would continue to benefit from mainland's economic development. The CCTV also interviewed the Director of the Hong Kong One Country Two Systems Economic Institute Cheung Chi-kong, who predictably gave all the optimistic forecast and analysis on Hong Kong. It also interviewed Jenny Lam, the TVB anchor, who surprisingly gave all the politically correct views on how the HKSAR performed successfully in all aspects.[37] Lam added at the end that some people left Hong Kong because of the serious environmental pollution problem — a point that appeared to be more independent and factually accurate. The CCTV also interviewed

Professor Albert Chen of the Basic Law Committee and he said that the HKSAR experience demonstrated the success of the "one country, two systems."[38] Apart from Chen, Jasper Tsang of the DAB was interviewed and his views interestingly were the most independent. Tsang said that the HKSAR government should develop new industries, such as the high-tech and value-added ones, rather than maintaining the "sunset" industries and the heavy reliance on the service industry.[39] Although Tsang shared his insights with the reporter, the latter was unfamiliar with the HKSAR circumstances and failed to engage Tsang by asking good questions at all. The CCTV showed a program entitled "Foreign Students in Hong Kong," emphasizing the globalized education setting of the HKSAR and the joy of foreign students in studying there.[40]

From a critical perspective, the CCTV (Channel 9) coverage of the HKSAR tenth anniversary was dry and one-sided. On July 1, 2007, one of the CCTV reporters revealed that he found it "extraordinary that Hong Kong people did not celebrate too much but they treated the anniversary as a festival;" nevertheless, he lacked any critical thinking to delve into why the people of Hong Kong had such an attitude.[41] Nor did he interview any independent Hong Kong expert on the phenomenon. The CCTV reporter and host did not appear to be knowledgeable on Hong Kong matters; the host said he did not really know the name of the location where the PLA paratroopers performed — in fact it was Happy Valley. Another host, during an interview with the Basic Law Committee member Wang Zhenmin, showed his lack of in-depth knowledge on Hong Kong by asking Wang questions on the background of Chief Executive Donald Tsang. Strictly speaking, media professionalism should be improved as both the reporters and hosts covering the HKSAR appeared to lack sufficient research prior to the formal coverage of the tenth anniversary.

The dry, monotonous, and superficial CCTV coverage of the HKSAR tenth anniversary represented a typical official propaganda. On July 1, 2007, its news report covered the events surrounding President Hu's meeting with the Hong Kong students. Two Hong Kong students said that they were becoming more nationalistic, while one sang the song "Dragon's Heart" to demonstrate his patriotism. Students were shown to voice the views on their visits to the motherland. In response, President Hu remarked that Hong Kong students should work hard, understand how to develop themselves, and that they should become talents contributing to both Hong Kong and China in the long-term future. This report on the interactions between Hu and Hong Kong students and the emphasis on patriotism demonstrated the CCTV's political correctness and conformity. The DAB core member Jasper Tsang publicly advocated that the CCTV news should be available free to the Hong Kong people. While this pro-Beijing political correctness is understandable, the deeper penetration of the official PRC propaganda into the HKSAR would perhaps be a long-term trend from now to 2047.

Comparatively, the Phoenix tended to have a more in-depth and better coverage of the HKSAR tenth anniversary, but its reports were by no means balanced. The Phoenix mobilized its reporters to cover the tenth anniversary of the HKSAR live to the viewers, but its reports had a number of features. First, it tended to focus on non-political issues such as the Buddhist leaders' celebration of the tenth anniversary during the firework display on the Lantau Island, and how the public in the HKSAR warmly received the two Pandas from Beijing. Second, one of its commentators severely criticized the political role of Cardinal Zen in mobilizing the masses to participate in protests, but then the program highlighted that the commentator's personal views did not represent the Phoenix. Ironically, the fact that the program allowed the commentator to voice such a view while simultaneously excluding a pro-Zen perspective from another independent commentator was indicative of its own political bias.[42] It was a myth of the political "neutrality" of the Phoenix when it broadcasted the anti-Cardinal Zen commentary without showing the opposing side of the argument. Third, the Phoenix overwhelmingly interviewed the establishment elites, such as Chief Executive Donald Tsang, the former secretary for justice Elsie Leung, the former director of the New China News Agency Zhou Nan, and the former PRC negotiator Shao Tianren. Interestingly, Tsang was allowed to use Cantonese during the Phoenix's interview. Surprisingly, Tsang appeared to implicitly criticize his predecessor C. H. Tung by saying that the Hong Kong bureaucracy was so large that "the business sector with its own work style and habit cannot move the civil service easily."[43] That Tsang's remark, critical of the business ignorance of the operation of the civil service, was broadcast through the Phoenix was perhaps an indication of some degree of media freedom within the Phoenix. Its media autonomy could also be seen in the interviews with other more independent commentators, notably Camoes Tam Chi-keung and Tim Hamlett, on their views toward the HKSAR.[44]

Nevertheless, such media autonomy in the Phoenix could not be overstated.[45] Tsang's implicit criticism of the business sector might not be taken as a political taboo by the editor of the Phoenix at all. On July 1, the Phoenix reported that mainland students in the HKSAR found a rise in patriotism in the territory. They all said that Mandarin was widely used in the HKSAR, that shops accepted *Renminbi*, and that the people of Hong Kong increased their identification with the motherland. The political correctness of Phoenix was further testified in its interview with Chris Patten. Its interview highlighted that Patten felt sad to leave Hong Kong, that he thought China "honored the 'one country, two systems' principle," that "the 'one country, two systems' is by and large well-developed."[46] It is well known that Patten hopes that democracy in Hong Kong can be developed further, but the interview avoided reporting on his pro-democracy views while emphasizing the success of the "one country, two systems." Obviously, selective coverage and emphasis served to achieve political correctness.

None of the democrats was interviewed by the PRC and Hong Kong electronic media on July 1. However, the CNN briefly interviewed Martin Lee and DW-TV interviewed Emily Lau. This phenomenon proved the local media's marginalization of the democrats, reversing the situation during the mid-1980s when both Lee and Lau were the darlings of the local press.

The coverage of the print media on the tenth anniversary of the HKSAR was ideologically diverse. The *Apple Daily* remained independent and critical. On June 30, when President Hu visited the HKSAR, the newspaper stressed in its headline that police protection of Hu was so tight that he could not hear pro-democracy voices.[47] On the same day, *Apple Daily* also reported Anson Chan's remark that she would take to the streets on July 1 so that President Hu would hear the voice of Hongkongers on universal suffrage.[48] On July 1, the newspaper's headline was Cardinal Zen's appeal to the people of Hong Kong to join the protests in the afternoon.[49] Its back page, which carried the words "We need universal suffrage," was designed for the participants in the July 1 protests. Other pro-Beijing newspapers, such as *Wen Wei Po* and *Ta Kung Pao*, overwhelmingly covered the activities and remarks of President Hu, and carried a large number of advertisements celebrating the tenth anniversary. The *Oriental Daily*, which now has branches of distribution and marketing in the mainland, also focused on Hu's remarks that encouraged the persistent diligence of the Hongkongers.[50] However, the *Oriental Daily* editorialized to emphasize the need to improve the salaries and working conditions of medical doctors — an indication that the newspaper was concerned about the welfare of the local people. However, its commentary, entitled "Kung Fu Tea," severely criticized the democrats such as Martin Lee, Lee Wing-tat, Yeung Sum, and Cardinal Zen as "anti-China and anti-Hong Kong."[51] The other more centralist newspapers such as the *Hong Kong Economic Journal* and *Ming Pao* editorialized to stress Hu's remark on the need for the protection of the interests of "one country," and to expect that the central government would care more about the concerns of the "two systems."⁵² While the *Hong Kong Economic Journal* has a respectable reputation of maintaining its independent and critical stance, the same comment cannot be applied to *Ming Pao,* whose editorials fluctuate from time to time. Most importantly, *Ming Pao*'s forum page in the past ten years has silently drifted toward a subtle process of self-censorship, deliberately or unintentionally sidelining some pro-democracy critics while regularly retaining the commentaries of the pro-Beijing elites.

Conclusion and Implications for Taiwan

The debate over the national security issue in the HKSAR had much wider implications. It was concerned about the difficulty of translating the cultural identity of Hong Kong people from Chinese into a political identification with the CCP — a difficult task for both the HKSAR and PRC governments because of the long period of colonial rule in Hong Kong, where Chinese nationalism and patriotism were downplayed. The debate over Article 23 of the Basic Law demonstrated the clash of Chinese and Western civilizations, the conflict between Chinese and Western values, the confrontations between the Hong Kong identity and the mainland Chinese political identity, and the persistent belief of the mainland Chinese ruling elites that economic modernization does not entail total Westernization. After all, the old Chinese belief in the Qing dynasty that mainland China can learn from Western technology but not Western values remains a hallmark shaping the debate over political reform in the HKSAR. Anti-foreignism remains the political element resisting any effort at implanting a Western-style democratic system, characterized by the rotation of political party in power and the direct elections of the chief executive through universal suffrage, into the HKSAR.

The policy failure of the National Security Bill forced the PRC officials responsible for Hong Kong affairs to change their united front tactics, while at the same time maintaining their xenophobic attitude toward the pro-democracy Hong Kong elites. The resurrection of the debate over patriotism highlighted the PRC united front work in the HKSAR. As long as the criteria of patriotism remain ambiguous, those who are patriots or not are determined more by the CCP demand for political loyalty and correctness rather than any objective yardstick for measurements. Under the prevailing atmosphere of the rise of mainland China and the pressure on Hongkongers to be more politically correct than ever before, the Hong Kong mass media have become the political battleground. While mainland media such as the

CCTV and Phoenix have made considerable inroads into the Hong Kong audience, the former remains an official propaganda whereas the latter appears to be more lively and autonomous. Yet their political correctness in reporting, commentaries, and coverage persists.

Such political correctness can also be seen increasingly in the TVB and ATV news, especially the Chinese channels where local reporters and editors are vulnerable to ownership change, self-censorship, and PRC united front work. The Cable TV, however, remains more autonomous than both the TVB and ATV news. Although current affairs programs of the TVB and ATV demonstrate media autonomy and professionalism, it is doubtful whether the editors and reporters will combat the invisible pressure on self-censorship and political correctness.

The print media in the HKSAR remain ideologically heterogeneous. Although *Apple Daily* and *Hong Kong Economic Journal* remain respectable and autonomous in their political coverage, commentaries, and editorials, other newspapers are under tremendous pressure to adhere to the line of political correctness and conformity. Perhaps fortunately, the need for all the newspapers to compete in the market place serves to constrain the tendency of the centralist newspapers to shift to the official PRC line. It remains to be seen whether the centralist newspapers, notably *Ming Pao*, are going to fall under the temptation of a large mainland Chinese advertising market and of the need to be more politically safe as well as correct in their coverage and editorial stance.

The implications of gradual identity change in the HKSAR, marked by the triumph of Hong Kong identity in the 2003 debate over the National Security Bill to the silent victory of political correctness in the media coverage of the tenth anniversary of the HKSAR, are significant for Taiwan. First and foremost, the Taiwanese identity remains relatively strong, perhaps much stronger than the Hong Kong identity.[53] Any attempt by the PRC to impose the mainland Chinese cultural-politico identity on Taiwan will backfire and have a boomerang effect on the Beijing-Taipei relationships. Second, the PRC united front work in the HKSAR is easier than that in Taiwan, where the pro-Taiwanese public will see such tactic as repugnant and counter-productive. The CCP united front work on the people of Taiwan, including both the pro-reunification and pro-independence supporters, will have to be conducted in a more subtle and skillful manner. Otherwise the pro-reunification supporters who are under the spell of the CCP united front tactics will run the risk of being politically condemned by their foes and marginalized by any pro-independence ruling elites. In the event that the pro-reunification elites grasp political power in Taiwan, the PRC united front tactics on them will perhaps generate severe opposition and negative reactions from the pro-Taiwan public. In short, the level of sophistication required for the PRC united front work in Taiwan is much higher than that in the HKSAR, where considerable elites and masses have already become the faithful clients of the most powerful patron, Beijing. Third, the mass media in Taiwan appear to be less susceptible to the PRC united front work than their counterpart in Hong Kong. If the PRC united front work were conducted on the Taiwan media, they would be politically divided, polarized, and politicized further. In brief, the effectiveness of PRC united front work on the HKSAR may not be easily translated into the more pro-Taiwanese setting in the ROC, where the local identity has already been elevated to the level of a "national" identity in conflict with the mainland cultural-politico identity.

7

The Election of the Hong Kong Deputies to the National People's Congress

The second election of the Hong Kong deputies to the Tenth NPC of the PRC was held on December 3, 2002 — five years after the first election had been held for the Hong Kong members of the Ninth NPC in the HKSAR.[1] The registration of contestants for the candidacy of Hong Kong deputies to the Tenth NPC was completed on November 18, 2002. There were 99 participants in the 15-day nomination period.[2] Of the 99 participants, 78 formally submitted their registration forms, which required at least ten nominations in order to make each registration effective. A total of 36 deputies were elected on December 3, 2002 by a 953-member Conference for Electing Deputies of the HKSAR to the Tenth NPC of the PRC.[3] The PRC Government appointed the Members of the Conference for Electing Deputies of the HKSAR without the involvement of the ordinary people of Hong Kong. The majority of the members of the Conference for Electing Deputies to the Tenth NPC came from the 800-member Election Committee that selected the second chief executive of the HKSAR in March 2002.[4]

Under the electoral arrangement, 54 candidates were first elected from among the members of the Election Conference in November 2002 for the second or final round of voting on December 3. The Central Committee of the Democratic Party (DP) endorsed four members — James To Kun-sun, Albert Ho Chun-yan, Anthony Cheung Bing-leung, and Sin Chung-kai — to stand in the election. Mr. Cheung ran in his own capacity whereas the others represented the party.[5] The DP Vice-Chairman Law Chi-kwong said the party should participate in the election because "Hong Kong people should have the right to stand for election of the NPC deputies."[6] Ho, a member of the Standing Committee of the Hong Kong Alliance in Support of the Patriotic and Democratic Movement in China, remarked: "We are a political party which got the community's support in the direct election here. If not even a single member from our party can get elected, that will be a problem of the NPC electoral system."[7]

Prior to the election, political observer Chris Yeung believed that its results would be "significant" because they "could reflect some interesting changes in the mindset of the local elite towards mainland–Hong Kong relations."[8] He predicted that "[w]ith the influence of a small, though vocal, group of pro-Beijing figures diluted in a larger panel, it is likely that most voters will put more weight on the qualities of the candidates rather than their political views."[9] As it turned out, however, Yeung's prediction became inaccurate because candidates' political orientations appeared to be the most important criterion shaping their chances of electoral success. This chapter aims at exploring the politics of selecting the Hong Kong members of the Tenth NPC, including the role of the Liaison Office in the election. The literature on elections in the HKSAR has focused on the Legislative Council and District Councils,[10] but little research has been conducted on the NPC elections except for Pepper's recent work. The study of the elections held for the Hong Kong members of the NPC, as this chapter will show, can demonstrate the uniqueness of mainland-style Chinese election in the politically pluralistic setting of the HKSAR.[11] Finally, the implications of the HKSAR NPC elections for Taiwan will be examined.

The First Round of Voting

The first round of voting was held on November 30, 2003 (see Table 7.1). Only 874 members of the 953-strong election panel turned up, but 870 cast their votes and 868 votes were valid.[12] All five of the democrats were defeated in the first round of voting amid unsubstantiated claims that some voters were under pressure not to support them. Democrats Albert Ho Chun-yan (64 votes), James To Kun-sun (81 votes), Sin Chung-kai (74 votes), Anthony Cheung (113 votes), and Frederick Fung Kin-kee (110 votes) were all defeated. Cheung, Fung, To, Sin, and Ho ranked at 57th, 58th, 61st, 65th, and 67th among the seventy-eight candidates respectively. Anthony Cheung said he was not surprised at the result given the fact that "some people are putting pressure on the voters not to vote for the democrats."[13] He also claimed that some members of the Election Conference were asked to abandon their support of the democrats.[14] His party colleague James To remarked: "I didn't have much expectation. I believe the results would be completely different if the candidates were elected by universal suffrage."[15]

Martin Lee, the former DP chairman, said that the failure of the three DP members to be elected in the first round of voting proved the "unrepresentative" nature of the Election Conference.[16]

Table 7.1 The 54 Winners in the First Round of Voting

Rank/Name	Number of Votes	Rank/Name	Number of Votes
1. Maria Tam*	687	28. Tsang Tak-sing*	463
2. Wang Rudeng	636	29. Wong Siu-yee	461
3. Rita Fan*	628	30. Ko Po-ling	458
4. Robin Chan Yau-hing*	615	31. Raymond Ho	453
5. Dennis Lam Shun-chiu	604	32. Ip Kwok-him	449
6. Raymond Wu*	601	33. Wong Yuk-shan	447
7. Raymond Chien	554	34. Wong Kwok-kin	443
8. David Chu Yu-lin	546	35. Ng Hong-man*	439
9. Allen Lee Peng-fei*	544	36. Leung Ping-chung*	436
10. Ng Ching-fai*	544	37. Hui Man-pok	434
11. Tsang Hin-chi*	537	38. Au Yeung Sing-chiu	428
12. Lam Kwong-siu	534	39. Joseph Lee Chung-tak*	422
13. Ma Lik*	528	40. Andrew Lam Siu-lo	419
14. Tso Wan-wai*	525	41. Peter Chan Chi-kwan	419
15. Ma Ho-fai	522	42. Lo Chung-hing*	417
16. Wilfred Wong*	517	43. Philip Wong Yu-hong*	414
17. Reverend Sik Chi-wai*	505	44. Victor Sit Fung-shuen*	414
18. Sophie Leung	502	45. Kan Fok-yee*	398
19. Peter Wong Man-kong*	486	46. Priscilla Lau Pui-king*	389
20. Yeung Yiu-chung*	484	47. Lee Chark-tim*	385
21. Cheng Yiu-tong*	484	48. Lo Suk-ching*	372
22. Howard Young	476	49. Wong Po-yan*	360
23. Ma Fung-kwok	473	50. Lee Lin-sang*	346
24. Ng Leung-sing	471	51. Fung Chi-kin	304
25. Fei Fih*	466	52. Ngai Shiu-kit*	299
26. Yuen Mo*	464	53. Stanley Ko Kam-chuen	298
27. Carson Wen	464	54. David Fang In-sheng	238

* Hong Kong deputies to the Ninth NPC.

Sources: *South China Morning Post*, November 30, 2002, p. 3; *Apple Daily*, November 30, 2002, p. A15; and *Ming Pao*, November 30, 2002, p. A6.

The pro-Beijing members of the Election Conference did not favor the democrats. An incumbent NPC local deputy and a member of the Election Conference, businessman Chan Wing-kee, said that those candidates who could communicate with the central government were the preferred ones. Chan revealed: "I have not voted for the democrats because they have difficulties in communicating with the central government. We need someone who can do so in order that the views of the public can be conveyed to the central government."[17] Prior to the first round of voting, Lee Cho-chak, a spokesman for the Chair Group that was in charge of the election, went so far as to state that there was a non-statutory requirement on NPC local deputies to love the nation.[18] He also asserted that the claim of loving China and loving Hong Kong needed action, not simply words.[19] Obviously, the political views of the candidates were seen as critical.

On the other hand, rumors were rife that some political forces put forward different candidates' lists for the voters. Lee himself admitted that he had received more than ten lists of candidates, but he did not know their origins.[20] According to Lee, "I don't believe the Beijing Liaison Office issued a recommended list."[21] Nonetheless, democrat Albert Ho claimed that voters had been issued with a list of recommended candidates. According to Ho, most voters marked the ballot papers on their desk rather than doing so in the booths provided, and thus "this was not a secret ballot election."[22] Anthony Cheung echoed Ho's claim:

> There was some maneuvering behind the scenes in the pre-election process and some lists were passed around to lobby against democrats. I have to admit that this is the reality, that it [is] unacceptable for the Election [Conference] to have democrat candidates elected. My point in running in the election is to show that I do care about national affairs.[23]

In fact, other reports indicated that some members of the Election Conference had brought name lists with them to cast their ballots in the first round of voting.[24]

Several days before the first round of voting, the mass media highlighted the determination of the Chinese side to "protect the old loyalists and friends, [and to] prevent the democrats from being elected."[25] Moreover, some pro-Beijing unions issued "authoritative" guidelines to members on how to vote; those elites who were recommended by "patriotic" unions included the Liaison Office's Assistant Director Wang Rudeng, General-Secretary of the Federation of Trade Union Wong Kwok-kin, and the 31 incumbent Hong Kong deputies to the NPC.[26] Some voters told the press that they had received "verbal" guidelines on how to vote.[27] A legislator and a member of the DAB, Ip Kwok-him, publicly admitted that the party and FTU had appealed to members to give their voting priorities to those candidates nominated by the two organizations.[28]

Only 874 members of the 953-member Election Conference turned up in the first round of voting — 870 cast their votes and 868 votes were valid. They were free to determine the number of candidates they chose. But they would have to choose 36 candidates for all the seats in the second or final round of voting.

The election result in the first round of voting was a surprise. Several newcomers performed impressively, including eye specialist and academic Dennis Lam who secured the fifth place with 604 votes, and Liberal Party legislator Sophie Leung who secured 502 votes.[29] It was rumored that Lam had served as an eye specialist for top PRC officials, thus elevating his political status. Another newcomer David Fang, the chief executive of St Paul's Hospital and brother of the former chief secretary for administration Anson Chan, narrowly secured the final seat with 238 votes. Surprisingly, a few pro-Beijing elites such as Tsang Tak-sing (463 votes) and Ng Hong-man (439 votes) obtained relatively much fewer votes than conventional wisdom assumed, for both of them were long-time supporters of the central government in Beijing. Both Tsang and Ng performed poorly in comparison with Sophie Leung of the Liberal Party. Allen Lee Peng-fei, the former chairman of the Liberal Party, was ranked the ninth candidate who got the highest number of votes. He outperformed Ma Lik, a die-hard supporter of Beijing and a member of the DAB. Surprisingly, Lee, Leung, and another member of the Liberal Party Howard Young also outperformed some long-time supporters of Beijing, such as Tsang, Ng, and Ip Kwok-him. Several incumbents like Ngai Shiu-kit, Wong Po-yan, and Lo Suk-ching performed poorly. It seemed as if the first round of voting would lead to the victory of many new faces and younger Hong Kong deputies in the final round.

The role of the Liaison Office remained a mystery in the first round of the voting. Some candidates who were elected in the first round but who got relatively fewer votes accused the Liaison Office of "making them lose face."[30] They pointed to the fact that although Raymond Chien Kuo-fung neither went to the election venue nor lobbied for support, he could be elected comfortably — an indication of the Liaison Office's support.[31] An "insider" told the press that a majority of the elected candidates were actually on the Liaison Office's recommended list.[32]

Critics said that it took five hours for vote counting in the first round of voting — a process that was much slower than the computerized method of vote counting in mainland NPC's elections at the provincial and municipal levels.[33] Moreover, some members of the Election Conference arrived late, including Chief Executive Tung, thus delaying the voting process by almost thirty minutes.[34]

The Second Round of Voting

After the first round of voting, the elected 54 candidates went to various forums to present their platforms to voters. While some candidates worked diligently in their lobbying activities, a minority did not make an effort at conducting their electioneering activities. Howard Yong, a member of the Liberal Party, used Hakka to appeal to voters for support from members of the rural advisory body, Heung Yee Kuk. Nevertheless, incumbent Wong Po-yan, who had obtained relatively few votes in the first round, expressed his indifferent attitude toward his electoral performance.[35] Some candidates distributed their name cards to voters and mobilized campaign assistants to lobby for political support on the voting day.[36]

The election results in the final round of voting were "surprising" in that the earlier results in the first round were turned around (see Table 7.2). However, the final results appeared to indicate that the candidates' political orientations tended to be a decisive factor paving the way for their victory. Allen Lee was ranked only twenty-seventh and he was defeated by Ma Lik, Tsang, Ip, Ng, and even Lau Pui-king (who got only 389 votes in the first round) who had all trailed behind him on November 30. Moreover, seven candidates who were in the top 36 places in the first round, such as Dennis Lam, legislator Ho Chung-tai, Howard Young, academic Wong Yuk-shan, and lawyer Ma Ho-fai were all defeated in the final round. Although two Liberal Party candidates, Allen Lee and Sophie Leung won, Leung's ranking in the candidates' list slumped dramatically from eighteenth in the first round of voting to a dangerously borderline thirty-third place.[37] In response to the election result, Anthony Cheung, who had been ousted in the first round, said:

> The election outcome means that Beijing still doesn't accept new blood that is professional, young and enthusiastic. It totally reflected the narrow representation of local NPC deputies. I suspect the pre-election result raised an alarm with those who fared poorly and prompted them to put pressure on the Central Government Liaison Office to give them more support.[38]

The Chairman of the Liberal Party, James Tien, publicly complained that the Liaison Office and pro-Beijing groups orchestrated the election results. He said:

> I am very unhappy that only two of our candidates were voted in. I believe the Beijing Liaison Office in Hong Kong, the Hong Kong Progressive

The Election of the Hong Kong Deputies to the National People's Congress   191

Table 7.2   Election Results of the Hong Kong Deputies to the Tenth National People's Congress

Rank	Candidate	Background	Votes in Second Round (Votes in First Round)	Change in the Number of Votes
1.	Rita Fan	President of Legislative Council	859 (628)	+231
2.	Wang Rudeng	Assistant Director of the Liaison Office	853 (636)	+217
3.	Ng Ching-fai	President of Baptist University	838 (544)	+294
4.	Cheng Yiu-tong	Chairman of Federation of Trade Unions	831 (484)	+347
5.	Maria Tam	Hong Kong Progressive Alliance	831 (687)	+144
6.	Wilfred Wong	Vice-Chair of Shui On Holdings	825 (517)	+308
7.	Ma Lik	Deputy Editor, Hong Kong Commercial Daily; DAB member	818 (528)	+290
8.	Yeung Yiu-chung	Legislator, DAB member	812 (484)	+328
9.	Peter Wong	Industrialist	810 (486)	+324
10.	Robin Chan Yau-hing	Chairman of Chinese General Chamber of Commerce	795 (615)	+180
11.	Raymond Wu	Hong Kong Progressive Alliance	783 (601)	+182
12.	Tsang Tak-sing	Adviser of Central Policy Unit	767 (463)	+304
13.	Fei Feh	Board member of Chinese Chamber of Commerce	748 (466)	+282
14.	Yuen Mo	Vice-President of China Merchants Holdings	731 (464)	+267
15.	Tso Wung-wai	Biochemist at Chinese University of Hong Kong; Hong Kong Progressive Alliance	731 (525)	+206
16.	Ip Kwok-him	Legislator, DAB member	725 (449)	+276
17.	Ma Fung-kwok	Legislator, New Century Forum	700 (473)	+227
18.	Ng Hong-mun	Director of Pui Kiu College; DAB member	697 (439)	+258

Table 7.2 (continued)

Rank	Candidate	Background	Votes in Second Round (Votes in First Round)	Change in the Number of Votes
19.	Carson Wen	Solicitor	694 (464)	+230
20.	Tang Hin-chi	Goldlion Holdings Chairman	676 (537)	+139
21.	Lam Kwong-siu	Bank of China (Hong Kong) Deputy Chief Executive	669 (534)	+135
22.	David Chu	Legislator, Member of Hong Kong Progressive Alliance	646 (546)	+100
23.	Sik Chi-wai	Abbot Reverend of Po Lin Monastery	642 (505)	+137
24.	Joseph Lee	Businessman, Former Youth Commission Board member	641 (422)	+219
25.	Lau Pui-king	DAB member, Academic at Polytechnic University	613 (389)	+224
26.	Lee Chark-tim	Adviser of Federation of Trade Unions	610 (385)	+225
27.	Allen Lee	Former Chairman of Liberal Party	593 (544)	+49
28.	Philip Wong	Legislator	584 (414)	+170
29.	Lo Suk-ching	General Secretary of New Territories Association of Societies	580 (372)	+208
30.	Wong Kwok-kin	General Secretary of Federation of Trade Unions	572 (443)	+129
31.	Victor Sit	Academic at the University of Hong Kong	554 (414)	+140
32.	Lee Lin-sang	Honorary President of New Territories Association of Societies	547 (346)	+201
33.	Sophie Lau	Legislator, member of Liberal Party	540 (502)	+38
34.	Ng Leung-sing	Legislator	539 (471)	+68
35.	Kan Fok-yee	Barrister	539 (398)	+141
36.	Ko Po-ling	Member of Equal Opportunities Commission, Chair of New Territories Association for Societies	530 (458)	+72

Sources: *Hong Kong iMail*, December 4, 2002, p. 9; *China Daily*, December 4, 2002, p. 1; *Hong Kong Economic Journal*, December 4, 2002, p. 7; *Ming Pao*, December 4, 2002, p. A4; *Oriental Daily*, December 4, 2002, p. A27; *Apple Daily*, November 30, 2002, p. A15.

Alliance, the Federation of Trade Unions and the DAB have coordinated the votes against us. On the one hand they said more people should participate in national affairs, but on the other they blockaded parties that are on good terms with the pro-Beijing camp and want to contribute to the mainland and the HKSAR. They have poured Beijing's rice away.[39]

Mr. Tien went so far as to assert that the pro-Beijing groups had circulated a number of candidates' lists among voters, and that none of the lists prior to the second round of voting had recommended the voters to support candidates of the Liberal Party. He also claimed that the central government in Beijing was not aware of the recommended lists that were prepared by the Liaison Office in Hong Kong.[40] While Tien was critical of the role of the Liaison Office, democrat Martin Lee viewed it as "a shadow government" meddling in "elections at every possible level," including the chief executive election, coordinating with pro-Beijing forces in Legislative Council and District Council elections, and raising funds for the DAB.[41]

In response to Tien's public remarks, some members of the Election Conference criticized him for being "mean" and "narrow-minded" in suggesting that political manipulations had been made to prevent his candidates from being elected as local NPC delegates.[42] Xu Ximin said that Tien's criticisms were "unfair," whereas Leung Fu-wah, a legislator of the FTU, suspected Tien of trying to trade favors with Beijing by making complaints.[43] Cheng Yiu-tong, Chairman of the FTU, denied telling members to vote against candidates of the Liberal Party. Yet the DAB Chairman Jasper Tsang Yok-sing implied that there were recommended lists. He said: "The DAB did not have its recommended list, but it was possible that my subordinates might have their own lists. I cannot exclude this possibility."[44] Tsang admitted that he had not supported any candidate of the Liberal Party, and that he had exchanged views with the FTU and the HKPA on who to vote for. Ip Kwok-him, the DAB vice-chairman, said: "Of course, we have our own lists of who to vote for, what's so special? Do we have to vote for the Liberal Party?"[45]

The Chairman of the Hong Kong Progressive Alliance (HKPA) Ambrose Lau reacted strongly to Tien's remarks, saying that the HKPA only had six of the twelve candidates elected in the first round, and that the Liberal Party should not adopt a mentality of acting as "a ruling party" in Hong Kong.[46] Lee Cho-chak, the spokesman for the Chair Group, said: "Many political groups want to have their representatives participate in ruling the country. I think you should not laugh because your candidates won, and cry foul when your candidates lost."[47] The pro-Beijing President of the Chinese Manufacturers' Association Chan Wing-kee, who abandoned to run for re-election, maintained that the Liaison Office had no recommended list.[48] Chan said it was possible for groups and parties to put forward recommended lists. According to Chan, someone had set him up and made it look as if he had circulated the candidate lists.[49]

Officials of the Liaison Office reacted to Tien's remarks cautiously. Wang Rudeng, who obtained the second highest number of votes in the final round, reacted to Tien's charges in a diplomatic way. Wang remarked that he expressed his gratitude to the Liberal Party whose recommended list had his name.[50] According to Wang, he himself had to lobby for political support from the members of the Election Conference, calling them and attending election forums. Gao Siren, the director of the Liaison Office, said: "I can definitely tell you that the Liaison Office has no lists."[51]

The mass media reacted to the election results in varying ways, ranging from criticism to applause. According to an editorial in *Ming Pao*,

> [S]ome incumbents of low reputation were re-elected though they had done poorly in the first round. Some candidates received vastly different numbers of votes in the first round and the second. Leftist newspapers ran stories giving electors guidance. And lists of "recommended candidates" circulated among electors. People therefore suspect the election was rigged. That will greatly damage local NPC deputies' credibility . . . [B]oth the first round of voting and the second seemed manipulated by an invisible hand. In the first round, Dennis Lam, Ma Ho-fai, Raymond Chien, Howard Young, Raymond Ho and Wong Yuk-shan won high votes. They ranked among the top 36 and seemed certain to be returned to the NPC. [But] none of them succeeded . . . The NPC election was convoluted. It involved political wresting and distribution of interests beyond candidates' comprehension. A winner need not hold himself accountable to any group. His re-election would have little to do with his performance. Such an election is not credible, nor would it make it easier for local NPC deputies to discharge their duties.[52]

Commenting on Tien's criticisms, Chris Yeung wrote:

> By accusing the pro-Beijing camp of blocking candidates through tactical voting . . . , he perhaps assumed all would be fair, which was never going to be the case . . . Many people are resigned to the fact that the NPC poll has always been a "small-circle election" with predictable results. Only candidates either in, or close to, the inner circle of the pro-Beijing camp are able to win a seat in the extremely competitive polls . . . It would be politically naïve of Mr. Lee and Mr. Tien if they ever believed the Liberal

Party was considered a member of the pro-Beijing camp. The truth is that the united front loosely pulled together by the Liaison Office remains a narrow-based coalition marked by factionalism and conflicting interests. This is despite token signs of liberalization in the electoral procedures, including the expansion of the size of the Election Conference from 440 members to 950. The fact that five democrats were able to secure enough nominations to stand for the first round of polls gave the sense of a genuine election, but not for long . . . [T]he complaint by Mr. Tien revealed the truth behind an election with Chinese characteristics.[53]

It appeared that Yeung revised his optimistic view prior to the elections and that he emphasized the NPC election "with Chinese characteristics." Nonetheless, the *China Daily* hailed the election as "open, impartial and fair."[54] It editorialized:

The election was a remarkable event in the political life of the Special Administrative Region. Through their deputies, the SAR's more than 6 million residents are able to make their voices heard at the country's supreme law-making body and, therefore, to have a meaningful say in running a country with a population of more than 1 billion. This was something impossible during the pre-handover era. Before 1997, Hong Kong deputies to the NPC were chosen in the neighboring constituency of Guangdong Province. Hong Kong as an independent constituency was only made possible after the handover . . . Another difference is that a candidate contesting the previous race needed only a relative majority or more than 50 percent of the votes cast to survive. This makes the election fairer and more impartial.[55]

Inside Politics of the Election

According to Allen Lee, there were three recommended name lists — A, B, and C as he called them — in the first round of voting.[56] List A was composed of twenty-one names, whose background included business and professional sectors. List B also had twenty-one names from the educational sector, representatives from the grassroots level, and working-class activists. According to Lee, his name was on List A during the first round of voting, whereas Ng Hong-man was on List B. List C comprised twelve people including Lam Shun-chiu, Ma Ho-fai, and Raymond Chien. Lee did not reveal the origins of the three lists. But he said that members of the Election Conference who received the three lists were encouraged to cast the ballots for one of the two following options: (1) List A and List C, or (2) List B and List C. Each of the two options had thirty-three candidates, while the three lists had a total of fifty-four candidates. The objective of the three lists, according to Lee, was to oust the democrats during the first round of voting.

When some members of the Election Conference followed the recommendations on how to vote for candidates of Lists A, B, and C, it was natural that candidates of List C would receive lots of votes in the first round of voting. The reason was that List C overlapped in the two options, according to Lee. In the second round of voting, however, there were about six lists prepared by political parties and groups. The four major lists, according to Lee, were prepared by (1) members of the Chinese People's Political Consultative Conference (CPPCC), (2) the DAB members, (3) the Hong Kong Progressive Alliance, and (4) the Fujian and Guangdong Federations of Societies. Lee remarked that the Liaison Office was like "another government" in the HKSAR.[57] Judging from the Liaison Office's close relationships with the CPPCC members, DAB, HKPA and the united front groups such as Fujian and Guangdong Federation of Societies, it was not surprising that the "shadow government" had probably endorsed the name lists. One DAB member who supported Lee expressed anger at the election results in which Lee's number of votes slightly increased but others' drastically improved.[58]

According to Chan Tung, a pseudonym for an insider of the pro-Beijing circle, the Liaison Office had two "duties" in the NPC election, namely to prevent the democrats from being elected and to guarantee the smooth process of electing some candidates.[59] The ability of the Liaison Office to "allocate votes" could be seen in the election of Rita Fan (859 votes) and in the success of Wang Rudeng (853 votes). To Chan, even if there were recommended lists prepared by the Liaison Office, they could not be very detailed because there were different interest groups under its influence.[60] If the Liaison Office had recommended lists, Ngai Shiu-kit and Lo Chung-hing seemed to be excluded from them, for Ngai was replaced by David Chu and Lo replaced by Lam Kwong-siu.[61] Chan concluded that the Liaison Office might put forward recommended name lists, but it could not control the election results.

While there is insufficient evidence to point to the Liaison Office's involvement in the dynamics of the electoral process, the fluctuating results appeared to indicate a considerable degree of influence from the Liaison Office. If Lee's claims were accurate, they could reflect the complexities behind the political calculations of the Liaison Office, which remained a powerful actor in shaping the election results.

Conclusion

There was no survey conducted by any research institute in Hong Kong on the representativeness of the Hong Kong NPC members; nevertheless, given the fact that the PRC Government handpicked them, their mandate remains limited and questionable. On the other hand, some of the Hong Kong NPC members are aware of their legitimacy problem and have thereby raised the question of setting up their offices in the HKSAR. Yet given the reluctance of the Liaison Office to consider enhancing the deputies' legitimacy in the minds of the Hong Kong people, their demand of having offices in Hong Kong remains an unfulfilled mission. In September 2005, the Liaison Office suggested that the Hong Kong NPC members could open their office inside its building in the Western District. Due to the concern amongst some NPC members that few citizens would like to enter the official Chinese representative office for help, they did not find the idea of the Liaison Office attractive. From the perspective of united front strategy, as long as the Hong Kong NPC members can be mobilized to support various PRC policies toward the HKSAR, they are politically instrumental. The election of the Hong Kong NPC members is of critical importance because their political loyalty can facilitate the PRC governing strategy toward the HKSAR. On the other hand, some Hong Kong NPC members do participate actively in the annual NPC meeting in Beijing, voicing their views that can contribute tremendously to the socio-economic development of the motherland.

The second election held for the Hong Kong deputies to the Tenth NPC showed that the election results were influenced by behind-the-scene political mobilization and strategic calculations. While different pro-Beijing groups and parties lobbied for support and tried to have their candidates elected, the pro-democracy candidates were politically excluded from participation in the final round of voting. However, the fact that the democrats were allowed to participate in the first round of voting showed a limited degree of political toleration. The entire election outcome appeared to be shaped, if not controlled, skillfully by the pro-Beijing elites who dominated the Election Conference. Although there was no concrete evidence to illustrate the role of the Liaison Office in the election process, it seemed to play the role of mobilizing members of the Election Conference to vote in certain ways. The selection of the Hong Kong delegates to the Tenth NPC of the PRC undoubtedly remained an election with "Chinese characteristics." Perhaps the most important "Chinese characteristic" in the election held for Hong Kong members of the NPC is that the political loyalty of candidates to the CCP appeared to be the decisive factor contributing to the greater chances of their electoral victory. Although there is no concrete evidence to prove that most of the elected candidates were affiliated with the CCP, all of them were consistently and largely supportive of Beijing's policy toward the Hong Kong Special Administrative Region. In brief, the degree of political loyalty of candidates emerged as the determining factor shaping their success in the election held for the Hong Kong deputies to China's NPC.

The Hong Kong NPC elections for Taiwan have an important bearing on the future cross-Strait negotiations. First, any Beijing-Taipei negotiation and settlement may consider the idea of allowing the people of Taiwan to select their deputies to the NPC on the mainland. It is unclear whether this idea will be accepted by the majority of the Taiwan elites and masses, but arguably having Taiwan deputies in the NPC can help the island articulate its interests more effectively, and it will also facilitate the mainland's socio-economic development. The crux of the problem is whether some Taiwan pro-independence elites will see the NPC as a mainland law-making body in which the Taiwanese should not get involved. From the perspective of the pro-Taiwan independence supporters, the Legislative Yuan is their own parliament, not the mainland NPC. Unless a strong political incentive can be established, many pro-independence Taiwanese will not see the usage and benefits of having their deputies represented in the NPC on the mainland.

Alternatively, any Taiwan deputies who are supposed to articulate their interest in the mainland, especially for those Taiwan business people and residents living in the PRC, may be elected by the Taiwan people and then represented in the CPPCC. But the problem is that the CPPCC is a consultative and not a law-making body. Ideally the Taiwanese will perhaps be persuaded to articulate their interests by selecting some representatives to the NPC in Beijing.

Finally, the possible involvement of Beijing's agents in the Hong Kong NPC election should arguably not be seen in any Taiwan counterpart in the future. Beijing will need to ensure that Taiwan's political autonomy will be substantial rather than cosmetic. In January 2008, 36 Hong Kong NPC members were elected by an Election Conference in which 1,169 of the 1,231 members cast their ballots. Four democrats failed to be elected due to the numerical majority of pro-Beijing loyalists. This mainland style of clients-dominated and limited electoral competition remains unappealing to the majority of the Taiwan citizens, who are imbued with a democratic culture of viewing elections as genuine competition among political parties for power.

8

A Fusion of Mainland Chinese and Hong Kong Political Cultures in the 2007 Chief Executive Election

Since the return of Hong Kong's sovereignty to the PRC, democratization in the HKSAR has been proceeding slowly mainly due to a serious clash of political cultures between the pro-democracy Hongkongers and Beijing.[1] The pro-democracy forces contend that the pace of democratic reforms in the HKSAR has to be accelerated immediately, including the selection of the chief executive by universal suffrage and the direct election of the entire LegCo. However, Beijing and the HKSAR government maintain that democratization has to proceed in a gradual and orderly manner. From Beijing's perspective, democratic reforms in the HKSAR cannot allow the pro-democracy forces to control half of the LegCo seats, for such democratic victory would constitute a serious menace to the executive-led nature of the HKSAR government and the politico-economic as well as the security interest of the central government.[2] Most democrats do not see their possible dominance in the legislature as a security threat to either the HKSAR administration or Beijing. Moreover, while Beijing views some democrats as an agent of foreign nation-states to shape and influence the pace and scope of democratization in the HKSAR, the democrats regard their communications with Western governments as natural without any conspiratorial motives. Above all, Beijing does not see democratization in the HKSAR as a necessity, for it believes that Hong Kong should not only be depoliticized but also focus on economic development. The Hong Kong democrats view democratization as a necessity because they argue that the maladministration of the Tung era proved that the institutional defect in the HKSAR has to be remedied by the acceleration of democratic reforms.

The divergent perspectives of Beijing and the Hong Kong democrats on the desirability, pace, scope, and impact of democratic reforms in the HKSAR reflect the underlying differences in the political cultures of the two sides. The political culture of Beijing is distrustful of Western-style democratization, wary of its impact on the HKSAR executive-led system, and sees economic prosperity as a substitute for political democracy. Vicky Randall argues convincingly that the traditional Chinese political culture is "antithetical to liberal democratic values."[3] As a political sandwich and a local administration upholding the principle of executive dominance over the legislature, the HKSAR leadership is destined to side with the central government's perspectives. While Beijing must back up the cautious position of the HKSAR government on democratization, the pro-democracy forces are bound to adopt a more confrontational attitude partly because of the need to appeal to their supporters in elections, and partly due to their bias in favor of Western-style democratic reforms as a political panacea. The clash of political culture between Beijing and the HKSAR ruling elite on the one hand and the Hong Kong pro-democracy forces on the other hand has remained the most prominent hallmark of Beijing-HKSAR relations since July 1, 1997.

Nevertheless, as this chapter will prove, the divergent political cultures of Beijing and the HKSAR ruling elite on the one hand and the Hong Kong democrats on the other can be amalgamated into a unique style of democratization. In other words, the ways in which the chief executive elections were conducted represented a fusion of the mainland Chinese and Hong Kong political cultures in the path of democratization in the HKSAR. Specifically, the mainland Chinese political culture of patrimonialism and the Hong Kong political tradition of pluralistic competition could be merged, representing an act and a spirit of compromise that will have further room for development in the future.

Democratization, Patrimonialism, and Pluralism

Little academic research has been conducted on Hong Kong's democratization by taking into account the mainland Chinese and Hong Kong political cultures. From a practical perspective, however, the pan-democrats and the Anson Chan group published their political reform blueprints, but no attempt was made to address the characteristics of mainland Chinese and Hong Kong political cultures.[4]

Patrimonialism can be defined as an exchange process in which the political patrons reward their supportive clients with politico-economic benefits. It is frequently "linked with or treated as synonymous with patron-client relations."[5] In a patrimonial state, "the ruler's power depend[s] on his capacity to win and retain the loyalty of key sectors of the political elite. Lacking sufficient coercive capacity to enforce acceptance of his rule, the ruler [seeks] to win voluntary allegiance by satisfying the aspirations — especially the material interests — of his supporters through the distribution of fiefs and benefices in exchange for tribute and loyalty."[6] Factional politics are another hallmark of patrimonial states, where the ruler has to maintain his or her political authority "by preserving the balance among the competing cliques."[7] While it is beyond the scope of this article to examine how the PRC factionalism may have shaped the HKSAR politics, patron-client relations have become the hallmark of Hong Kong politics since its retrocession to the motherland.[8]

Mainland Chinese politics have traditionally been characterized by patrimonialism, including extensive patron-client networks and factional struggle.[9] Factional struggle characterized the politics of Tang, Sung, Yuan, Ming, and Ching dynasties.[10] It also persists throughout the history of the CCP.[11] Patron-client networks have been shaping the leadership of the CCP, the recruitment of its members, and Beijing's personnel control over the HKSAR.[12] To ensure the selection of a politically loyal chief executive of the HKSAR, the central government in Beijing has to rely on patron-client networks in the process of the chief executive election.

On the other hand, the HKSAR is marked by a political culture that emphasizes governmental responsiveness, transparency, accountability, the rule of law, and pluralistic competition. These values are arguably incompatible with the mainland Chinese political culture punctuated by governmental authority, secrecy, clientelism, the rule by law, and loyal opposition.[13] Yet in the context of the 2007 chief executive elections, as this chapter will show, the long-cherished Hong Kong value of pluralistic competition was mixed practically with the mainland Chinese proclivity toward political control and patrimonialism. The HKSAR democrats were divided into two groups: a mainstream faction willing to nominate a candidate in a politically constrained competition, and another non-mainstream group advocating a boycott of the "undemocratic" election. The former group believed that by participating in the "undemocratic election," it would project an image of loyal opposition and maximize its bargaining power *vis-à-vis* both the HKSAR government and Beijing in the long run.

The Transformation of Democrats from Confrontational Politics to Loyal Opposition

The relationships between the pro-democracy forces, including both the mainstream and non-mainstream factions, and the Tung Chee-hwa administration from July 1997 to March 2005 were sour and marked by mutual distrusts. The abortive attempt of the Tung regime to legislate on Article 23 of the Basic Law, which requires the HKSAR government to enact laws on its own to combat treason, subversion, and sedition, led to a public outcry and the protests by an estimate of one million citizens on July 1, 2003.[14] This misrule of the Tung regime could not pacify the anger of the public, culminating in another massive protest by at least 250,000 people on July 1, 2004. The sudden resignation of Tung Chee-hwa on the grounds of personal health in March 2005 paved the way for the succession of the former British-trained bureaucrat-turned-politician Donald Tsang Yam-kuen. Tsang and his lieutenant Raphael Hui came up with a political reform blueprint, which was unfortunately rejected by 24 pro-democracy legislators on December 21, 2005.[15] The government proposals sought to double the size of the Election Committee from 800 to 1,600 in 2007, including a move to add all 529 District Councillors. The second part of the proposals was to add ten seats to the Legislative Council, including five from geographical constituencies and another five from functional constituencies. The democrats argued that the 102 appointed District Councils members should be excluded from the reform proposals. The government needed at least six of the 25 democrats in the legislature to break ranks so that the reform proposals could be passed.[16] Yet it failed. The pan-democratic camp's blockage to Tsang's reform package brought their relationship to a nadir.

The decision of the pan-democratic camp's candidate Alan Leong Ka-kit to participate in the 2007 chief executive election had a significant bearing in repairing the damage done on Tsang's reform plan in December 2005. Critics of Leong, notably the members of the League of Social Democrats, argued that his participation served to legitimize the "small-circle election," and that boycotting the election would maximize the political leverage of the pan-democratic camp *vis-à-vis* the Tsang regime. This stance, however, was rejected by the mainstream democrats, who believed that they would have to win back the confidence of the moderate Hongkongers by participating in the chief executive elections as a loyal opposition. A survey conducted by the Hong Kong Transition Project showed that 67 percent of the 800 respondents in December supported Tsang's political reform proposal of enlarging the number of Election Committee members.[17] Another poll demonstrated that 36 percent of 403 respondents in November supported LegCo members to pass the Tsang reform proposals, whereas 37 percent opposed.[18] Due to the split in public opinion, some citizens did have reservations about the pan-democratic camp's rejection of Tsang's democratic reform blueprint. In early 2007, the mainstream democrats had two options in face of the chief executive elections: participation or boycott. Participation would prove to the people of Hong Kong that they were rational and accepted the confines of the "small-circle election." Nonetheless, the democrats could still maximize the limited political space within a "bird cage democracy." Above all, the pan-democratic camp's participation would demonstrate to Beijing that they were moderates rather than "pro-independence" radicals, fighting for more democratic reforms within the parameters of the Basic Law. In a nutshell, participation could turn the pan-democrats into a loyal opposition acceptable to both Beijing and the HKSAR ruling elites. As the pan-democratic camp's candidate Alan Leong Kah-kit argued, although he would certainly be defeated, his participation would represent a win-win situation in which the people of Hong Kong enjoyed the fruits of their participation. The "small-circle election" was forced to be more transparent, more accountable to the public, and more competitive than ever before. The most prominent benefit of the pan-democratic camp's participation was an amalgamation of Hong Kong's political culture of pluralistic competition with the mainland Chinese tradition of personnel control and acceptance of a loyal opposition.

The Politics of Nomination

During the election of the members of the Election Committee on December 10, 2006, the political supporters and clients of Beijing unexpectedly encountered setbacks. The legal profession witnessed the defeat of moderate and pro-Beijing barristers, including the famous barrister Cheng Huan. In the higher education sector, a number of university administrators were defeated, including Lee Chack-fan of the University of Hong Kong and Wong Yuk-shan of the City University of Hong Kong. All the pro-democracy academics were elected, including Kuan Hsin-chi, Joseph Cheng Yu-shek, Michael DeGolyer, and Kenneth Chan Ka-lok. The pro-democracy academics formed a united front, diligently sending emails to seek the support of the voters in the higher education sub-sector.[19] The victory of the pan-democrats in key sectors such as higher education and law indicated that they would have a golden opportunity of nominating a pro-democracy candidate to compete with Donald Tsang.

Nevertheless, a closer look at the composition of the Election Committee and its competitiveness in the selection process can reveal the mainland Chinese style of political control. The 800 members of the Election Committee came from four sectors: 664 were elected from 35 sub-sectors; 40 members were nominated by the religious sub-sectors; and 96 were actually ex-officio members including the Hong Kong deputies to the NPC and members of the Legislative Council.[20] However, many sub-sectors did not have to hold any election. Of the 200 members returning from the first sector, 105 of them were uncontested.[21] Those sub-sectors that witnessed competition included financial services, hotel, insurance, real estate and construction, textile and garment, tourism, transport, and wholesale and retail. The second sector tended to be the most competitive because all of its members had to compete in the elections. The third sector, however, was far less competitive; 40 of the 160 members in the sector did not have to compete in elections, notably the uncontested candidates in the labor, sports, and agriculture and fisheries sub-sectors. The fourth sector was equally non-competitive as 62 of the total of 104 "elected" members were uncontested. Overall, a total of 387 members out of 800 members of the Election Committee underwent the electoral competition — almost half of the electors who voted for the chief executive candidates. Furthermore, while 204,646 citizens registered as voters in the selection of the Election Committee members, the voter turnout was merely 27.43 percent.[22] From the perspective of pluralism, the process of selecting members of the Election Committee was only partially democratic and combined with a certain degree of political control. Those sub-sectors that did not envisage any election simply fielded in uncontested candidates through hidden political compromises, particularly the business professions and many grassroots-level occupations such as agriculture and fisheries. The lack of competitiveness in many sub-sectors was a testimony to the mainland Chinese style of political restrictions, whereas the partially competitive sub-sectors demonstrated the pluralistic side of Hong Kong's political culture.

Leong announced in late January 2007 that he secured the support of at least 100 members of the Election Committee and therefore could participate in the chief executive election.[23] On the other hand, Donald Tsang visited the DAB and Liberal Party (LP) headquarters, trying to garner a high number of nominations for his re-election bid. According to the LP Chairman James Tien, Tsang promised that if he were re-elected, his cooperation with the Liberal Party would be enhanced further.[24] Tien said that the LP would provide the support of 110 members of the Election Committee. This reciprocal exchange between the Liberal Party and Tsang was a testimony to the patrimonial style of politics in the HKSAR.

Before Tsang's visit, Tien had strategically predicted that there would be 50 blank votes in the chief executive election, implying that his LP members might not fully support Tsang. When Tsang arrived at the LP headquarters on February 6, Tien denied that he had made such prediction, and that his party members would select one of the "much sweeter apples."[25] Tien played a critical role in the Article 23 debacle in July 2003, when he suddenly withdrew from the Executive Council so that the Tung Chee-hwa administration would not be able to secure the LP support in the Legislative Council for the national security legislation. Isolated by Tien so abruptly, Tung was forced to postpone the enactment of Article 23 of the Basic Law indefinitely. Viewing his LP as a "kingmaker" and the second largest political client following the pro-Beijing Democratic Alliance for Betterment of Hong Kong (DAB), Tien deliberately showed his political muscle before the March 2007 chief executive election so that Tsang would have to reciprocate the LP support later.

The DAB, being more loyal to the central government in Beijing than the LP, did not intentionally project a patron–client network with Tsang during his electioneering. The pro-Beijing party's previously critical attitude toward Tsang's "pro-British" background when he ran for the chief executive election in 2004 embarrassed Beijing, which did not want to envisage an outright struggle between its clientelist party and preferred chief executive in the HKSAR. In 2007, the DAB Chairman Ma Lik said that Tsang responded to his party's concerns "satisfactorily," and that 40 DAB members of the Election Committee supported Tsang.[26] The DAB also urged Tsang to listen to the views of the public and to improve their already "friendly relationships."[27] It acted as a channel through which Tsang tapped the views of the ordinary citizens. For example, the party orchestrated an activity named "how to do better on this job" for Tsang to interact with ordinary citizens in eighteen districts. The DAB Vice-Chairman Ip Kwok-him admitted that the party coordinated Tsang's campaign office so that he would be able to visit some households and conduct his "direct election campaign" at the grassroots level.[28]

Prior to the nomination period, Beijing and Tsang's supporters were worrying whether the former chief secretary Anson Chan Fang On-sang would participate in the chief executive election. Due to her popularity and charisma, Chan's participation could have been a serious threat to

Tsang. Chan announced her decision not to participate in September 2006 due to the major concern that the election result was already "predetermined."[29] Given that most members of the Election Committee were pro-Beijing and would vote for her former colleague Donald Tsang, Chan decided to avoid contesting in an unwinnable and clientelist political show. Since Chan's decision not to participate in the chief executive election, her influence on Hong Kong politics has declined, according to the Hong Kong NPC member Allen Lee Peng-fei.[30] Chan's victory over Regina Ip in the LegCo by-election in December 2007 helped her regain some degree of political influence.

Tsang worked hard to secure the nominations of the Election Committee members. When he met the representatives of the entertainment, culture, fisheries, and religious sectors, he expressed his determination to hold a high-level meeting that would involve societal enterprises, business and non-governmental organizations so that the unemployed would have their situation improved.[31] One Taoist member of the Election Committee complained that Tsang had never attended Taoist activities since the HKSAR return to the PRC, and Tsang promised that he would attend their functions despite the fact that he is a Catholic.[32]

The nomination of Tsang and Leong was viewed as a crucial pre-election battle. Tsang got 641 nominations whereas Leong obtained 132 supporters from the Election Committee. From the perspective of pluralistic competition, Leong scored an impressive victory as the 132 nominations surprised most observers. In Table 1, Leong succeeded in getting the support of the members of the Election Committee from the education, higher education, health, information and technology, legal, and social welfare sectors. Tsang got the overwhelming support of the business professions, which were the *de facto* clients of Beijing, but he failed to achieve any inroads into the education, higher education, social welfare, and particularly the legal profession where none of the lawyers nominated him (see Table 8.1). Leong's nomination success was hailed as "a democratic milestone," for it was the first time in the HKSAR history that a pro-democracy candidate could compete in the chief executive elections.[33] Nevertheless, four pro-democracy legislators who boycotted the chief executive elections did not nominate Leong. They included Emily Lau, Leung Yiu-chung, Albert Chan Wai-yip, and Leung Kwok-hung. Moreover, Albert Cheng King-hon openly said that he nominated Tsang.[34]

Table 8.1 The Support of Donald Tsang and Alan Leong in the Nomination Process

Sector	Number of Electors	Number Supportive of Tsang	Number Supportive of Leong	Abstention
The First Sector				
Financial Services	12	12	0	0
Hotel	11	11	0	0
Insurance	12	12	0	0
Real Estate and Construction	12	12	0	0
Textile and Garment	12	12	0	0
Tourism	12	12	0	0
Transport	12	12	0	0
Wholesale and retail	12	12	0	0
Catering	11	11	0	0
Commerce	24	24	0	0
Employers	11	11	0	0
Mainland Chinese Enterprises				
Finance	12	12	0	0
Import and Export	12	12	0	0
Industry	24	24	0	0
The Second Sector				
Accountancy	20	11	7	2
Architecture, surveying and planning	20	18	1	1
Chinese Medicine	20	20	0	0
Education	20	3	15	2
Engineering	20	12	8	0
Health Services	20	14	6	0
Higher Education	20	2	16	2
Information Technology	20	11	9	0
Legal	20	0	19	1
Medical	20	17	1	2
The Third Sector				
Labor	40	38	0	2
Social Welfare	40	9	31	0
Sports, Performing Arts, Culture and publications	40	40	0	0
Agriculture and fisheries	40	40	0	0
The Fourth Sector				
Hong Kong and Kowloon District Councils	21	21	0	0
New Territories District Councils	21	21	0	0
Chinese People's Political Consultative Conference	41	41	0	0

Table 8.1 *(continued)*

Sector	Number of Electors	Number Supportive of Tsang	Number Supportive of Leong	Abstention
Heung Yee Kuk	21	21	0	0
Religious Catholics	7	6	1	0
Confucius	7	7	0	0
Islamic	6	6	0	0
Taoist	6	6	0	0
Buddhist	7	7	0	0
Christian	7	4	3	0
Legislators	60	35	18	7★
Hong Kong Members of National People's Congress	36	31	0	1★★

Source: *Sing Tao Daily*, February 17, 2007, p. B7.

★ They included Legislative Council President Rita Fan, Lau Chin-shek, Leung Yiu-chung, Leung Kwok-hung, Chan Wai-yip, Emily Lau, and Leong Kah-kit.

★★ He was Allen Lee Peng-fei.

The Pluralistic Style of Political Campaign

The campaign styles of both Tsang and Leong, however, were in conformity with Hong Kong's tradition of pluralistic competition. At the early phase of his campaign, Tsang appeared to have difficulties in garnering the unquestionable support of the business elites. One businessman challenged him, saying that being the chief executive was not simply fulfilling the duties and responsibilities of a job, but the position entailed ideals and leadership.[35] Many other business members of the Election Committee shared this view in the closed-door discussion with Tsang on February 3 and 4. Some businessmen requested that Tsang clarify his new batch of principal officials if he were re-elected. Tsang responded to the queries, saying that the new line-up of principal officials would be younger and that he would groom a team of new leaders for the HKSAR.

The annual budget prepared by Financial Secretary Henry Tang was criticized by the democrats as a deliberate preparation for Tsang's re-election bid. Tang delivered a number of tax benefits to the people of Hong Kong, including the reduction of stamp duty and other taxes, such as the rates, the salary tax and the tax on red wine.[36] About 1.35 million tax payers enjoyed various tax reductions, while 1 million elderly and needy citizens were the beneficiaries of tax refunds and of additional welfare payment.[37] The feel-good factor acted as a morale booster for Tsang, whose victory in the chief executive elections was arguably preceded by additional rewards to citizens in the midst of economic prosperity. Critics charged that the budget distributed "a can of candy" to the middle class but meager benefits to the lower classes, but Tang denied that his budgetary policy was shaped by any intention of campaigning for Tsang, and that he autonomously made budgetary decisions.[38] Intentionally or unintentionally, Tang's budget served as a pre-election campaign move to help his patron, Tsang, buy the political support of the ordinary citizens.

Assisted by the budgetary policy of his client Tang, Tsang was emboldened to launch an aggressive attack on Leong. Tsang criticized Leong and the democrats for being preoccupied with political slogans and for using the "two systems" as a shield to confront with one country.[39] During the campaign debate, Tsang also angrily denied that the government was biased in favor of the big business. He remarked that his bosses embraced those "who are rich and not rich, who have power and who do not have power, and who have votes and those who have no votes."[40] What Tsang emphasized was in conformity with the principle of harmony advocated by his patron, Beijing.

Leong challenged the authority of the central government in Beijing by raising the idea that the Basic Law's stipulation of requiring the central government to approve the appointment of principal officials made by the chief executive should be repealed. This suggestion provoked the angry response from the pro-Beijing media, some moderate commentators, and the patriotic Hong Kong elites such as the Hong Kong member of the NPC Standing Committee Tsang Hin-chi.[41] Defending his proposal, Leong contended that communications between Beijing, the people of Hong Kong and various sectors could be enhanced prior to any implementation of his long-term suggestion of repealing the stipulation. In a sense, Leong deliberately put forward a provocative idea that challenged Beijing's authority.

Leong and Tsang's political platforms were very different. In Table 8.2, Leong projected a much clearer image in his fight for democratization in the HKSAR, whereas Tsang adopted a procrastinating attitude. Leong skillfully emphasized the fact that although he would surely lose, the people of Hong Kong would win the election.[42] What he meant was that the people of Hong Kong should realize the "ridiculous" aspect of the "small circle election," namely a directly elected legislator could not have a realistic possibility of defeating the central government-supported but non–directly elected incumbent Tsang.[43] Leong also forced Tsang to tackle policy issues raised in the live televised debate forums, including education, the policy toward the poor and the needy, environmental protection, and the question of poverty.

Table 8.2 Comparison of Tsang and Leong's Political Platforms

Issues	Leong's Position	Tsang's Position
Date of Direct election	Not later than 2012	No direct response, but emphasized the need for further study
Chief Executive Election	1. Change the Election Committee into a Nomination Committee but 400 members directly elected by citizens should be added. 2. Lower the threshold of nominating the chief executive candidates from 100 to 50 members. 3. The Nominating Committee would not screen out the eligible candidates.	A consultative document would be published in mid-2007 and a full report would be submitted to the central government in Beijing by December 2007.
Legislative Council Election	1. Narrowing the currently five geographical constituencies and using the single vote single constituency system to elect 30 directly elected legislators. 2. Abolishing all functional constituencies in one single stroke, but using the entire HKSAR as a large constituency to allow political parties grasp the rest of the 30 seats through the proportional representation system. 3. Voters can cast their ballots in both the directly elected geographical constituencies and also the large territorial constituency that returns 30 members from the proportional representation system.	Same as above.

Apart from the varying campaign platforms, the most Hongkong-ized or Westernized style of the chief executive election could be seen in the candidates' debate forums. During the first live televised debate in early March, Leong adopted an aggressive tactic and succeeded in displaying his debating skills. Tsang adopted an overly conservative style and remained defensive throughout the debate. His conservatism was in conformity with a tendency of shunning a public forum held by members of the pan-democrats. Yet Leong did not shy away from participation in all forums and tried to force Tsang to appear publicly. Both went to different districts and interacted with ordinary citizens, attempting to bring about an ingredient of direct elections to the chief executive elections.

At the first candidates' campaign platform held by the Election Committee, Tsang introduced his plans to the electors, but nine pan-democrats protested against the requirement that voters had to submit written questions in advance to the candidates.[44] They requested that the host of the forum, Executive Council member Leung Chun-ying, should allow them to ask questions verbally, but their demand was rejected. Infuriated by Leung's decision, the nine democrats stood up and continued to raise their hands, but none of them was chosen to ask a question. The setting of the Election Committee's campaign platform was restrictive, mirroring the mainland Chinese style of political control.

During the second live televised debate on March 15, Tsang adopted a far more assertive approach to tackling Leong's arguments and positions. Tsang scored political points by emphasizing that Leong should not instigate class struggle in Hong Kong society, that universal suffrage was by no means a panacea to all the problems, that social harmony should be the developmental objective, and that Leong himself did not really understand the statistics and complexities of the government's budgetary and monetary policies.[45] When asked by the mass media whether the enactment of Article 23 of the Basic Law would be a priority before the issue of direct elections, Tsang answered that "this assumption is fundamentally flawed."[46] Even prior to the debate, he had revealed that "its enactment would be a necessity as the HKSAR has an obligation to do so, but the question is that the government will have to look for the ripe time."[47]

While Tsang shunned the issue of the national security law during the last debate, Leong maintained his outstanding performance in the second forum by pointing to the absence of any pro–Hong Kong independence activists, by exposing the governmental failure of tackling educational reform, by appealing to the poor and the powerless for the need to have universal suffrage, and by stressing the feasibility of using the massive HK$3,500 billion foreign reserves in local development.⁴⁸ He ended his concluding speech passionately by asking the audience to support universal suffrage — a powerful message that he succeeded in achieving his campaign objective.

Although the two forums were broadcast live to the public through major television and radio stations, only 196 ordinary citizens could participate in the second forum.⁴⁹ In the first debate, twenty-two questions were raised by Election Committee members, while six were selected at random from questions submitted by the public in advance.⁵⁰ Before the second debate, the campaign teams of Leong and Tsang negotiated with the media representatives and the organizers of the debate on whether more citizens should be allowed to participate in the second forum. Yet representatives of the local mass media publicly accused the Leong campaign team of politicizing the discussions. Given that many media representatives, proprietors, and editors prefer to choose the path of political correctness, it was perhaps natural that they tended to be critical of the Leong team rather than the Tsang supporters.⁵¹

Although Tsang's victory in the chief executive election was pre-determined due to the undemocratic nature of the composition of the Election Committee, the mass media depicted the campaign as pluralistic and competitive. Tsang's campaign strategy was described as a design to win the hearts and minds of the civil servants.⁵² The "turning point" in Tsang's campaign strategy took place in early February when he put forward a "concrete program" of tax reduction and poverty alleviation.⁵³ At that juncture, 68 percent of the 861 respondents in a survey conducted by the University of Hong Kong supported him, an increase of 7.5 percent compared to Tsang's popularity in December 2006.⁵⁴ Eighty-eight percent thought Tsang's harmonious relationship with Beijing was his most significant asset compared with Leong, who failed to get into the top ten popular legislators even in February 2007.⁵⁵ The print media cited all the findings in the opinion polls in such a way as to portray the whole campaign and election as competitive. In reality, the campaign appeared to be competitive, but the election result was clear from the outset.

The Business Elites and Professionals

An overwhelming majority of business people in the HKSAR is Beijing's clients and pro-establishment, but a minority is pro-democracy. Members of the Chinese People's Political Consultative Conference, such as Chan Wing-kei, were openly critical of Leong's idea of annulling the stipulation in the Basic Law that allows Beijing to approve the nomination of the principal officials by the chief executive. Chan pointed to Leong's attempt at "violating the Basic Law" and his "ineligibility" of becoming the chief executive.[56] While Victor Li, the eldest son of tycoon Li Ka-shing, openly supported Tsang, Richard Li tended to be more pro-democracy and called for the direct election of the chief executive as soon as possible.[57] Richard Li explained that he nominated Tsang, but his constituents expected that the Hong Kong polity would be democratized further.[58]

Other big businessmen were explicitly pro-Tsang. Business tycoon Stanley Ho said that if any member of the Election Committee cast a blank vote, his or her identity could be investigated and revealed easily.[59] He later denied making such remark, pointing to the media distortion of his view. However, PRC officials such as Qiao Xiaoyang, the deputy general-secretary of the NPC Standing Committee, said that members of the Election Committee should not cast blank votes.[60] Qiao's comment indicated that Beijing distanced itself from Ho's remark.

The professionals were divided into two groups, one pro-Leong and the other pro-Tsang. On March 24, ten members of the Election Committee who had nominated Tsang as the candidate for the chief executive publicly said that they would vote for him again because a survey of 12,200 medical professionals showed that 60.5 percent of the 3,000 respondents supported him, whereas only 32.2 percent voted for Leong.[61] About 7.2 percent of the respondents remarked they would cast blank votes. Based on the survey results, the ten members decided to vote in accordance with the majority wish of the medical professionals.

The Role of Political Parties

The pro-democracy parties were split into the mainstream moderates and the minority radicals. The moderates supported Leong to maximize the democratic limits tolerated by the central government, but the radical League of Social Democrats argued that it was "disgraceful" for the mainstream democrats to participate in the "undemocratic" election.[62] Two members disrupted a rally led by the pan-democrats on March 18. Even within the Civic Party, it was reported that some academics were dissatisfied with the control of party affairs by legislators.[63] Leong's political platform was the product of his brainchild Margaret Ng, whose attitude toward outside criticisms was defiant and whose input into his campaign was much greater than academics Kuan Hsin-chi and Joseph Cheng.[64]

The pan-democratic camp mobilized its supporters to call for the direct election of both the chief executive and the entire Legislative Council. While they claimed to have 4,000 people participating in the pro-democracy parade on March 18, the police put the estimate to only 1,800.[65] The number of participants was clearly no match for the half a million people's parade on July 1, 2003 and the estimated 250,000 demonstrators on July 1, 2004.

The democrats attempted to pressure Tsang into implementing democratic reform by publicizing a consensus model in mid-March. According to the consensus model reached by the democrats, the HKSAR should have direct elections of both the chief executive and the whole legislature by 2012. Specifically, the functional constituencies in the legislature should be abolished; the Election Committee selecting the chief executive should be turned into a nomination committee and be expanded by incorporating 360 directly elected District Councils members to the existing 800-member body.[66] In fact, the pan-democrats appeared to return to the Tsang's abortive political reform model in December 2005 by incorporating District Councils members into the Election Committee. From a critical perspective, although the pan-democratic camp tried to project an image of unity, their political consensus had negligible impact on Leong's campaign. A few radicals such as Leung Kwok-hung and Albert Chan Wai-yip rejected the consensus model, thus exposing the rift within the pro-democracy movement.

To fend off the pan-democratic appeal to the government for democratization, Tsang adopted a skilful political finesse by not excluding the likelihood of having direct elections of both the chief executive and the Legislative Council by 2012.[67] However, he warned the people of Hong Kong of being overly pessimistic, for he did not foresee the possibility that the HKSAR would be economically marginalized and that it would lose its competitiveness. Tsang's ploy was to refuse to admit the difficulties of getting Beijing's support to accelerate democratization in 2012 on the one hand and to stimulate the Hong Kong identity by highlighting the economic strength and potential endowed upon the HKSAR. His campaign strategy brought about resonance from the public, especially those who had a relatively strong Hong Kong identity.

As early as mid-January, the Tsang government announced its action plan of developing the HKSAR economy, including 207 proposals that would boost the financial services, industry, commerce, shipping, infrastructure, and tourism. Critics argued that the action plan looked like a pre-election campaign platform of Tsang and that it aimed at buying the support of the business sector.[68] In practice, the action blueprint was a follow-up implementation of the central government's eleventh five-year plan, demonstrating the result of a harmonious partnership between the public and private sectors.[69] The situation in 2007 was favorable to Tsang's electoral contest. The HKSAR economy changed drastically after the PRC government implemented the CEPA and the mainlanders' free visit scheme to Hong Kong in the summer of 2003. The economic measures succeeded in bolstering the economy of the HKSAR, restoring the societal morale in the wake of the havoc incurred by the SARS in the early half of 2003.

Political groups supportive of Tsang, including the FTU, the DAB, and the pro-business Liberal Party, appeared to act in a way critical of Tsang, but their support of him was unwavering. The DAB even proposed the idea of helping Tsang to "wash the floors" of various households and buildings, treating the chief executive election as a direct election in which the incumbent Tsang had to reach out to the populace.[70] At the District Council level, Tsang secured the support of 82 DAB members, 30 Liberal Party members, and 10 FTU members. Alan Leong, on the other hand, acquired the support of 77 Democratic Party members, 25 members of the Association for Democracy and People's Livelihood, and 4 Civic Party members.[71]

Tsang himself adopted a skillful campaign strategy by first visiting the DAB's 111 members of the Election Committee and lobbying for their political support.[72] The DAB's demands on the new chief executive were so moderate that they could fit into Tsang's profile easily: having the idea of "loving China and loving Hong Kong," securing the trust of Hong Kong people, getting the support of the central government, and acquiring the confidence of civil servants. Tsang had secret meetings with Chairman of the DAB Ma Lik, Chairman of the Liberal Party James Tien, FTU leader Cheng Yiu-tong, and leader of the Legislative Council's coalition of independent legislators Shek Lai-him. Ma said that the DAB had to express its expectations of the new chief executive quickly because, if it did not support Tsang earlier, the media would have mistakenly regarded the DAB stance as the position of Beijing.[73]

Tsang's Political Patron: Beijing

When Tung Chee-hwa stood for the second HKSAR chief executive election, many mainland officials openly endorsed him, notably the former PRC president Jiang Zeming who reprimanded a Hong Kong reporter as being "too simple" and "too naïve" when Jiang was asked whether Mr. Tung had already been "crowned". In the 2007 chief executive elections, many PRC officials heaped praise on Donald Tsang, giving a clear indication of Beijing's political preference.

From January to early February 2007, PRC officials who expressed their appreciation of Tsang's diligent work included Deputy Director of the Liaison Office in the HKSAR Li Gang, State Councillor Tang Jiaxun, Foreign Minister Li Zhaoxing, and the head of the PRC Foreign Ministry in Hong Kong Lu Xinhua.[74] One Hong Kong member of the Chinese People's Political Consultative Conference, who made his comment on the condition of anonymity, said that it became a "convention" by the central government to express its support of a particular candidate so that it would be a reference to the people of Hong Kong who would make their choices.[75] In retrospect, during the first chief executive election in 1997, Beijing did not wish to express its preference over any candidate, although it was widely believed that the Hong Kong and Macao Affairs Office supported Tung Chee-hwa and that the Liaison Office backed up Sir Ti-Liang Yang.

Prior to the chief executive election, Premier Wen Jiabao openly expressed his wish that the HKSAR would become more open, more inclusive, and more harmonious — code words that referred to the need for political harmony.[76] Wen avoided giving an explicit endorsement of Tsang — a progressive step compared to Jiang Zeming's open support of the unpopular Tung in 2002. Wen left the task of offering unequivocal endorsement of Tsang to his subordinates. In support of Tsang's campaign and opposition to Leong's and Anson Chan's democratic reform blueprints, Deputy Director of the Hong Kong and Macao Affairs Office Chen Zuo'er criticized them as being "pseudo-democratic heroes."[77] Chen argued that the NPC had long raised the issue of considering the direct elections of both the chief executive and the Legislative Council as the ultimate objectives. Jia Qinglin, the chairman of the Chinese People's Political Consultative Conference, commented that he believed the people of Hong Kong would select a patriot who "loves China and loves Hong Kong," and who supports the Basic Law.[78] Jia listed three conditions for the chief executive: the improvement of economic development and people's livelihood, the adoption of the people-based principle, and the attempt at getting the recognition and support of the ordinary citizens."[79] Immediately after Alan Leong proposed the idea of annulling the Basic Law's stipulation that empowered Beijing to approve the appointment of principal officials nominated by the chief executive, Deputy Secretary-General of the NPC Qiao Xiaoyang said that the Basic Law had its bottom line and that political reform in the HKSAR could not bring about any revision of the mini-constitution.⁸⁰ Finally, Wu Bangguo, a member of the NPC Standing Committee, appealed to the Hong Kong NPC members to select a "patriotic" chief executive.⁸¹ Echoing Qiao, Wu emphasized that the Basic Law could not be challenged, especially the stipulations that the Hong Kong political system had to be accountable to the central government, and that the executive-led polity had to be guaranteed.

The Political Bias of the Mass Media

The print media in the HKSAR, except for the pro-democracy *Apple Daily*, portrayed the chief executive election as not only competitive but also a progressive step toward democratization in Hong Kong. The most notable example was *Ming Pao*, whose editorial went so far as to criticize Alan Leong for putting forward a blueprint that was like "neither a donkey nor a horse."⁸² It severely criticized Leong for his "shocking" ideas of revising the Basic Law substantially, abolishing the Election Committee that would nominate the chief executive, appointing directly elected legislators to be some of the principal officials, and calling for the direct elections of both the chief executive and the entire Legislative Council in 2012. The editorial stance of *Ming Pao* was clearly titled toward the central government in Beijing, displaying the preference of most Hong Kong media to remain politically "correct" rather than violating Beijing's bottom line.

Some press media conducted opinion polls whose results unintentionally or intentionally facilitated the mobilization of public opinion in support of the more popular Tsang — an old phenomenon that could be found in the previous chief executive elections. For instance, *Ming Pao* conducted a poll of 947 citizens and showed 62 percent support of Tsang and 21 percent siding with Leong.⁸³ The poll result also demonstrated that Leong's public support plummeted from 32 percent on March 19 to 21 percent on March 25.⁸⁴ The March 25 poll revealed 42 percent public perception that the chief executive elections were competitive and that it would enhance the legitimacy of the elected candidate. However, 39 percent thought that it would have no impact on the elected chief executive's legitimacy, while 5 percent viewed the election as delegitimizing.⁸⁵ Although 58 percent hoped that the chief executive would be directly elected by universal suffrage in 2012, the overall poll result did favor Tsang.

Above all, representatives of eight electronic media organizations suddenly criticized some people, implicitly Leong's campaign team members, for politicizing the discussion over the rules of the second televised candidates' forum. They said that the consensus was to forbid the supporters of the two candidates to clap their hands, but it did not restrict those ordinary citizens who would attend the debate from doing so. However, Ronny Tong of the Civic Party argued that the stipulation forbidding electors to clap their hands had political considerations. A member of the Election Committee told the author that during the first candidates' forum, Leong's supporters were more organized and their applause aroused the anger of an influential and a stanch supporter of Tsang, who lobbied behind the scene for more restrictive regulations in the second forum.[86] The way in which the eight media representatives criticized the pro-democracy camp for politicization appeared to damage their reputation and image as impartial professionals handling the election forum.

The print media's portrayal of Tsang's debate performance was undoubtedly helpful to his entire campaign. Immediately after the first publicized debate, *Sing Tao Daily* used its headline to accuse Leong of mistakenly equating the government's "assets" with "financial reserves."[87] The criticism was actually leveled by economist Francis Lui. Strictly speaking, an objective print media would not have used an academic's one-sided criticism as a headline, but *Sing Tao Daily*'s political bias in favor of Tsang was vividly shown. It extensively quoted James Tien's comment that Tsang outperformed Leong in the debate, saying that Leong "actively shoe-shined Beijing but deadly criticizing the business sector."[88] The remarks of two academics — Ma Ngok and Ivan Choy — critical of Tsang's inferior debating skills were played down by the newspaper and relegated to the bottom section of the reporting page.[89] Another report of *Sing Tao Daily* used the headline, entitled "The social welfare sector views Donald Tsang as more pragmatic than Leong." A careful reading of the report showed that it relied on the remark of only one elector of the social welfare sub-sector, and that his comment actually carried a reservation about the government's lack of vision on the HKSAR social welfare.[90] The biased headline that was inconsistent with the report's content demonstrated not only the poor quality of editorial gate-keeping but also the sloppy coverage on the chief executive election. The explicitly pro-Tsang and pro-Beijing stance of *Sing Tao Daily* was a huge contrast to its pro-Taiwan and anti-Beijing position during the 1970s and the early 1980s, when the newspaper's editorial position and proprietors were still outside the influence and control of the PRC. No wonder Raymond Wong, a leading organizer of the League of Social Democrats, criticized the Hong Kong media for showing self-censorship and quality problems ranging from reporting skills to editorial refinement.[91]

Similar to *Sing Tao Daily*, *Ming Pao* depicted Leong's debating skills as more superior to Tsang during the last public forum in mid-March, but the latter's ability to win the hearts and minds of the ordinary people was stronger.[92] It cited the remarks of "experts," such as Ivan Choy and Leung Man-to to claim that Tsang scored his victory over Leong.[93] The editorial of *Ming Pao* was more subtle and implicit in its support of Tsang, referring to Leong as "better" in his televised performance.[94] Yet the headline of the editorial was balanced by its content that stressed *Ming Pao*'s overriding concern about whether the platforms and ideals of the two candidates would trigger the resonance of the public. The editorial actually referred to Tsang as "more mature," "confident" and "concrete."[95] Reading between the lines, the editorial apparently praised Leong but substantially emphasized the experience and pragmatism of Tsang. Another editorial of *Ming Pao* apparently criticized both Tsang's and Leong's platforms as unsatisfactory, but its content stressed the expansion of governmental functions in Tsang's governing ideal and criticized Leong for adopting a "left-wing" ideology.[96] By depicting Leong as both supportive of governmental interventionism and expansion, the editorial unintentionally or intentionally made him inferior to Tsang. In fact, *Ming Pao*'s poll of 796 members of the Election Committee showed that the 144 respondents ranked Tsang's platform as having 6.8 marks out of ten marks, slightly higher than the average 6.1 marks given to Leong's platform.[97] Supplementing the editorial with the poll result, *Ming Pao* implicitly sided with Tsang.

Both *Ming Pao* and *Sing Tao Daily* emphasized that 2 million viewers watched the first publicized debate, thus intentionally or unintentionally providing legitimacy to the entire chief executive elections whose "small-circle" aspect was prominently downplayed by the two newspapers. As a matter of fact, public opinion in the HKSAR tended to favor Tsang over Leong. According to the survey conducted by the University of Hong Kong, Tsang on the eve of the election garnered 80 percent support whereas Leong merely got 10 percent support.[98] The surveys conducted by Lingnan University pointed to the constantly strong public support of Tsang (see Table 8.3).

When asked why they supported Tsang or Leong, 35.6 percent of those who supported Tsang in a survey conducted by a group named City Think-Tank from February 2 to 9 viewed him as possessing a higher governing capacity. Meanwhile, 43.8 percent who would vote for Leong emphasized the importance of his ability to promote democratic development (see Table 8.4). The supporters of Tsang had different concerns compared to the Leong counterparts. Other factors favorable to Tsang embraced his

Table 8.3 Surveys Conducted by Lingnan University and the University of Hong Kong on the Performance of Candidates in the Chief Executive Election

Lingnan University's Surveys

1. If the Chief Executive election were held tomorrow, who would you choose if you could vote?

	Survey on March 1 (N=611)	Survey on March 15 (N=633)
Donald Tsang	61.4%	63.8%
Alan Leong	25.9%	26.4%
Would support both	1.5%	1.5%
Would not support both	3.4%	2.9%

2. After you listened to the debate forum, what is Tsang's impression on you?

	Survey on March 1	Survey on March 15
Changing better	26.7%	33.6%
Changing worse	13.1%	10.7%
No change	57.4%	53.8%

3. After you listened to the debate forum, what is Leong's impression on you?

	Survey on March 1	Survey on March 15
Changing better	36.5%	33.3%
Changing worse	20.9%	18.3%
No change	35.2%	42.8%

The University of Hong Kong's Survey on March 15 (N=477)

1. Who performed better? Tsang 36.9% Leong 39.8%
2. Who would you vote for if you were asked to do so tomorrow? Tsang 63.9% Leong 23.3%
3. Before the debate, who did you support? Tsang 65% Leong 20.2%
4. Compared to March 1, what is your view of Tsang's performance? Better 54.1% Worse 10.1%
5. Compared to March 1, what is your view of Leong's performance? Better 38.3% Worse 15.2%

Source: *Sing Tao Daily*, March 16, 2007, p. B1.

blueprint of governing the HKSAR, ability to communicate with Beijing, and the degree of societal recognition. Leong's strengths lay in his ability to promote democratization, enjoy party support, and show a roadmap of governing Hong Kong.

Table 8.4 The Reasons Why Respondents Supported Tsang or Leong

Why do you support Tsang or Leong? (N=1,324)

	Leong	Tsang
Number supporting	322	815
Reasons		
1. Having party support	10.2%	2.3%
2. Having higher degree of governing capacity	5.9%	35.6%
3. Gaining societal recognition	12.1%	16.3%
4. Having a blueprint of ruling Hong Kong	10.9%	20.6%
5. Beneficial to Hong Kong's harmony	4.7%	7%
6. Can communicate with the central government	0.9%	10.7%
7. Can promote democratic development	43.8%	0.7%
8. Others	5.3%	3.6%

Source: *Sing Tao Daily*, February 15, 2007, p. B4.

Furthermore, those who supported Tsang tended to come from wide political spectrums, including citizens identifying themselves as democrats, pro-Beijing, and independents (see Table 8.5). Leong's political support stemmed more from the democrats and independents than the pro-Beijing patriots. Another survey conducted by the University of Hong Kong showed that 83.2 percent of the public would have voted for Tsang, while only 10.3 percent supported Leong.[99] Tsang's popularity did mean that even if the 2007 chief executive election were held in the form of universal suffrage, he would have defeated Leong comfortably.

Table 8.5 Public Support of Tsang and Leong

Supporters' Self-Identification	Marks Given to Tsang	Marks to Leong
N=1,011		
Democrats (N=250)	68.7 out of 100 marks	44.3
Pro-China (N=64)	79.2	31.5
Independents (N=376)	68.5	42.2
No political tendency (N=281)	72.3	38.5

Source: *Ming Pao*, February 10, 2007, p. A21.

Note: The full marks given to Tsang and Leong were 100.

A minority of democrats organized a mock referendum for secondary school students to vote for their chief executive. Led by Human Rights Monitor's chairwoman Cyd Ho Sau-lan, the mock referendum prepared 100,000 to 150,000 votes and mobilized 800 helpers to manage the "voting" process on March 25, the day when the chief executive election was simultaneously held. Four secondary schools withdrew from the mock referendum, for they were reportedly under pressure from the schools' management.[100] However, both the print and electronic media did not highlight the mock referendum, perhaps reflecting a certain degree of self-censorship. Pro-democracy legislator Emily Lau accused the ATV of exercising self-censorship in mid-February, when a program that interviewed Democratic Party chairman Albert Ho and Hong Kong NPC member Allen Lee — both criticizing the chief executive elections as "unfair" and "undemocratic" — was suddenly withdrawn.[101] Although ATV claimed that the move was due to "technical problems," Lau questioned whether the decision was an outcome of self-censorship.[102]

Election Result

On March 25, Tsang obtained 649 votes, defeating Leong who garnered 123 votes.[103] Tsang succeeded in getting eight more votes than the number of nominators, whereas Leong lost nine votes compared to his nomination. There were 16 invalid votes, including 11 blank votes. After being elected, Tsang vowed to prepare a consultative document on democratization, solve the problem of direct elections within five years, and seek to reach compromise on a political reform blueprint acceptable to 60 percent of Hong Kong people.[104] In terms of poverty, Tsang promised to promote employment, decrease unemployment to a level below 4 percent, and encourage the development of social enterprises. His economic agendas included the strengthening of Hong Kong's relations with the mainland and the reduction of profit and salary taxes to 15 percent, thus increasing the competitive edge of the HKSAR. Finally, Tsang was determined to enhance resources in health care, develop the education system, and minimize the ratio between students and teachers at both the primary and secondary levels.

Immediately after the chief executive election, patron-client politics took the form of Tsang's appointment of James Tien as the new chairman of the Hong Kong Tourism Board. Rumors were rife that Jasper Tsang would be appointed as the next head of the Education and Manpower Bureau or Home Affairs. However, due to DAB Chair Ma Lik's controversial remark on the June Fourth tragedy in the PRC in 1989, it was reported in May that Jasper Tsang would not join the Donald Tsang administration as a principal official. In any case, the exchange between Donald Tsang and James Tien was described as "gifts" given to the Liberal Party after the chief executive election.[105] While patronage politics was commonplace throughout the British colonial era, the most prominent feature of clientelism in the HKSAR has been the extensive appointments of the friends and supporters of the chief executive, including both Tung Chee-hwa and Donald Tsang, without regard to the maladministration of the political appointees. The Tourism Board under the former chairperson Selina Chow was severely criticized by the mass media for appointing her friend, Clara Chong, as the executive director. Chong's leadership was severely questioned as the Board spent a huge amount in its publicity. Without addressing the issue of alleged maladministration and over-spending, Donald Tsang continued to regard the Board's as the fiefdom of the Liberal Party — a vivid demonstration of the seriousness of clientelism in Hong Kong politics.

The final episode of the chief executive election was the central government's endorsement of Tsang. On April 2, the PRC Premier Wen Jiabao formally appointed Tsang as the chief executive from July 1, 2007 to 2012.[106] The appointment also symbolized patron Beijing's coronation of its client Donald Tsang as the third chief executive of the HKSAR from July 1, 2007 onwards.

The Merger of Two Political Cultures

The amalgamation of the mainland Chinese and Hong Kong political cultures was recognized by Jasper Tsang, the former DAB chairman. He wrote:

> Although this Chief Executive election does not adopt the one person one vote system, the electioneering activities have largely used the format of universal suffrage. At the end, the election result would most probably the same as one conducted under universal suffrage. Viewed from any angle, this election can achieve the best result in the context without universal suffrage. This is also the outcome of the rational decision adopted by the central government. The central government accepts "competitive election" without any attempt at interference. Although Donald Tsang is surely to be elected, he has tried his best to conduct his public campaigns. Alan Leong and his team adopt a proper attitude and put up with a strong performance. Both campaign teams have not relied on negative propaganda, thus avoiding unhappy conflicts. The mass media's editorials, reports and

commentaries have remained civilized, healthy and they earn the public support, thereby creating a sense of good political atmosphere.[107]

Tsang's comments summed up the mix of mainland Chinese and Hong Kong political cultures: Beijing's acceptance of Hong Kong's loyal opposition on the one hand and the positive campaigns conducted by the pluralistically-minded Hongkongers on the other.

Similarly, the *South China Morning Post* hailed the election as a progressive step in Hong Kong's democratization. It said:

> This was a historic election campaign that marked a small, yet significant, step forward in our city's political development. For the first time, a challenger from the pro-democracy camp secured enough nominations to stand. As a result, this election was livelier than those in the past. Civic Party member Alan Leong Kah-kit can take much credit for his performance. He has achieved what he set out to do. Mr. Leong introduced a little competition to the campaign.[108]

Indeed, having a party member compete in the chief executive election was unprecedented in the HKSAR. It signaled an important recognition from Beijing that the pluralistic Hong Kong polity could have a party candidate contesting with its preferred chief executive.

The campaign style of both Tsang and Leong was in conformity with the Hong Kong electoral culture. After his victory, Tsang toured the territory on an open-top double-decker bus to thank his supporters, acting like a candidate participating in a direct election.[109] Although most citizens received him positively, one of them said, "The only opinion I have is against Beijing appointing our Chief Executive."[110] His view echoed many members of the silent majority of the Hongkongers, dreaming that one day they will be able to elect the chief executive directly.

Conclusion and Implications for Taiwan

The 2007 chief executive election was a manifestation of a Hong Kong style of democratization, marked by pluralistic competition and open campaigns whereby the two candidates had to make their platforms and proposals accountable to the public. Most importantly, it represented a testimony of the merge of mainland political culture with the Hong Kong politico-electoral tradition. The PRC political culture is marked by personnel control, loyal opposition, and patrimonialism. In the HKSAR chief executive election, personnel control was ensured through the selection of the members of the Election Committee, whereas loyal opposition could be seen in Leong's participation. Another aspect of the mainland political culture is patriomonialism, which could be seen in the automatic election of almost half of the Election Committee members, and in the political appointment of James Tien into the chairmanship of the Hong Kong Tourism Board shortly after the election.

Leong and the democratic camp's participation in the chief executive election served to rebuild the trust that was impaired in LegCo's rejection of the political reform blueprint proposed by Donald Tsang in December 2005. Their partaking is auspicious for the relationships with both Beijing and the HKSAR government in the medium term. Indeed, it remains to be seen whether the improved relationship will be translated into a positive force bringing about any breakthrough in the political reform discourse and negotiations.

From the broader perspective of democratization, the 2007 chief executive election had a significant bearing on Hong Kong's political development. For the first time in the political history of the HKSAR, the party-affiliated candidate Alan Leong could challenge the authority of the Beijing-preferred candidate Donald Tsang. Accepting the confines of the Basic Law, Leong and his supporters projected a loyal opposition that could maximize the limited democratic space and win the trust of the central government. If the pan-democratic camp continues to adopt this moderate approach, the HKSAR democratic development will continue to proceed in a piecemeal but acceptable way to the central government. Unless the PRC undergoes significant breakthrough in its political liberalization and democratization, Hong Kong's political development is destined to work within the constrained political space tolerated by Beijing at least in the foreseeable future.

The way in which the Hong Kong chief executive is selected and politically hamstrung by the PRC patron cannot be applied to Taiwan. Expecting any Taiwan leader to be the client of Beijing is and will be politically unrealistic. Any Taiwan leader who is viewed by the Taiwanese as Beijing's client will be politically denounced and severely criticized. Hence, in the event of any breakthrough in the Beijing-Taipei agreement, the top Taiwan leader's relationships with Beijing will be different from the HKSAR chief executive's patron-clientelist connections with the central government. Nor can the constrained election method in the HKSAR be adopted in Taiwan, where the president has already been directly elected by all Taiwan citizens through universal suffrage.

9

Applying the Spirit of "One Country, Two Systems" to Taiwan's Political Future

As argued in the previous chapters, the content of Hong Kong's "one country, two systems" cannot be applied to the resolution of Taiwan's political future. The political system of the HKSAR is vastly different from that of Taiwan. Therefore, any attempt by the PRC to exert political control on the Taiwan polity will surely be counter-productive. Although the "one country, two systems" is practised in the HKSAR, and less so in the Macao Special Administrative Region (MSAR) where the polity, economy, and society have all been integrated into the PRC, the spirit of tolerating systemic differences and their existence between the PRC and the two SARs can still be applied to tackle Taiwan's political future creatively.

This chapter adopts a creative and constructive approach to examine whether and how the "one country, two systems" formula can be applied to solve the problem of Taiwan's political future. Indeed, the problematic governance in the Hong Kong case is an easy justification that the "one country, two systems" cannot be applied to deal with Taiwan's future. Nevertheless, if we treat the "one country, two systems" as a broad concept entailing the devolution of some degree of political power to a different region, it does have an element of creativity to tackle Taiwan's political destiny. The crux of the problem is how to adjust the content and context of "one country, two systems" to the unique Taiwan circumstances. Moreover, this chapter will argue that the Hong Kong model does not simply embrace governance; the ways in which Britain and China reached the Joint Declaration in 1984 have been totally neglected.[1] The processes of building trust, conducting secret negotiations, making concessions, and meeting the bottom lines of both negotiating sides can surely be replicated in the possible peaceful resolution of Taiwan's political future.

The Current Impasse in Beijing-Taipei Relations

The crux of the problem lies in the varying bottom lines held by Beijing and Taipei. From Beijing's perspective, the Taiwan leaders have to recognize that Taiwan is part of mainland China. The rise of the pro-Taiwan independence forces, especially the victory of the DPP since the 2000 presidential elections, has heightened Beijing's trepidations that the path of Taiwan independence has become politically entrenched. As a result, Beijing has never renounced the use of force to reunify Taiwan. On the other hand, Taiwan insists that the PRC should renounce the use of force so that both sides would be able to return to the bargaining table, as with the situation in 1992 when both sides appeared to set aside the meaning of one China.

Another critical issue hindering any breakthrough in the relationships between Taiwan and the PRC is that both sides have been making claims and demands in public since the former Taiwan president Lee Teng-hui adopted a more provocative style than his predecessor Chiang Ching-kuo. The fact that Taiwan's leaders and officials in charge of cross-Strait relations often make assertions in public is by no means conducive to a harmonious and trustful relationship between Taipei and Beijing. First and foremost, such public comments and remarks on cross-Strait relations often lead to immediate reactions from Beijing's officials responsible for Taiwan matters. Most importantly, Beijing's public response is usually marked by a stiff reaction and reiteration of its position. In other words, neither Beijing nor Taipei can have any breakthrough in their relations because of excessive public positioning and assertions. What Beijing and Taipei need is a kind of secret negotiation through the despatch of emissaries to either side of the two regimes. Although it is reported that secret emissaries are occasionally used by the Taiwan government to tap the views and policy line of Beijing, both sides remain deadlocked over the island's political future.

Quite often Taiwan and the PRC have problems of perceptions that, if mismanaged, could spark military conflict across the two straits. In November 2004, when Taiwan President Chen Shui-bian paid a visit to one of the outlying islands, 28 jet fighters from the PRC were said to create "disturbance" in the air.[2] At that time, Taiwan accused the PRC of stationing 610 missiles along the eastern coast, targeting the island. Moreover, Taiwan also detected a mainland nuclear submarine entering into Japanese waters in November 2004, prompting the Japanese navy to track down the Chinese submarine. Taiwan reportedly provided Japan with the military intelligence detected on the mainland nuclear submarine. From the PRC perspective, Taiwan appeared to play the Japanese card to check and balance against Beijing. After all, Taiwan had been ruled by Japan for 50 years from 1895 to 1945.[3] Some Taiwan politicians, notably the former president Lee Teng-hui, have more political affinity with Japan than with the PRC. The Chen Shui-bian regime proposed to enhance Taiwan's missile defence capability in defiance of strong opposition from some members of the public.[4] This attempt at adopting a deterrent strategy surely met with the PRC's remobilization of missiles along the mainland's coastal provinces. While the PRC perceives Taiwan as not only nurturing and fostering moves tantamount to exercising its independence, Taiwan has been mobilizing the support of Japan and the United States to act as an anti-communist and democratic bulwark against the authoritarian and socialist regime in mainland China. This problem of perception, if it persists, is by no means beneficial to a peaceful resolution of the conflicts between Taiwan and the PRC.

The final problem that poses an obstacle to any substantial breakthrough in Taipei-Beijing relations is the U.S. policy. Traditionally, the U.S. has adopted a two-pronged strategy. On the one hand, it recognizes that there is only one China and that Taiwan is part of China. However, on the other hand, the U.S. government has continued arms sales to Taiwan for the sake of allowing the island to defend itself militarily. With the onset of democracy in Taiwan, Washington has found Taipei an important ideological ally. Not only are many Congressmen supportive of Taiwan's democracy, but the U.S. administration has become relatively tolerant of the emergence of pro-Taiwan independence forces on the island. Although sometimes the U.S. government diplomatically tries to restrain the Taiwan leaders from making any move or gesture too provocative to Beijing, overall the American policy has perhaps made the island's leaders much bolder in making their public assertions and demands on cross-Strait relations.

As a result, there has been a cyclical pattern in the triangular relationships between the U.S., Taiwan, and the PRC. Since the U.S. has maintained a relatively supportive policy toward Taiwan's government, the latter has adopted a relatively and publicly assertive policy toward the PRC. In turn, Beijing has been reacting negatively to Taiwan's public assertions. The missile crisis across the Taiwan Strait in 1996 could be attributable mainly to the hawkish position adopted by the PRC, especially the military, in response to President Lee's visit to the U.S. However, it could also be argued that had the U.S. sensitivity toward Lee's visit been raised, the missile test in the Taiwan Strait could have been avoided. In response to the PRC military threat to Taipei, the U.S. despatched its seventh fleet to the Taiwan Strait as a gesture of political support for the island. The triangular relationships between the US, Taiwan, and the PRC are trapped in a vicious circle in which any move from Taiwan, tacitly supported by the U.S., is bound to trigger a knee-jerk reaction from the PRC. Unless this vicious circle in U.S.-Taiwan-PRC relationships is managed in a cautious and skilful way that would bring about negotiations between Beijing and Taipei, the ongoing deadlock between Taiwan and the PRC will persist. Most alarmingly, with a globally emerging PRC, there are concerns that the new leadership under President Hu Jintao may toy with the idea of solving the problem of Taiwan's political future in a "surprising" way before 2009.[5] While all the Chinese residents in Greater China, which is composed of mainland China, Taiwan, Hong Kong, and Macao, are imbued with the hope that such a "surprise" solution would become peaceful, the likelihood of a military conflict, full-scale or limited skirmishes, cannot be easily dismissed.

The U.S. administration has expressed its concern about the heightened tensions between Taiwan and the PRC, especially since the re-election of DPP President Chen Shui-bian in Taiwan in March 2004. President Chen installed a group of pro-Taiwan independence supporters as his lieutenants responsible for cross-Strait relations — a move by no means beneficial to any constructive breakthrough in the diplomatic impasse. On the other hand, with the gradual withdrawal of the former PRC president Jiang Zemin from formal politics, Hu Jintao is now commanding the Military Affairs Commission (MAC). However, it is misleading to jump to the conclusion that Jiang does not and will not have a final say on the PRC Taiwan policy. In 2004, the MAC expressed its support of Jiang once he stepped down from its chairmanship. Although some observers see Hu Jintao as a young Chinese leader adopting a more appeasement or soft-line policy toward Taiwan,[6] the fact that Jiang and some other CCP elders still have a say in the conduct of Chinese politics means that Beijing's policy toward Taipei could suddenly or unexpectedly turn hard-line, as with the unexpected and surprise missile tests in 1996. In particular, the new Hu-Wen leadership is perhaps intent on carving a niche in Chinese history by tackling the Taiwan issue in a more determined manner.

If the relationships between Taiwan and the PRC remain fluid, volatile, unstable, and potentially conflict-ridden, it is in the interest of three parties — the PRC, Taiwan and the U.S. — to search for a peaceful settlement of Taiwan's political future. A Sinologist in the U.S., Kenneth Liberthal, proposed the idea of both Taiwan and the PRC reaching an intermediate solution of abandoning military build-up and renouncing the use of force, respectively.[7] This idea is undoubtedly constructive, but the crux of the problem is how the two parties return to the negotiating table, as with the situation in 1992 when both sides put aside their differences on the meaning of one China and started negotiating a series of cross-Strait issues in Singapore.

From a conflict resolution perspective, the Hong Kong model and the "one country, two systems" need to be properly understood for the sake of using them to solve the problem of Taiwan's political future. The Hong Kong model, as mentioned above, does not embrace simply the governance of the HKSAR; it is actually characterized by a long and difficult negotiating process between Britain and China from 1982 to 1984. Moreover, the "one country, two systems" cannot only be seen as the relationships between a superior overlord and an inferior dependent polity, albeit the previous chapters have argued that the HKSAR is becoming more mainlandized and Sinified, and that the content of Hong Kong governance cannot be implanted onto Taiwan. Adopting a conflict resolution perspective, however, the "one country, two systems" can be seen as a small step toward federalism or a progressive move toward the devolution of political power to a different political system. In the event that the PRC, Taiwan, and the U.S. see the Hong Kong model as a hallmark of trust-building between two negotiating parties and the "one country, two systems" as an experiment with Chinese-style federalism, perhaps all the parties concerned would appreciate the virtues of flexibility, creativity, and innovation in the ongoing search for a peaceful resolution of Taiwan's political future. The sections below will discuss the conceptual problems of the Hong Kong model and the "one country, two systems," examine the processes of trust-building during the Sino-British negotiation over Hong Kong, and will finally propose a number of measures that can be taken by mainland China, Taiwan, and the U.S. to achieve a genuine breakthrough in Taipei-Beijing relationships.

Conceptual Ambiguity of the "One Country, Two Systems" Formula

In the first place, the Chen administration in Taiwan rejected the use of Hong Kong's "one country, two systems" for the PRC to negotiate with the island regime, for Taiwan's status is different from the HKSAR. True, Taiwan's *de facto* nation-state status which receives the diplomatic recognition of some countries in the world is a far cry from the local government status of Hong Kong. But the problem of status should not be an obstacle to the discussions and negotiations between the PRC and Taiwan. The reason is that on the negotiating table, the question of Taiwan's status can be discussed in exchange for another contentious matter, such as whether the PRC will renounce the use of military force to deal with Taiwan's political future. If both sides agree to disagree with the mutual perspectives on Taiwan's status, then they can and should sit down at the bargaining table so that every bone of contention can be negotiated imaginatively without prejudiced or rigid assumptions.

Critics of the application of the Hong Kong's "one country, two systems" model look to the unequal nature of the formula and the ways in which it was applied in the HKSAR. To quote from Byron Weng,

> By design, "one country" is the premise and "two systems" the promise. "Two systems" cannot be juxtaposed unless the "one China principle" is upheld first. Moreover, the "one country" is not just China. It is certainly not the Republic of China. It is the People's Republic of China. The central government will be in Beijing, under the continuing control of the Chinese Communist Party, and not open to democratic change. Whatever is said about "two systems," one side is at the mercy of the other. A Special Administrative Region exists at the central authorities' pleasure . . . . To Beijing, "one country, two systems" is but an instrument for unification; to Taipei, it is Taiwan's lot after unification. Unification is not likely to materialize if the Taiwanese people have a say in it.[8]

Weng's arguments are only partially accurate. It is true that the HKSAR polity is inferior to the central government, which as previous chapters have proved is exerting political control and influence upon the territory. However, Weng looks to the weakest part of the "one country, two systems" — governance and patron–clientelist relationships between Hong Kong and Beijing. The "one country, two systems," as argued below, is premised on the assumption of a more *de facto* federal system, whose spirit can be applied to the case of Taiwan's future. Moreover, the difference over the definition of one China can be discussed at the negotiating table and it is by no means the ultimate obstacle to a peaceful resolution of Taiwan's political future. Hence, while Weng correctly points to the subordinate nature and problematic governance of the HKSAR and to its inferior status *vis-à-vis* Beijing, the spirit of having two different systems coexist has been neglected.

The concept of "one country, two systems" is vague and predicated on the co-existence of two different economic systems, namely Hong Kong and Macao's capitalism and the PRC's "socialism with Chinese characteristics." This assumption was valid in the mid-1980s when the late supreme Chinese leader, Deng Xiaoping, foresaw a long path of mainland China's economic development and when he anticipated that the "one country, two systems" would become a long-term solution for the PRC to converge with Taiwan economically. Deng also assumed that mainland China would perhaps need fifty years to develop its capitalist system or productive forces to catch up with Hong Kong and Macao. However, since the late 1990s and especially after the death of Deng in 1997, this assumption of the coexistence between socialist China and capitalist Hong Kong/Macao has rapidly become shaky. The PRC has been adopting capitalist means to achieve its modernization programmes. The question is no longer the coexistence between Chinese socialism and capitalism in Hong Kong and Macao. Instead, the rise of China and the corresponding decline in the economic performances of both Hong Kong and Macao, which were seriously affected by the Asian financial crisis, has meant that China is economically surpassing the two Special Administrative Regions. The HKSAR, in particular, has adopted the policy of economic dependence on mainland China, relying on the investment from mainland investors and consumer spending spree from the mainland tourists. Both Hong Kong and Macao have benefited from the Closer Economic Partnership Arrangements signed with the motherland. Moreover, China's participation in the World Trade Organization in 2001 signalled its deeper integration into the global capitalist orbit. While the late Deng might anticipate fifty years for China to catch up economically with capitalist Hong Kong and Macao, the reality is that ten years after the transfer of sovereignty of Hong Kong, mainland China has already surpassed the economic performance of the two capitalist enclaves. Economically, China's rise is narrowing its economic gap with Taiwan. In the past, the Taiwan government argued that the economic gap between the PRC and ROC meant that any negotiation over Taiwan's political future would have little incentives. Yet with more Taiwanese investing and residing in the mainland, especially Fujian province and Shanghai city, the economic gap thesis is no longer a justification for Taiwan to maintain a non-negotiating approach to the mainland.

However, economic convergence between mainland China and Taiwan is not tantamount to any smooth transition to political convergence, namely reunification. The PRC political system remains authoritarian; its regime tackles political dissidents in a much more intolerant manner than either the HKSAR government or the MSAR administration.[9] The control over the Internet in the mainland and the suppression of religious dissidents like the Falun Gong members persist in the PRC, whereas the HKSAR and the MSAR have appeared to tolerate, albeit monitor, the activities of Falun Gong supporters. As discussed in Chapter 6, the determination of the HKSAR authorities to enact Article 23 of the Basic Law, which outlaws subversion, sedition, treason, and secession in post-1997 Hong Kong, encountered fierce opposition in mid-2003. Due to public outcry, the HKSAR government indefinitely postponed the enactment of the anti-subversive law. The MSAR, on the other hand, was also forced by the chaotic circumstances in Hong Kong to shelve the enactment of the anti-subversion article in its Basic Law. Although Macao is going to legislate on Article 23 soon, such anti-subversion law would not be applied to the Taiwan scenario, where the strong Taiwan identity must reject any intrusion of mainland Chinese practices and political identity. Predictably, any Beijing-Taipei agreement on Taiwan's future will perhaps have to be more flexible with regard to any provision on anti-subversion. As long as Taiwan accepts that it is part of the China mainland, every problem can be negotiated with an open-minded acumen — a position held by the PRC but in the first place rejected by the Taiwan side. The challenge for both sides is how to open up dialogue regardless of the vastly different premises held by their negotiators.

Unlike China, Hong Kong, and Macao where the polities remain undemocratic in the sense that the chief executive is by no means directly elected by citizens through universal suffrage, Taiwan has a Western-style democratic and party system in which the president is directly elected by the ordinary citizens.[10] From the perspective of political development, the Taiwan government has no real incentive to discuss the issue of reunification with the PRC. It is uncertain when and highly doubtful whether mainland China will develop its political system along the line of Taiwan-style democracy, which however is punctuated by extensive bribery in elections and controversial electoral administration as witnessed in the attempted "assassination" of presidential candidate Chen Shui-bian in 2004. Indeed, there are virtues in Taiwan's democratic system, for its independent judiciary has been assertive toward any impropriety of Chen's subordinates and relatives, as the case of Chao Chien-ming showed.[11] Yet as argued in Chapter 6, so long as the PRC exhibits strong xenophobic sentiments, it is unlikely that Western-style democracy will be developed on the mainland at least in the short and medium terms. If the PRC is not going to be a Western-style democracy in the short and medium terms, the political justification for Taiwan to delay the negotiations with the CCP remains relatively strong.

Since the PRC economic renaissance is not accompanied by a full-scale democratization, the "one country, two systems" originally designed to incorporate capitalist Hong Kong and Macao into the mainland's socialist ambit is *de facto* generating economic, and to some extent political, convergence between Beijing on the one hand and Hong Kong as well as

Macao on the other. In the meantime, as argued in previous chapters, the "one country, two systems" in Hong Kong is gradually moving toward "one country, one system" in which capitalism and "soft" authoritarianism (occasional resort to the repression of political dissidents) coexist. Still, mainland China is arguably characterized by a "hard" authoritarian regime where the legal system remains underdeveloped and where the state suppresses dissidents in a much larger scale and a prominent manner.[12]

However, if the Chinese in mainland China, Hong Kong, Macao, and in overseas countries are yearning for an eventual reunification with Taiwan in the future, the coexistence of two different political systems between the PRC and Taiwan is not an excuse for prolonged separation. Arguably, if Taiwan's democracy means that it has a spirit of accommodating and tolerating opinion differences and of accepting diversities, then it will be by no means harmful to Taiwan if its negotiators discuss the island domain's future with the mainland counterparts. Ideally, a full-fledged democracy like Taiwan should at least attempt to look for creative and imaginative solutions to resolve the sovereignty dispute with the mainland over the island. A prolonged non-negotiating stance is by no means conducive to the development of a creative and tolerant democracy. Any delaying tactic on the part of Taiwan with regard to dialogue with the mainland is arguably a demonstration of a passive and an uncreative democracy.

In the same vein, if the PRC policy-makers on Taiwan do not come up with imaginative and creative solutions, their niche in the history of China will not only be tarnished, but the wish of the Chinese all over the world for a peaceful reunification with Taiwan will permanently turn up in smoke. The PRC think-tank on Taiwan should perhaps realize that Taiwan is indeed very different from the cases of Hong Kong and Macao. As this book has argued, the content of "one country, two systems" in the HKSAR cannot be copied mechanically to the Taiwan case. As the Taiwanese identity is very strong and as the island has a Western-style democratic system that respects the aspiration of the populace, any solution on Taiwan's political future demands more imagination than what the PRC think-tank might traditionally assume. In short, both the Taiwan and PRC authorities need to liberalize their thinking for the sake of achieving a real breakthrough in the current political and diplomatic impasse.

Regardless of the conceptual ambiguity and changing meanings of "one country, two systems," the spirit of delegating some degree of political and administrative powers to special regions remains a central idea in the formula. Beijing does attempt to delegate political and administrative powers to both the HKSAR and MSAR governments, but the problem is that maladministration and poor leadership in the HKSAR administration, as witnessed in the massive protests against Tung Chee-hwa in July 1, 2003 and 2004, meant that the central government has been forced by the circumstances to intervene in Hong Kong affairs. The weaknesses of the Tung administration were characterized by chaotic policy-making priorities, incompetent handling of crises like the bird flu and SARS, and serious patron-clientelism that rewarded politically loyal but relatively inept supporters.[13] In contrast, the Edmund Ho administration in the MSAR did not demonstrate such weaknesses from December 20, 1999 to the labour confrontation with the police on May 1, 2007, thus avoiding the need for the central government to interfere with Macao affairs in a way as explicitly as the case of Hong Kong.[14] In short, the fact that Beijing interferes with the affairs of the HKSAR does not necessarily mean that the idea of delegating political and administrative powers to special regions is impracticable. The inept administration of the HKSAR leadership appeared to render the concept of "one country, two systems" impracticable, but the strong Hong Kong identity has been maintaining a relatively high degree of civil liberties in the HKSAR, except for the surveillance on pro-democracy activists.

Refocusing the "One Country, Two Systems" on the Negotiation Process

Objectively speaking, the Hong Kong model and the Macao formula of "one country, two systems" have been punctuated by a long process of negotiation between mainland China and Britain on the one hand, and Beijing and Portugal on the other. Although the process of negotiation between China and Portugal on Macao's political future was much smoother due to the absence of any dispute over the question of sovereignty (Lisbon had long admitted that Beijing had the sovereignty over Macao and that Portugal merely administered the enclave), both sides needed to build up their mutual trust for the sake of facilitating the process of give and take at the bargaining table.[15] Britain, however, originally insisted that it possessed the sovereignty of Hong Kong — a position held by the former prime minister Margaret Thatcher. This British stance led to not only the deadlock between both sides in the early phase of the negotiation, but it also precipitated a crisis of public confidence in Hong Kong in 1982–1983.[16] The Chinese government rejected the initial British stance, insisting that sovereignty could not be separated from administration. In 1983, when Thatcher wrote to the late Chinese premier Zhao Ziyang that Britain would be willing to surrender its claim on sovereignty in exchange for a solution acceptable to both sides and supportive of Hong Kong's existing lifestyle, the diplomatic impasse was broken.[17] During this difficult phase of negotiation, the British diplomats and the Chinese counterparts remained tight-lipped in public about their tense negotiation. At the same time, both sides continued their talks at the bargaining table despite opinion differences. In other words, secret negotiations and persistent talks on deadlocked issues marked the Sino-British negotiation over Hong Kong's future.

Comparatively speaking, the current diplomatic impasse between the PRC and Taiwan can be attributable to open pronouncements without the political will to build up mutual trust, thus exacerbating the relationships between the two sides. It is common to envisage Taiwan officials and their mainland Chinese counterparts making claims in public, thus provoking reciprocal shouting matches and vociferous reactions from the other side. Arguably, this open "negotiating" style and political posturing are by no means conducive to any breakthrough in their relationships. In the event that both sides rely more on secret emissaries to exchange their views, the process can perhaps establish some degree of trust prior to formal negotiations.

The 1992 negotiations between Taiwan's and the PRC's emissaries in Hong Kong were characterized by one principle dominant in the Sino-British negotiations over Hong Kong, namely an agreement to disagree on certain thorny issues. The negotiation in Hong Kong in 1992 was marked by the gentlemen's agreement to disagree on the precise meaning of one China. Both sides did not waste time arguing over their interpretations of China. Instead they proceeded to discuss issues of mutual concerns. Similarly, the Sino-British negotiations were also marked by the agreement of both Britain and China to disagree on the question of sovereignty at the early stage of discussions. Even in the Sino-Portuguese talks on Macao's future, both sides at one time disagreed on whether Portugal should leave Macao at a later stage rather than 1999, on the complicated nationality issue of Macao residents, and on whether the People's Liberation Army needed to be stationed in Macao. Both Portugal and China could hammer out solutions to tackle all these issues not only during the negotiation from 1986–87 but also during the last years of Portuguese rule. Hence, the political will on the part of the two negotiating parties to reach a satisfactory and compromising solution is necessary in the case of cross-Strait disputes.

In fact, there have been signs that the meaning of China can be discussed further. Some analysts from mainland China suggested that China can be "United China." Alternatively, both sides may consider using Greater China as the basis for negotiation. Even if both sides disagree on the precise meaning of one China, this baffling problem can be put aside, as with the 1992 "consensus" between Taipei and Beijing talks in Hong Kong, so that potential breakthroughs can be made. Alternatively, one China can refer to the Chinese civilization, so that both sides can perhaps achieve a fundamental advance. If the "one country, two systems" is rejected outright by Taiwan, both the mainland and the Taipei side may consider "one country, three systems" without worrying about the political baggage of the late Deng's insistence that the Hong Kong and Macao model would be applied to Taiwan.

It seems that President Hu's remarks on the HKSAR during its tenth anniversary adopted an open-minded attitude toward the reunification formula on Taiwan. His speech surprisingly did not mention that the Hong Kong model of "one country, two systems" would have to be used to reunify Taiwan in the longer term.[18] This important phenomenon might have been neglected by Taiwan experts, but Hu's comment appeared to slightly depart from his predecessor Jiang Zemin who was keen to use the "one country, two systems" model to tackle Taiwan's political future.

While the concept of "one country, two systems" is ambiguous, its vagueness is embedded with inherent flexibility, thus opening the opportunities for interpretation and innovation.[19] That the content of "one country, two systems" cannot be spelt out clearly by any PRC leader and official, including the late Deng Xiaoping, proves that there are opportunities for innovation and experimentation. Kim Richad Nossal has argued that the ambiguities in Hong Kong's Basic Law actually provide room for the HKSAR to explore the ways in which it can become an international actor.[20] As the events have unfolded, the HKSAR does have considerable autonomy in dealing with other nation-states with the approval of Beijing. In this aspect, Beijing can consider granting Taiwan more latitude in handling its existing diplomatic relations while helping the island explore new international relations by using the term, "Taiwan, China," or another term acceptable to the Taiwan side.

In fact, there can be different types of "one country, two systems," including not simply Hong Kong and Macao but also Taiwan. If the Macao model of "one country, two systems" is already different from the Hong Kong version, the Taiwan case is bound to be unique. From this perspective, the Taiwan officials may perhaps look to the creativity and the federal ingredient embedded in the "one country, two systems." It is dogmatic for some Taiwan officials to harp on the same theme that the Hong Kong situation is characterized by broken promises. Beijing does intervene extensively in Hong Kong's political arena, but this does not mean that all the promises laid out in the Sino-British Joint Declaration have been broken. Instead, as argued in the chapter on the implementation of the Basic Law, the HKSAR generally retains its civil liberties, the rule of law and societal freedom, although political mainlandization and media self-censorship have become more prominent than ever before. In short, the Taiwanese should not easily dismiss the Hong Kong model, whose early elements of negotiation, trust, and compromises between the PRC and British diplomats have all been forgotten by critics of the "one country, two systems."

The Will of the Taiwan People: Lessons from the Hong Kong Model

The most thorny problem of the Taiwan side is that any secret negotiations between Taipei and Beijing may be unacceptable to the will of the Taiwan people, and thus at some stage of the negotiations, the Taiwan policy-makers will need to consult the views of the populace by various means, including the possibility of a referendum. Nevertheless, any referendum conducted by the Taiwan government on the island domain's future can be interpreted by Beijing as an act of *de facto* and *de jure* independence. The desire of the Chen Shui-bian administration to promulgate a constitution for Taiwan signalled another sign of an inevitable confrontation between the strong Taiwan identity and Beijing. Some Taiwan academics have already drafted the constitution for Taiwan, embracing a stipulation that the people in Taiwan will have to be consulted prior to any decision on the future of the island.

Creatively speaking, having a broad agreement laying out the principles of the peace agreement between Taipei and Beijing will achieve greater legitimacy and acceptability if it is put forward to the Taiwan public for a plebiscite or referendum. Allowing the Taiwanese to decide the draft agreement between the PRC and Taiwan will realize the spirits of attempting to make compromises and concessions. It will also demonstrate to the people of Taiwan that the PRC is open-minded toward their political choice. Moreover, even if the agreement were rejected by most Taiwan people, the negotiators from both sides would be able to return to the negotiating table to hammer out a solution for another possible agreement. The crux of the problem lies with the political will from both sides. Ideally, both sides should adopt an open-minded acumen of accepting a possible Taiwan public rejection of what they negotiate. If not, any draft agreement including key principles reached by the negotiators would be subject to the opposition's accusation of imposing a top-down and arbitrary solution without public consultation. Of course, if the PRC makes a crucial concession of allowing the people of Taiwan to vote for a draft cross-Strait agreement, the Taiwan side must exchange a concession acceptable to the PRC, such as reaching a 50-year peace settlement or refraining from forging any military alliance with any foreign states that would jeopardize the national security interest of mainland China. The concrete mutual concessions will have to be negotiated by both sides with goodwill.

Indeed, if any draft Beijing-Taipei agreement were put to the Taiwan people for a vote and yet rejected, the result would be frustrating to the negotiators. One possible middle-range solution to tackle the danger of having an entire draft agreement rejected by the Taiwan people is to dissect the content into several items for a plebiscite. For example, the referendum vote can contain several principles and voters are asked to cast their ballots on each of them, including the principle of peaceful coexistence, the status of Taiwan, the relationship with the mainland, and the need to retain Taiwan's existing polity, society, and lifestyle. This way, having a draft agreement "split" into several key items for a referendum will perhaps avoid the likelihood of being rejected as a whole.

In 2005, the thaw between the PRC and the opposition parties in Taiwan — the New People's Party and the Kuomintang — resulted in the visits of James Soong and Lien Chan, the leaders of the two parties respectively, to the PRC. Yet obstacles to further breakthrough persisted. Taiwan's pro-independence activists labelled Soong and Lien as "traitors," implying that any move by the Taiwan authorities toward reunification with the PRC in the future is bound to be conflict-ridden and controversial. Predictably, Taiwan's internal politics will become a severe constraint on the peaceful settlement between Beijing and the Taipei government in the short run.

Given the fact that Taiwan is already a democracy where politicians can play the public opinion card, such card will have to be handled in a cautious way to avoid infuriating the PRC. During the Sino-British negotiations over Hong Kong's future, the British Hong Kong government was at one time accused of playing the public opinion card in Hong Kong, for opinion surveys found that a majority of the people of Hong Kong preferred to maintain the *status quo* — an implication that many Hong Kong people might reject any agreement reached by Britain and China on Hong Kong's future.[21] During the tenth anniversary of the HKSAR, Lu Ping revealed that the British in September 1983 deliberately leaked out the PRC intention of resuming its sovereignty over Hong Kong, thus plunging the

Hong Kong economy into chaos.[22] Yet the PRC government persisted and eventually the British had no choice but to link the Hong Kong dollar to the U.S. currency so as to stabilize the economy.[23] The lesson from the Hong Kong case is that any attempt by the Taiwan side to play the public opinion card would perhaps incur hard-line response from the PRC negotiators — a sensitive issue that can perhaps derail the entire process of negotiations. Strictly speaking, unlike the British who could play the economic card of Hong Kong by challenging the patience of the PRC authorities in 1983, the Taiwanese side will not be able to do the same thing, for any decline in the economic confidence of the Taiwan people would only weaken the island without increasing any bargaining power *vis-à-vis* Beijing.

From the perspective of some Hong Kong people who had a strong sense of belonging in the territory, they thought that, during the Sino-British negotiations, the Hongkongers were deprived of the right of self-determination and had to accept whatever agreement reached by the British colonizers and the Chinese overlord. As a result, when mainland China and Britain formally initialled the Joint Declaration, the British consulted the people of Hong Kong only cosmetically while emphasizing the fact that the alternative to the agreement was no agreement at all. Under these circumstances, the people of Hong Kong had no choice but to accept the Sino-British Joint Declaration. The deprival of self-determination on the part of Hongkongers cannot be applied to Taiwan. Indeed, from the PRC perspective, the people of Taiwan cannot have the right of self-determination as Taiwan is not an independent nation-state. However, the Taiwanese may disagree with this mainland Chinese stance, arguing that they do have the right of self-determination. If a deadlock emerges with regard to whether the Taiwan people possess the right of self-determination, both sides should ideally avoid raising this sensitive, delicate, and thorny issue. Otherwise, the dispute over the right of self-determination could perhaps severely undermine the dialogue of both sides.

The timing of consulting the views of the people of Taiwan on any draft agreement between the PRC and Taiwan will also be a delicate matter that demands political finesse, judgement, and foresight. In the event that the Taiwan negotiators, regardless of whether some of them are from the pro-Taiwan independence DPP or the pro-unification Kuomintang or both, fail to consult the people of Taiwan at some point during the closed-door negotiations, they will perhaps plunge the regime into disrepute and unpopularity. How to keep the people of Taiwan informed of the progress of any cross-Strait negotiations will become a tricky issue. In the event that the PRC and Taiwan sides reach a temporary agreement in closed-door discussions, the nuts and bolts of such agreement will have to be presented to the Taiwan public for discussions. Given the fact that Taiwan remains a deeply divided society that is polarized between pro-unification and pro-independence sentiments, any public consultation will ironically encounter the risk of being turned into a deadlock in which citizens, groups and parties will bitterly bicker over the draft agreement's provisions. Under these circumstances, setting a deadline for public consultations in Taiwan will facilitate the development of any cross-Strait agreement. Otherwise, the debate over democratic procedures in Taiwan will drag on and perhaps jeopardize the potential of reaching the cross-Strait peace agreement. The technicalities of how the Taiwan people can be consulted, and of when such consultations should be held and terminated, will be extremely critical to the success of the Beijing-Taipei agreement.

To prevent Taiwan's public opinion from plunging the Beijing-Taipei negotiations into a sour atmosphere or a deadlocked scenario, both the diplomats from the PRC and Taiwan side will require their political will to persist in reaching a satisfactory solution, taking into account the wishes of the Taiwan public. However, it is easier said than done, for such political will of the representatives from Taipei and Beijing will demand considerable patience, tenacity, and mutual understandings. Under the existing circumstances in which both Taiwan and mainland China lack sufficient trust to initiate dialogue, it is perhaps too early to expect the emergence of the political will from both sides to persevere in the negotiation process.

Still, the Hong Kong model of negotiations, albeit secretive, did offer some lessons for any Taipei-Beijing talks on Taiwan's political future. Ideally, the process of Beijing-Taipei negotiations should be closed door and secretive, thus avoiding public accusations, politicization, and megaphone-style diplomacy from both sides. The mass media will, however, be kept in the dark about the details of negotiations, unless it will be necessary to leak out the content to the public through the press. During the Sino-British negotiations, both sides used terms such as "useful" and "constructive" to calm the fears of the public. Such terms will also be crucial to the need to convey a message of productive negotiations to the people of Taiwan.

Moreover, the timing and the mode of consulting the views of the Taiwan Legislative Yuan on any draft agreement between the PRC and Taiwan will also be critical. Given that the Legislative Yuan has been highly politicized and divided into pro-independence and pro-unification factions, the technical issue of when and how to consult the legislature on any draft agreement will be controversial.

An important political uncertainty is whether some citizens, individuals, or groups may launch a legal challenge to the government if it reaches any draft agreement with the PRC over the island regime's future, on the grounds that the Taiwan people are not sufficiently consulted. As Taiwan has its rule of law, the right of citizens and groups to file lawsuits against the government is inevitable. However, if proper public consultations are held, the legality of any possible lawsuit against the government will be a weak one. In view of all these potential pitfalls in the process of Beijing-Taipei negotiations over Taiwan's political future, it will be perhaps wise for the PRC to adopt a more flexible approach on the bargaining table. Taiwan's internal politics are so complicated that it will have the grave danger of derailing the negotiations.

While the Hong Kong model tended to deny the input of public opinion from Hong Kong, the case of Beijing-Taipei negotiations will have to take into account some, if not all, divisive opinions of the Taiwan people. For any negotiations between mainland China and Taiwan to succeed and achieve a genuine breakthrough, confidence-building and mutual trustful relationships are necessary conditions in the short run. In the medium and long terms, both sides will need considerable patience, persistence, and understandings. The negotiations predictably would become far more conflict-ridden than the Sino-British talks on Hong Kong, thus leading to a higher possibility of a sudden breakdown in the negotiating process.

The Role of Third Parties: The U.S. and Singapore

However, trust-building may be enhanced between Beijing and Taipei through the selective and skilful intervention of third parties, including both the U.S. and Singapore. During the process of negotiating Taiwan's future, there would be two major options for the participation of the U.S. and Singapore. Given that the PRC insists Taiwan's future belongs to its domestic issue, excessive intervention from either the U.S. or Singapore would definitely be detrimental to the negotiating process. The first option for third parties like the U.S. and Singapore is to maintain a neutral status, but intervening in a critical stage whenever the negotiations reach the point of no return or breakdown. Such intervention, however, will require the support of both Taiwan and the PRC. On the other hand, Beijing will be reluctant to see any intervention from foreign nation-states because of the assumption that the PRC-Taiwan negotiations remain a "domestic" matter. The second option is to allow third parties to participate in the negotiations as observers, while keeping the principle of maintaining the confidentiality of the entire negotiating process. Here, Singapore may be more suitable than the U.S. to be an observer, mainly because of its friendly relations with both the PRC and Taiwan. In any event, both the U.S. and Singapore, or any third party involved, will have to maintain an apparently neutral attitude, refraining from making any unnecessary public comments unless the situation of the negotiations turns into a very tense scenario. Overall, any third party's involvement in Beijing-Taipei negotiations will have to be extremely cautious and selective, thus facilitating its role as a constructive partner and a trust-building booster who will help both sides bring about a peaceful settlement over Taiwan's political future.

Indeed, the U.S. or Singapore, which can play a crucial bridging role between mainland Beijing and Taipei diplomatically, will need to consider the capacity of any representatives who are sent to observe the Beijing-Taipei negotiations. Having American or Singaporean officials observe the negotiations between Beijing and Taipei would appear to be a foreign government's explicit intervention in the PRC domestic affairs. Hence, the representatives of either the U.S. government or the Singaporean administration can come from either the academia or the semi-official sector. One may argue that it will make no difference whether the third party sends officials, semi-government officials, or academics to observe the negotiations. What I propose here is to inject an ingredient of flexibility in the format of any third party's observer status, thus avoiding the problem of arousing any unnecessary displeasure and discomfort on the part of the PRC government.

This suggested alternative of having a third party's involvement in the observation of Beijing-Taipei negotiations is a departure from the Hong Kong model. While the Hong Kong model was simple and straightforward in terms of the actual involvement of the parties whose interests were directly impacted, the Taiwan case obviously calls for more sophistication and creativity from the perspective of conflict resolution. As the most influential player shaping mainland China-Taiwan relations, the United States has the capability of facilitating a peaceful settlement on Taiwan's political future provided that it can intervene at the ripe time and at the right place. However, the PRC perception of the American hegemony in the world and in East Asia is not conducive to the actual U.S. involvement in any Beijing-Taipei negotiations. Perhaps the Americans will only be briefed by both the PRC and Taiwan after a certain round of negotiation. On the other hand, Singapore, which has traditionally been the close friends of both the PRC and Taiwan, has tremendous potential of becoming a middleman in the predictably hazardous path of Beijing-Taipei negotiations. If face is an essential ingredient of Chinese political culture, any third party involvement would perhaps be rejected in the first place.

The Beijing-Taipei Pact or Accord

From the vantage point of conflict resolution, Taiwan and the PRC can perhaps reach a memorandum of understanding parallel to the Sino-British Memorandum of Understanding on the new Chek Lap Kok airport. Alternatively and ideally, both Taiwan and the PRC can sign a Peace Accord on Taiwan's political future. However, regardless of whether the first agreement would take the form of a memorandum or a Joint Declaration as with the Hong Kong case, both sides will need to reach the bottom line of each negotiating party. Then a Basic Law for Taiwan — a constitution for Taiwan — can be promulgated later in order to allow Taiwan people a high degree of self-governance. The crux of the problem is, firstly, that both sides have not yet met the bottom line of the other party. Taiwan demands that the PRC should first renounce the use of military force against the island domain, whereas the latter demands the former to abandon the call for any move towards Taiwan's independence. Ideally, the third party, such as Singapore, may like to intervene in the first stage of the negotiation, helping both sides reach the bottom line of the other negotiating party. For example, Taiwan recognizes the fact that the island is part of China mainland. In return, the PRC will have to renounce the use of military force to deal with Taiwan's political future. Once the first stage of exchanging mutual concession is reached, a quick agreement with very broad principles can be reached. Arguably, the goal of meeting the bottom line of each side can be achieved without the need for both the PRC and Taiwan to agree on the meaning of one China. The PRC side occasionally floated the idea that even the definition of China could perhaps be discussed, including the likelihood of uniting Taiwan under the umbrella concept of United China or Greater China. On the other hand, Taiwan has reiterated the importance of both sides returning to the so-called 1992 consensus in Hong Kong, meaning that both sides can agree to disagree on thorny issues such as the meaning of one China. If the political will to reach an agreement does exist, it is a matter of time for both the PRC and Taiwan to hammer out a solution to their differences over the definition of one China. Arguably, the hurdle is not so insurmountable as conventional wisdom may assume.

Ideally, both mainland China and Taiwan can exchange their bottom lines, thus paving the way for a smooth negotiation on other issues. But given the frequent shouting matches and public posturing of both sides, it is perhaps beneficial to both Taiwan and mainland China if Singapore can play the role of facilitator at the first critical stage. As with the Hong Kong and Macao examples, once the bottom lines of negotiating parties were reached, other issues of lesser importance, like aviation rights, nationality, and the formal status of participation in international organizations would be solved without great difficulties.

The second stumbling block for a breakthrough in cross-Strait relations is the question of sovereignty. While China insists that it possesses the sovereignty over Taiwan, meaning that Taiwan is part of mainland China, the Chen Shui-bian administration reiterated that the island regime has its own sovereignty and that it is an undeniable entity. The baffling problem of sovereignty needs to be skilfully tackled in any negotiations by perhaps allowing both sides to agree to disagree. From an objective point of view, the PRC view of sovereignty over Taiwan tends to be absolute, insisting that Taiwan belongs to China. This mainland Chinese perspective reflects the traditional Chinese view of rights, which are conferred upon the citizenry by the state. Yet the Taiwanese view of sovereignty tends to be relatively "modern," insisting that the people of Taiwan have been residing in the island for such a long time that some countries in the world have recognized the *de facto* sovereignty of Taiwan. Sovereignty change, to the Taiwan leaders, must require the endorsement of the Taiwan public. It is extremely difficult for both Taipei and Beijing to reconcile their conflicting notions of sovereignty. The PRC top-down and absolute perspective on sovereignty is in contrast to the bottom-up and pro-Taiwanese view held by Taipei. It will be wise to shelve the issue of sovereignty at the early stage of the negotiations, thus avoiding a possible breakdown and deterioration of diplomatic talks. Given the fact that the Chinese traditionally have attached importance to face, neither Taiwan nor mainland China would be willing to make concessions on their perspectives of sovereignty easily. Yet if both sides agree to disagree even on the issue of sovereignty, once they reach a consensus in the first stage — Taiwan exchanging its recognition of the island as part of China mainland for the PRC renouncement of employing military force — the other issues will perhaps be easier tackled.

The third problem hindering any cross-Strait negotiations is that the Taiwan government may promulgate a pro-independence constitution — a move that will surely endanger any Beijing-Taipei negotiation and complicate the PRC perception of Taiwan. If the PRC sees Taiwan's pro-independence constitutional move as too provocative, the danger of military conflict will be a real one, especially if the hard-line PRC leaders on Taiwan affairs dominate the mainland political arena. To prevent the Beijing-Taipei relations from deteriorating further, the United States can play a critical role of refraining Taiwan from going too far along the path of *de jure* independence. It seems that the Bush administration has already played this important diplomatic role of warning against any move by the Chen Shui-bian administration to drift away from the mainland Chinese orbit in a *de jure* independent manner. Continuous American pressure on Taiwan so as to restrain its pro-independence constitutional move will be a must.

In the event that the Hu Jintao regime in the PRC encounters constant challenges from groups and citizens at the grassroots level, as witnessed in a spate of ongoing citizen protests and confrontations between citizens and police in various provinces, it is not surprising that the PRC regime will perhaps witness the dominance of hard-liners on Taiwan affairs. In particular, in the event that the civilian-military relations in the PRC were suddenly tipped in favour of the military hard-liners, Beijing will perhaps resort to more high-profile and tougher measures to tackle any Taiwan move in promulgating a pro-independence constitution.

Once both Taiwan and mainland China reach the most important bottom line of each side, as suggested before, a Peace Accord stating the principles of the agreement can be drafted. Both Taipei and Beijing can sign an accord with a major principle that both sides will continue to negotiate a settlement on peaceful reunification. The second principle is that with regard to the form of reunification, details can be discussed further between Taiwan and the PRC. One option is perhaps to imitate the Hong Kong or Macao model in which a Basic Law — a mini-constitution for the Special Administrative Region — was drafted immediately following the initialling of the Joint Declaration. Since the relationships between Taiwan and mainland China are far more complicated and politically delicate than the Hong Kong or Macao model, any Peace Agreement reached between the two sides should be brief, with its content far more concise than the parallel Sino-British and Sino-Portuguese Joint Declaration. In a sense, the first step of any Beijing-Taipei negotiation is to defuse the time bomb of any military conflict or confrontation, while at the same time stipulating their intentions to reach a satisfactory agreement immediately after the bottom lines of the two parties are reached.

The second stage of Beijing-Taipei negotiations will involve the nuts and bolts of the peaceful settlement, including perhaps the concrete definition of one China. In September 1997, Beijing was reportedly drafting a Hong

Kong–style "Taiwan Basic Law" to wean the island into reunification by 2010.[24] While the Hong Kong model of drafting the Basic Law was characterized by a top-down approach initiated from Beijing, which grasped the veto power to decide the content of the mini-constitution, a more bottom-up model should perhaps be adopted in the Taiwan case. Nevertheless, any Basic Law for Taiwan will likely take a much longer process than the Hong Kong case, which drafted the Basic Law in 1985 and saw its promulgation in 1990. There will be four options for Taiwan and mainland China to draft the Taiwan Basic Law. The first alternative is to keep it very brief so as to prevent rocking the Beijing-Taipei negotiation process, leaving the detailed issues to a Joint Liaison Group to hammer out various solutions. The second alternative is for both sides to reach a more detailed agreement, but perhaps a bit less detailed than the Basic Law of Hong Kong or Macao; nevertheless, the diplomats from both sides will need to be very patient and persistent in negotiations. Otherwise, the involvement of the Taiwan public opinion in the process of drafting a satisfactory Basic Law will have the danger of bringing about an abrupt deadlock on the negotiating table between Taipei and Beijing. The third option of the Taiwan Basic Law is that it will include only principles, such as Taiwan being allowed to maintain its own military, so that all the potentially contentious issues will be shunned. Symbolic reunification rather than detailed reunification, unlike the model of Hong Kong and Macao, can be reached between the PRC and Taiwan. The final option is that there will be simply no Taiwan Basic Law. Once the Beijing-Taipei Peace Accord or Pact is initiated, it will stipulate that Taiwan will be allowed to maintain its existing constitution (of course not a pro-independence constitution), and that all the existing lifestyle and freedom as well as politico-economic and legal systems will all be retained on the island.

Yet if a Taiwan Basic Law were accepted as a step forward, the process of drafting the Basic Law will require the Taiwan Legislative Yuan to debate its content. Again, given the polarized nature of Taiwan's legislative politics, disputes will be inevitable and the crux of the question is whether the Taiwan government, regardless of the party in power, will have the persuasive power and political will to convince the Legislative Yuan of the acceptability of the Basic Law. During the process of finalizing the Basic Law, the Taiwan government will have to consider incorporating the mini-constitution into a referendum in a very circumspect manner. In the event that the Taiwan public rejects the entire Basic Law, the Taiwan government will perhaps waste considerable time negotiating with the PRC administration. Arguably, a referendum will not be suitable because the issues discussed in the mini-constitution cannot be voted through a referendum easily. Any referendum, if needed, will be more suitable immediately after the Peace Accord. The public endorsement of the major principles of the Joint Peace Pact will confer a powerful mandate upon the Taiwan government to proceed with the detailed negotiations with the PRC on other unresolved issues.

Another critical issue in the drafting process of a possible Basic Law is that the Taiwan government will have to be very cautious in avoiding any image of internationalizing the negotiating issues, say in the form of making inappropriate public announcements or even seeking the intervention of other parties not recognized by the PRC. This political sensitivity will be especially important when both sides encounter arguments and deadlock over issues such as the proper name of Taiwan's participation in international organizations. Internationalization in the form of seeking outside help other than the third parties acceptable to Beijing will plunge the negotiations into uncertainty and tense circumstances. Even if Taiwan may seek the help of the U.S. or Singapore at any critical stage of the negotiation over the Basic Law, such solicitation should ideally be cautious, low-key, and silent. A hallmark of the Sino-British negotiation on Hong Kong's future from 1982 to 1984 was that the British government did not internationalize the issue of Hong Kong's future. The British and the PRC governments reached an agreement without any foreign intervention, although the U.S. government was kept informed of the events through the British channel. Although the British government attempted to internationalize the future of Hong Kong after the Tiananmen tragedy in the PRC in June 1989, the absence of internationalization — foreign intervention without the PRC endorsement — made the Sino-British negotiation relatively smooth.

Above all, de-internationalization means that during the talks between the PRC and Taiwan, the latter will have to abandon any move to lobby other countries in support of Taipei's participation in the United Nations (UN). Taiwan has been lobbying some countries for support of its participation in the UN since 1992. To the PRC, the ROC's lobbying activities represent an internationalization of Taiwan's future and an act of outright separatism. From Taiwan's perspective, its entry to the UN would legally recognize the sovereignty status of the island domain. Abandoning its effort to participate in the UN could become a bargaining chip for Taiwan to exchange for the PRC support of its participation in more international organizations by using the name of either "United China, Taiwan" or "Greater China, Taiwan." The crux of the problem is that Taiwan's negotiators will have to be extremely sensitive toward the need to avoid any provocative move, such as adopting the dollar diplomacy to lobby Third

World states to raise the issue of Taipei's participation in the UN, which would infuriate Beijing and thus undermine the entire negotiating process.

Any Taiwan Basic Law may have to consider the issue of how to link Taiwan's representatives to the mainland NPC. In the cases of Hong Kong and Macao, local deputies are elected to the NPC. However, Taiwan's politicians must recognize the need for a linkage between the deputies of the island and their counterparts of the NPC. In the event that some Taiwanese regard the NPC not only as a political rubber-stamp dominated by the CCP but also as an unnecessary link that would lower the political status of Taiwan, the issue would become a baffling problem during the long negotiating process. Given the fact that the NPC has recently become more politically assertive with better educated and qualified deputies who raise critical questions on various government issues,[25] the Taiwan government and people should arguably view the NPC in a more positive manner, thus reducing the likelihood of an unexpected *cul-de-sac* during the negotiations.

Indeed, some of the issues that can be discussed during the drafting process of any Taiwan Basic Law should be relatively easy, such as the fact that Taiwan will be able to retain its own military for defensive purpose — a point that was emphasized by many PRC leaders in the past. Other issues such as the maintenance of Taiwan's judicial, legislative, and executive autonomy as well as the current lifestyle should be relatively simple. The question of Taiwan holders of Taiwanese passports, however, may become a tricky issue, for the name of the existing Taiwan passports can become a bone of contention. Yet if the PRC side is keen to achieve reunification with Taiwan symbolically but not dogmatically, any contentious issue can be handled in a more flexible and compromising manner. For the sake of reaching a Taiwan Basic Law, both sides should adopt the principle of temporarily shelving the difficult and deadlocked issues while simultaneously searching for satisfactory solutions in the near future. The principle of agreeing to disagree, arguably, should pervade throughout the entire process of the Beijing-Taipei negotiations.

With the benefit of hindsight, many of the nine points presented by the late SCNPC Chairman Ye Jianying in 1981 can be transplanted into a solution on Taiwan's political future. They include the three links (postal, commercial, and aviation/navigation links), the four exchanges (academic, tourist, cultural, and sports exchanges), Taiwan's maintenance of its armed forces, Beijing's non-interference with Taiwan's domestic affairs, the continuation of Taiwan's socio-economic rights and property rights, Taiwan representatives' participation in the PRC governance, China's financial aid to Taiwan if the latter encounters difficulties, and Taiwanese investment and residence in the mainland. Ye's point on the "third KMT-CCP cooperation" needs a degree of flexibility, for Taiwan's ruling party may or may not be the KMT by the time both Beijing and Taipei resume negotiations. Furthermore, Taiwan should perhaps not be made a Special Administrative Region as with the status of Hong Kong and Macao. If Taiwan desires another higher status different from Hong Kong and Macao, the PRC can adopt a more open-minded attitude toward its demand on the condition that Taiwan eventually will have to accept that the island is a part of the United or Greater China, or China mainland. In short, Ye's nine points can be slightly modified and it is too far to argue that under the "one country, two systems," "Taiwan must acquiesce to being a local unit of China — the ROC would cease to exist."[26] Although the HKSAR experience shows that its autonomy *vis-à-vis* the central government is bound to be politically restricted, some elements of Ye's nine points and the spirit of the Hong Kong and Macao "one country, two systems" can still be applicable to a possible resolution of Taiwan's political future.

Conclusion

If we view the "one country, two systems" in terms of the way in which the HKSAR government has ruled itself since July 1, 1997, it is easy to jump to the conclusion that the Hong Kong model cannot be applied to solve Taiwan's political future, as my earlier chapters have also argued. Nor does Macao's political and economic dependency on the PRC offer a solution for the PRC to appeal to Taiwan for reunification. However, this chapter adopts a redefinition and re-focus of the "one country, two systems" by tracing the ways in which the Sino-British and Sino-Portuguese agreements on Hong Kong and Macao were reached respectively. If "one country, two systems" refers to the spirit of delegating some degree of political power to a special region with certain ingredients of ambiguity, flexibility, and creativity, this formula can arguably be applied to deal with Taiwan's political future in a more innovative manner. Similarly, if the Hong Kong model is defined in terms of how Britain and China reached the agreement over Hong Kong's future by maintaining the principle of agreeing to disagree and the tenet of reaching a satisfactory final solution, it can certainly be applied to the resolution of Taiwan's political future.

Adopting an innovative and a constructive perspective, this chapter has proposed a number of steps in which Taiwan, mainland China, and perhaps third parties like the United States and even Singapore can trigger trust-building and negotiations. The political pitfalls of the road to a peaceful settlement will be numerous and hazardous. Both mainland China and Taiwan will have to abide by the principle of agreeing to disagree, the tenet of patience, and the motto of reaching a final satisfactory solution. During the entire processes of pre-negotiation and negotiation, both sides, especially Taiwan's democracy, will have to adopt a self-restrained and extremely cautious attitude. Public political positioning, unnecessary internationalization, and hyper-politicization in the form of mobilizing Taiwan's public opinion through any referendum will have to be handled in an extremely circumspect manner. On the other hand, fundamental issues that cannot be resolved include the question of sovereignty and the precise meaning of one China. However, if these thorny issues were handled under the rubric of agreeing to disagree, the prospects for a peaceful settlement may not be as pessimistic as conventional wisdom may assume. Viewed from the perspective of conflict resolution, mainland China and Taiwan will have to face the daunting challenges of reaching consensus on various contentious issues, whereas the United States and Singapore can perhaps play a far more constructive role than what they are doing.

The inevitable mainlandization of the HKSAR is one thing, but the applicability of the spirit of the "one country, two systems" to Taiwan's political future is arguably another matter that should and can be pursued further. Mainland China's attempt at using the Hong Kong model of "one country, two systems" to appeal to Taiwan's reunification is understandable. Yet the experience of the HKSAR is actually unattractive to Taiwan, where a Western-style democracy with the rotation of party in power is firmly entrenched, and where many citizens are expecting the realization of their rights of self-determination. If the PRC is keen on reunifying Taiwan in an imaginative and innovative way, it should be more flexible in terms of the names of Taiwan and the united China after their reunification, the content of a possible Taiwan Basic Law, and the need for the people of Taiwan to vote on the principles of any cross-Strait agreement. If the new PRC leadership realizes the uniqueness of Taiwan, which remains vastly different from the cases of Hong Kong and Macao, the Beijing-Taipei impasse will be resolved perhaps surprisingly and unpredictably. However, the KMT Chairman Ma Ying-jeou said in January 2008 that he would adopt a policy of no unification, no independence and no force. The Taiwan elite has no incentive to negotiate the island's future with the PRC leaders, who do not have a political solution acceptable to both sides.

10
Conclusion

The innovative concept of "one country, two systems" was used by the late Chinese reformer Deng Xiaoping to tackle Hong Kong's and Macao's political future in the short run and to deal with Taiwan's reunification matter in the long term. Although he passed away in 1997 and failed to witness the transfer of Hong Kong's and Macao's sovereignty and administration to Beijing respectively, his concept has evolved rapidly. The concept was implemented unskillfully by both the Tung leadership and Beijing's clients in the HKSAR, leading to chaotic governance and public outcry, thus discrediting the "one country, two systems" model. Fortunately, under the Donald Tsang administration and with the economic support of Beijing, Hong Kong's "one country, two systems" appeared to be a "success" during its tenth anniversary of the return to the motherland — a phenomenon politically overstated by the official PRC media and the increasingly self-censored HKSAR mass media. The case of Macao, however, is very different from Hong Kong's.[1] Despite the fact that Macao's governance was smoother and did not necessitate the rescue from Beijing, its politico-economic convergence with the PRC has been faster than Hong Kong. Politically, Hong Kong remains more pluralistic than Macao, which is more tolerant of dissent than the PRC polity. Economically, both Hong Kong and Macao have become increasingly dependent on the PRC, thus diluting their economic uniqueness. Although Hong Kong's rule of law and civil liberties are generally retained, and social groups' assertiveness remains impressive, the legal system has been highly politicized and its decisions have been judged by political actors in a hyper-politicized manner. Due to the clash of Western and Chinese civilizations, the pro-democracy elites who strongly identify themselves as Hong Kong people are constantly under the watchful eyes of the central government's agents. Yet the explosion of civil society as manifested on July 1, 2003 has remained a bulwark against any political encroachment on civil liberties. Arguably, the implementation of the "one country, two systems" has not been as smooth and "successful" as the official propaganda portrays. The political experience of the HKSAR has failed to attract Taiwan back to the PRC orbit.

If the "one country, two systems" in the HKSAR during its first decade was viewed as "successful," the phenomenon could be attributable to the existence of civil liberties in general and the tenacity of the rule of law in particular. Yet the persistence of civil liberties and the rule of law is by no means the political gifts endowed upon the people of Hong Kong by either the PRC state or the HKSAR regime. They are arguably the products of the fierce struggle of those Hong Kong people who maintain a strong degree of Hong Kong identity and who oppose any state intervention in the erosion of civil liberties. The loyal political clients of Beijing often accuse the pro-democracy elites in the HKSAR of being "anti-China" and creating a "chaotic Hong Kong." This argument is a testimony of political correctness in conformity with patron-clientelism in both the HKSAR and the PRC. But Beijing's political clients in Hong Kong have totally neglected the fact that, without the staunch opposition from those pro-democracy elites and masses to any sign of state encroachment upon their civil liberties, the rule of law and societal freedom in the HKSAR could not have thrived so easily.

Deng's concept of "one country, two systems" entails a dialectical process filled with contradictions. These contradictions are manifested in the ongoing capitalist revolution in the PRC, whose economic system is more akin to the Hong Kong counterpart than ever before. Yet politically, the HKSAR polity is under tremendous pressure to converge with the mainland system, although the former remains more pluralistic than the latter. The synthesis of the "two systems" will be clear when both Hong Kong and the mainland will be prepared for a closer politico-economic integration in the year 2047. From now to 2047, the tensions between Hong Kong's pluralistic setting and the PRC monolithic polity will continue to be shown in the HKSAR judicial politics, constitutional debate, identity transformations, media development, and electoral participation. In any case, the "one country, two systems" in Hong Kong is gradually drifting toward "one country, one system" in which the economy of both the HKSAR and the mainland is basically capitalist whereas their polities are increasingly converging. The hallmarks of the "two systems" can still be found in the societal defense of civil liberties and the rule of law.

Interestingly, during the tenth anniversary of the HKSAR, both Britain and the United States announced that the "one country, two systems" in

Hong Kong was "successful." Western powers like Britain and the United States, which hope that the HKSAR will envisage the direct election of the chief executive through universal suffrage as soon as possible, are adopting a double standard. On the one hand, they push for democratization in the HKSAR. On the other hand, they accept the superficiality of the persistence of most civil liberties without critically assessing the trend of mainlandization of the HKSAR under the "one country, two systems." Perhaps the lucrative economic market in the PRC has induced both Britain and the United States to pragmatically accept the superficiality of the "successful" operation of the "one country, two systems" with total ignorance of Hong Kong's drift toward media self-censorship, political Sinification or recolonization, economic dependency on the mainland, and the politicization of judicial decisions.

Beijing's clients in the HKSAR do not see the process of mainlandization as an erosion of the Hong Kong identity, for they have already been politically co-opted, culturally assimilated, and endowed with economic interests in both Hong Kong and the mainland. From a critical perspective, Beijing's political clients in the HKSAR are imbued with a colonial mentality. While they staunchly opposed the British colonialists from the 1960s to the 1990s, they have turned to be the politically loyal but absolutely uncritical agents of Beijing. At the apex of the Tung regime's misrule in the HKSAR, the pro-Beijing elites continued to provide an inaccurate assessment of Hong Kong's political circumstances to the central government. The Liaison Office and the HKMAO made errors in their over-optimistic assessment of Hong Kong's political situation — a phenomenon partly ascribable to the failure of the pro-Beijing elites to wake up to the evident governing crisis from 1999 to 2004. The pro-Beijing elites enjoyed political power to such an extent that they were intolerant of any public criticisms during the Tung regime. If colonial mentality is conceptually defined as a politically opportunistic mindset toeing the official line of the overlord, it does exist among the HKSAR's patriotic elites. If political opportunism marked the pro-British elites in Hong Kong before July 1, 1997, then a blind patriotism that amalgamates politico-cultural identifications with the PRC is characterizing Beijing's clients in the HKSAR. In the event that mainland Chinese politics undergo drastic changes in the form of significantly reducing the value and influence of patron-clientelism, the pro-Beijing elites in the HKSAR will perhaps experience a very painful process of self-evaluations, self-criticisms, and self-adjustment.

Some of the elites and masses with strong Hong Kong identity, however, view the rapid mainlandization of the HKSAR with great concerns. Unlike the pro-Beijing elites, the pro-Hong Kong elites tend to be less patriotic toward the motherland and continue to be the critical activists in Hong Kong. They are concerned about the influx of tens of thousands of mainland-born Chinese into the HKSAR since its retrocession, the constant political restrictions, the increasingly self-censored mass media, and the politicization of judicial judgments. Interestingly, the celebrations of the HKSAR tenth anniversary emphasized the superficial triumph of the mainland national Chinese identity and de-emphasized the existence of the strong Hong Kong identity. The message from the central government was clear: the HKSAR leadership will have to accelerate patriotic education so that the local Hong Kong identity will hopefully be diluted whereas the politico-cultural identification with the PRC will be enhanced. The process of mainlandizing the mindset of most Hong Kong people who have strong local identity will by no means be easy. To them, patriotism has to proceed naturally without any sign of compulsion. The tug of war between the local Hong Kong identity and the mainland Chinese identity will persist. Indeed, they can also coexist and amalgamate, as with the case of the 2007 chief executive election where the mainland and Hong Kong political cultures were merged.

The publication of a consultative document on political reform in the HKSAR in July 2007 showed that the Donald Tsang regime has been adopting a delaying tactic to postpone the direct election of both the chief executive and the entire legislature.[2] Specifying various options for political reform, the document has encouraged the people of Hong Kong to ponder the ways forward. Nonetheless, without revealing any mainstream political models for the direct election of the chief executive and the entire legislature, the *Green Paper* symbolized the predicament of the Tsang regime, which is bound to be a loyal client of the central government. Beijing does not want to envisage any Taiwanization of Hong Kong's polity. Nor does it wish to witness any popular directly elected chief executive who will no longer be a politically correct and obedient client. The debate over Hong Kong's democratization is destined to be protracted, illustrating firstly the patron-client relations between the HKSAR regime and Beijing and secondly the central government's fear of having a Taiwan-style democratic polity in Hong Kong. The controversy reveals a deep-rooted rift between those pro-democracy Hongkongers imbued with a very strong Hong Kong identity and those pro-Beijing elites and masses inculcated with an equally strong politico-cultural PRC identity.

On December 12, 2007, Chief Executive Tsang submitted a report on Hong Kong's constitutional development to Beijing. The report says that there is a need for amending the methods of selecting the chief executive and the Legislative Council in 2012, and that implementing universal suffrage for the chief executive first by no later than 2017 will have a better chance of being accepted by most Hong Kong people. In response to the report, the SCNPC reached a decision on December 29. According to the decision, the chief executive and the entire legislature would not be returned by universal suffrage in 2012; the HKSAR government would maintain the half-and-half ratio of legislators returned from geographical constituencies and those from functional constituencies in 2012; and that any future amendment on the method of selecting the chief executive must be reported to the SCNPC for a decision, which would be followed by a government bill to the Legislative Council where a two-thirds majority vote, the chief executive's consent and finally the SCNPC approval would be required. The SCNPC decision opens the door to the possibility of electing the chief executive by universal suffrage in 2017. For the HKSAR government, the earliest possible year of having the chief executive directly elected by universal suffrage would be 2017 and that of having the entire legislature directly elected by universal suffrage would be 2020. The Taiwan government reacted to the SCNPC decision swiftly and expressed its regret that there would not be the direct elections of both the chief executive and the whole legislature in 2012. The HKSAR government issued a statement and said that Taiwan had no role in Hong Kong's internal development. The content of the SCNPC decision on Hong Kong's constitutional reform had little demonstration effect on Taiwan, where the president is directly elected by citizens through universal suffrage.

However, Beijing's decision on Hong Kong's democratization has implications for the PRC's relations with Taiwan. It allows the HKSAR government to tackle the relatively "easier" issues on political reforms, followed by the technically difficult and politically controversial ones. The practice of dealing with the less contentious matters first in political negotiations can be constructively applied to Beijing-Taipei relations. Meanwhile, although there is a deep mutual distrust between the Hong Kong democrats and the HKSAR government, and between the democrats and Beijing, the SCNPC decision gives at least ten years to all sides in designing a political model for Hong Kong. Arguably, the spirit of trying to reach agreements amidst mutual distrust is a dynamic aspect of Beijing-HKSAR relations that can be applied to Beijing-Taipei negotiations in the future.

Beijing favors a controllable model of having the Hong Kong chief executive directly elected by universal suffrage. As the deputy secretary-general of the SCNPC, Qiao Xiaoyang, explained the SCNPC decision on December 29, a "broadly representative nominating committee" shall nominate the candidates for the chief executive election in the future. As long as the composition of the nominating committee is controlled by Beijing's representative Liaison Office in the HKSAR, the nominated candidates would be politically acceptable to the central government—a mainland Chinese style of democratization in a pluralistic Hong Kong setting. This mainland Chinese political culture will clash with the vision of the pan-democratic camp, which rejects a filtering mechanism that would exclude any moderate democrat from running in the chief executive direct election. The democrats will face a dilemma of either accepting a bird-cage type of democracy, which will run contrary to their Western values, or rejecting it but discrediting themselves in the eyes of the pragmatically-minded public and the increasingly politically correct Chinese media. If the democrats remain disunited and excessively individualistic, they would be easily politically marginalized and constantly portrayed by the mainstream media as destructive rather than constructive oppositionists. If democracy embraces the spirit of making concessions and consensus, it will be imperative for the democrats to negotiate with the HKSAR government from now to 2017. On the other hand, Chief Executive Donald Tsang will likely complete his last term of office with political glory. He has skillfully utilized the colonial policy of elite co-optation and patron-clientelism to establish a much stronger power base than his predecessor Tung Chee-hwa; tried to portray an image of fighting for the interest of Hong Kong *vis-à-vis* Beijing; and secured patron Beijing's consent for the likelihood of having a chief executive directly elected by universal suffrage in HKSAR in 2017. Overall, the SCNPC decision on Hong Kong's political reform on December 29, 2007 was a testimony to the operation of patron-client pluralism in the new politics of post-colonial Hong Kong.

This book argues that although the implementation of the "one country, two systems" in the HKSAR has been seemingly "successful," it hides the rapid underlying and irresistible process of mainlandization. Despite this prominent development, the spirit of the "one country, two systems" formula can still be applied to deal with Taiwan's political future. The "one country, two systems" is predicated on the devotion of power to a locality and the coexistence of two different systems. This spirit does contain a tinge of *de facto* federalism, albeit in reality Beijing's political culture tends to exert control over the HKSAR through its direct intervention and its loyal clients. Some elements of the nine points raised by the late Marshal Ye, as discussed in Chapter 9, can be modified and applied to resolve Taiwan's political future. Somehow the people of Taiwan appear to be ignorant of the concept of "one country, two systems." While critics of the concept accurately point to the real difficulties of Hong Kong's autonomy *vis-à-vis* Beijing, they have overstated the aspect of governance and neglected the ways in which Britain and the PRC reached the Sino-British Joint Declaration on Hong Kong's political future.

If we look back to the ways in which Britain and Portugal reached the agreements with China on the future of both Hong Kong and Macao respectively, the concept of "one country, two systems" can be interpreted broadly so that steps can be taken to solve the problem of Taiwan's political future. As the last chapter suggests, the PRC and Taiwan can build up a trustful relationship perhaps with the help of third parties. Hopefully, trust-building can be an interim solution that will narrow the differences of the PRC and Taiwan. The visits of opposition party leaders in Taiwan, including the Kuomintang, to the PRC were the first step toward official rapprochement in the long run. However, the obstacle to Taiwan's political future is not really the turbulent implementation of "one country, two systems" in the HKSAR. Rather, the island's democratic politics has unleashed strong pro-independence forces critical of any move toward eventual reunification with the PRC. If so, the PRC will have to devise a solution far more flexible than the "one country, two systems" formula as applied to Hong Kong and Macao.

When the PRC National People's Congress enacted the Anti-Secession Law in March 2005, it did not really mention using the concept of "one country, two systems" to deal with Taiwan's political future. Perhaps this was a sign that the PRC leadership is open-minded toward other alternatives in dealing with Taiwan's reunification with the mainland. Another optimistic sign was that President Hu's remarks on the HKSAR during its tenth anniversary also did not mention the utilization of the "one country, two systems" to tackle Taiwan's political future. Beijing is perhaps studying various options that can lure the island regime back to the orbit of a united China or Greater China.

Taiwan's democratic operation, however, is by no means a model for both Hong Kong and Macao. Although some democrats in Hong Kong and Macao hope that the chief executive would be directly elected by universal suffrage, just like the political model of Taiwan, the island's chaotic governance and elite corruption are not attractive to many ordinary citizens of Hong Kong and Macao. In order to prove that the Taiwan model of governance is attractive to Hong Kong and Macao, the Taiwan elites and masses will have to consolidate democratic governance, reduce elite corruption, and reach harmonious consensus in a deeply politically divided society. From the perspective of governance, neither the Hong Kong model nor the Taiwan one is politically attractive to each other. It is unfortunate that advocates of either the Hong Kong model or the Taiwan example have been focusing on its governance.

In a nutshell, the "one country, two systems" in the HKSAR has evolved in a way that is by no means conducive to its rigid application to tackle Taiwan's baffling political future. The mainlandization of the HKSAR is inevitable, partly because of the rapid rise of a global China and partly because of the political correctness of Beijing's clientelist rulers and supporters in Hong Kong. However, if we step back to learn a lesson from how Sino-British diplomats reached an agreement on Hong Kong's future in the early half of the 1980s, we can put aside the problem of having "one system" currently eroding the uniqueness of the "two systems" in the HKSAR. Nor do we need to look for those "successes" from the cases of Hong Kong and Macao to justify a solution to deal with Taiwan's political future. It is the spirit of mutual trust, compromise, concessions, consensus, and understandings that are critical to the resolution of the differences between the PRC and Taiwan. Ultimately, in the event that the political leaders of the PRC and Taiwan have the political will to settle their differences, their historical reunification is not really an insurmountable problem. Perhaps generational change in both the PRC and Taiwan leadership will propel the two sides to explore creative, innovative, and feasible solutions to solve the problem of Taiwan's political future. No Chinese in Greater China and overseas countries in the world would like to witness any military skirmishes and conflicts between the PRC and Taiwan, who have been traditionally brothers in the same Chinese family. If democracy in Taiwan demands an unprecedented degree of creativity, tolerance, and consensus, any forward-looking Taiwan leaders should not procrastinate in the quest for a solution to the island's political future. Similarly, if the principles of the PRC governance are now embracing political tolerance and social harmony, its leaders should explore a more flexible solution to deal with the future of Taiwan. This book has argued for the need for both the PRC and Taiwan to meet the bottom lines of the other side, as with the Sino-British negotiation over Hong Kong. In the event that both sides adopt a liberalizing political acumen, a solution under the spirit of mutual understandings, tolerance, compromise, concessions, and coexistence should not be too far away from the current impasse. In conclusion, although the "one country, two systems" in the HKSAR proves to be turbulent and marked by political mainlandization and convergence with the PRC, its spirit can be applied boldly and creatively to resolve the political stalemate between Beijing and Taipei.

Notes

Introduction

1. Personal observations of the CCTV and Phoenix coverage of the tenth anniversary of the HKSAR, July 1, 2007 in Hong Kong.

1   Patron-Client Pluralism and Beijing's Relations with Hong Kong

1. Jae Ho Chung and Lo Shiu-hing, "Beijing's Relations with the Hong Kong Special Administrative Region: An Inferential Framework For the Post-1997 Arrangement," *Pacific Affairs*, vol. 68, no. 2 (Summer 1995), pp. 167–186; Sonny Lo Shiu-hing, "Five Perspectives on Beijing's Policy Towards Hong Kong," in Joseph Y. S. Cheng, ed., *Political Development in the HKSAR* (Hong Kong: City University of Hong Kong, 2001), pp. 41–60; and Ting Wai, "HKSAR's Relations with its Chinese Sovereign," in James C. Hsiung, ed., *Hong Kong the Super Paradox: Life after Return to China* (London: Macmillan, 2000), pp. 265–288.
2. Vicky Randall and Robin Theobald, *Political Change and Underdevelopment: A Critical Introduction to Third World Politics* (London: Macmillan, 1985), p. 52; Robert D. Putnam, *The Comparative Study of Political Elites* (New Jersey: Prentice Hall, 1976), pp. 157–160; and James Scott, "Patron-Client Politics and Political Change in Southeast Asia," *American Political Science Review*, vol. 66 (1972), pp. 90–113.
3. Randall and Theobald, *Political Change and Underdevelopment*, p. 52. Also see Robin Theobald, "Patrimonialism," *World Politics*, vol. XXXIV, no. 4 (July 1982), pp. 548–559; and Harold Crouch, "Patrimonialism and Military Rule in Indonesia," *World Politics*, vol. XXXI, no. 4 (July 1979), pp. 571–587.
4. James Scott, "Corruption, Machine Politics, and Political Change," *American Political Science Review*, vol. LXIII, no. 4 (December 1969), pp. 1142–1158.
5. See, for example, Andrew Scobell, "Hong Kong's Influence on China: The Tail That Wags the Dog?," *Asian Survey*, vol. XXVIII, no. 6 (June 1988), pp. 599–612; and also Michael DeGolyer, "Hong Kong tail wags dog," *The Hong Kong Standard*, May 17, 2007.
6. Liu Wei, "Hong Kong's Impact on Shenzhen Real Property Law," *Hong Kong Law Journal*, vol. 27 (1997), pp. 356–373; and Lo Shiu-hing, "Hong Kong's Political Influence on South China," *Problems of Post-Communism*, vol. 46, no. 4 (July/August 1999), pp. 33–41.

7. *Yazhou Zhoukan*, July 6, 2007 (it is called *Zhonghua Tansuo* or *China Exploration* in Toronto), pp. 6–19.
8. For the political development of the PRC, see Bruce Gilley, "Elite-led Democratization in China: Prospects, Perils and Policy Implications," *International Journal*, vol. 61, no. 2 (Spring 2006), pp. 341–358; and also Winberg Chai, "China's 2005 White Paper: 'Building of Political Democracy' in China," *Asian Affairs*, vol. 33, no. 1 (Spring 2006), pp. 3–36.
9. Some mainlanders secretly attended the candlelight vigil and admitted the failure of the PRC regime to deal with the demands of student demonstrators in May–June 1989 peacefully. See *Ming Pao*, June 5, 2007.
10. One member of the mainland Chinese Communist Party said that she did not participate in the Hong Kong protests, which to her would upset political stability. See *Sing Tao Daily*, June 28, 2007, p. B5.
11. Shirley Lau, "Migrants shaping Hong Kong's new face," CNN, June 30, 2007.
12. Ibid.
13. See Deng Xiaoping, "One Country, Two Systems," in *Deng Xiaoping On the Question of Hong Kong* (Beijing: New Horizon Press, 1993), pp. 6–11, in which he stressed that the capitalist Hong Kong would coexist with socialist China (p. 7). In June 2007, President Hu Jintao reportedly rejected "democratic socialism" as the PRC political objective.
14. Lo Shiu-hing, Yu Wing-yat, and Wan Kwok-Fai, "The 1999 District Councils Elections," in Ming K. Chan and Alvin So, eds., *Crisis and Transformation in China's Hong Kong* (New York: M. E. Sharpe, 2002), pp. 139–165.
15. One of the key organizers of the rescue of the student democrats from mainland China after the June 1989 Tiananmen tragedy, Chan Tat-ching, who denied that he was and is a triad member, openly said he expected the inevitable transformations of the PRC in a recent interview. For the details regarding his rescue operations which secured the support of Western governments, some mainland security officials, and mainland citizens sympathetic of the student leaders, see *China Times*, June 4, 2007 and http://peacehall.com/news/gb/pubvp/2007/06/200706020001.shtml, June 20, 2007.
16. When Democratic Party leader Albert Ho and Civic Party member Margaret Ng visited Toronto in late May 2007, they both expressed the view that the PRC would change democratically in the long run.
17. For all the details, see http://www.hxem.com. They included the Bank of China, the Bank of Communications, the China Construction Bank Corporation, China Telecom, and the Petro China Company, to name a few.
18. This situation reversed the phenomenon of Hong Kong as a "socioeconomic center" of the PRC. See Alvin So and Reginald Kwok, "Socioeconomic Center, Political Periphery: Hong Kong's Uncertain Transition Toward the Twenty-first Century," in Reginald Kwok and Alvin So, eds., *The Hong Kong–Guangdong Link: Partnership in Flux* (Hong Kong: Hong Kong University Press, 1995), pp. 251–257.

19. For dependent development, see Peter Evans, *Dependent Development: The Alliance of Multinational, State and Local Capital in Brazil* (Princeton: Princeton University Press, 1979).
20. Raymond Wong accurately pointed to the self-censorship trend of the Chinese print and electronic media in the HKSAR when he visited Toronto in June 2007. A careful observation of the TVB news and ATV news, especially the former, demonstrated a high degree of political correctness in their coverage of Hong Kong's politics.
21. Remarks made by Mrs. Regina Ip in a course on Hong Kong's tenth anniversary at the University of Hong Kong's School of Professional And Continuing Education, April 28, 2007.
22. For the survey result, see "Hong Kong, SAR: The first 10 years under China's rule," a report of the Hong Kong Transition Project and the national Democratic Institute for International Affairs, June 2007, p. 72.
23. For an insightful discussion of the relationships between taxation and democracy in Hong Kong, see Richard Cullen and Tor Krever, *Taxation and Democracy in Hong Kong* (Hong Kong: Civic Exchange, November 2005), pp. 1–35.
24. For this argument, see Lo Shiu-hing, *Governing Hong Kong: Legitimacy, Communication and Political Decay* (New York: Nova Science, 2001), p. 245.
25. Samuel P. Huntington, *The Clash of Civilizations and the Remaking of World Order* (New York: Simon & Schuster, 1996), pp. 70–72.
26. Michel C. Oksenberg, Michael D. Swaine, and Daniel C. Lynch, "China Faces the Twenty-First Century," in Orville Schell and David Shambaugh, eds., *The China Reader: The Reform Era* (New York: Vintage Books, 1999), p. 515; and Walter C. Clemens, Jr., "China: Alternative Futures," *Communist and Post-Communist Studies*, vol. 32 (1999), p. 17.
27. *Ming Pao*, June 15, 2007.
28. Personal communication with Wang, May 2006.
29. *Ibid*.
30. See You Tube for the detailed coverage of Jiang's public outburst in front of the Hong Kong reporters.
31. For *nomenklatura* in Hong Kong, see John P. Burns, "The Role of the New China News Agency and China's Policy Toward Hong Kong," in John P. Burns, Victor C. Falkenheim, and David M. Lampton, eds., *Hong Kong and China in Transition* (Toronto: Canada and Hong Kong Research Project, University of Toronto–York University, 1994), pp. 17–60; John Burns, "The Structure of Communist Party Control in Hong Kong," *Asian Survey*, vol. 30, no. 8 (August 1990). For the recent studies on China's united front work in Hong Kong, see Jamie Allen, *Seeing Red: China's Uncompromising Takeover of Hong Kong* (Singapore: Butterworth-Heinemann Asia, 1997), pp. 68–111; Holly Porteous, "Beijing's United Front Strategy in Hong Kong," *Commentary*, no. 72 (Winter 1998); Benson Wong, "Can Cooptation Win Over the Hong Kong People?," *Issues & Studies*, vol. 33, no. 5 (May 1997); and Sonny Lo, Eilo Yu,

Bruce Kwong, and Benson Wong, "The 2004 Legislative Council Elections in Hong Kong: The Triumph of China's United Front Work after the July 2003 and 2004 Protests," *Chinese Law & Government*, vol. 38, no. 1 (January/February 2005), pp. 3–29.

32. See the official PRC government's website and also the website of the Liaison Office, in http://www.locpg.gov.hk (accessed June 19, 2007).
33. *Open Magazine*, no. 200 (August 2003), pp. 38–39.
34. Bruce Kwong, "Patron-Client Politics in Hong Kong: a study of the 2002 and 2005 Chief Executive Elections," *Journal of Contemporary China*, vol. 16, no. 52 (July 2007); and Lo Shiu-hing, "The Political Cultures of Mainland China and Hong Kong: Democratization, Patrimonialism and Pluralism in the 2007 Chief Executive Elections," *Asia Pacific Journal of Public Administration*, forthcoming (July 2007).
35. *Open Magazine*, no. 200 (August 2003), pp. 40–41.
36. Man Cheuk-fei, "The Model of the Chinese Communist Control on Hong Kong's Leftwing Newspapers: A Study of Party Newspapers in an Enclave, 1947–1982," unpublished M.Phil thesis, Department of Government and Public Administration, the Chinese University of Hong Kong, December 1998.
37. *Open Magazine*, no. 200 (August 2003), pp. 38–40.
38. *Ibid.*, p. 39.
39. Carrie Chan, "Ex-convict picked as next secretary for home affairs," *The Standard*, June 15, 2007. It must be noted that the home affairs secretary is more or less playing the same functions as the director of the PRC United Front Department.
40. *Ming Pao*, June 17, 2007.
41. *Open Magazine*, no. 200 (August 2003), pp. 40–41.
42. Xu Jiatun, *Xu Jiatun's Hong Kong Memoir* (in Chinese), volumes 1 and 2 (Taipei: United Daily News, 1993); and Lo Shiu-hing, "The Chinese Communist Party Elite's Conflict over Hong Kong, 1983–1990," *China Information*, vol. 8, no. 4 (Spring 1994).
43. Lo, *Governing Hong Kong*, pp. 142–144.
44. TVB interview with C. H. Tung, June 8, 2007.
45. *The Trend Magazine*, no. 215 (July 2003), pp. 6–8.
46. *Ming Pao*, June 17, 2007.
47. *The Trend Magazine*, June 2007.
48. *Ming Pao*, June 17, 2007.
49. *Ming Pao*, June 15, 2007.
50. Remarks made by a mainland researcher who interviewed the author twice in September and October 2003.
51. "What is 9+2? Pan-PRD: A Diversified Single Market — an enlarged hinterland of Hong Kong," in *Bauhinia Gala: A Celebration of the 10th Anniversary of the Establishment of the Hong Kong Special Administrative Region* (Toronto: Best Deal Graphic & Printing, 2007), p. 35.

52. For "policy wind" in the PRC, see David Zweig, *Agrarian Radicalism in China, 1968–1981* (Cambridge, Massachusetts: Harvard University Press, 1989).
53. *Ming Pao*, May 27, 2007, p. A35.
54. Personal discussion with Chief Executive Edmund Ho, December 2004.
55. "Special Meeting of the House Committee on 27 February 2004: Background Brief Prepared by Legislative Council Secretariat. Main Issues Relating to Cooperation between Guangdong and Hong Kong discussed with the Chief Secretary for Administration," LC Paper No. CB(2)1442/03–04.
56. *Sing Tao Daily*, June 2, 2007, p. B17. Also see *Today Daily News* (Toronto), June 2, 2007, p. A11.
57. See *Sing Tao Daily*, June 2, 2007, p. B7.
58. Lo Shiu-hing, *The Politics of Cross-Border Crime in Greater China*, forthcoming (M. E. Sharpe).
59. *Ming Pao*, May 28, 2007, p. A15.
60. Lo Shiu-hing, *Political Development in Macau* (Hong Kong: The Chinese University Press, 1995).
61. *Ming Pao*, May 28, 2007, p. A15.
62. *Ibid.*
63. *Hong Kong Standard*, July 2, 2007, p. A3.
64. *Zhonghua Tansuo (China Exploration)*, the overseas Chinese (Toronto) version of *Yazhou Zhoukan*, no. 88 (July 13, 2007), p. 11.
65. Zhang Ran, "QDII expanded to include securities, fund companies," *China Daily*, June 21, 2007.
66. A notable exception was Bruce Kwong, "Patron-Client Politics and Elections in Hong Kong," unpublished PhD thesis, Department of Politics and Public Administration, the University of Hong Kong, 2004.
67. Scott, "Corruption, Machine Politics, and Political Change," pp. 1142–1158.
68. A. Weingrod, "Patrons, Patronage and Political Parties," *Comparative Studies in Society and History*, vol. 10 (July 1968), pp. 377–400.
69. J. D. Powell, "Peasant Society and Clientelist Politics," *American Political Science Review*, vol. 64 (June 1970), pp. 411–425.
70. Scott, "Corruption, Machine Politics, and Political Change," p. 1144.
71. On the Article 23 debate, see Anthony B. L. Cheung, "The Hong Kong System under One Country Being Tested: Article 23, Governance Crisis and the Search for a New Hong Kong Identity," in Joseph Cheng, ed., *The July 1 Protest Rally: Interpreting a Historic Event* (Hong Kong: City University of Hong Kong, 2005), pp. 33–70; and Sonny Lo, "Hong Kong, 1 July 2003 — Half a Million Protestors: The Security Law, Identity Politics, Democracy and China," *Behind the Headlines*, vol. 60, no. 4 (April 2004), pp. 1–14.
72. Carrie Chan, "Beijing to announce new Tsang team," *The Standard*, June 23, 2007.
73. Scott, "Corruption, Machine Politics, and Political Change," pp. 1150–1158.

2 The Mainlandization of Hong Kong

1. *Ming Pao*, March 11, 2005.
2. *Yizhoukan* (*Next Magazine*), no. 782 (March 3, 2005), pp. 46–53.
3. *Sing Tao Daily*, March 4, 2005.
4. *Dongzhoukan* (*Eastweek*), May 26, 2004, pp. 19–28. Also see *Cheng Ming*, no. 215 (July 2003), pp. 6–8; *Guangjiaojing* (Wide Angle), no. 371 (August 15–September 16, 2003), pp. 6–10; and *Qianshao* (Frontline), no. 162 (August 2004), pp. 6–8. For the debate over Article 23 of the Basic Law, see Fu Hualing, Carole J. Petersen, and Simon N. M. Young, eds., *National Security and Fundamental Freedoms: Hong Kong's Article 23 Under Scrutiny* (Hong Kong: Hong University Press, 2005).
5. See *Sing Pao*, July 24, 2003. Also see Liam Fitzpatrick, "The Long March," *Time*, July 14, 2003, pp. 18–23. The central government criticized its officials in Hong Kong for failure in understanding the problems of the territory and the degree of public discontent. Political commentator and Hong Kong member to the National People's Congress, Allen Lee Peng-fei, publicly unveiled that Gao Siren, the director of the Liaison Office in the HKSAR, was criticized by Beijing. Lee made the remarks on his program at the Commercial Radio, July 25, 2003 at 9:25 am.
6. *Sing Pao*, July 18, 2003.
7. See *Dongzhoukan*, June 9, 2004, pp. 14–29.
8. For the intimidation incidents, see *Yizhoukan*, June 3, 2004, which dealt with Allen Lee's story. A former mainland Chinese official of the PRC's Hong Kong and Macao Affairs Office called Lee's home and he appeared to be intimidated. Raymond Wong was reportedly in debt, whereas the threats issued to Cheng and Lee appeared to be purely political. Both Wong and Cheng were staunchly anti-Communist, but Lee tended to be an independent commentator critical of the Tung regime.
9. Wang Wenfang, *China's Resumption of Sovereignty over Hong Kong* (Hong Kong: David C. Lam Institute for East-West Studies, Hong Kong Baptist University, 1997).
10. *Mingbao Zhoukan* (Ming Pao Sunday Supplement), no. 616 (March 6, 2005), pp. 28–33. One unsubstantiated report said Tung had offered to resign five times (2002, 2003, 2004, January 2005, and March 2005). See *Cheng Ming*, no. 235 (March 2005), pp. 16–17.
11. Alfred G. Meyer, "Theories of Convergence," in Chalmers Johnson, ed., *Change in Communist Systems* (Stanford, California: Stanford University Press, 1970), pp. 336–337.
12. *Ibid.*, p. 323. Also see Alan J. Foster, *Political Convergence: The Theory* (London: Politics Association, 1978); and Johan K. Vree, *Political Integration: The Formation of Theory and Its Problems* (The Hague: Mouton, 1972).
13. See Andrew Jack, *Inside Putin's Russia: Can There Be Reform without Democracy?*

(New York: Oxford University Press, 2004); and Lilia Shevtsova, *Putin's Russia* (Washington, D.C.: Carnegie Endowment for International Peace, 2003).

14. For an optimistic view, see Su Shaozhi, "Problems of Democratic Reform in China," in Edward Friedman, ed., *The Politics of Democratization: Generalizing East Asian Experiences* (Boulder, Colorado: Westview, 1994), pp. 225–230; and Zibigniew Brzezinski, "Will China Democratize? Disruption without Disintegration," *Journal of Democracy*, vol. 9, no. 1 (January 1998): pp. 3–4. For a pessimistic perspective, see, for example, Pei Minxin, "Is China Democratizing?" *Foreign Affairs*, vol. 77, no. 1 (January/February 1998), p. 81; and Tatsumi Okabe, "China's Prospects for Change," in Larry Diamond and Marc F. Plattner, eds., *Democracy in East Asia* (Baltimore: Johns Hopkins University Press, 1998), pp. 175–176.

15. On Hong Kong's convergence or divergence with China, see an earlier study by James Cotton, "Hong Kong: Convergence or Divergence?" *Journal of Northeast Asian Studies* 6, no. 4 (Winter 1987). Also see Gerald Segal, *The Fate of Hong Kong* (London: Simon & Schuster, 1993), pp. 207–210.

16. On China's authoritarian system, see Michel Oksenberg, "China's Political System: Challenges of the Twenty-First Century," in Jonathan Unger, ed., *The Nature of Chinese Politics: From Mao to Jiang*, (New York: M. E. Sharpe, 2002), pp. 193–208. On Hong Kong's semi-competitive system, see William Overholt, "Hong Kong: Between Third World and First," *Hong Kong Democratic Foundation Newsletter*, no. 17 (January 2001).

17. For a discussion of Hong Kong's dependence on China, see Ian Holliday, Ma Ngok, and Ray Yep, "After 1997: The Dialectics of Hong Kong Dependence," *Journal of Contemporary Asia* 34, no. 2 (2004), pp. 254–270.

18. Indeed, the HKSAR can also influence the political culture of the PRC, especially in South China. See Andrew Scobell, "After Deng, What? Reconsidering the Prospects for a Democratic Transition in China," *Problems of Post-Communism* 44, no. 5 (September/October 1997), pp. 27–28; and Michel Oksenberg, "Will China Democratize? Confronting a Classic Dilemma," *Journal of Democracy* 9, no. 1 (January 1998), pp. 31–32.

19. The Party-state in the PRC remains "quite heavy-handed in controlling activities by religious groups, educated professionals, labor, youth, and women." See Carol Lee Hamrin, "Social Dynamics and New Generation Politics," in David M. Finkelstein and Maryanne Kivlehan, eds., *China's Leadership in the 21st Century* (New York: M. E. Sharpe, 2003), pp. 205–211.

20. Anthony B.L. Cheung, "Civil Service Reform in Post-1997 Hong Kong: Political Challenges, Managerial Responses?" *International Journal of Public Administration* 24, no. 9 (2001), pp. 929–950; and Wilson Wong, "From a British-Style Administrative State to a Chinese-Style Political State: Civil Service Reform in Hong Kong After the Transfer of Sovereignty" (Paper written for the Brookings Institution, June 2003), http://www.brookings.edu/fp/cnaps/papers/wong2003.pdf (accessed June 2, 2005).

21. Martin Lee, "Letter to Hong Kong," RTHK Radio 3, September 5, 1999, http://www.martinlee.org.hk/lettersToHK9.5.99.htm (accessed May 15, 2005).
22. Melinda Liu and Alexandra A. Seno, "Getting the Word Out," *Newsweek*, July 12, 2004.
23. See "Research Team on the Compendium of Submissions on Article 23 of the Basic Law" (report prepared by Robert Chung and his research team at the University of Hong Kong), http://www.hkupop.hku/Chinese/resources/bl23/bl23gp/report/app8.pdf (accessed May 10, 2005).
24. Tung's governing strategy was shaped by Confucian values such as harmony, benevolence, and peace, but it was out of touch with the increasingly politicized environment of Hong Kong. See Lau Siu-kai, "Government and Political Change in the Hong Kong Special Administrative Region," in James C. Hsiung, ed., *Hong Kong the Super Paradox: Life After Return to China* (London: Macmillan, 2000), pp. 35–57; and Lau Siu-kai, "Tung Chee-hwa's Governing Strategy: The Shortfall in Politics," in Lau Siu-kai, ed., *The First Tung Chee-hwa Administration: The First Five Years of the Hong Kong Special Administrative Region* (Hong Kong: The Chinese University Press, 2002), pp. 1–40.
25. For the crisis of legitimacy in Hong Kong before the retrocession, see Ian Scott, *Political Change and the Crisis of Legitimacy in Hong Kong* (Hong Kong: Oxford University Press, 1990). With regard to the PRC's intervention in Hong Kong's political reform in the 1990s, see Jermain T. M. Lam, "Democracy or Convergence: The Dilemma of Political Reform in Hong Kong," *Asian Journal of Public Administration,* vol. 15, no. 2 (December 1993), pp. 225–253.
26. *Cheng Ming*, no. 183 (November 2000), pp. 6–8; and *Kaifang (Open Magazine)*, no. 158 (February 2000), p. 18.
27. Beijing also decided that the term of the replacement chief executive should be two years rather than five years, generating a debate in Hong Kong over whether the Basic Law's stipulation concerning the five-year term of office of the chief executive was violated. Eventually, on April 27, 2005, the NPC had to interpret the Basic Law saying that the term of office of the replacement chief executive would be two years. For the entire debate, see *Sing Tao Daily*, April 28, 2005; Editorial, "Court Need Not Anticipate NPC," *Ming Pao*, April 5, 2005; and "Rule of Law a Necessity, Not a Luxury," *South China Morning Post*, April 20, 2005, A14. For a critique of the NPC interpretation of the Basic Law by the democrats such as Margaret Ng and Martin Lee, see *Xinbao* (Hong Kong Economic Journal), May 2, 2005, 4 and *Ming Pao*, April 20, 2005, p. D13. The Catholic Church's Bishop Joseph Zen criticized the NPC interpretation as a move that "failed to respect the Basic Law." See *Hong Kong Economic Journal*, April 9, 2005, p. 4.
28. The British colonial administration relied heavily on patronage too. See Ambrose King Yeo-chi, "Administrative Absorption of Politics in Hong Kong: Emphasis on the Grass-roots Level," *Asian Survey,* vol. 15, no. 5 (May 1975), p. 424;

and S. N. G. Davies, "One Brand of Politics Rekindled," *Hong Kong Law Journal* 7 (1977), pp. 69–70. The post-handover political absorption can be found in Anthony B. L. Cheung and Paul C. W. Wong, "Who Advised the Hong Kong Government? The Politics of Absorption before and after 1997," *Asian Survey*, vol. 44, no. 6 (December 2004), pp. 874–894.

29. Raymond Wu was removed from the Equal Opportunities Commission and Tam Yiu-chung was stripped of his chairmanship of the Vocational Training Council, thus sparking suspicion that the Tsang alienated some pro-Beijing elites. The pro-Beijing elites such as Wu and Choy So-yuk publicly expressed their displeasure with Tsang, triggering an attempt by officials of the Liaison Office — China's representative office in the HKSAR — to persuade them to support Tsang. See *Sing Tao Daily*, May 20, 2005, p. B3.

30. *Sing Tao Daily*, June 28, 2007, p. B4.

31. Ibid., March 11, 2005.

32. Tan Ee Lyn, "Hong Kong Tung says Falun Gong evokes Jonestown suicide," *Reuters*, May 22, 2001; and Stella Lee and Kong Lai-fun, "Tung Steps Up Attack on Sect," *South China Morning Post*, April 26, 2001. The rise of Falun Gong in China can be seen as a confrontation between the Party-state and society. See Clemens Stubbe Ostergaard, "Governance and the Political Challenge of the Falun Gong," in Jude Howell, ed., *Governance in China* (Lanham, Maryland: Rowman & Littlefield, 2004), pp. 297–225.

33. *Wen Wei Po*, July 2, 2007, p. A20.

34. The former financial secretary Antony Leung was involved in a car scandal; the former secretary for health Yeoh Eng-kiong was severely criticized for his mishandling of the outbreak of the Severe Acute Respiratory Syndrome; and the former secretary for security Regina Ip was enmeshed in the debate over Article 23 of the Basic Law. Tung did not ask any of the three to resign until they themselves took the initiative to do so.

35. See Editorial, "First-Rate Good Man But Not First-Class Leader, Wholeheartedly Working for Hong Kong But Lacking in Capability," *Ming Pao*, March 11, 2005.

36. Alvin Y. So and Ming K. Chan, "Conclusion: Crisis and Transformation in the Hong Kong SAR — Toward Soft Authoritarian Developmentalism?" in Ming K. Chan and Alvin Y. So, eds., *Crisis and Transformation in China's Hong Kong* (New York: M. E. Sharpe, 2002), pp. 363–384; and Anthony B. L. Cheung, "The Changing Political System: Executive-led Government or 'Disabled' Governance?" in Lau, *The First Tung Chee-hwa Administration*, pp. 41–68.

37. Michael E. DeGolyer, "How the Stunning Outbreak of Disease Led to a Stunning Outbreak of Dissent," in Christine Loh and Civic Exchange, eds., *At the Epicentre: Hong Kong and the SARS Outbreak* (Hong Kong: Hong Kong University Press, 2004), pp. 117–138.

38. *Yizhoukan*, no. 749 (July 15, 2004), pp. 42–48.

39. See Editorial, "The Organizer of the 1967 Riots Should Not Receive the Medal," *Ming Pao*, July 2, 2001.
40. See *Taiyang Bao* (*The Sun*), July 6, 2003.
41. Carrie Chan and Diane Lee, "Ma critics use June 4 row to attack DAB," *The Standard*, May 17, 2007.
42. Ibid.
43. For Chan's disagreement with Tung, see *Yizhoukan*, no. 567 (January 18, 2001), p. 52; and *Dongzhoukan*, no. 407 (August 10, 2000), p. 26.
44. For the Principal Officials Accountability System, see Christine Loh and Richard Cullen, "Political Reform in Hong Kong: The Principal Officials Accountability System: The First Year (2002–2003)," *Journal of Contemporary China* 14, no. 42 (February 2005), pp. 153–176.
45. *Taiyang Bao*, July 7, 2003.
46. *Ibid.*, July 8, 2003.
47. *Ibid.*, July 10, 2003.
48. For a discussion that Chinese nationalism is compatible with authoritarianism, see Suisheng Zhao, "Chinese Nationalism and Authoritarianism in the 1990s," in Suisheng Zhao, ed., *China and Democracy: Reconsidering the Prospects of a Democratic China* (New York: Routledge, 2000), pp. 253–270.
49. *Dongxiang* (*The Trend Magazine*), no. 235 (March 2005), pp. 16–17. For China's united front work, see Holly Porteous, "China's United Front Strategy in Hong Kong," *Commentary*, no. 72 (Winter 1998), pp. 1–10. The aim of united front is to isolate the minority and to win the majority. See Van Slyke Lyman, *Enemies and Friends: The United Front in Chinese Communist History* (Stanford, California: Stanford University Press, 1967), pp. 3–6. For a good review of China's united front work in Hong Kong before the handover, see Jamie Allan, *Seeing Red: China's Uncompromising Takeover of Hong Kong* (Singapore: Butterworth-Heinemann Asia, 1997), pp. 68–111; and Wai-kwok Wong, "Can Co-optation Win Over the Hong Kong People? China's United Front Work in Hong Kong Since 1984," *Issues & Studies* 33, no. 5 (May 1997), pp. 102–137.
50. Editorial, "Cyber Priorities," *South China Morning Post*, August 5, 2000; and *Yizhoukan*, no. 473 (April 2, 1999), pp. 30–38.
51. *Dongxiang* (*The Trend Magazine*), no. 235 (March 2005): 17. Interestingly, when Donald Tsang was tipped as the replacement chief executive in April and May 2005, the Hong Kong reports said he was close to Liao Hui. However, when Hong Kong reporters asked Gao for his view on Tsang, the former refused to say anything in public — a move apparently contrary to most PRC officials dealing with Hong Kong affairs. Therefore, the report on the opinion differences between Liao and Gao appeared to be accurate.
52. John Flowerdew, *The Final Years of British Hong Kong: The Discourse of Colonial Withdrawal* (London: Macmillan, 1998), pp. 178–186.
53. *Dongxiang*, no. 183 (November 2000), pp. 6–8.

54. The DAB and the rural advisory body Heung Yee Kuk publicly endorsed the nomination of Tsang as the candidate for the chief executive election scheduled to be held on July 10, 2005. See TVB news, June 1, 2005.
55. For details, see "Framework of accountability for principal officials," press release, http://www.info.gov.hk/gia/general/200204/17/0417251.htm (accessed August 1, 2002). Interesting, in March 2004, the PRC's legal expert, the late Xiao Weiyun, visited Hong Kong and he argued that the POAS actually violated the Basic Law.
56. Leung's letter of resignation to Chief Executive Tung Chee-hwa, March 10, 2003, in LC Paper No. CB(2)1526/02–03(01), Annex; Chris Yeung, "I Forgave an Honest Mistake, Says Tung," *South China Morning Post*, March 22, 2003; Editorial, "Chief Executive Must Let Antony Leung Go," *South China Morning Post*, March 19, 2003, p. 12; Editorial, "A Time of Reckoning," *The Standard*, May 7, 2003, p. A2; "Credibility Crisis," *The Standard*, March 26, 2003, p. A15; Margaret Ng, "The Case against Antony Leung," *South China Morning Post*, March 28, 2003, p. 16; and Yeung Sum, "Abuse of Power?" *South China Morning Post*, April 15, 2003, p. 14.
57. Carole J. Petersen, "National Security Offences and Civil Liberties in Hong Kong: A Critique of the Government's 'Consultation' on Article 23 of the Basic Law," *Hong Kong Law Journal* 32, Part 3 (2002), pp. 457–470.
58. A survey found that 90 percent of the 1,154 protestors opposed the legislation on Article 23 of the Basic Law, and that 60 percent of them came from the middle class. See *Taiyang Bao*, July 7, 2003.
59. For Bishop Zen's political defiance, see Beatrice Leung and Chan Shun-hing, *Changing Church and State Relations in Hong Kong, 1950–2000* (Hong Kong: Hong Kong University Press, 2003), pp. 117–124. In October 2000, Zen publicly unveiled that the Liaison Office's officials tried to warn him of his contacts with the mainland Catholics. See *Apple Daily*, October 5, 2000, p. 21.
60. Some students of the pro-Beijing schools, such as the Fukien Secondary Schools, participated in the mass protests. Their teachers reportedly used the justification of the absence from school to "penalize" them. See *Taiyang Bao*, July 9, 2003.
61. *Apple Daily*, July 2, 2003.
62. Allen Lee Peng-fei's remarks at the University of Hong Kong SPACE course on April 28, 2007.
63. *Yizhoukan*, no. 708 (October 2, 2003), pp. 46–52. Since July 1, 2003, Liao's public profile has become so low that his subordinate Chen Zuo'er is the spokesman of the HKMAO in public.
64. I am indebted to Sister Beatrice Leung for this point. Also see Beatrice Leung and Marcus Wang, "Hong Kong and Vatican Relations in the Chinese Context," paper presented at the conference "Hong Kong Ten Years After," on June 29–30, 2007 at the City University of Hong Kong and jointly sponsored by the CNRS-CERI/Po, Paris.

65. *Ibid.*
66. He remarked on the July 1, 2007 protest in which he was one of the participants: "We really wait for a long time to see the direct elections of the Chief Executive and the entire Legislative Council. We hope to envisage their realization as soon as possible." TVB news, July 1, 2007.
67. *Hong Kong iMail*, August 28, 2005. For an overview of the debate on Hong Kong's constitutional reforms, see Johannes Chan, "Some Thoughts on Constitutional Reform in Hong Kong," *Hong Kong Law Journal* 34, Part 1 (2004), pp. 1–12; and Albert Chen, "The Constitutional Controversy of Spring 2004," *Hong Kong Law Journal*, Part 2 (2004), pp. 215–225.
68. *Apple Daily*, July 2 and July 3, 2004.
69. Ambrose Leung, Cheung Chi-fai, and Carrie Chan, "United Front Cadre Seeks to Heal Rift," *South China Morning Post*, May 27, 2004, p. 1.
70. For the full results of the elections, see http://www.elections.gov.hk/elections/legco2004/eindes.html. Also see Christine Loh, "Hong Kong Legislative Council Elections: Overcoming the System," *China Brief* 4, no. 18 (September 16, 2004), published by the Jamestown Foundation, http://www.jamestown.org (accessed June 2, 2005).
71. *Cheng Ming*, no. 330 (April 2005), p. 87.
72. For China's market transition, see Barry Naughton, "China's Transition in Economic Perspective," in Merle Goldman and Roderick MacFarquhar, eds., *The Paradox of China's Post-Mao Reforms*, (Cambridge, Massachusetts: Harvard University Press, 1999), pp. 30–44.
73. Patten's assumptions can be seen in Chris Patten, *East Meets West: The Last Governor of Hong Kong on Power, Freedom and the Future* (London: McClelland & Stewart, 1998), pp. 292–300.
74. *Ibid.*, pp. 104–105.
75. Beijing set up the Provisional Legislative Council to veto the political reform introduced by Patten. Members of the Provisional Legislative Council were all appointed by the PRC and none of the democrats could ride the "through train" to cross over the legislature beyond July 1, 1997. However, the democrats were able to return to the legislature in the 1988 Legislative Council elections. See Leo Goodstadt, "China and the Selection of Hong Kong's Post-Colonial Political Elite," *The China Quarterly*, no. 163 (September 2000), pp. 721–741. Also see Leo Goodstadt, *Uneasy Partners: The Conflict between Public Interest and Private Profit in Hong Kong* (Hong Kong: Hong Kong University Press, 2004).
76. Lau Siu-kai, "The Making of the Electoral System," in Kuan Hsin-chi, Lau Siu-kai, Louie Kin-sheun, and Timothy Ka-ying Wong, eds., *Power Transfer and Electoral Politics: The First Legislative Election in the Hong Kong Special Administrative Region* (Hong Kong: The Chinese University Press, 1999), pp. 3–35.
77. Alvin Y. So, *Hong Kong's Embattled Democracy: A Societal Analysis* (Baltimore: The Johns Hopkins University Press, 1999), pp. 231–232; and Lo Shiu-hing

and Yu Wing-yat, "The Politics of Electoral Reform in Hong Kong," *Commonwealth & Comparative Politics* 39, no. 2 (July 2001), pp. 99–108.
78. Choi Chi-keung, "The Decisive Effect of the Proportional Representation System: From Inter-party Competition to Intra-party Competition," in Kuan Hsin-chi, Lau Siu-kai, and Timothy Ka-ying Wong, eds., *Out of the Shadow of 1997? The 2000 Legislative Council Election in the Hong Kong Special Administrative Region* (Hong Kong: The Chinese University Press, 2002), pp. 99–124.
79. *Dongzhoukan*, no. 372 (December 9, 1999), p. 45.
80. Also see Craig N. Canning, "Hong Kong: 'One Country, Two Systems' in Troubled Waters," *Current History* 103, no. 674 (September 2004), pp. 295–296.
81. *Ta Kung Pao*, July 20, 2003.
82. President Hu Jintao said Beijing opposed any intervention from foreign forces into Hong Kong's domestic affairs. See *Taiyang Bao*, July 20, 2003.
83. See *The First Report of the Constitutional Task Force: Issues of Legislative Process in the Basic Law Relating to Constitutional Development* (March 2004), www.info.gov.hk/cab (accessed June 1, 2005). The first report in March also focused on the technical issue of amending the Basic Law and local ordinances.
84. *The Second Report of the Constitutional Task Force: Issues of Legislative Process in the Basic Law Relating to Constitutional Development* (April 2004), pp. 18–19, www.info.gov.hk/cab. The report came up with a number of rules governing political reform, including the need to maintain the central government's authority and the executive-led system. Also see *South China Morning Post*, April 16, 2004.
85. See "Decision of the Standing Committee of the National People's Congress on Issues Relating to the Methods for Selecting the Chief Executive of the Hong Kong Special Administrative Region in the Year 2007 and for Forming the Legislative Council of the Hong Kong Special Administrative Region in the Year 2008. Adopted by the Standing Committee of the Tenth National People's Congress at its Ninth Session on 26 April 2004," S. S. No. 5 to Gazette Extraordinary No. 8/2004, http://www.info.gov.hk/cab/cab-review/eng/basic/pdf/es5200408081.pdf (accessed December 29, 2004). Also see "The Fourth Report of the Constitutional Development Task Force: Views and Proposals of Members of the Committee on the Methods for Selecting the Chief Executive in 2007 and for Forming the Legislative Council in 2008 (December 2004)," http://www.info.gov.hk/cab/cab-review/eng/report4/pdf/fourthreport.pdf, 2 n. 1 (accessed December 29, 2004).
86. "The Decision of the Standing Committee of the National People's Congress . . . ," E9.
87. *Ming Pao*, June 3, 2005, revealing national security agents, Public Security Bureau officers, and many other researchers from Beijing, Shanghai, and Guangdong were sent to Hong Kong to collect intelligence on the territory, because the intelligence provided by the Liaison Office had proved to be inaccurate.

88. *South China Morning Post,* February 2004, p. 1.
89. For a full debate over patriotism, see Ming Pao, ed., *Aiguo lunzheng* ("The debate over patriotism") (Hong Kong: Ming Pao, April 2004).
90. *South China Morning Post*, May 28, 2004, 1. Also see Editorial, "Freedom of Speech Must Be Defended," *South China Morning Post*, May 28, 2004, p. 12.
91. The retired mainland official, Cheng Shousan, denied that he had intimidated Lee, but later reports said he was one of the Chinese officials who were asked to conduct stronger united front work on the people of Hong Kong. See *South China Morning Post*, June 1, 2004, p. 1.
92. *South China Morning Post*, August 17and 24, 2004.
93. *Apple Daily*, September 14, 2004.
94. *Ibid.*, February 27, 1999, p. 1.
95. The HKSAR Government Daily Information Bulletin, "The Chief Executive Report to the State Council" (June 10, 1999).
96. *Sing Tao Daily*, March 21, 2004.
97. *Hong Kong Economic Times*, March 30, 2005, p. 33.
98. Chan withdrew his legal challenge after the SCNPC's interpretation of the Basic Law.
99. Leung said, "If Aw Sian was prosecuted, it would be a serious obstacle for restructuring. If the group should collapse, its newspapers would be compelled to cease operation." See *South China Morning Post*, February 5, 1999, p. 1. For critiques of Leung's position, see Editorial, "Secretary Leung Should Take a Rest," *Apple Daily*, February 5, 1999, p. A8; Editorial, "This Good Person Has Done a Wrong Thing," *Ming Pao*, February 5, 1999, p. A2; and Editorial, "Question of Justice," *South China Morning Post*, February 5, 1999, p. 18. For a critical review of the rule of law in Hong Kong, see Margaret Ng, "Post-handover Rule of Law: A New Interpretation," in Chris Yeung, ed., *Hong Kong China: The Red Dawn* (Sydney: Prentice Hall, 1998), pp. 99–120.
100. Byron S. J. Weng has argued that the Basic Law "provides a weak basis for judicial independence." See Weng, "Judicial Independence under the Basic Law," in Steve Tsang, ed., *Judicial Independence and the Rule of Law in Hong Kong* (Hong Kong: Hong Kong University Press, 2001), p. 69.
101. See *Apple Daily*, June 31, 2003; and *Hong Kong Economic Times*, July 2, 2003.
102. The term is borrowed from Guillermo O'Donnell and Philippe C. Schmitter, *Transitions from Authoritarian Rule: Tentative Conclusions about Uncertain Democracies* (Baltimore: The Johns Hopkins University Press, 1986), p. 49.
103. Sidney Tarrow, *Power in Movement: Social Movements and Contentious Politics* (Cambridge: Cambridge University Press, 1998), p. 23.
104. For social movements in Hong Kong, see Lui Tai-lok and Stephen Wing-kai Chiu, "Introduction: Changing Political Opportunities and the Shaping of Collective Action: Social Movements in Hong Kong," in Stephen Wing-kai Chiu and Lui Tai-lok, eds., *The Dynamics of Social Movement in Hong Kong* (Hong Kong: Hong Kong University Press 2000), pp. 1–20.

105. Writing before July 1, 1997, Ip Po-keung had already argued that the civil society in Hong Kong would at best be "tamed," but not "crushed." See Ip Po-keung, "Development of Civil Society in Hong Kong: Constraints, Problems and Risks," in Li Pang-kwong, ed., *Political Order and Power Transition in Hong Kong* (Hong Kong: The Chinese University Press, 1997), p. 183. For the civil society's quest for autonomy in the HKSAR, see Agnes S. Ku, "Negotiating the Space of Civil Autonomy in Hong Kong: Power, Discourses and Dramaturgical Representation," *The China Quarterly*, no. 179 (September 2004), pp. 647–664.
106. In general, the public believes that the English language "is the key to preparing the young people for a successful career." See Chao Fen Sun, "Hong Kong's Language Policy in the Postcolonial Age: Social Justice and Globalization," in Ming K. Chan and Alvin Y. So, eds., *Crisis and Transformation in China's Hong Kong* (New York: M. E. Sharpe, 2002), p. 295.
107. It must be noted that the British colonial officials originally viewed the Catholic Church with either "contempt" or political suspicion. See Beatrice Leung and Chan Shun-hing, *Changing Church and State Relations in Hong Kong, 1950–2000* (Hong Kong: Hong Kong University Press, 2003), p. 27.
108. Thomas Tse-kwan Choi, "Civic and Political Education," in Mark Bray and Ramsey Koo, eds., *Education and Society in Hong Kong and Macao: Comparative Perspectives on Continuity and Change* (Hong Kong: Comparative Education Research Centre, University of Hong Kong, 2004), p. 189.
109. Yet recent surveys have found that patriotism of the Hong Kong people has slightly increased; 73 percent of a survey of 1,054 citizens identified themselves as "feeling proud of being a Chinese." See *Ming Pao*, June 2, 2005.
110. Civic Exchange, "Listening to the Wisdom of the Masses: Hong Kong People's Attitude toward Constitutional Reform" (January 2004), http://www.hkbu.edu.hk/~hktp, 16 (accessed June 1, 2005).
111. See Elaine Chan, "Defining Fellow Compatriots as 'Others': National Identity in Hong Kong," *Government and Opposition* 35, no. 4 (2000), pp. 499–519.
112. Gordon Matthews, "Heunggongyahn: On the Past, Present and Future of Hong Kong Identity," *Bulletin of Concerned Asian Scholars* 29, no. 3 (1997), p. 13.
113. David Akers-Jones, *Feeling the Stones: Reminiscences by David Akers-Jones* (Hong Kong: Hong Kong University Press, 2004), p. 268.
114. Chu Yun-han and Chang Yu-tzung, "Culture Shift and Regime Legitimacy: Comparing Mainland China, Taiwan, and Hong Kong," in Hua Shiping, ed., *Chinese Political Culture, 1989–2000* (New York: M. E. Sharpe, 2001), pp. 331–332.
115. This phenomenon is contrary to Hong Kong as a "socioeconomic center" before the handover. See Alvin Y. So and Reginald Yin-wang Kwok, "Socioeconomic Center, Political Periphery: Hong Kong's Uncertain Transition toward the Twenty-first Century," in Reginald Yin-wang Kwok and Alvin

Y. So, eds., *The Hong Kong–Guangdong Link: Partnership in Flux* (Hong Kong: Hong Kong University Press, 1995), pp. 251–257.

116. Intermarriage between the people of Hong Kong and mainlanders, especially between Hong Kong men and mainland women, has become commonplace since retrocession. More Hong Kong women have visited the mainland and searched for male partners too.

117. Sung Yun-wing, *The Emergence of Greater China: The Economic Integration of Mainland China, Taiwan and Hong Kong* (London: Palgrave, 2004); Sung Yun-wing, *Hong Kong and South China: The Economic Synergy* (Hong Kong: City University Press, 1998); and Sung Yun-wing and Song Enrong, *The China–Hong Kong Connection: The Key to China's Open-Door Policy* (Cambridge: Cambridge University Press, 1991).

118. The criticism leveled at Anson Chan came mainly from the pro-Beijing elites, but whether Chan really was an obstacle to closer economic integration between Hong Kong and China was debatable. For a good review of the multifaceted Hong Kong–China integration, see Anthony Gar-on Yeh, Yok-shiu F. Lee, Tunney Lee, and Nien Dak Sze, eds., *Building a Competitive Pearl River Delta Region: Cooperation, Coordination, and Planning* (Centre of Urban and Environmental Management, University of Hong Kong, 2002).

119. His remarks made at the conference "Hong Kong Ten Years After" at the City University of Hong Kong, June 29, 2007. I am indebted to Professor Ting Wai for this insightful point.

120. Some mainland visitors were amazed at the mass protests in the HKSAR on July 1, 2003 and July 1, 2004. Some participated in the annual candlelight vigil held at the Victoria Park to commemorate the Tiananmen incident in the PRC.

121. Information provided by a mainland student to the author, April 16, 2005.

122. *Ming Pao*, July 5, 2007, p. A15.

123. For the British colonial legacy, see Ming Chan, "The Imperfect Legacy: Defects in the British Legal System in Colonial Hong Kong," *University of Pennsylvania Journal of International Economic Law* 18, no. 1 (Spring 1997); and Ming Chan, "The Legacy of the British Administration of Hong Kong: A View from Hong Kong," *The China Quarterly*, no. 151 (September 1997).

124. In the British colonial era, the business people adapted to the transfer of sovereignty by looking for mainland Chinese partners, enhancing their links with the mainland and retaining a politically conservative outlook. See C. K. Lau, *Hong Kong's Colonial Legacy: A Hong Kong Chinese View of the British Heritage* (Hong Kong: The Chinese University Press, 1997), pp. 83–100.

125. Hong Kong Cable Television program on the tenth anniversary of the HKSAR, "Hong Kong Connection," broadcast in Canada's Fairchild Television on June 22, 2007 at 10:45 pm.

126. Remarks made by Martin Lee in "Hong Kong Connection," Cable TV program, broadcast in Toronto on June 24, 2007.

127. See *Sing Tao Daily*, December 22, 2005. Lau Chin-shek has moderated his political views and stance since he had to visit his ailing mother in mainland China in the late 1990s. His vote share in the direct elections held for the Legislative Council also declined gradually, pointing to his gradual political eclipse.
128. For the most recent survey on self-censorship in Hong Kong, see Hong Kong Journalist Association, "Survey on Press Freedom in Hong Kong, January 2007," in http://www.hkja.org.hk (accessed January 12, 2007).
129. Joseph S. Nye, *Soft Power: The Means to Success in World Politics* (New York: Public Affairs, 2004).
130. *Ibid.*
131. *Ibid.*, p. 5.
132. *Ibid.*, p. 7.
133. *Ibid.*, p. 8.
134. See *Ming Pao*, November 23, 2005.
135. "The Fifth Report of the Constitutional Development Task Force: Package of Proposals for the Methods for Selecting the Chief Executive in 2007 and for Forming the Legislative Council in 2008," October 2005, in els/ca/papers/ca1021cb2-rpt-e.pdf" http://www.legco.gov.hk/yr05-06/english/panels/ca/papers/ca1021cb2-rpt-e.pdf (accessed 25 November 2005).
136. Bruce Gilley, "Elite-led democratization in China: Prospects perils and policy implications," *International Journal*, Spring 2006, pp. 341–358.

3 The Politics of Judicial Autonomy

1. One observer said that politicization could be seen from "the beginning [of the government's attempt to ask for the NPC's interpretation] to the end." See Anthony Cheung Bing-leung, "Interpretation from a political beginning to a political end," *Ming Pao*, June 30, 1999, p. A25.
2. Byron S. J. Weng, "Judicial Independence under the Basic Law," in Steve Tsang, *Judicial Independence and the Rule of Law in Hong Kong* (Hong Kong: Hong Kong University Press, 2001), p. 50.
3. See *Apple Daily*, February 27, 1999, p. A1. Also see Xiao Weiyun and others, "Why the Court of Final Appeal Was Wrong: Comments of the Mainland Scholars on the Judgment of the Court of Final Appeal," in Johannes M. M. Chan, H. L. Fu, and Yash Ghai, eds., *Hong Kong's Constitutional Debate: Conflict Over Interpretation* (Hong Kong: Hong Kong University Press, 2000), pp. 53–60.
4. *Hong Kong Economic Journal*, February 27, 1999, p. 1. Also see the CFA's judgment on January 29, 1999. Final Appeal Numbers 14, 15, and 16.
5. Remarks made by Cheung Tat-ming, a lecturer at the Faculty of Law, University of Hong Kong. See *Oriental Daily*, February 27, 1999, p. A20. Also

see Yash Ghai, "Court must explain its power but stand firm against a review," *Hong Kong Standard*, February 26, 1999, p. 11. Margaret Ng believed that the CFA should not yield to the demand of those people who were dissatisfied with its decision. See her article "When people write the history of this moment in the future," *Ming Pao*, March 10, 1999, p. E10.

6. Chung Ching-tin, "The central government adopts a retrained attitude toward the CFA's judgment," *Hong Kong Economic Journal*, March 10, 1999, p. 14.
7. *Hong Kong Standard*, June 27, 1999, p. 13. Also see Qiao Xiaoyang, "Explanatory Note on 'The Interpretation by the Standing Committee of the National People's Congress of Articles 22(4) and 24(2)(3) of the Basic Law of the HKSAR of the PRC (Draft)' at the Tenth Session of the Standing Committee of the Ninth National People's Congress on 22 June 1999," in Chan, Fu, and Ghai, eds., *Hong Kong's Constitutional Debate: Conflict Over Interpretation*, pp. 483–484. When the CFA judges discussed Article 22 in the landmark case in January 1999, Judge Charles Ching and Judge Henry Litton remarked that Article 22 belonged to "the affairs under the mainland's jurisdiction." See *Hong Kong Economic Journal*, January 13, 1999, p. 8.
8. *Hong Kong Standard*, June 27, 1999, p. 13. Also see Qiao's "Explanatory Note . . . ," pp. 484–485.
9. *Sunday Morning Post*, June 27, 1999, p. 1.
10. *Ibid*.
11. The five judges of the CFA are Andrew Li Kwok-nang, Justice Henry Litton, Justice Anthony Mason, Justice Kemal Bokhary, and Justice Charles Ching. See *South China Morning Post*, February 26, 1999, p. 1.
12. Wong On-yin, "It is wise for Li Kwok-nang to resign," *Apple Daily*, June 28, 1999, p. D1. Another letter from a citizen, however, said that Li should resign in a bid to protest against the reversal of the verdict of the CFA by the NPC. See Lee Shek-keung, "Li Kwok-nang should resign to protest," Letter to the editor, *Apple Daily*, May 22, 1999, p. F1.
13. *Hong Kong Standard*, February 8, 1999, p. 2.
14. *Hong Kong Economic Journal*, May 13, 1999, p. 7.
15. *Apple Daily*, February 12, 1999, p. A15.
16. *Ming Pao*, February 12, 1999, p. A9.
17. *Ming Pao*, 26 May 1999, p. A9. However, one CFA judge, Anthony Mason, said on 30 January during a seminar at the University of Hong Kong that the court had made a "purposive interpretation" of the Basic Law. The CFA's judgment said: "It is generally accepted that in the interpretation of a constitution such as the Basic Law a purposive approach is to be applied. The adoption of a purposive approach is necessary because a constitution states general principles and expresses purposes without condescending to particularity and definition of terms. Gaps and ambiguities are bound to arise and, in resolving them, the courts are bound to give effect to the principles and purposes declared in, and to be ascertained from, the constitution and relevant extrinsic materials." See

the CFA's judgment in Appeal Numbers 14, 15, and 16 of 1998. *Ng Ka Ling, Ng Tan Tan v. The Director of Immigration; Tsui Kuen Nang v. The Director of Immigration; The Director of Immigration v. Cheung Lai Wah.*
18. *Ibid.*
19. *Hong Kong Economic Journal*, May 26, 1999, p. 8. Shiu also opposed the idea of amending the Basic Law, saying that "if we were to amend the Basic Law because you, she or I misinterpret the Basic Law, where would the dignity of the Basic Law be? The law enjoys a supreme position under the rule of law. You and I are under it — even Li Kwok-nang and Tung Chee-hwa are under the Basic Law." See *South China Morning Post*, May 16, 1999, p. 2.
20. *Hong Kong Standard*, May 16, 1999, p. 2.
21. *Hong Kong Standard*, January 8, 1999, p. 5. Also see *Hong Kong Economic Journal*, January 8, 1999, p. 7.
22. *Hong Kong Standard*, January 8, 1999, p. 5. Judge Ching was critical of the government's immigration law introduced after the handover. He said that the law was "totally absurd" as it could split family members who were born before and after a parent had met the seven-year permanent residency requirement. See *South China Morning Post*, January 13, 1999, p. 4.
23. The Honourable Mr Justice Godfrey, Justice of Appeal, "Legal issue is what is at stake," Letter to the editor, *South China Morning Post*, May 12, 1999, p. 16.
24. Reproduced in English in *Apple Daily*, May 20, 1999, p. A2. Godfrey's letter was dated May 19, 1999. Also see *Ming Pao*, May 20, 1999, p. A8. A spokesperson for the Judiciary said it had no comment on Godfrey's letter, which was just "an individual opinion." *Hong Kong Standard*, May 20, 1999, p. 3. Godfrey's letter aroused the concern of three mainland Chinese legal academics researching comparative law at the City University of Hong Kong. The three academics interpreted his letter as "implying that it is procedurally inappropriate for the government to request the NPC to interpret the Basic Law." For this interpretation of Godfrey's letter, see Lin Leifan, Ku Minkang, and Zhu Guobin, "Judges cannot resist the NPC's interpretation," *Ming Pao*, May 25, 1999, p. B13.
25. *South China Morning Post*, May 4, 1999, p. 3. Also see *Apple Daily*, May 4, 1999, p. A4.
26. *South China Morning Post*, May 17, 1999, p. 3.
27. *Ibid.*
28. This was one of the sections in the CFA's judgment in the Final Appeal Numbers 14, 15, and 16 of 1998. The judgment was made on January 29, 1999.
29. *Ibid.*
30. See *Oriental Daily*, February 7, 1999, p. A19. *Ming Pao*, February 7, 1999, p. A4. *Hong Kong Economic Journal*, February 8, 1999, p. 1.
31. *South China Morning Post*, February 8, 1999, p. 1.
32. *Hong Kong Standard*, February 8, 1999, p. 2.

33. *South China Morning Post*, February 26, 1999, p. 1.
34. *Ibid.* Also see *Ming Pao*, April 30, 1999, p. A6.
35. Cited in Felix Lo, "NPC a good option to help settle abode issue," *China Daily*, May 17, 1999, p. 1. *China Daily* used the word "reinterpretation," which was not a term accepted by the HKSAR government. I therefore use the word interpretation instead of reinterpretation. The HKSAR government said that the term reinterpretation "is only apt to describe the situation where the same body interprets the relevant legal provisions for a second time. The present case does not fit that description. The NPC Standing Committee, as a higher authority, will be interpreting the provisions for the first time." See Pamela Tan, Director of Administration and Development, Department of Justice, "Interpreting provisions," Letter to the editor, *South China Morning Post*, June 26, 1999, p. 14.
36. *Hong Kong Economic Journal*, June 21, 1999, p. 4 and *South China Morning Post*, June 21, 1999, p. 4.
37. *Hong Kong Standard*, February 8, 1999, p. 2.
38. *Hong Kong Standard*, February 8, 1999, p. 2.
39. *Ming Pao*, May 5, 1999, p. A6.
40. *Hong Kong Economic Journal*, April 29, 1999, p. 2.
41. *Hong Kong Standard*, February 8, 1999, p. 2.
42. *Hong Kong Standard*, June 27, 1999, p. 2. See the remarks made by Maria Tam and Anthony Neoh, the Hong Kong members of the Basic Law Committee.
43. See the remarks of Maria Tam in *Oriental Daily*, June 27, 1999, p. 1.
44. The most effective way, according to Maria Tam and Raymond Wu, was the government's request of the NPC to interpret the Basic Law. See *Hong Kong Commercial Daily*, May 9, 1999, p. A12. For Tam's similar remarks, see *Hong Kong Economic Journal*, May 10, 1999, p. 7.
45. *South China Morning Post*, May 3, 1999, p. 1.
46. *Hong Kong Economic Journal*, February 8, 1999, p. 5.
47. *Apple Daily*, February 13, 1999, p. F2.
48. *Apple Daily*, February 27, 1999, p. A1.
49. *Ming Pao*, May 19, 1999, p. A6.
50. *South China Morning Post*, May 16, 1999, p. 2.
51. *Oriental Daily*, March 1, 1999, p. A19.
52. *Ibid.*
53. *Ibid.*
54. Editorial, "It is time constitutional row ended," *Ming Pao*, March 1, 1999, p. E8.
55. See Chen's article, "The survival of the rule of law rests on one idea," *Ming Pao*, February 9, 1999, p. A8. Another Committee member, Anthony Neoh, attempted to play down the incident by saying that the mainland legal experts might "misunderstand" the CFA's judgment, which according to him did not intend to challenge the NPC authority. *Ibid.*

56. See his "Participating in revising the Basic Law, developing the spirit of self-governance," *Ming Pao*, March 15, 1999, p. E9.
57. *Ming Pao*, May 22, 1999, p. A9.
58. *Ibid*.
59. *Oriental Daily*, February 26, 1999, p. A19.
60. *Apple Daily*, May 22, 1999, p. A19.
61. *Oriental Daily*, May 30, 1999, p. A19. Also see *The Sun*, May 30, 1999, p. A11.
62. *Ming Pao*, May 21, 1999, p. A6.
63. See *Ming Pao*, May 30, 1999, p. A8.
64. *Ibid*.
65. See *Hong Kong Economic Journal*, May 22, 1999, p. 4. Tam said that the time might not be ripe for the establishment of constitutional convention, for the right of abode issue was only one court case.
66. See Ng, "Horrifying Constitutional Convention," *Ming Pao*, June 2, 1999, p. A32.
67. *Ibid*.
68. *Ibid*.
69. Liu is with the Faculty of Law at the University of Hong Kong. See his "Writing before the interpretation by the NPC Standing Committee," *Ming Pao*, May 22, 1999, p. B12.
70. Remarks made by Democratic Party member and legislator Cheung Man-kwong. *Hong Kong Standard*, May 18, 1999, p. 4.
71. See Michael Allen, Brian Thompson, and Bernadette Walsh, *Cases & Materials On Constitutional & Administrative Law* (London: Blackstone, 1994), p. 247.
72. *Hong Kong Standard*, June 13, 1999, p. 2.
73. Six of them were from Hong Kong and the other half from the PRC.
74. *Apple Daily*, June 19, 1999, p. A15. *South China Morning Post*, June 19, 1999, p. 2.
75. *Hong Kong Standard*, June 19, 1999, p. 1.
76. *Ibid*. Also see *Hong Kong Economic Journal*, June 19, 1999, p. 4.
77. See Yash Ghai, "Framework to judge law," *South China Morning Post*, October 6, 1997, p. 21.
78. *Ming Pao*, May 18, 1999, p. A6. Nine Hong Kong NPC members did not sign their names. They included Jiang Enzhu (the head of the NCNA who did not want to express his view), Rita Fan (the President of the Legislative Council), Allen Lee (who opposed the NPC interpretation), Wong Po-yan, Ng Hong-mun, Maria Tam, Raymond Wu (who were the Hong Kong members of the Basic Law Committee and who did not want to express their views), Tso Wang-wai and Wong Man-kong (who both advocated the idea of asking the CFA to "rectify" its decision). Also see *Hong Kong Economic Journal*, May 17, 1999, p. 5.
79. *Hong Kong Economic Journal*, May 18, 1999, p. 7.
80. He was one of the outspoken Hong Kong NPC members on the right of abode issue. Ma, a member of the pro-China Democratic Alliance for Betterment of Hong Kong, advocated that the central government should help

the HKSAR government to deal with the influx of population. See his "The central government should assist [us] in solving the CFA incident," *Ming Pao*, March 16, 1999, p. E6. Ma also argued in February that "[i]f the CFA refuses to clarify or gives a clarification which is unacceptable, that means the mistakes have not been corrected and action should be taken to get the problem fixed." See *South China Morning Post*, February 26, 1999, p. 4. Ma at one point insisted that he would initiate a motion to the NPC to "clarify" issues related to the CFA's ruling. See *Oriental Daily*, February 26, 1999, p. A19.

81. *Hong Kong Economic Journal*, March 15, 1999, p. 5. Also see *Apple Daily*, March 15, 1999, p. A6.
82. *Hong Kong Economic Journal*, March 15, 1999, p. 5.
83. *South China Morning Post*, June 14, 1999, p. 4.
84. *Ibid.*
85. *Hong Kong Standard*, May 21, 1999, p. 2.
86. *Ibid.*
87. *Hong Kong Economic Journal*, May 4, 1999, p. 10. Also see *Hong Kong Standard*, April 30, 1999, p. 1.
88. *Apple Daily*, February 13, 1999, p. A6.
89. *Apple Daily*, May 4, 1999, p. A4.
90. *South China Morning Post*, June 21, 1999, p. 4.
91. *Hong Kong Standard*, June 22, 1999, p. 2.
92. *South China Morning Post*, May 3, 1999, p. 1; June 10, 1999, p. 19 and June 23, 1999, p. 1. Also see *Oriental Daily*, May 3, 1999, p. A19. Allen Lee, "We have to fight for the rule of law," *Ming Pao*, May 29, 1999, p. B14. Also see *Apple Daily*, May 17, 1999, p. A12.
93. See his "Only hope that the NPC will make an impartial decision," *Ming Pao*, May 8, 1999, p. B12.
94. *Hong Kong Standard*, May 3, 1999, p. 3. Also see *Oriental Daily*, May 3, 1999, p. A19.
95. *South China Morning Post*, February 8, 1999, p. 4.
96. Chris Yeung and No Kwai-yan, "The ties that bind our NPC deputies," *South China Morning Post*, March 16, 1999, p. 19.
97. See Lau Yui-shiu, "The central government does not need to worry about the uncontrollable Hong Kong NPC members," *Hong Kong Economic Journal*, March 17, 1999, p. 9.
98. *Ibid.*
99. Terry Cheng, "NPC deputies face dilemma on dual roles," *Hong Kong Standard*, March 17, 1999, p. 11.
100. *South China Morning Post*, January 9, 1999, p. 5.
101. *South China Morning Post*, February 2, 1999, p. 1.
102. Daily Information Bulletin of the HKSAR Government, "Government Statement on CFA's Judgment," January 29, 1999.
103. See Editorial, "Happily accepting the judgment, calmly facing the

consequences," *Hong Kong Economic Journal*, February 6, 1999, p. 1. Also see Editorial, "Ending confusion," *South China Morning Post*, February 2, 1999, p. 16, which said "One of the most encouraging aspects of the CFA's decision on right of abode for mainland-born children is the way it has been so unhesitatingly accepted by the Government."

104. *South China Morning Post*, February 5, 1999, p. 19.
105. Margaret Ng, "Justice speaks with a clear voice," *South China Morning Post*, February 5, 1999, p. 19.
106. Daily Information Bulletin, "Chief Executive's media session on the CFA ruling," February 10, 1999.
107. The word "inform" was from *Apple Daily*, February 27, 1999, p. A14. The word "forewarn" was from "Statement by the Secretary for Justice at Legislative Council House Committee Meeting, March 5, 1999."
108. Remarks made by Martin Lee Chu-ming, Margaret Ng, and Emily Lau. See *Apple Daily*, February 27, 1999, p. A14. However, Leung argued that "[t]o regard the application itself as applying political pressure on the court is entirely wrong. The CFA itself regarded the application as proper in the exceptional circumstances." See "Statement by the Secretary for Justice at the Legislative Council House Committee Meeting, May 5, 1999."
109. Daily Information Bulletin, "Government applies by motion to CFA for clarification." February 24, 1999.
110. *Hong Kong Economic Journal*, May 3, 1999, p. 6.
111. *Apple Daily*, May 4, 1999, p. A4.
112. *South China Morning Post*, May 6, 1999, p. 6.
113. *Hong Kong Economic Journal*, May 6, 1999, p. 7.
114. *Ming Pao*, May 3, 1999, p. A2.
115. *Ibid.*
116. Daily Information Bulletin, "Interpretation: A legal and constitutional option," May 18, 1999.
117. *Ibid.*
118. Ip's remarks in the legislature on May 19, 1999, broadcast live at the Cable TV.
119. *Hong Kong Economic Journal*, May 20, 1999, p. 7.
120. *South China Morning Post*, May 20, 1999, p. 3.
121. *Oriental Daily*, June 3, 1999, p. A19.
122. Daily Information Bulletin, "Chief Executive's report to State Council," June 10, 1999.
123. *Ibid.*
124. Remarks made by Cheung Tat-ming, see *Ming Pao*, May 13, 1999, p. A11. He also questioned whether the HKSAR government had the right to request the State Council to ask the NPC to interpret the Basic Law.
125. Daily Information Bulletin, "Chief Secretary for Administration's Transcript," May 19, 1999.

126. *South China Morning Post*, May 20, 1999, p. 3.
127. Daily Information Bulletin, "Secretary for Justice calls for understanding to implement 'One Country, Two Systems,'" May 22, 1999.
128. Daily Information Bulletin, "Transcript of media session on the NPC Standing Committee's interpretation of the Basic Law," June 26, 1999.
129. *Oriental Daily*, May 5, 1999, p. A19.
130. *Oriental Daily*, June 30, 1999, p. A19.
131. *Hong Kong Economic Journal*, June 30, 1999, p. 6.
132. *South China Morning Post*, June 30, 1999, p. 1.
133. *The Sun*, June 28, 1999, p. A6.
134. *Ming Pao*, May 26, 1999, p. A9.
135. *Ming Pao*, May 5, 1999, p. A6.
136. *The Sun*, May 10, 1999, p. A4.
137. *Oriental Daily*, June 28, 1999, p. A19.
138. See his "Rule of law is intact," *Hong Kong Standard*, June 26, 1999, p. 11.
139. *Hong Kong Standard*, May 4, 1999, p. 3.
140. *Apple Daily*, February 27, 1999, p. A14.
141. *Hong Kong Standard*, June 22, 1999, p. 2.
142. *Hong Kong Standard*, February 2, 1999, p. 1.
143. *Apple Daily*, February 9, 1999, p. A1. *Oriental Daily*, February 9, 1999, p. A19.
144. *Hong Kong Economic Journal*, March 8, 1999, p. 6.
145. *Hong Kong Standard*, May 6, 1999, p. 1. *Apple Daily*, May 6, 1999, p. A2.
146. *Oriental Daily*, May 4, 1999, p. A19. Also see *Wen Hui Pao*, May 4, 1999, p. A12.
147. *Ming Pao*, May 1, 1999, p. A3.
148. *South China Morning Post*, June 24, 1999, p. 1.
149. *Hong Kong Standard*, June 23, 1999, p. 1.
150. *South China Morning Post*, June 28, 1999, p. 1. *Hong Kong Economic Journal*, June 28, 1999, p. 5. *Apple Daily*, June 28, 1999, p. A8.
151. *Ming Pao*, June 24, 1999, p. A10.
152. *South China Morning Post*, May 6, 1999, p. 6.
153. *Hong Kong Economic Journal*, June 23, 1999, p. 5.
154. *Ming Pao*, June 23, 1999, p. A1 and p. B13.
155. Letter to the editor (name and address of the author supplied), "Farcical to ask judges to change their tune," *South China Morning Post*, February 27, 1999, p. 14.
156. *Hong Kong Standard*, February 26, 1999, p. 4.
157. *South China Morning Post*, March 16, 1999, p. 6. But Chang Hsin, a legal researcher at the Chinese University, said it was unrealistic to propose a referendum because its result might embarrass the central government.
158. *South China Morning Post*, 26 February 26, 1999, p. 1.
159. Wong Man-tai, "Clarifying the judgement undermines the rule of law," *Hong Kong Economic Journal*, March 1, 1999, p. 6. Also see Editorial, "Undermining

the rule of law, having serious consequences," *Hong Kong Economic Journal*, February 27, 1999, p. 1.
160. Yash Ghai, "The theatre of the law," *South China Morning Post*, March 1, 1999, p. 23.
161. Editorial, "Best Way Out," *South China Morning Post*, February 27, 1999, p. 14.
162. Cited in Quinton Chan and Samantha Wong, "Judges 'left in awkward position,'" *South China Morning Post*, June 27, 1999, p. 3. Also see the article by Cheung Man-kwong, a member of the Democratic Party led by Martin Lee, "The Tung clique's inauspicious bell over the rule of law," *Ming Pao*, May 21, 1999, p. B13.
163. *Hong Kong Standard*, May 20, 1999, p. 3.
164. *Apple Daily*, May 18, 1999, p. A2.
165. *Apple Daily*, May 11, 1999, p. A20.
166. *Ming Pao*, June 14, 1999, p. A10 and June 16, 1999, p. A9.
167. Editorial, "Judgment may open floodgates," *Hong Kong Standard*, June 12, 1999, p. 14. The editorial criticized the Court of Appeal's judgment on June 11 that 17 appellants could not be deported by the government which had not set up a scheme to verify their claim to the right of abode in Hong Kong.
168. Editorial, "Judges must not play at politics," *Hong Kong Standard*, May 20, 1999, p. 10.
169. Editorial, "The situation is decided and do not believe in dangerous remarks," *Oriental Daily*, May 20, 1999, p. A19.
170. See "Speak out for the law," *South China Morning Post*, May 30, 1999, p. 10.
171. Chris Yeung, "Judicial powers bound," *South China Morning Post*, June 28, 1999, p. 19.
172. Chris Tsang Chi-ping, "Principle will be undermined," Letter to the editor, *South China Morning Post*, June 21, 1999, p. 16.
173. Colin Campbell, "Court should have sought NPC interpretation," Letter to the editor, *South China Morning Post*, May 21, 1999, p. 16.
174. Richard Lord, "Government's bold decision," *South China Morning Post*, May 21, 1999, p. 16.
175. Ng Chi-sum, "Invite the Basic Law drafters to apologize," *Apple Daily*, May 7, 1999, p. F3.
176. See Poon Kwok-sum, "Drafters become criminals for thousand years," Letter to the editor, *Apple Daily*, February 5, 1999, p. F3.
177. *The Sun*, May 14, 1999, p. A18.
178. *South China Morning Post*, May 8, 1999, p. 4.
179. *Apple Daily*, May 9, 1999, p. A6.
180. *Hong Kong Economic Journal*, June 29, 1999, p. 7.
181. For a detailed discussion about constitutional conventions, see Colin R. Munro, *Studies in Constitutional Law* (London: Butterworths, 1987), Chapter 3, pp. 35–60. For an argument that other constitutional conventions, such as the need

for "ministers" to resign in the event of making blunders and having personal scandals, should be seriously studied and implemented by the HKSAR government, see Lo Shiu-hing, Yu Wing-yat, Kwong Kam-kwan, Wan Kwok-fai, and Cheung Yat-fung, *The Tung Chee-Hwa Government's Governing Crisis and its Solutions* (in Chinese) (Hong Kong: Ming Pao Publisher, 2002), Chapter 2.

4 The Emergence of Constitutional Conventions

1. The earlier version of this chapter was an article published in the *Hong Kong Law Journal* (Part 1, 2005), pp. 103–128.
2. See A. V. Dicey, *Introduction to the Study of the Law of the Constitution* (London: Macmillan, 10th Edition, 1959), pp. 23–24. Numerous experts in constitutional law analyze the question of conventions. For examples, see Colin R. Munro, *Studies in Constitutional Law* (London: Butterworths, 1987), pp. 35–39; Colin Turpin, *British Government and the Constitution: Text, Cases and Materials* (London: Weidenfeld and Nicolson, 1990), pp. 96–115; Peter W. Hogg, *Constitutional Law of Canada* (Toronto: Carswell, 1985), pp. 9–20; Joseph Jaconelli, "The Nature of Constitutional Convention," *Legal Studies*, vol. 19, no. 1 (March 1999), pp. 24–46; Geoffrey Marshall, *Constitutional Conventions: The Rules and Forms of Political Accountability* (Oxford: Clarendon Press, 1986); Andrew Heard, *Canadian Constitutional Conventions: The Marriage of Law and Politics* (Toronto: Oxford University Press, 1991); Geoffrey Marshall and Graeme Moodie, *Some Problems of the Constitution* (London: Hutchinson, 1959); Eugene A. Forsey, "The Courts and the Conventions of the Constitution," *UNB Law Journal*, 33 (1984); Stanley De Smith and Rodney Brazier, *Constitutional and Administrative Law* (London: Penguin, 1994), pp. 35–48.
3. Sir Ivor Jennings, *The Law and the Constitution* (London: University of London Press 1959), pp. 39–40.
4. John P. Mackintosh, *The British Cabinet* (London: Stevens, 1977).
5. For a similar approach to identifying the variety of constitution conventions, see Andrew Heard, "Recognizing the Variety among Constitutional Conventions," *Canadian Journal of Political Science*, vol. XXII, no. 1 (1989).
6. Hilaire Barnett, *Constitutional & Administrative Law* (London: Cavendish, 1995), p. 30.
7. Hogg, *Constitutional Law of Canada* (n 1 above), p. 16.
8. *Ibid.*, p. 16.
9. Jennings, *The Law and the Constitution* (n 2 above), p. 136.
10. Geoffrey Marshall, ed., *Ministerial Responsibility* (Oxford: Oxford University Press, 1989).
11. See Robert F. Adie and Paul G. Thomas, eds., *Canadian Public Administration: Problematic Perspectives* (New Jersey: Prentice-Hall, 1982), Chapter 8,

pp. 261–300. Also see S. L. Sutherland, "Responsible Government and Ministerial Responsibility: Every Reform Is Its Own Problem," *Canadian Journal of Political Science*, vol. XXIV, no. 1 (March 1991), pp. 91–120.
12. Yash Ghai, *Hong Kong's New Constitutional Order: The Resumption of Chinese Sovereignty and the Basic Law* (Hong Kong: Hong Kong University Press, 1997), p. 17.
13. *Ibid*.
14. Stephen Davies with Elfed Roberts, *Political Dictionary for Hong Kong* (Hong Kong: Macmillan, 1990), p. 85.
15. *Ibid*.
16. Yash Ghai, "Framework to judge law," *South China Morning Post*, October 6, 1997, p. 21.
17. See Lo Shiu-hing, "The Politics of Judicial Autonomy in Hong Kong," paper presented at a conference on Hong Kong at the University of Warwick, July 1999. For the earlier controversies over the composition and powers of the Court of Final Appeal, see Lo Shiu-hing, "The Politics of the Court of Final Appeal Debate in Hong Kong," *China Quarterly*, no. 161 (March 2000).
18. For details of the protests, see John P. Burns, *Government Capacity and the Hong Kong Civil Service* (Hong Kong: Oxford University Press, 2004), pp. 173–176; and Sonny Lo, "Hong Kong, 1 July 2003 — Half a million protestors: The Security Law, Identity Politics, Democracy and China," *Behind the Headlines*, vol. 60, no. 4 (2004), pp. 1–14.
19. See "Decision of the Standing Committee of the National People's Congress on Issues Relating to the Methods for Selecting the Chief Executive of the Hong Kong Special Administrative Region in the Year 2007 and for Forming the Legislative Council of the Hong Kong Special Administrative Region in the Year 2008: Adopted by the Standing Committee of the Tenth National People's Congress at its Ninth Session on 26 April 2004," S. S. No. 5 to Gazette Extraordinary No. 8/2004, in http://www.info.gov.hk/cab/cab-review/eng/basic/pdf/es5200408081.pdf (accessed December 29, 2004). Also see "The Fourth Report of the Constitutional Development Task Force: Views and Proposals of Members of the Committee on the Methods for Selecting the Chief Executive in 2007 and for Forming the Legislative Council in 2008 (December 2004)," in report4/pdf/fourthreport.pdf" http://www.info.gov.hk/cab/cab-review/eng/report4/pdf/fourthreport.pdf, p. 2, note 1 (accessed December 29, 2004).
20. "The Interpretation by the Standing Committee of the National People's Congress of Article 7 of Annex I and Article III of Annex II to the Basic Law of the Hong Kong Special Administrative Region of the PRC: Adopted by the Standing Committee of the Tenth National People's Congress at its Eighth Session on 6 April 2004," L. S. No. 2 to Gazette Ext. No. 5/2004, in http://www.info.gov.hk/cab/cab-review/eng/basic/pdf/es22004080554.pdf (accessed December 29, 2004).

21. For details of the British government's concessions made to the PRC over the issue of direct election of the Legislative Council, see Ian Scott, *Political Change and the Crisis of Legitimacy in Hong Kong* (Hong Kong: Oxford University Press, 1989); and Lo Shiu-hing, *The Politics of Democratization in Hong Kong* (London: Macmillan, 1997).
22. For Patten's confrontation with China over his political reform blueprint, see John Flowerdew, *The Final Years of British Hong Kong: The Discourse of Colonial Withdrawal* (London: Macmillan, 1998); Jonathan Dimbleby, *The Last Governor: Chris Patten & The Handover of Hong Kong* (London: Little, Brown and Company, 1997); and Lo Shiu-hing, *Governing Hong Kong: Legitimacy, Communication and Political Decay* (New York: Nova Science, 2001), pp. 161–168.
23. For details, see "Framework of accountability for principal officials," press release, http://www.info.gov.hk/gia/general/200204/17/0417251.htm (accessed August 1, 2002).
24. Their post titles were Chief Secretary for Administration; Financial Secretary; Secretary for Justice; Secretary for the Civil Service; Secretary for Commerce, Industry and Manpower; Secretary for Constitutional Affairs; Secretary for Economic Development; Secretary for Education; Secretary for the Environment, Health and Welfare; Secretary for Financial Services and the Treasury; Secretary for Home Affairs; Secretary for Housing, Planning and Lands; Secretary for Security; and Secretary for Transport and Works. See *Ibid*. These principal officials are hired on contract terms, unlike those civil servants who are on permanent terms of service. The term of their contract would not exceed the term of the chief executive, who nominated them for appointment.
25. The primary objectives of the accountability system, according to the government, are: "to strengthen the accountability of principal officials; ensure better response to the needs of the community; enhance coordination in policy formulation; strengthen the cooperation between the Executive and the Legislature; ensure effective implementation of policies and provide quality services to the public." See *Ibid*.
26. See, for example, Cheung Chor-yung, "The Quest for Good Governance: Hong Kong's Principal Officials Accountability System," *China: An International Journal*, vol. 1, no. 2 (September 2003), pp. 249–272.
27. Andrew Wong, "Political Accountability and Constitutional Conventions (in Chinese)," unpublished paper, October 2001. Lo Shiu-hing, Yu Wing-yat, Kwong Kam-kwan, Wan Kwok-fai, and Cheung Yat-fung, *The Tung Chee-hwa Government: Governing Crisis and Solutions* (in Chinese) (Hong Kong: Ming Pao, 2002), Chapter 2.
28. *Ibid*.
29. See Scott, *Political Change and the Crisis of Legitimacy in Hong Kong* (see note 21 above).
30. For a review of the role of the LegCo President, see Max Wong Wai-lun,

"The meaning of 'charge': private member's bills in the Legislative Council," *Hong Kong Law Journal*, vol. 28 (1988), pp. 230–247.
31. For Patten's political discourse, see John Flowerdew, *The Final Years of British Hong Kong: The Discourse of Colonial Withdrawal* (London: Macmillan, 1998).
32. See *The Central Committee's Work Report* (in Chinese) (Hong Kong: The Democratic Alliance for Betterment of Hong Kong, December 2002). For a discussion of the "partial" neutrality of Hong Kong civil servants, see Lo Shiu-hing, *Governing Hong Kong: Legitimacy, Communication and Political Decay* (New York: Nova Science, 2001), pp. 106–112.
33. For a more in-depth discussion of the dimensions of "political neutrality" of civil servants in the HKSAR, see Lo, *Governing Hong Kong*, pp. 106–112. For the myth of "political neutrality" of civil servants in Hong Kong under British rule, see Ian Scott, "Civil Service Neutrality in Hong Kong," in Haile K. Asmerom and Elisa P. Reis, eds., *Democratization and Bureaucratic Neutrality* (London: Macmillan, 1996).
34. Margaret Ng, "Loyalty is no substitute for accountability," *South China Morning Post*, May 8, 2001, p. 18.
35. Chief Executive Office, "Code For Principal Officials Under the Accountability System," G. N. 3845, attached in Panel on Constitutional Affairs, "Background Brief prepared by Legislative Council Secretariat: Prevention of conflict of interest of principal officials and related issues," LC Paper No. CB(2)1497/02–03(01), Chapter 2, especially 2.7 to 2.11.
36. See the commentaries of the two pro-Beijing and pro-government newspapers months prior to the formal establishment of the POAS on July 1, 2002.
37. Cannix Yau, "LegCo shamed by Leung vote," *The Standard*, May 8, 2003, p. A3.
38. See *Eastweek*, May 26, 2004, pp. 19–20.
39. *Ibid.*
40. Response of Leung to LegCo members' questions, see "The Financial Secretary's response to some of the matters raised by Legislative Council members at the meeting of the Panel on Constitutional Affairs on 17 March 2003 and at the House Committee meeting on 21 March 2003," LC Paper No. CB(2)1692/02–03(03).
41. Leung's letter of resignation to Chief Executive Tung Chee-hwa, March 10, 2003, in LC Paper No. CB(2)1526/02–03(01), Annex.
42. Chris Yeung, "I forgave an honest mistake, says Tung," *South China Morning Post*, March 22, 2003.
43. *Ibid.*
44. See, for example, Editorial, "Chief Executive must let Antony Leung go," *South China Morning Post*, March 19, 2003, p. 12. Also see Editorial, "A time of reckoning," *The Standard*, May 7, 2003, p. A2; "Leung the Albatross," *Sing Tao Daily*, March 25, 2003, p. F7; "Credibility Crisis," *The Standard*, March 26,

2003, p. A15; Margaret Ng, "The case against Antony Leung," *South China Morning Post*, March 28, 2003, p. 16; and Yeung Sum, "Abuse of Power?," *South China Morning Post*, April 15, 2003, p. 14.
45. Personal discussion with Stephen Lam Sui-lun, the Secretary for Constitutional Affairs, on May 6, 2003.
46. On July 25, 2002, the Hong Kong Exchanges and Clearing Limited proposed that prices of listed companies' shares quoted at below HK$0.5 should be consolidated, failing which, delisting would follow. On July 26, 577 of the 761 stocks recorded a loss. On July 27, the Hong Kong Exchanges and Clearing Limited announced its decision to withdraw its delisting proposal. This penny-stock incident prompted a panel of inquiry to investigate the role of Frederick Ma, the financial secretary, the Hong Kong Exchanges and Clearing Limited, the Securities and Futures Commission, and other related civil servants. For details of the report, see *Report of the Panel of Inquiry on the Penny Stocks Incident by Robert G. Kotewall and Gordon C. K. Kwong, September 2002* (Hong Kong: Printing Department, the HKSAR Government, 2002).
47. In March 2003, the PRC President Hu Jintao promised support for Tung and said he believed the chief executive would be able to properly handle Leung's alleged conflict-of-interest scandal. See *The Standard*, March 20, 2003, p. B4.
48. Frank Ching, "Spin master," *South China Morning Post*, August 1, 2003, p. 12.
49. Ip once claimed that taxi drivers and MacDonald workers were uninterested in the debate over Article 23 of the Basic Law. She also asserted that direct elections brought about Adolf Hitler's rise to power in Nazi Germany. Her public remarks offended many ordinary citizens. See Editorial, "Why Regina Ip should not take all the blame," *South China Morning Post*, July 25, 2003, p. 12.
50. Michael Ng, "Yeoh urged to resign," *The Standard*, July 6, 2004, p. B1.
51. *Ibid*.
52. For a discussion of the SARS crisis, see Christine Loh, ed., *At the Epicentre: Hong Kong and the SARS Outbreak* (Hong Kong: Hong Kong University Press, 2004).
53. Dr. Yeoh Eng-kiong, "I fully accepted responsibility," *South China Morning Post*, March 19, 2004, p. 14.
54. See Editorial, "Passing the buck won't fix health system," *South China Morning Post*, March 17, 2004, p. 14; and Patsy Moy and Carrie Chan, "Health minister washes his hands of SARS battle," *South China Morning Post*, March 7, 2004.
55. See Dr. Wilson Fung Yee-leung, Vice-President of the Hong Kong Medical Association, "Dr. Yeoh should step down," *South China Morning Post*, March 29, 2004, p. 2. Also see the remarks made by Lo Wing-lok, a former legislator, in Cannix Yau, "There's hope if they quit," *The Standard*, October 10, 2003, p. B2.
56. *Ming Pao*, July 6, 2004.

57. *Ibid.*
58. *Ibid.*, July 8, 2004.
59. The Tung administration's legitimacy crisis could be seen even before the mass protests on July 1, 2003. See Lo, *Governing Hong Kong: Legitimacy, Communication and Political Decay* (n 22 above).
60. Scarlett Chiang, "Law quits ICAC," *The Standard*, June 21, 2007.
61. *Ibid.*
62. For the Robert Chung incident in 1999, see Carole J. Petersen and Jan Currie, "Higher Education Restructuring and Academic Freedom in Hong Kong," *The Journal of Comparative Asian Development*, vol. 6, no. 1 (Spring 2007), pp. 143–163.
63. See *Sudden Weekly*, no. 493, January 7, 2005. Also see http://en.wikipedia.org/wili/Sudden_Weekly (accessed March 14, 2005).
64. *Ibid.* Also see "Tung Chee-hwa's top aide resigns, reasons unclear," *Taipei Times*, January 8, 2005, p. 5.
65. Gianni Griveller, "The (not so glorious) end to Tung Chee-hwa's political career," *The Star*, March 14, 2005, in ectionId=132&fArticleId=2446499" http://www.thestar.co.za/index.php?fSectionId=132&fArticleId=2446499 (accessed March 14, 2005).
66. TVB news, July 9, 2007. Also see "Union backs RTHK chief despite 'out of character' action," *The Standard*, July 9, 2007.
67. Una So and Diane Lee, "RTHK chief quits amid media frenzy," *The Standard*, July 10, 2007.
68. Chu's scandal came at a time when the HKSAR government tried to replace the RTHK, which was severely criticized for his financial mismanagement, with a new public service broadcaster as suggested by the Committee on Review of Public Service Boradcasting.
69. For Tung's formal resignation letter see *Sing Tao Daily*, March 13, 2005. In fact, it was reported that after the protests of half a million Hong Kong people on the streets against the HKSAR government on July 1, 2003, Tung twice offered to resign. But Beijing declined his resignation offers. See *Next Magazine*, no. 708, October 2, 2003, pp. 46–52.
70. *Ming Pao*, March 13, 2005.
71. *Ibid.*
72. See, for example, Audrey Eu's remarks, TVB News, March 14, 2005. Also see the remarks made by Ronny Tong, *Ming Pao*, March 12, 2005.
73. See Elsie Leung's statement reported in *Sing Tao Daily*, March 13, 2005.

5 The Implementation of the Basic Law

1. For a general discussion of the constitutional "positioning" and "repositioning" on Chapter 1 of the Basic Law, see Benny Y. T. Tai, "Chapter 1 of Hong

Kong's New Constitution: Constitutional Positioning and Repositioning," in Ming Chan and Alvin So, eds., *Crisis and Transformation in China's Hong Kong* (Armonk: M. E. Sharpe, 2002), pp. 189–219.
2. *The Basic Law of the Hong Kong Special Administrative Region of the People's Republic of China* (hereafter *The Basic Law*) (Hong Kong: The Consultative Committee for the Basic Law of the Hong Kong Special Administrative Region of the People's Republic of China, April 1990), p. 6.
3. For a useful study of Hong Kong's democracy movement, see Alvin So, *Hong Kong's Embattled Democracy* (Baltimore: The Johns Hopkins University Press, 1999); and Lo Shiu-hing, *The Politics of Democratization in Hong Kong* (London: Macmillan, 1997).
4. Ibid.
5. *Ming Pao*, May 27, 2007.
6. *Deng Xiaoping On the Question of Hong Kong* (Hong Kong: New Horizon Press, 1993), pp. 7–8.
7. Three major perspectives on China's democratic future are advanced by Pei Minxin, Gordan Chang, and Bruce Gilley. Pei Minxin argues that China's developmental autocracy has its limits in the difficult process of democratization. Gordan Chang has predicted the coming collapse of the mainland Chinese regime. Bruce Gilley argues that democratization in mainland China will be a matter of time. See Pei Minxin, *China's Trapped Transition: The Limits of Developmental Autocracy* (Cambridge: Harvard University Press, 2006); Gordan Chang, *The Coming Collapse of China* (New York: Random House, 2001); and Bruce Gilley, *China's Democratic Future: How it will happen and where it will lead* (New York: Columbia University Press, 2004).
8. Rao Geping, "'One Country' Must Dominate the Two Systems," in http://www.hkjouurnal.org, April 2006, pp. 1–6; Wang Zhenmin, "Why Does Hong Kong Still Matter?," in http://www.hkjournal.org, April 2006, pp. 1–6; Rao Geping, "Hong Kong can develop its capitalist system only under the framework of the 'One Country, Two Systems' policy," paper presented at the international conference "The Evolution of 'One Country, Two Systems' in Hong Kong and Macao: Implications for Canada," held on March 24, 2006 at the University of Waterloo; and Wang Zhenmin, "China's Legal/Constitutional Approach Toward Hong Kong and Macao," paper presented at the international conference, "The Evolution of 'One Country, Two Systems' in Hong Kong and Macao: Implications for Canada," held on March 24, 2006 at the University of Waterloo.
9. "Close cooperation established between police and PLA Hong Kong Garrison Commander," *People's Daily*, May 12, 2007.
10. For a study of how the police handled the anti-WTO protests, see Lo Shiu-hing, "The Politics of Policing the Anti-WTO Protests in Hong Kong," *Asian Journal of Political Science*, vol. 14, no. 2 (December 2006), pp. 140–162.
11. It was rumored that the Executive Council member who toyed with such idea

was the leader of the pro-Beijing Federation of Trade Unions Cheng Yiu-tong. For the half a million protestors on July 1, 2003, see John P. Burns, *Government Capacity and the Hong Kong Civil Service* (Hong Kong: Oxford University Press, 2004), pp. 173–176; and Sonny Lo, "Hong Kong, 1 July 2003 — Half a Million Protestors: The Security Law, Identity Politics, Democracy, and China," *Behind the Headlines*, vol. 60, no. 4 (April 2004), pp. 1–14.
12. *Sing Tao Daily*, May 22, 2007, p. B3.
13. *Ibid*.
14. *Ibid*.
15. *Ming Pao*, May 23, 2007, p. A12.
16. *The Basic Law*, p. 12.
17. For details of how the Liaison Office shaped the local elections, see Lo Shiu-hing, Yu Wing-tat, and Wan Kwok-fai, "The 1999 District Councils Elections," in Ming Chan and Alvin So, eds., *Crisis and Transformation in China's Hong Kong* (Armonk: M. E. Sharpe, 2002); and Sonny Lo, Yu Wing-yat, Kwong Kam-kwan, and Wong Wai -kwok, "The 2004 Legislative Council Elections in Hong Kong: The Triumph of China's United Front Work After the July 2003 and 2004 Protests," in *Chinese Law & Government*, vol. 38, no. 1 (January/February 2005), pp. 19–24.
18. *The Basic Law*, p. 13.
19. For a detailed analysis of the development of civil liberties and the rule of law in the HKSAR, see Johannes Chan, "Civil Liberties, Rule of Law and Human Rights: The Hong Kong Special Administrative Region in Its First Four Years," in Lau Siu-kai, ed., *The First Tung Chee-hwa Administration: The First Five Years of the Hong Kong Special Administrative Region* (Hong Kong: The Chinese University Press, 2002), pp. 89–122.
20. See the critical remarks made by Raymond Wong in all his short videos mounted onto www.youtube.com.
21. See Human Rights Monitor, "Surveillance, Basic Law Article 30, and the Right to Privacy in Hong Kong: A Briefing Paper," Legislative Council LC Paper No. CB(2)259i/05–06(01), October 2005, pp. 10–22.
22. H. L. Fu and Richard Cullen, "Political Policing in Hong Kong," *Hong Kong Law Journal*, vol. 33, Part 1 (2003), pp. 199–230.
23. Thomas E. Kellogg, "A Flawed Effort? Legislating on Surveillance on Hong Kong," in http://www.hkjournal.com (accessed May 24, 2007).
24. *Ibid.*, p. 5.
25. *Apple Daily*, May 5, 2006.
26. *Sing Tao Daily*, May 21, 2007, p. B4.
27. *Deng Xiaoping on the Question of Hong Kong* (Hong Kong: New Horizon Press, 1993), p. 19.
28. Albert Ho's interview by OMNI news (Toronto, Canada) on May 28, 2007 at 9:00 pm.

29. Lo Shiu-hing, "Colonial Policy-makers, Capitalist Class and China: Determinants of Electoral Reform in Hong Kong's and Macau's Legislatures," *Pacific Affairs*, vol. 62, no. 2 (Summer, 1989), pp. 204–218.
30. *Apple Daily*, December 12, 2005, p. A6.
31. In July 2007, the DAB vowed to support the direct election of the chief executive in 2017, but it was reported that its party heavyweight Tam Yiu-chung visited Beijing to consult the central government on the party's new position. After his visit to Beijing, the DAB stressed that candidates for the chief executive elections would have to undergo "democratic procedures," a term that appears to be favored by Beijing authorities. See *Sing Tao Daily*, July 7, 2007, p. B5 and *Today Daily News* (Toronto), July 7, 2007, p. B12.
32. *The Basic Law*, p. 38.
33. *The Basic Law*, p. 40.
34. *Today Daily News*, May 28, 2007.
35. Yash Ghai, "Framework to Judge Law," *South China Morning Post*, October 6, 1997, p. 21.
36. For the complexities of the NPC Standing Committee's legislative and constitutional interpretations, see Albert Chen, *An Introduction to the Legal System of the People's Republic of China* (Hong Kong: Butterworths, 2004), pp. 118–128.
37. Wang Zhenmin, "The Roman Law Tradition and Its Future Development in China," *Frontier Law China*, vol. 1, no. 1 (2006), p. 74.
38. *Ibid.*, p. 75.
39. *Ibid.*, p. 77.
40. *Deng Xiaoping On the Question of Hong Kong*, pp. 17–18.
41. For a classic work on the clash of Hong Kong's legal system with China's, see Michael Davies, *Constitutional Confrontation in Hong Kong* (Hong Kong: Macmillan, 1989).
42. Remarks made by Martin Lee, and cited by Margaret Ng during her visit to Toronto and in her public forum on May 25, 2007.

6 Identity Change from the National Security Debate to Celebrations of the Tenth Year Anniversary

1. For details of the debate over Article 23 of the Basic Law, see Cheung, "The Hong Kong System under One Country Being Tested: Article 23, Governance Crisis and the Search for a New Hong Kong Identity," in Cheng, ed., *The July 1 Protest Rally: Interpreting a Historic Event*, pp. 33–69.
2. *Apple Daily*, July 17, 2003.
3. *Apple Daily*, July 6, 2003, p. A6.
4. *Apple Daily*, July 5, 2003, p. A2.
5. *Apple Daily*, July 5, 2003, p. 1.

6. Personal observations of LegCo's committee meetings on the National Security Bill from April to June 2003.
7. *Apple Daily*, July 1, 2003.
8. *Apple Daily*, July 9, 2003.
9. *Apple Daily*, July 5, 2003, p. A1.
10. Personal discussion with Tien's aide, August 2003.
11. *Apple Daily*, July 7 and July 8, 2003.
12. *Sing Pao*, July 8, 2003, p. A2.
13. *Apple Daily*, July 9, 2003, p. A2.
14. Although Ian Scott and Anthony Cheung insightfully trace the policy deadlocks in the HKSAR to the disarticulated nature of the political system and policy environment, neither of them has adopted a patron-clientelist approach to critically assess the failure of the National Security Bill. See Ian Scott, "Legitimacy, Governance in Post-1997 Hong Kong," *The Asia Pacific Journal of Public Administration*, vol. 29, no. 1 (June 2007), pp. 29–50; Ian Scott, "The Disarticulation of Hong Kong's Post-handover Political System," *The China Journal*, no. 43 (January 2000); and Anthony Cheung, "Policy Capacity in Post-1997 Hong Kong: Constrained Institutions Facing a Crowding and Differentiated Polity," *The Asia Pacific Journal of Public Administration*, vol. 29, no. 1 (June 2007), pp. 51–76.
15. Personal observations of LegCo's committee hearings on the public views with regard to the National Security (Legislative Provisions) Bill from April to June 2003.
16. Lo Shiu-hing, *Governing Hong Kong: Legitimacy, Communication and Political Decay* (New York: Nova Science, 2001).
17. *Apple Daily*, July 8, 2003, p. A2.
18. *Apple Daily*, July 5, 2003.
19. Mao Zedong, "The Role of the Chinese Communist Party in the National War," October 1938, in Mao Zedong, *Selected Readings From the Works of Mao Zedong* (Beijing: Foreign Languages Press, 1971), p. 144.
20. For Xiao's detailed remarks, see Ming Pao, ed., *The Controversial Discussions on Patriotism* (Hong Kong: Ming Pao, April 2004) pp. 20–34.
21. *The Controversial Discussion on Patriotism*, pp. 59–118.
22. *Ibid.*, pp. 107–112.
23. *Ibid.*, pp. 174–178.
24. *Ibid.*, pp. 165–173.
25. Lo Shiu-hing and Yu Wing-yat, "The 2000 Legislative Council Elections in Hong Kong," *Representation*, vol. 38, no. 4 (2002), pp. 327–339.
26. Kwok had a sex scandal involving his assistant and this case was interestingly investigated by a democrat who became a journalist.
27. For details of the elections, see Sonny Lo, Yu Wing Yat, Kwong Kam Kwan, and Wong Wai Kwok, "The 2004 Legislative Council Elections in Hong Kong: The Triumph of China's United Front Work After the July 2003 and 2004

Protests," in Sonny Lo, Eilo Yu, Bruce Kwong, and Benson Wong, eds., "The 2004 Legislative Council Election in the HKSAR," *Chinese Law and Government*, vol. 38, no. 1 (January/February 2005), pp. 3–29.

28. The Hong Kong Journalists Association found in 2007 that 60 percent of the journalists believed that at least some of their colleagues were exercising self-censorship. Francis Moriarty also wrote: "If journalists are playing safe, that suggests self-censorship." See Francis Moriarty, "Press Freedom in Hong Kong: The Trend is Down," in moriarty.pdf" www.hkjournal.org/PDF/2002_summer/moriarty.pdf, no. 2 (April 2007), p. 2.
29. Personal observations as I have access to TVB and ATV news every day in Ontario, Canada.
30. Personal discussion with a reporter in the HKSAR, July 2, 2007.
31. Personal observations in the HKSAR, July 1, 2007.
32. Cable TV news, July 1, 2007.
33. "Hong Kong Current Affairs," ATV, June 30, 2007 at 11:00 pm.
34. TVB Sunday File, June 30, 2007.
35. TVB (Pearl) on July 1, 2007 and ATV Newsline program, July 1, 2007.
36. CCTV coverage of the tenth anniversary of the HKSAR, July 1 and July 2, 2007.
37. CCTV (Channel 9), July 2, 2007.
38. *Ibid*.
39. *Ibid*., July 1, 2007 at 8:00 pm.
40. *Ibid*., "Rediscovering China: Foreign Students in Hong Kong," July 1 and July 2, 2007.
41. CCTV (Channel 9), July 1, 2007.
42. The Phoenix's coverage of the HKSAR tenth anniversary on July 1, 2007.
43. The Phoenix interview with Donald Tsang, July 1, 2007 at 1:00 pm. It was then broadcasted again on July 2, 2007.
44. Tam is a very knowledgeable commentator on mainland China, Taiwan, Hong Kong and Macao. For his blog, see http://blog.phoenixtv.com/index.php/uid_674350_action_viewspace_itemid_33059. Tim Hamlett is a professor at the Department of Journalism at the Hong Kong Baptist University.
45. A reporter in the Phoenix revealed to the author that there was a "political gatekeeper" overseeing the remarks of the commentators and reporters, who needed a rehearsal and detailed discussion prior to the formal live broadcast. Personal discussion with the reporter, July 2005. A careful analysis of the views of the commentators is that most of their views tended to be politically safe and correct, notably the remarks of Peter Qiu on both Hong Kong affairs and mainland China's relations with foreign nation-states. Qiu's commentaries on China's foreign relations can be regularly seen in *Today Daily News* (Toronto). On July 1, 2007, Qiu commented on the remarks made by President Hu on the HKSAR, and he praised the President's emphasis on social harmony and tolerance. With the benefit of hindsight this was a politically correct comment,

although some Hong Kong print media (such as the *Apple Daily*) on the following day highlighted, in fact inaccurately, President Hu's "emphasis" on Beijing's veto over Hong Kong's political reforms. For President Hu's speech, see *Wen Wei Po*, July 2, 2007.
46. The Phoenix interview with Chris Patten, July 1, 2007.
47. *Apple Daily*, June 30, 2007, p. A1.
48. *Ibid.*, p. A2.
49. *Ibid.*, July 1, 2007, p. A1.
50. *Oriental Daily*, July 1, 2007, p. A1.
51. *Ibid.*, p. A30.
52. "Persisting Four Principles. Is it 'one country' or 'two systems'?," *Hong Kong Economic Journal*, July 2, 2007, p. 1. Also see "No dispute over the 'one country' principle, but 'two systems' need to take care of Hong Kong's circumstances," *Ming Pao*, July 2, 2007, p. A4.
53. For the strong Taiwan identity, see Daniel C. Lynch, "Taiwan's Self-Conscious Nation-Building Project," *Asian Survey*, vol. 44, no. (2004), pp. 513–533.

7   The Election of Hong Kong Deputies to the National People's Congress

1. For the first election held for the Hong Kong members of the NPC, see Suzanne Pepper, "Hong Kong Joins the National People's Congress: a first test for one country with two political systems," *Journal of Contemporary China*, vol. 8, no. 21 (July 1999), pp. 319–343.
2. *Xinhua News Agency*, November 18, 2002.
3. A candidate needed to obtain ten nominations. Ma Lik, a local NPC deputy from the DAB, claimed that some of the 953 NPC election panel members asked to nominate him. Thus, he said, "it amounts to a vote of confidence in our work." See *South China Morning Post*, November 2, 2002, p. 3.
4. For details, see Lo Shiu-hing, "'Legitimizing' the Selection of the Second HKSAR Chief Executive: From the Election Committee to the Chief Executive Election Bill," *China Perspectives*, no. 38 (November–December 2001), pp. 44–59.
5. Cheung obtained the nominations of 14 members of the Election Committee, more than the required ten nominations for a candidate to run in the election held for the Hong Kong NPC members. See *Hong Kong Economic Journal*, November 11, 2002, p. 5.
6. *South China Morning Post*, September 27, 2002, p. 2.
7. *South China Morning Post*, July 17, 2002, p. 6. However, the DP had four members who were eligible to register as voters in the NPC election but did not do so, including Szeto Wah and Andrew Cheng Kar-foo. See *South China Morning Post*, July 17, 2002, p. 6.

8. Chris Yeung, "Observer," *South China Morning Post*, November 20, 2002, p. 16.
9. *Ibid.*
10. See Kuan Hsin-chi, Lau Siu-kai, and Timothy Ka-ying Wong, eds., *Out of the Shadow of 1997? The 2000 Legislative Council Election in the Hong Kong Special Administrative Region* (Hong Kong: The Chinese University Press, 2000); Kuan Hsin-chi, Lau Siu-kai, Louie Kin-sheun, and Timothy Ka-ying Wong, eds., *Power Transfer And Electoral Politics: The First Legislative Election in the Hong Kong Special Administrative Region* (Hong Kong: The Chinese University Press, 1999); Ma Ngok, "The First HKSAR Election: Changed System, Changed Results, Changing Electioneering Techniques," in Joseph Y. S. Cheng, ed., *Political Development in the HKSAR* (Hong Kong: City University of Hong Kong, 2001), pp. 139–164; and Shiu-hing Lo, Wing-yat Yu, and Kwok-fai Wan, "The 1999 District Councils Elections," in Ming K. Chan and Alvin Y. So, eds., *Crisis and Transformation in China's Hong Kong* (Armonk, New York: M. E. Sharpe, 2002), pp. 139–165. For earlier studies on Hong Kong's elections, see Lau Siu-kai and Louie Kin-sheun, eds., *Hong Kong Tried Democracy: The 1991 Elections in Hong Kong* (Hong Kong: The Chinese University of Hong Kong, 1993); and Rowena Kwok, Joan Leung, and Ian Scott, eds., *Votes Without Power: The Hong Kong Legislative Council Elections 1991* (Hong Kong: Hong Kong University press, 1992). For Pepper's work, see her "Hong Kong Joins the National People's Congress: a first test for one country with two political systems (see endnote 1)."
11. Usually, candidates who are CCP members or who are supported by the CCP have a greater chance to be elected than non-CCP members. For the recent local elections in China, see for example Li Lianjiang, "Elections and Popular Resistance in Rural China," *China Information*, vol. 15, no. 2 (2001), pp. 1–19; Kelvin J. O'Brien, "Villages, Elections, and Citizenship in Contemporary China," *Modern China*, vol. 27, no. 4 (October 2001), pp. 407–35; Li Lianjiang and Kevin O'Brien, "The Struggle over Village Elections," in Merle Goldman and Roderick MacFarquhar, eds., *The Paradox of China's Post-Mao Reforms* (Massachusetts: Harvard University Press, 1999), pp. 129–144.
12. *South China Morning Post*, November 30, 2002, p. 3.
13. *South China Morning Post*, November 30, 2002, p. 3.
14. *Hong Kong Economic Journal*, November 30, 2002, p. 6.
15. *South China Morning Post*, November 30, 2002, p. 3.
16. *Apple Daily*, November 30, 2002, p. A15. The new chairman of the DP is Yeung Sum.
17. *South China Morning Post*, November 30, 2002, p. 3.
18. *Hong Kong Economic Journal*, November 26, 2002, p. 7. The Chair Group had 15 members, including Chong Sai-ping, Li Ka-shing, Cha Chi-min, Chung Sze-yuen, Xu Ximin, Leung Chun-ying, Tung Chee-hwa, and Fok Ying-tung. They were elected in Hong Kong on November 1, 2002. Only 759 members attended the meeting on November 1, 2002. About one-fifth of the

953 members were absent. While 744 members of the Election Committee voted for their support of a list of the members of the Chair Group, Democratic Party member Chan Wai-yip voted against the members. Fourteen members abstained, including barrister Alan Leong and horse trainer Kan Ping-chee. The members of the Chair Group then elected Tung Chee-hwa as the Group's chairman. See *Apple Daily*, November 2, 2002, p. A6.
19. *Wen Wei Po*, November 26, 2002, p. A4.
20. See *Oriental Daily*, November 2, 2002, p. A27; and *Hong Kong Economic Journal*, November 2, 2002, p. 7.
21. *South China Morning Post*, November 30, 2002, p. 3.
22. *Ibid.*
23. *The Standard*, November 30, 2002.
24. *Apple Daily*, November 30, 2002, p. A15.
25. *Ming Pao*, November 29, 2002, p. A8. *Wen Wei Po* criticized the democrats for putting up a "political show." See *Wen Wei Po*, November 28, 2002, p. A11.
26. *Ming Pao*, November 29, 2002, p. A8.
27. *Ibid.*
28. *Ibid.*
29. Cannix Yau, "Democrats fall at first hurdle in NPC ballot," *The Standard*, November 30, 2002.
30. *Oriental Daily*, November 30, 2002, p. A31.
31. *Ibid.*
32. *Ibid.*
33. *Oriental Daily*, November 30, 2002, p. A31.
34. *Ibid.*
35. *Oriental Daily*, December 1, 2002, p. A31.
36. *Wen Wei Po*, November 30, 2002, p. A4.
37. Leung became "the queen of nominations" when she got a total of 270 nominations from the 953-strong election panel, but it would have "no bearing on her election chances." See Chris Yeung, "Observer," *South China Morning Post*, November 20, 2002, p. 16.
38. *The Standard*, December 4, 2002.
39. *South China Morning Post*, December 5, 2002, p. 3.
40. *Ming Pao*, December 5, 2002, p. A2.
41. *The Standard*, December 6, 2002.
42. *South China Morning Post*, December 6, 2002, p. 2.
43. Xu accused the democrats of creating troubles. He wrote: "Most of the 900 members of the Election Committee are experienced elites nominated by different sectors. Their interest cannot be bought. Apart from the need to take care of the overall situation of loving China and loving Hong Kong, it was difficult to manipulate the process. This time, in the nominating list, there were several people who publicly opposed the Chinese constitution and the Hong Kong Basic Law. Most members of the Election Committee did not

have to be reminded about these people. Most members had the automatic ability to resist the virus and poison . . . In fact, Hong Kong people's ability to distinguish the good from the bad has increased since the transfer of sovereignty. It was also impossible to distribute or allocate votes amongst the members of the Election Committee. In fact, in the first round of the election, voters were free to choose between one and thirty-six candidates, thus allowing several people who were against China to penetrate. But the second round needed a voter's choice of all 36 candidates. Otherwise the vote would be invalid . . . This election is successful, open, fair, just, reasonable and legal." See his "It is self-contradictory to talk about 'manipulating the election,'" *Wen Wei Po*, December 6, 2002, p. A18.
44. *South China Morning Post*, December 6, 2002, p. 2.
45. *South China Morning Post*, December 5, 2002, p. 3.
46. *Ibid*.
47. *South China Morning Post*, December 6, 2002, p. 2.
48. *Hong Kong Economic Journal*, December 6, 2002, p. 7.
49. *South China Morning Post*, December 6, 2002, p. 2.
50. *Hong Kong Economic Journal*, December 6, 2002, p. 7.
51. *South China Morning Post*, December 6, 2002, p. 2.
52. Editorial, "Was NPC election rigged?," *Ming Pao*, December 5, 2002, p. E4.
53. Chris Yeung, "James Tien puts NPC election in perspective," *South China Morning Post*, December 8, 2002, p. 8.
54. Editorial, "Open, fair election, a credit to new era in Hong Kong," *China Daily*, December 4, 2002, p. 6.
55. *Ibid*.
56. Personal interview with Allen Lee, December 20, 2002. These lists were confirmed by Johnny Lau, who is a commentator on Chinese politics and who is very close to the pro-Beijing camp. Personal discussion with Lau, December 22, 2002.
57. Personal interview with Allen Lee, December 20, 2002.
58. *Ming Pao*, December 5, 2002, p. A2.
59. Chan Tung, "Is there any recommended list from the Liaison Office?,"*Ming Pao*, December 5, 2002, p. A32.
60. *Ibid*.
61. *Ibid*.

8 A Fusion of Mainland Chinese and Hong Kong Political Cultures in the 2007 Chief Executive Election

1. For Hong Kong's pro-democracy movement and its political hurdles, see Kuan Hsin-chi, "The Pro-Democracy Movement in Hong Kong," in C. L. Chiou and Leong H. Liew, eds., *Uncertain Future: Taiwan–Hong Kong–China Relations*

After Hong Kong's Return to Chinese Sovereignty (Aldershot: Ashgate, 2000), pp. 1–22.
2. Ting Wai accurately captures the essence of Beijing's political relations with the HKSAR: "Some basic tenets of Chinese Communist rule are steadfast: the CCP controls the state, while the state controls society, although such control has slackened somewhat since the open-door and reform initiative began 20 years ago. The Chinese consider that national independence, territorial integrity, and reunification are national goals of utmost importance. Having integrated into the Chinese political order, Hong Kong is supposed to uphold the same principles governing the whole country." Ting Wai, "Hong Kong's Relations with Its Chinese Sovereign," in James C. Hsiung, ed., *Hong Kong the Super Paradox: Life after Return to China* (London: Macmillan, 2000), p. 267.
3. Vicky Randall, "Why have the political trajectories of India and China been different?," in David Potter, David Goldblatt, Margaret Kiloh, and Paul Lewis, eds., *Democratization* (Cambridge: Polity Press, 1997), pp. 208–214.
4. See Anson Chan and Her Core Group, *The Road to Universal Suffrage* (Hong Kong: The Anson Chan Core Group, March 5, 2007), pp. 1–22. Also see *Toward Full Universal Suffrage: A Reform Model for Public Consultation on the Political System in 2012* (Hong Kong: The Democratic Party of Hong Kong, March 2007), pp. 1–22.
5. Robin Theobald, "Patrimonialism," *World Politics*, vol. XXXIV, no. 4 (July 1982), p. 548.
6. Harold Crouch, "Patrimonialism and Military Rule in Indonesia," *World Politics*, vol. XXXI, no. 4 (July 1979), p. 572.
7. *Ibid.*
8. See Bruce Kwong, "Patron-Client Politics and the Chief Executive Elections in Hong Kong," *Journal of Contemporary China*, forthcoming 2007. For another discussion of Hong Kong's patron-client politics, see Lo Shiu-hing, *Governing Hong Kong: Legitimacy, Communication and Political Decay* (New York: Nova Science, 2001), pp. 199–203 and pp. 273–280.
9. Lucian Pye, *The Spirit of Chinese Politics* (Cambridge: Harvard University Press, 1992), pp. 197–232.
10. Ch'ien Mu, *Traditional Government in Imperial China: A Critical Analysis*, translated by Chu-tu Hsueh and George O. Totten (Hong Kong: The Chinese University Press, 1982), pp. 67–142.
11. Jing Huang, *Factionalism in Chinese Communist Politics* (Cambridge: Cambridge University Press, 2000).
12. For the PRC case, see Benjamin C. Ostrov, "Clientage in the PRC's National Defense Research and Development Sector," in Lowell Dittmer, Haruhiro Fukui, and Peter N. S. Lee, eds., *Informal Politics in East Asia* (Cambridge: Cambridge University Press, 2000), pp. 215–233. A recent study has found that the CCP recruitment is showing a gradual decline in orthodox communist ideology and a more technocratic ruling party. See Gang Guo, "Party

Recruitment of College Students in China," *Journal of Contemporary China*, vol. 14, no. 43 (May 2005), pp. 371–393.
13. For the changes China's loyal opposition, see Merle Goldman, *Sowing the Seeds of Democracy in China: Political Reform in the Deng Xiaoping Era* (Cambridge: Harvard University Press, 1994), pp. 356–360. On the Chinese state's control of the loyal opposition, see Anita Chan, "The changing ruling elite and political opposition in China," in Garry Rodan, ed., *Political Opposition in Industrializing Asia* (London: Routledge, 1996), pp. 161–187.
14. Sonny Lo, "Hong Kong, 1 July 2003 — Half a million protestors: The Security Law, Identity Politics, Democracy, and China," *Behind the Headlines*, vol. 60, no. 4 (April 2004), pp. 1–14.
15. Cannix Yau, "Back to square one for Tsang," *The Standard*, December 22, 2005.
16. The only democrat who abstained in the voting was Lau Chin-shek. Bishop Joseph Zen felt happy with the outcome of the vote. See Jonathan Cheng, "Zen happy about LegCo's rejection of proposals," *The Standard*, December 23, 2005.
17. "Hong Kong Constitutional Reform: What Do the People Want?," Survey Report of the Hong Kong Transition Project, commissioned by the Civic Exchange (December 2005), p. 38.
18. *Ibid.*, p. 59.
19. Personal communication with Professor Michael DeGolyer, December 2006.
20. For details, see http://www.eac.gov.hk (accessed May 14, 2007).
21. I calculated the figure based on the statistics from http://www.eac.gov.hk/en/ecse/ecse_2006_electionresult.htm (accessed May 14, 2007).
22. See http://www.eac.gov.hk/en/ecse/ecse_2006_turnout.htm (accessed May 14, 2007).
23. *Ming Pao*, January 31, 2007, p. A14.
24. *Ming Pao*, February 7, 2007, p. A15.
25. *Ibid.*
26. *Sing Tao Daily*, February 6, 2007, p. B6.
27. *Ibid.*
28. *Ibid.*
29. "Anson Chan will not contest election for Chief Executive," September 23, 2006, in http://www.asianews.it/index.php?l=en&art=7297 (accessed May 14, 2007).
30. *Sing Tao Daily*, March 10, 2007, p. B12.
31. *Sing Tao Daily*, February 5, 2007, p. B1.
32. It is interesting to note that Anson Chan and Alan Leong are also Catholics.
33. *The Epoch Times*, February 16, 2007, p. A4.
34. *Ming Pao*, February 15, 2007, p. A14.
35. *The World Journal*, February 4, 2007, p. A22.
36. *Sing Tao Daily*, March 1, 2007, p. B3.

37. *Sing Tao Daily*, March 1, 2007, p. B1.
38. *Ming Pao*, March 1, 2007, p. A17.
39. *Sing Tao Daily*, February 6, 2007, p. B6.
40. *Sing Tao Daily*, March 18, 2007, p. A19.
41. *Ming Pao*, February 14, 2007, p. A14 and also *Ming Pao*, February 14, 2007, p. D13.
42. *Ming Pao*, February 16, 2007, p. A14.
43. *Ibid.*
44. *Sing Tao Daily*, February 3, 2007, p. B1.
45. *Today Daily News*, March 16, 2007, p. B8. Also see RTHK's program on the chief executive election forum on the night of March 15, 2007.
46. *World Journal*, March 16, 2007, p. A21.
47. *Ming Pao*, February 2, 2007, p. A21.
48. *Sing Tao Daily*, March 16, 2007, p. B3.
49. *Sing Tao Daily*, March 16, 2007, p. B3.
50. "Sparks fly in face-off," *The Standard*, March 2, 2007.
51. If political correctness in the HKSAR comes from the media representatives, who are intellectuals, the situation is no different from mainland China where intellectuals are the target of co-optation. See Joseph Fewsmith, "Where Do Correct Ideas Come From? The Party School, Key Think Tanks, and the Intellectuals," in David M. Finkelstein and Maryanne Kivlehan, eds., *China's Leadership in the 21st Century* (New York: M. E. Sharpe, 2003), pp. 152–164.
52. *Sing Tao Daily*, February 3, 2007, p. B1.
53. *Sing Tao Daily*, February 7, 2007, p. B1.
54. *Sing Tao Daily*, February 7, 2007, p. B1.
55. The top ten legislators in February 2007 were consecutively Rita Fan, Audrey Eu, Selina Chow, James Tien, Lee Cheuk-yan, Jasper Tsang Yok-sing, Emily Lau, Martin Lee, Leung Kwok-hung, and Albert Cheng King-hon.
56. *Sing Tao Daily*, February 13, 2007, p. B4.
57. For Victor Li's stance during the nomination period, see *Ming Pao*, February 5, 2007, p. A14.
58. *Today Daily News*, February 17, 2007, p. B1.
59. *Ming Pao*, March 15, 2007, p. A 16.
60. *Sing Tao Daily*, March 13, 2007, p. B4.
61. *Sing Tao Daily*, March 24, 2007, p. B4.
62. *Ming Pao*, March 19, 2007, p. A11.
63. *Sing Tao Daily*, January 23, 2007, p. B6.
64. *Sing Tao Daily*, February 15, 2007, p. B4.
65. *Sing Tao Daily*, March 19, 2007, p. B6.
66. "Democrats unveil suffrage proposals," *The Standard*, March 14, 2007, p. E19.
67. *Ming Pao*, February 2, 2007, p. A24.
68. Joseph Cheng, "'Eleventh 5-year' Action Plan Similar to Election Platform," *Sing Tao Daily,* January 26, 2007, p. B8.

69. "Optimistic blueprint will take courage," *The Standard*, January 16, 2007.
70. *Ming Pao*, January 26, 2007, p. A18.
71. *Ibid*.
72. *Ming Pao*, February 1, 2007, p. A24.
73. *Ibid*.
74. *Sing Tao Daily*, February 7, 2007, p. B1 and March 12, 2007, p. B6.
75. *Sing Tao Daily*, February 7, 2007, p. B1.
76. *Today Daily News*, March 17, 2007, p. B4.
77. *Sing Tao Daily*, March 7, 2007, p. B8.
78. *Ibid*.
79. *Ming Pao*, March 7, 2007, p. A11.
80. *Sing Tao Daily*, March 12, 2007, p. B6.
81. *Ming Pao*, March 8, 2007, p. A13.
82. Editorial, "Empty talk on ideals without help on democracy, big changes in the constitution add more difficulties to the future of direct elections," *Ming Pao*, February 13, 2007, p. A13.
83. *Ming Pao*, March 25, 2007, p. A9.
84. *Ibid*.
85. *Ibid*.
86. Personal communication with a member of the Election Committee, March 2007.
87. *Sing Tao Daily*, March 3, 2007, p. B3.
88. *Ibid*.
89. *Ibid*., March 2, 2007, p. B3.
90. *Sing Tao Daily*, February 10, 2007, p. B3.
91. OMNI News (Toronto, Ontario), May 11, 2007.
92. See *Ming Pao*, March 16, 2007, p. A20.
93. *Ming Pao*, March 16, 2007, p. A15.
94. Editorial, "Public debate creates history, Leong's performance better than Tsang," *Ming Pao*, March 2, 2007, p. A14.
95. *Ibid*.
96. Editorial, "Donald Tsang apparently small but practically large, Alan Leong stylistically right but realistically left," *Ming Pao*, February 26, 2007, p. A11.
97. *Ming Pao*, February 26, 2007, p. A14.
98. *Sing Tao Daily*, March 24, 2007, p. B4.
99. *Sing Tao Daily*, March 26, 2007, p. B4.
100. *Ming Pao*, February 23, 2007, p. A16.
101. *Ming Pao*, February 16, 2007, p. A14.
102. *Ibid*.
103. *Ming Pao*, March 25, 2007, p. A1.
104. *Sing Tao Daily*, March 26, 2007, p. A1.
105. "Government gifts make tourism sector a Liberal Party fiefdom," *South China Morning Post*, March 31, 2007, p. 14.

106. Jimmy Cheung, "Tsang gets glowing report from Beijing," *South China Morning Post*, April 3, 2007.
107. Tsang Yok-sing, "Still Observing the Election Result," *Sing Tao Daily*, March 23, 2007, p. B1.
108. Editorial, "Tsang's legacy tied to universal suffrage," *South China Morning Post*, March 26, 2007.
109. Albert Wong, "Savoring victory on an open-top double-decker," *South China Morning Post*, March 26, 2007.
110. *Ibid.*

9 Applying the Spirit of "One Country, Two Systems" to Taiwan's Political Future

1. Jamie Allen, *Seeing Red: China's Uncompromising Takeover of Hong Kong* (Singapore: Butterworth-Heinemann Asia, 1997); and Ian Scott, *Political Change and the Crisis of Legitimacy in Hong Kong* (Hong Kong: Oxford University Press, 1990).
2. *Shijie Ribao*, November 14, 2004.
3. Yu-ming Shaw, ed., *The Republic of China on Taiwan Today* (Taipei: Kwang Hwa, 1989).
4. Chen Wei, "Taiwan unveils missile defences to a wary public," *Globe and Mail*, October 23, 2004.
5. *Shijie Ribao*, November 15, 2004.
6. Peter Goodspeed, "China's President now a player on world stage," *National Post*, November 11, 2004.
7. Kenneth Liberthal, "Preventing a War Over Taiwan," *Foreign Affairs*, vol. 84, no. 2 (March/April 2005), pp. 53–63. Also see *Shijie Ribao*, November 11, 2004.
8. Byron S. J. Weng, "'One Country, Two Systems' From A Taiwan Perspective," *Orbis*, vol. 46, no. 4 (Fall 2002), pp. 730–731.
9. Tony Saich, *Governance and Politics in China* (New York: Palgrave, 2001); and Jonathan Unger, ed. *The Nature of Chinese Politics: From Mao to Jiang* (New York: M. E. Sharpe, 2002).
10. Yu Wing-yat, *Intra-Party Democracy and Democratization in Taiwan*, unpublished PhD Thesis, the University of Hong Kong, 2004.
11. "Taiwan Chen's son-in-law charged," BBC news, July 10, 2006.
12. Steven Mosher, *Hegemon* (San Francisco: Encounter Books, 2000).
13. Bruce Kwong, *Patron-Client Politics and Elections in Hong Kong*, unpublished PhD Thesis, the University of Hong Kong, 2004.
14. Macao's problem of governance can be seen in Sonny Lo, "Macao's Looming Crisis of Governance: The Deeper Problems Underlying the Labor-Police Confrontations," *Macau Closer*, June 2007, pp. 18–21. For an earlier work on

how Edmund Ho built up his legitimacy, see Sonny Lo and Herbert Yee, "Legitimacy-Building in the Macao Special Administrative Region: Colonial Legacies and Reform Strategies," *Asian Journal of Political Science*, vol. 13, no. 1 (June 2005), pp. 51–79.
15. Chang Jaw-ling, *Settlement of the Macao Issue: Distinctive Features of Beijing's Negotiating Behavior (With Test of 1887 Protocol and 1987 Declaration)*, no. 4 (Baltimore: School of Law, University of Maryland, 1988), pp. 1–37.
16. Joseph Cheng, ed., *Hong Kong in Transition* (Hong Kong: Oxford University Press, 1986).
17. *Ibid.*
18. See his speech on *Wen Wei Po*, July 2, 2007.
19. Kim Richard Nossal, "A High Degree of Ambiguity: Hong Kong as an International Actor after 1997," *Pacific Review*, vol. 10, no. 1 (1997), pp. 84–103.
20. *Ibid.*
21. Cheng, ed., *Hong Kong in Transition*.
22. ATV interview with Lu Ping, June 30, 2007.
23. For details, see Chung Sze-yuen, *Hong Kong's Journey to Reunification* (Hong Kong: The Chinese University Press, 2001), pp. 70–71.
24. *South China Morning Post*, September 27, 1997.
25. Murray Scott Tanner, "The National People's Congress," in Merle Goldman and Roderick MacFarquhar, eds., *The Paradox of China's Post-Mao Reforms* (Cambridge: Harvard University Press, 1999). In fact, during the March 2007 NPC meeting, mainland deputies became far more open to media questions and public criticisms — a positive sign of the PRC political development.
26. Weng, "'One Country, Two Systems' From A Taiwan Perspective," p. 715.

10 Conclusion

1. For the governing differences between Hong Kong and Macao, see Sonny Shiu-hing Lo, "One Formula, Two Experiences: political divergence of Hong Kong and Macao since retrocession," *Journal of Contemporary China*, vol. 16, no. 52 (August 2007), pp. 359–387.
2. *Green Paper on Constitutional Development* (Hong Kong: The HKSAR Government, July 2007).

Bibliography

Government Documents

Chief Executive Office, "Code For Principal Officials Under the Accountability System," G. N. 3845, attached in Panel on Constitutional Affairs, "Background Brief prepared by Legislative Council Secretariat: Prevention of conflict of interest of principal officials and related issues," LC Paper No. CB(2)1497/02–03(01).
Daily Information Bulletin of the HKSAR Government, "Government Statement on CFA's Judgment," January 29, 1999.
Daily Information Bulletin, "Chief Executive's report to State Council," June 10, 1999.
Daily Information Bulletin, "Chief Secretary for Administration's Transcript," May 19, 1999.
Daily Information Bulletin, "Government applies by motion to CFA for clarification," February 24, 1999.
Daily Information Bulletin, "Secretary for Justice calls for understanding to implement 'One Country, Two Systems,'" May 22, 1999.
Daily Information Bulletin, "Transcript of media session on the NPC Standing Committee's interpretation of the Basic Law," June 26, 1999.
"Decision of the Standing Committee of the National People's Congress on Issues Relating to the Methods for Selecting the Chief Executive of the Hong Kong Special Administrative Region in the Year 2007 and for Forming the Legislative Council of the Hong Kong Special Administrative Region in the Year 2008. Adopted by the Standing Committee of the Tenth National People's Congress at its Ninth Session on 26 April 2004," S. S. No. 5 to Gazette Extraordinary No. 8/2004, http://www.info.gov.hk/cab/cab-review/eng/basic/pdf/es5200408081.pdf (accessed December 29, 2004).
"Framework of accountability for principal officials," press release, http://www.info.gov.hk/gia/general/200204/17/0417251.htm (accessed August 1, 2002).
Leung, Anthony, Letter of resignation to Chief Executive Tung Chee-hwa, March 10, 2003, in LC Paper No. CB(2)1526/02–03(01), Annex.
Report of the Panel of Inquiry on the Penny Stocks Incident by Robert G. Kotewall and Gordon C. K. Kwong, September 2002 (Hong Kong: Printing Department, the HKSAR Government, 2002).
"Special Meeting of the House Committee on 27 February 2004: Background Brief Prepared by Legislative Council Secretariat. Main Issues Relating to Cooperation

between Guangdong and Hong Kong discussed with the Chief Secretary for Administration," LC Paper No. CB(2)1442/03–04.

The Basic Law of the Hong Kong Special Administrative Region of the People's Republic of China (hereafter *The Basic Law*) (Hong Kong: The Consultative Committee for the Basic Law of the Hong Kong Special Administrative Region of the People's Republic of China, April 1990).

"The Fifth Report of the Constitutional Development Task Force: Package of Proposals for the Methods for Selecting the Chief Executive in 2007 and for Forming the Legislative Council in 2008," October 2005, in http://www.legco.gov.hk/yr05-06/english/panels/ca/papers/ca1021cb2-rpt-e.pdf (accessed November 25, 2005).

"The Financial Secretary's response to some of the matters raised by Legislative Council members at the meeting of the Panel on Constitutional Affairs on 17 March 2003 and at the House Committee meeting on 21 March 2003," LC Paper No. CB(2)1692/02–03(03).

The First Report of the Constitutional Task Force: Issues of Legislative Process in the Basic Law Relating to Constitutional Development (March 2004), www.info.gov.hk/cab (accessed June 1, 2005).

"The Fourth Report of the Constitutional Development Task Force: Views and Proposals of Members of the Committee on the Methods for Selecting the Chief Executive in 2007 and for Forming the Legislative Council in 2008 (December 2004)," in http://www.info.gov.hk/cab/cab-review/eng/report4/pdf/fourthreport.pdf, p 2, note 1 (accessed December 29, 2004).

The HKSAR Government Daily Information Bulletin, "The Chief Executive Report to the State Council" (June 10, 1999).

"The Interpretation by the Standing Committee of the National People's Congress of Article 7 of Annex I and Article III of Annex II to the Basic Law of the Hong Kong Special Administrative Region of the PRC: Adopted by the Standing Committee of the Tenth National People's Congress at its Eighth Session on 6 April 2004," L. S. No. 2 to Gazette Ext. No. 5/2004, in http://www.info.gov.hk/cab/cab-review/eng/basic/pdf/es22004080554.pdf (accessed December 29, 2004).

The Second Report of the Constitutional Task Force: Issues of Legislative Process in the Basic Law Relating to Constitutional Development (April 2004), pp. 18–19, www.info.gov.hk/cab.

"What is 9+2? Pan-PRD: A Diversified Single Market—an enlarged hinterland of Hong Kong," in *Bauhinia Gala: A Celebration of the 10th Anniversary of the Establishment of the Hong Kong Special Administrative Region* (Toronto: Best Deal Graphic & Printing, 2007).

News Reports

Apple Daily.
BBC news.
Cable TV news.
Cheng Ming.
China Daily.
China Times.
Dongxiang (*The Trend Magazine*).
Dongzhoukan (*Eastweek*).
Globe and Mail.
Guangjiaojing (*Wide Angle Magazine*).
Hong Kong Commercial Daily.
Hong Kong Economic Times.
Hong Kong Standard.
Hong Kong iMail.
Ming Pao.
Mingbao Zhoukan (*Ming Pao Sunday Supplement*).
National Post.
OMNI News (Toronto, Ontario).
Oriental Daily.
People's Daily.
Qianshao (*Frontline*).
Shijie Ribao.
Sing Pao.
Sing Tao Daily.
South China Morning Post.
Sudden Weekly.
Ta Kung Pao.
Taipei Times.
Taiyang Bao (*The Sun*).
The Epoch Times.
The Hong Kong iMail.
The Hong Kong Standard.
Today Daily News.
TVB news.
Wen Wei Po.
Yizhoukan (*Next Magazine*).

Books and Articles

Akers-Jones, David, *Feeling the Stones: Reminiscences by David Akers-Jones* (Hong Kong: Hong Kong University Press, 2004).
Allen, Jamie, *Seeing Red: China's Uncompromising Takeover of Hong Kong* (Singapore: Butterworth-Heinemann Asia, 1997).
Allen, Michael; Thompson, Brian; and Walsh, Bernadette, eds., *Cases & Materials On Constitutional & Administrative Law* (London: Blackstone, 1994).
Barnett, Hilaire, *Constitutional & Administrative Law* (London: Cavendish, 1995).
Burns, John P., "The Role of the New China News Agency and China's Policy Toward Hong Kong," in John P. Burns, Victor C. Falkenheim, and David M. Lampton, eds., *Hong Kong and China in Transition* (Toronto: Canada and Hong Kong Research Project, University of Toronto–York University, 1994), pp. 17–60.
Burns, John P., *Government Capacity and the Hong Kong Civil Service* (Hong Kong: Oxford University Press, 2004).
Burns, John, "The Structure of Communist Party Control in Hong Kong," *Asian Survey*, vol. 30, no. 8 (August 1990).
Canning, Craig N., "Hong Kong: 'One Country, Two Systems' in Troubled Waters," *Current History* 103, no. 674 (September 2004), pp. 295–96.
Chai, Winberg, "China's 2005 White Paper: 'Building of Political Democracy' in China," *Asian Affairs*, vol. 33, no. 1 (Spring 2006).
Chan, Anita, "The Changing Ruling Elite and Political Opposition in China," in Garry Rodan, ed., *Political Opposition in Industrializing Asia* (London: Routledge, 1996).
Chan, Anson and Her Core Group, *The Road to Universal Suffrage* (Hong Kong: The Anson Chan Core Group, March 5, 2007).
Chan, Elaine, "Defining Fellow Compatriots as 'Others': National Identity in Hong Kong," *Government and Opposition* 35, no. 4 (2000).
Chan, Johannes, "Civil Liberties, Rule of Law and Human Rights: The Hong Kong Special Administrative Region in Its First Four Years," in Lau Siu-kai, ed., *The First Tung Chee-hwa Administration: The First Five Years of the Hong Kong Special Administrative Region* (Hong Kong: The Chinese University Press, 2002).
Chan, Johannes, "Some Thoughts on Constitutional Reform in Hong Kong," *Hong Kong Law Journal* 34, Part 1 (2004), pp. 1–12.
Chan, Ming K., "The Imperfect Legacy: Defects in the British Legal System in Colonial Hong Kong," *University of Pennsylvania Journal of International Economic Law* 18, no. 1 (Spring 1997).
Chan, Ming K., "The Legacy of the British Administration of Hong Kong: A View from Hong Kong," *The China Quarterly*, no. 151 (September 1997).
Chang, Gordan, *The Coming Collapse of China* (New York: Random House, 2001).

Chang, Jaw-ling, *Settlement of the Macao Issue: Distinctive Features of Beijing's Negotiating Behavior (With Test of 1887 Protocol and 1987 Declaration)*, no. 4 (Baltimore: School of Law, University of Maryland, 1988).

Chao, Fen Sun, "Hong Kong's Language Policy in the Postcolonial Age: Social Justice and Globalization," in Ming K. Chan and Alvin Y. So, eds., *Crisis and Transformation in China's Hong Kong* (New York: M. E. Sharpe, 2002).

Chen, Albert, "The Constitutional Controversy of Spring 2004," *Hong Kong Law Journal*, Part 2 (2004)

Chen, Albert, *An Introduction to the Legal System of the People's Republic of China* (Hong Kong: Butterworths, 2004).

Cheng, Joseph, ed., *Hong Kong in Transition* (Hong Kong: Oxford University Press, 1986).

Cheung, Anthony, "Policy Capacity in Post-1997 Hong Kong: Constrained Institutions Facing a Crowding and Differentiated Polity," *The Asia Pacific Journal of Public Administration*, vol. 29, no. 1 (June 2007).

Cheung, Anthony B. L., "The Hong Kong System Under One Country Being Tested: Article 23, Governance Crisis and the Search for a New Hong Kong Identity," in Joseph Y. S. Cheng, ed., *The July 1 Protest Rally: Interpreting a Historic Event* (Hong Kong: City University of Hong Kong, 2005).

Cheung, Anthony B. L. and Wong, Paul C. W., "Who Advised the Hong Kong Government? The Politics of Absorption before and after 1997," *Asian Survey*, vol. 44, no. 6 (December 2004).

Cheung, Anthony B. L., "Civil Service Reform in Post-1997 Hong Kong: Political Challenges, Managerial Responses?" *International Journal of Public Administration* 24, no. 9 (2001).

Cheung, Chor-yung, "The Quest for Good Governance: Hong Kong's Principal Officials Accountability System," *China: An International Journal*, vol. 1, no. 2 (September 2003).

Choi, Chi-keung, "The Decisive Effect of the Proportional Representation System: From Inter-party Competition to Intra-party Competition," in Kuan Hsin-chi, Lau Siu-kai, and Timothy Ka-ying Wong, eds., *Out of the Shadow of 1997? The 2000 Legislative Council Election in the Hong Kong Special Administrative Region* (Hong Kong: The Chinese University Press, 2002).

Chu, Yun-han and Chang, Yu-tzung, "Culture Shift and Regime Legitimacy: Comparing Mainland China, Taiwan, and Hong Kong," in Shiping Hua, ed., *Chinese Political Culture, 1989–2000* (New York: M. E. Sharpe, 2001).

Chung, Jae Ho and Lo, Shiu-hing, "Beijing's Relations with the Hong Kong Special Administrative Region: An Inferential Framework for the Post-1997 Arrangement," *Pacific Affairs*, vol. 68, no. 2 (Summer 1995).

Chung, Robert and his research team at the University of Hong Kong, "Research Team on the Compendium of Submissions on Article 23 of the Basic Law" report/app8.pdf" http://www.hkupop.hku/Chinese/resources/bl23/bl23gp/report/app8.pdf (accessed May 10, 2005).

Chung, Sze-yuen, *Hong Kong's Journey to Reunification* (Hong Kong: The Chinese University Press, 2001).

Civic Exchange, "Listening to the Wisdom of the Masses: Hong Kong People's Attitude toward Constitutional Reform" (January 2004), http://www.hkbu.edu.hk/~hktp (accessed June 1, 2005).

Cotton, James, "Hong Kong: Convergence or Divergence?" *Journal of Northeast Asian Studies* 6, no. 4 (Winter 1987).

Crouch, Harold, "Patrimonialism and Military Rule in Indonesia," *World Politics*, vol. XXXI, no. 4 (July 1979).

Cullen, Richard and Krever, Tor, *Taxation and Democracy in Hong Kong* (Hong Kong: Civic Exchange, November 2005).

Davies, Michael, *Constitutional Confrontation in Hong Kong* (Hong Kong: Macmillan, 1989).

Davies, S. N. G., "One Brand of Politics Rekindled," *Hong Kong Law Journal* 7 (1977).

Davies, Stephen and Roberts, Elfed, *Political Dictionary for Hong Kong* (Hong Kong: Macmillan, 1990).

De Smith, Stanley and Brazier, Rodney, *Constitutional and Administrative Law* (London: Penguin, 1994).

DeGolyer, Michael, "Hong Kong tail wags dog," *The Hong Kong Standard*, May 17, 2007.

DeGolyer, Michael, "Hong Kong Constitutional Reform: What Do the People Want?," Survey Report of the Hong Kong Transition Project, commissioned by the Civic Exchange (December 2005).

DeGolyer, Michael E., "How the Stunning Outbreak of Disease Led to a Stunning Outbreak of Dissent," in Christine Loh and Civic Exchange, eds., *At the Epicentre: Hong Kong and the SARS Outbreak* (Hong Kong: Hong Kong University Press, 2004).

Deng Xiaoping on the Question of Hong Kong (Hong Kong: New Horizon Press, 1993).

Deng, Xiaoping, "One Country, Two Systems," in *Deng Xiaoping on the Question of Hong Kong* (Beijing: New Horizon Press, 1993).

Dicey, A. V., *Introduction to the Study of the Law of the Constitution* (London: Macmillan, 10th Edition, 1959).

Dimbleby, Jonathan, *The Last Governor: Chris Patten & The Handover of Hong Kong* (London: Little, Brown and Company, 1997).

Evans, Peter, *Dependent Development: The Alliance of Multinational, State and Local Capital in Brazil* (Princeton: Princeton University Press, 1979).

Fewsmith, Joseph, "Where Do Correct Ideas Come From? The Party School, Key Think Tanks, and the Intellectuals," in David M. Finkelstein and Maryanne Kivlehan, eds., *China's Leadership in the 21st Century* (New York: M. E. Sharpe, 2003).

Flowerdew, John, *The Final Years of British Hong Kong: The Discourse of Colonial Withdrawal* (London: Macmillan, 1998).

Forsey, Eugene A., "The Courts and the Conventions of the Constitution," *UNB Law Journal*, 33 (1984).
Foster, Alan J., *Political Convergence: The Theory* (London: Politics Association, 1978).
Fu, H. L. and Cullen, Richard, "Political Policing in Hong Kong," *Hong Kong Law Journal*, vol. 33, Part 1 (2003).
Fu, Hualing; Petersen, Carole J.; and Young, Simon N. M., eds., *National Security and Fundamental Freedoms: Hong Kong's Article 23 under Scrutiny* (Hong Kong: Hong University Press, 2005).
Gang, Guo, "Party Recruitment of College Students in China," *Journal of Contemporary China*, vol. 14, no. 43 (May 2005).
Ghai, Yash, *Hong Kong's New Constitutional Order: The Resumption of Chinese Sovereignty and the Basic Law* (Hong Kong: Hong Kong University Press, 1997).
Gilley, Bruce, "Elite-led Democratization in China: Prospects, Perils and Policy Implications," *International Journal*, vol. 61, no. 2 (Spring 2006).
Gilley, Bruce, *China's Democratic Future: How it will happen and where it will lead* (New York: Columbia University Press, 2004).
Goldman, Merle, *Sowing the Seeds of Democracy in China: Political Reform in the Deng Xiaoping Era* (Cambridge: Harvard University Press, 1994).
Goodspeed, "China's President now a player on world stage," *National Post*, November 11, 2004.
Goodstadt, Leo, *Uneasy Partners: The Conflict between Public Interest and Private Profit in Hong Kong* (Hong Kong: Hong Kong University Press, 2004).
Goodstadt, Leo, "China and the Selection of Hong Kong's Post-Colonial Political Elite," *The China Quarterly*, no. 163 (September 2000), pp. 721–741.
Hamrin, Carol Lee, "Social Dynamics and New Generation Politics," in David M. Finkelstein and Maryanne Kivlehan, eds., *China's Leadership in the 21st Century* (New York: M. E. Sharpe, 2003).
Heard, Andrew, "Recognizing the Variety Among Constitutional Conventions," *Canadian Journal of Political Science*, vol. XXII, no. 1 (1989).
Heard, Andrew, *Canadian Constitutional Conventions: The Marriage of Law and Politics* (Toronto: Oxford University Press, 1991).
Hogg, Peter W., *Constitutional Law of Canada* (Toronto: Carswell, 1985).
Holliday, Ian; Ma, Ngok; and Yep, Ray, "After 1997: The Dialectics of Hong Kong Dependence," *Journal of Contemporary Asia* 34, no. 2 (2004).
Hong Kong Journalist Association, "Survey on Press Freedom in Hong Kong, January 2007," in http://www.hkja.org.hk (accessed January 12, 2007).
Huang, Jing, *Factionalism in Chinese Communist Politics* (Cambridge: Cambridge University Press, 2000).
Human Rights Monitor, "Surveillance, Basic Law Article 30, and the Right to Privacy in Hong Kong: A Briefing Paper," Legislative Council LC Paper No. CB(2)259i/05–06(01), October 2005.
Huntington, Samuel P., *The Clash of Civilizations and the Remaking of World Order* (New York: Simon & Schuster, 1996).

Ip, Po-keung, "Development of Civil Society in Hong Kong: Constraints, Problems and Risks," in Li Pang-kwong, ed., *Political Order and Power Transition in Hong Kong* (Hong Kong: The Chinese University Press, 1997).

Jaconelli, Joseph, "The Nature of Constitutional Convention," *Legal Studies*, vol. 19, no. 1 (March 1999).

Jennings, Sir Ivor, *The Law and the Constitution* (London: University of London Press, 1959).

Kellogg, Thomas E., "A Flawed Effort? Legislating on Surveillance on Hong Kong," in http://www.hkjournal.com (accessed May 24, 2007).

King, Ambrose Yeo-chi, "Administrative Absorption of Politics in Hong Kong: Emphasis on the Grass-roots Level," *Asian Survey*, vol. 15, no. 5 (May 1975).

Ku, Agnes S., "Negotiating the Space of Civil Autonomy in Hong Kong: Power, Discourses and Dramaturgical Representation," *The China Quarterly*, no. 179 (September 2004), pp. 647–664.

Kuan, Hsin-chi, "The Pro-Democracy Movement in Hong Kong," in C. L. Chiou and Leong H. Liew, eds., *Uncertain Future: Taiwan–Hong Kong–China Relations after Hong Kong's Return to Chinese Sovereignty* (Aldershot: Ashgate, 2000).

Kuan, Hsin-chi; Lau, Siu-kai; and Wong, Timothy Ka-ying, eds., *Out of the Shadow of 1997? The 2000 Legislative Council Election in the Hong Kong Special Administrative Region* (Hong Kong: The Chinese University Press, 2000).

Kuan, Hsin-chi; Lau, Siu-kai; Louie, Kin-sheun; and Wong, Timothy Ka-ying, eds., *Power Transfer and Electoral Politics: The First Legislative Election in the Hong Kong Special Administrative Region* (Hong Kong: The Chinese University Press, 1999).

Kwok, Rowena; Leung, Joan; and Scott, Ian, eds., *Votes Without Power: The Hong Kong Legislative Council Elections 1991* (Hong Kong: Hong Kong University press, 1992).

Kwong, Bruce, "Patron-Client Politics in Hong Kong: a study of the 2002 and 2005 Chief Executive Elections," *Journal of Contemporary China*, vol. 16, no. 52 (July 2007).

Kwong, Bruce, "Patron-Client Politics and Elections in Hong Kong," unpublished PhD thesis, Department of Politics and Public Administration, the University of Hong Kong, 2004.

Lam, Jermain T. M., "Democracy or Convergence: The Dilemma of Political Reform in Hong Kong," *Asian Journal of Public Administration*, vol. 15, no. 2 (December 1993).

Lau Siu-kai, "The Making of the Electoral System," in Kuan Hsin-chi, Lau Siu-kai, Louie Kin-sheun, and Timothy Ka-ying Wong, eds., *Power Transfer and Electoral Politics: The First Legislative Election in the Hong Kong Special Administrative Region*s (Hong Kong: The Chinese University Press, 1999).

Lau, C. K., *Hong Kong's Colonial Legacy: A Hong Kong Chinese View of the British Heritage* (Hong Kong: The Chinese University Press, 1997).

Lau, Siu-kai and Louie, Kin-sheun, eds., *Hong Kong Tried Democracy: The 1991 Elections in Hong Kong* (Hong Kong: The Chinese University of Hong Kong, 1993).

Lau, Siu-kai, "Government and Political Change in the Hong Kong Special Administrative Region," in James C. Hsiung, ed., *Hong Kong the Super Paradox: Life after Return to China* (London: Macmillan, 2000).

Lau, Siu-kai, "Tung Chee-hwa's Governing Strategy: The Shortfall in Politics," in Lau Siu-kai, ed., *The First Tung Chee-hwa Administration: The First Five Years of the Hong Kong Special Administrative Region* (Hong Kong: The Chinese University Press, 2002), pp. 1–40.

Lee, Martin, "Letter to Hong Kong," RTHK Radio 3, September 5, 1999, http://www.martinlee.org.hk/lettersToHK9.5.99.htm (accessed May 15, 2005).

Leung, Beatrice and Chan, Shun-hing, *Changing Church and State Relations in Hong Kong, 1950–2000* (Hong Kong: Hong Kong University Press, 2003).

Leung, Beatrice and Wong, Marcus, "Hong Kong and Vatican Relations in the Chinese Context," paper presented at the conference "Hong Kong Ten Years After," on June 29–30, 2007 at the City University of Hong Kong and jointly sponsored by the CNRS-CERI/Po, Paris.

Liberthal, Kenneth, "Preventing a War Over Taiwan," *Foreign Affairs*, vol. 84, no. 2 (March/April 2005).

Liu, Wei, "Hong Kong's Impact on Shenzhen Real Property Law," *Hong Kong Law Journal*, vol. 27 (1997).

Lo, Shiu-hing, "One Formula, Two Experiences: political divergence of Hong Kong and Macao since retrocession," *Journal of Contemporary China*, vol. 16, no. 52 (August 2007).

Lo, Shiu-hing, "The Politics of Policing the Anti-WTO Protests in Hong Kong," *Asian Journal of Political Science*, vol. 14, no. 2 (December 2006).

Lo, Shiu-hing, "The Emergence of Constitutional Conventions in the Hong Kong Special Administrative Region," *Hong Kong Law Journal*, Part 1 (2005).

Lo, Shiu-hing, "'Legitimizing' the Selection of the Second HKSAR Chief Executive: From the Election Committee to the Chief Executive Election Bill," *China Perspectives*, no. 38 (November–December 2001).

Lo, Shiu-hing, *Governing Hong Kong: Legitimacy, Communication and Political Decay* (New York: Nova Science, 2001).

Lo, Shiu-hing, "The Politics of the Court of Final Appeal Debate in Hong Kong," *China Quarterly*, no. 161 (March 2000).

Lo, Shiu-hing, "Hong Kong's Political Influence on South China," *Problems of Post-Communism*, vol. 46, no. 4 (July/August 1999).

Lo, Shiu-hing, *The Politics of Democratization in Hong Kong* (London: Macmillan, 1997).

Lo, Shiu-hing, *Political Development in Macau* (Hong Kong: The Chinese University Press, 1995).

Lo, Shiu-hing, "The Chinese Communist Party Elite's Conflict over Hong Kong, 1983–1990," *China Information*, vol. 8, no. 4 (Spring 1994).

Lo, Shiu-hing and Yu, Wing-yat, "The 2000 Legislative Council Elections in Hong Kong," *Representation*, vol. 38, no. 4 (2002).

Lo, Shiu-hing and Yu, Wing-yat, "The Politics of Electoral Reform in Hong Kong," *Commonwealth & Comparative Politics* 39, no. 2 (July 2001).

Lo Shiu-hing, Yu Wing-yat, Kwong Kam-kwan, Wan Kwok-fai, and Cheung Yat-fung, *The Tung Chee-Hwa Government's Governing Crisis and its Solutions* (in Chinese) (Hong Kong: Ming Pao Publisher, 2002).

Lo, Shiu-hing, Yu Wing-yat, and Wan, Kwok-fai, "The 1999 District Councils Elections," in Ming Chan and Alvin So, eds., *Crisis and Transformation in China's Hong Kong* (Armonk: M. E. Sharpe, 2002).

Lo, Sonny, "Macao's Looming Crisis of Governance: The Deeper Problems Underlying the Labor-Police Confrontations," *Macau Closer*, June 2007.

Lo, Sonny, "Hong Kong, 1 July 2003 — Half a million protestors: The Security Law, Identity Politics, Democracy and China," *Behind the Headlines*, vol. 60, no. 4 (April 2004).

Lo, Sonny and Yee, Herbert, "Legitimacy-Building in the Macao Special Administrative Region: Colonial Legacies and Reform Strategies," *Asian Journal of Political Science*, vol. 13, no. 1 (June 2005).

Lo, Sonny; Yu, Eilo; Kwong, Bruce; and Wong, Benson, "The 2004 Legislative Council Elections in Hong Kong: The Triumph of China's United Front Work after the July 2003 and 2004 Protests," *Chinese Law & Government*, vol. 38, no. 1 (January/February 2005).

Lo, Sonny Shiu-hing, "Five Perspectives on Beijing's Policy Towards Hong Kong," in Joseph Y. S. Cheng, ed., *Political Development in the HKSAR* (Hong Kong: City University of Hong Kong, 2001).

Loh, Christine, "Hong Kong Legislative Council Elections: Overcoming the System," *China Brief* 4, no. 18 (September 16, 2004), published by the Jamestown Foundation, http://www.jamestown.org (accessed June 2, 2005).

Loh, Christine, ed., *At the Epicentre: Hong Kong and the SARS Outbreak* (Hong Kong: Hong Kong University Press, 2004).

Loh, Christine and Cullen, Richard, "Political Reform in Hong Kong: The Principal Officials Accountability System: The First Year (2002–2003)," *Journal of Contemporary China* 14, no. 42 (February 2005).

Lui, Tai-lok and Chiu, Stephen Wing-kai, "Introduction: Changing Political Opportunities and the Shaping of Collective Action: Social Movements in Hong Kong," in Stephen Chiu and Lui Tai-lok, eds., *The Dynamics of Social Movement in Hong Kong* (Hong Kong: Hong Kong University Press 2000).

Lyman, Van Slyke, *Enemies and Friends: The United Front in Chinese Communist History* (Stanford, California: Stanford University Press, 1967).

Lynch, Daniel C., "Taiwan's Self-Conscious Nation-Building Project," *Asian Survey*, vol. 44, no. 4 (2004).

Mackintosh, John P., *The British Cabinet* (London: Stevens, 1977).

Man, Cheuk-fei, "The Model of the Chinese Communist Control on Hong Kong's Leftwing Newspapers: A Study of Party Newspapers in an Enclave, 1947–

1982," unpublished M.Phil thesis, Department of Government and Public Administration, the Chinese University of Hong Kong, December 1998.
Mao, Zedong, "The Role of the Chinese Communist Party in the National War," October 1938, in Mao Zedong, *Selected Readings From the Works of Mao Zedong* (Beijing: Foreign Languages Press, 1971).
Marshall, Geoffrey, ed., *Ministerial Responsibility* (Oxford: Oxford University Press, 1989).
Marshall, Geoffrey, *Constitutional Conventions: The Rules and Forms of Political Accountability* (Oxford: Clarendon Press, 1986).
Marshall, Geoffrey and Moodie, Graeme, *Some Problems of the Constitution* (London: Hutchinson, 1959).
Matthews, Gordon, "Heunggongyahn: On the Past, Present and Future of Hong Kong Identity," *Bulletin of Concerned Asian Scholars* 29, no. 3 (1997).
Meyer, Alfred G., "Theories of Convergence," in Chalmers Johnson, ed., *Change in Communist Systems* (Stanford, California: Stanford University Press, 1970).
Ming, Pao, ed., *Aiguo lunzheng (The debate over patriotism)* (Hong Kong: Ming Pao, April 2004).
Moriarty, Francis, "Press Freedom in Hong Kong: The Trend is Down," in www.hkjournal.org/PDF/2002_summer/moriarty.pdf, no. 2 (April 2007).
Mosher, Steven, *Hegemon* (San Francisco: Encounter Books, 2000).
Mu, Ch'ien, *Traditional Government in Imperial China: A Critical Analysis*, translated by Chu-tu Hsueh and George O. Totten (Hong Kong: The Chinese University Press, 1982).
Munro, Colin R., *Studies in Constitutional Law* (London: Butterworths, 1987).
Naughton, Barry, "China's Transition in Economic Perspective," in Merle Goldman and Roderick MacFarquhar, eds., *The Paradox of China's Post-Mao Reforms* (Cambridge, Massachusetts: Harvard University Press, 1999).
Ng, Margaret, "Post-handover Rule of Law: A New Interpretation," in *Hong Kong China: The Red Dawn*, ed. Chris Yeung (Sydney: Prentice Hall, 1998).
Nossal, Kim Richard, "A High Degree of Ambiguity: Hong Kong as an International Actor after 1997," *Pacific Review*, vol. 10, no. 1 (1997).
Nye, Joseph S., *Soft Power: The Means to Success in World Politics* (New York: Public Affairs, 2004).
O'Donnell, Guillermo and Schmitter, Philippe C., *Transitions from Authoritarian Rule: Tentative Conclusions about Uncertain Democracies* (Baltimore: The Johns Hopkins University Press, 1986).
Okabe, Tatsumi, "China's Prospects for Change," in Larry Diamond and Marc F. Plattner, eds., *Democracy in East Asia* (Baltimore: Johns Hopkins University Press, 1998).
Oksenbert, Michel, "China's Political System: Challenges of the Twenty-First Century," in Jonathan Unger, ed., *The Nature of Chinese Politics: From Mao to Jiang* (New York: M. E. Sharpe, 2002).

Oksenbert, Michel, "Will China Democratize? Confronting a Classic Dilemma," *Journal of Democracy* 9, no. 1 (January 1998).

Ostergaard, Clemens Stubbe, "Governance and the Political Challenge of the Falun Gong," in Jude Howell, ed., *Governance in China* (Lanham, Maryland: Rowman & Littlefield, 2004).

Ostrov, Benjamin C., "Clientage in the PRC's National Defense Research and Development Sector," in Lowell Dittmer, Haruhiro Fukui, and Peter N. S. Lee, eds., *Informal Politics in East Asia* (Cambridge: Cambridge University Press, 2000).

Overholt, William, "Hong Kong: Between Third World and First," *Hong Kong Democratic Foundation Newsletter*, no. 17 (January 2001).

Patten, Chris, *East Meets West: The Last Governor of Hong Kong on Power, Freedom and the Future* (London: McClelland & Stewart, 1998).

Pei, Minxin, "Is China Democratizing?" *Foreign Affairs*, vol. 77, no. 1 (January/February 1998).

Pei, Minxin, *China's Trapped Transition: The Limits of Developmental Autocracy* (Cambridge: Harvard University Press, 2006).

Pepper, Suzanne, "Hong Kong Joins the National People's Congress: a first test for one country with two political systems," *Journal of Contemporary China*, vol. 8, no. 21 (July 1999).

Petersen, Carole J., "National Security Offences and Civil Liberties in Hong Kong: A Critique of the Government's 'Consultation' on Article 23 of the Basic Law," *Hong Kong Law Journal* 32, Part 3 (2002).

Petersen, Carole J. and Currie, Jan, "Higher Education Restructuring and Academic Freedom in Hong Kong," *The Journal of Comparative Asian Development*, vol. 6, no. 1 (Spring 2007).

Porteous, Holly, "Beijing's United Front Strategy in Hong Kong," *Commentary*, no. 72 (Winter 1998).

Powell, J. D., "Peasant Society and Clientelist Politics," *American Political Science Review*, vol. 64 (June 1970).

Putnam, Robert D., *The Comparative Study of Political Elites* (New Jersey: Prentice Hall, 1976).

Pye, Lucian, *The Spirit of Chinese Politics* (Cambridge: Harvard University Press, 1992).

Randall, Vicky, "Why have the political trajectories of India and China been different?," in David Potter, David Goldblatt, Margaret Kiloh, and Paul Lewis, eds., *Democratization* (Cambridge: Polity Press, 1997).

Randall, Vicky and Robin Theobald, *Political Change and Underdevelopment: A Critical Introduction to Third World Politics* (London: Macmillan, 1985).

Rao, Geping, "Hong Kong can develop its capitalist system only under the framework of the 'One Country, Two Systems' policy," paper presented at the international conference "The Evolution of 'One Country, Two Systems' in Hong Kong and Macao: Implications for Canada," held on March 24, 2006 at the University of Waterloo.

Rao, Geping, " 'One Country' Must Dominate the Two Systems," in jouurnal.org" http://www.hkjouurnal.org, April 2006.

Saich, Tony, *Governance and Politics in China* (New York: Palgrave, 2001).

Scobell, Andrew, "After Deng, What? Reconsidering the Prospects for a Democratic Transition in China," *Problems of Post-Communism* 44, no. 5 (September/October 1997).

Scobell, Andrew, "Hong Kong's Influence on China: The Tail That Wags the Dog?," *Asian Survey*, vol. XXVIII, no. 6 (June 1988).

Scott, Ian, "Legitimacy, Governance in Post-1997 Hong Kong," *The Asia Pacific Journal of Public Administration*, vol. 29, no. 1 (June 2007).

Scott, Ian, "The Disarticulation of Hong Kong's Post-handover Political System," *The China Journal*, no. 43 (January 2000).

Scott, Ian, "Civil Service Neutrality in Hong Kong," in Haile K. Asmerom and Elisa P. Reis, eds., *Democratization and Bureaucratic Neutrality* (London: Macmillan, 1996).

Scott, Ian, *Political Change and the Crisis of Legitimacy in Hong Kong* (Hong Kong: Oxford University Press, 1990).

Scott, James, "Patron-Client Politics and Political Change in Southeast Asia," *American Political Science Review*, vol. 66 (1972).

Scott, James, "Corruption, Machine Politics, and Political Change," *American Political Science Review*, vol. LXIII, no. 4 (December 1969).

Segal, Gerald, *The Fate of Hong Kong* (London: Simon & Schuster, 1993).

Shaw, Yu-ming, ed., *The Republic of China on Taiwan Today* (Taipei: Kwang Hwa, 1989).

So, Alvin Y., *Hong Kong's Embattled Democracy: A Societal Analysis* (Baltimore: The Johns Hopkins University Press, 1999).

So, Alvin Y. and Chan, Ming K., "Conclusion: Crisis and Transformation in the Hong Kong SAR—Toward Soft Authoritarian Developmentalism?" in Ming Chan and Alvin So, eds., *Crisis and Transformation in China's Hong Kong* (New York: M. E. Sharpe, 2002).

So, Alvin and Kwok, Reginald, "Socioeconomic Center, Political Periphery: Hong Kong's Uncertain Transition toward the Twenty-first Century," in Reginald Kwok and Alvin So, eds., *The Hong Kong–Guangdong Link: Partnership in Flux* (Hong Kong: Hong Kong University Press, 1995).

Su, Shaozhi, "Problems of Democratic Reform in China," in Edward Friedman, ed., *The Politics of Democratization: Generalizing East Asian Experiences* (Boulder, Colorado: Westview, 1994).

Sung, Yun-wing, *The Emergence of Greater China: The Economic Integration of Mainland China, Taiwan and Hong Kong* (London: Palgrave, 2004).

Sung, Yun-wing, *Hong Kong and South China: The Economic Synergy* (Hong Kong: City University Press, 1998).

Sung, Yun-wing and Song, Enrong, *The China–Hong Kong Connection: The Key to China's Open-Door Policy* (Cambridge: Cambridge University Press, 1991).

Sutherland, S. L., "Responsible Government and Ministerial Responsibility: Every Reform Is Its Own Problem," *Canadian Journal of Political Science*, vol. XXIV, no. 1 (March 1991).

Tai, Benny Y. T., "Chapter 1 of Hong Kong's New Constitution: Constitutional Positioning and Repositioning," in Ming Chan and Alvin So, eds., *Crisis and Transformation in China's Hong Kong* (Armonk: M. E. Sharpe, 2002).

Tanner, Murray Scott, "The National People's Congress," in Merle Goldman and Roderick MacFarquhar, eds., *The Paradox of China's Post-Mao Reforms* (Cambridge: Harvard University Press, 1999).

Tarrow, Sidney, *Power in Movement: Social Movements and Contentious Politics* (Cambridge: Cambridge University Press, 1998).

The Central Committee's Work Report (in Chinese) (Hong Kong: The Democratic Alliance for Betterment of Hong Kong, December 2002).

Theobald, Robin, "Patrimonialism," *World Politics*, vol. XXXIV, no. 4 (July 1982).

Ting, Wai, "Hong Kong's Relations with Its Chinese Sovereign," in James C. Hsiung, ed., *Hong Kong the Super Paradox: Life after Return to China* (London: Macmillan, 2000).

Toward Full Universal Suffrage: A Reform Model for Public Consultation on the Political System in 2012 (Hong Kong: The Democratic Party of Hong Kong, March 2007).

Tse, Thomas Kwan-choi, "Civic and Political Education," in Mark Bray and Ramsey Koo, eds., *Education and Society in Hong Kong and Macao: Comparative Perspectives on Continuity and Change* (Hong Kong: Comparative Education Research Centre, University of Hong Kong, 2004).

Turpin, Colin, *British Government and the Constitution: Text, Cases and Materials* (London: Weidenfeld and Nicolson, 1990).

Unger, Jonathan, ed., *The Nature of Chinese Politics: From Mao to Jiang* (New York: M. E. Sharpe, 2002).

Vree, Johan K., *Political Integration: The Formation of Theory and Its Problems* (The Hague: Mouton, 1972).

Wang, Wenfang, *China's Resumption of Sovereignty over Hong Kong* (Hong Kong: David C. Lam Institute for East-West Studies, Hong Kong Baptist University, 1997).

Wang, Zhenmin, "Why Does Hong Kong Still Matter?," in http://www.hkjournal.org, April 2006.

Wang, Zhenmin, "China's Legal/Constitutional Approach toward Hong Kong and Macao," paper presented at the international conference, "The Evolution of 'One Country, Two Systems' in Hong Kong and Macao: Implications for Canada," held on March 24, 2006 at the University of Waterloo.

Wang, Zhenmin, "The Roman Law Tradition and Its Future Development in China," *Frontier Law China*, vol. 1, no. 1 (2006).

Weingrod, A., "Patrons, Patronage and Political Parties," *Comparative Studies in Society and History*, vol. 10 (July 1968).

Weng, Byron S. J., "'One Country, Two Systems' from a Taiwan Perspective," *Orbis*, vol. 46, no. 4 (Fall 2002).

Weng, Byron S. J., "Judicial Independence under the Basic Law," in Steve Tsang, ed., *Judicial Independence and the Rule of Law in Hong Kong* (Hong Kong: Hong Kong University Press, 2001).

Wong, Andrew, "Political Accountability and Constitutional Conventions (in Chinese)," unpublished paper, October 2001.

Wong, Benson Wai-kwok, "Can Cooptation Win Over the Hong Kong People?," *Issues & Studies*, vol. 33, no. 5 (May 1997).

Wong, Max Wai-lun, "The meaning of 'charge': private member's bills in the Legislative Council," *Hong Kong Law Journal*, vol. 28 (1988).

Wong, Wilson, "From a British-Style Administrative State to a Chinese-Style Political State: Civil Service Reform in Hong Kong after the Transfer of Sovereignty" (Paper written for the Brookings Institution, June 2003), http://www.brookings.edu/fp/cnaps/papers/wong2003.pdf (accessed June 2, 2005).

Xiao, Weiyun and others, "Why the Court of Final Appeal Was Wrong: Comments of the Mainland Scholars on the Judgment of the Court of Final Appeal," in Johannes M. M. Chan, H. L. Fu, and Yash Ghai, eds., *Hong Kong's Constitutional Debate: Conflict Over Interpretation* (Hong Kong: Hong Kong University Press, 2000).

Xu, Jiatun, *Xu Jiatun's Hong Kong Memoir* (in Chinese), volumes 1 and 2 (Taipei: United Daily News, 1993).

Yeh, Anthony Gar-on; Lee, Yok-shiu; Lee, Tunney; and Sze, Nien Dak, eds., *Building a Competitive Pearl River Delta Region: Cooperation, Coordination, and Planning* (Centre of Urban and Environmental Management, University of Hong Kong, 2002).

Yu, Wing-yat, *Intra-Party Democracy and Democratization in Taiwan*, unpublished PhD Thesis, the University of Hong Kong, 2004.

Zhang, Ran, "QDII expanded to include securities, fund companies," *China Daily*, June 21, 2007.

Zhao, Suisheng, "Chinese Nationalism and Authoritarianism in the 1990s," in Suisheng Zhao, ed., *China and Democracy: Reconsidering the Prospects of a Democratic China* (New York: Routledge, 2000).

Zweig, David, *Agrarian Radicalism in China, 1968–1981* (Cambridge, Massachusetts: Harvard University Press, 1989).

Index

Academic freedom   128, 291, 318
Accountability   3, 30, 31, 33, 47, 115, 116, 120, 121, 122, 123, 124, 125, 126, 127, 131, 132, 139, 201, 270, 271, 286, 288, 289, 307, 311, 316, 317, 321
Administrative officers   33, 34, 51
American   41, 56, 71, 171, 229, 244, 247
Annexation   7, 8, 10, 34, 37
Anti-democratic   12, 15, 67, 75
Anti-foreignism   173, 181
Anti-Japanese protests   63
Apple Daily   62, 67, 85, 105, 153, 157, 165, 180, 182, 187, 192, 217
Article 23 of the Basic Law   122, 124, 126, 131, 138, 139, 140, 141, 151, 152, 153, 154, 155, 156, 157, 168, 159, 160, 161, 162, 163, 164, 165, 173, 181, 202, 205, 211, 233, 234, 265, 266, 268, 269, 271, 290, 294, 311, 318
Article 23 Concern Group   60, 164
Asian financial crisis   12, 23, 28, 44, 45, 233
ATV   1, 175, 176, 177, 182, 222, 263, 296, 306
Authoritarianism   8, 10, 34, 174, 235, 270, 321
Autonomy   14, 16, 17, 19, 22, 23, 28, 37, 54, 59, 60, 61, 67, 73, 76, 79, 81, 83, 85, 87, 88, 89, 91, 93, 95, 96, 97, 99, 100, 101, 103, 104, 105, 107, 108, 113, 116, 123, 124, 134, 135, 136, 142, 143, 144, 145, 146, 147, 148, 157, 174, 179, 182, 198, 238, 250, 251, 259, 275, 277, 287, 314

Chinese definition of   145
economic autonomy   142
in external relations   143, 144
fiscal autonomy   28, 37
Hong Kong autonomy   14, 16, 17, 22, 23, 54, 81, 88, 96, 100, 103, 113, 116, 123, 124, 134, 135, 144, 145, 147, 148, 158, 251, 259, 275
judicial autonomy   14, 59, 60, 61, 67, 73, 76, 81, 83, 85, 87, 89, 91, 93, 95, 97, 99, 100, 103, 105, 107, 108, 146
legislative autonomy   136
media autonomy   179, 182
personal autonomy   19
political autonomy   198
Taiwan's autonomy   79, 250

Bar Association   103
Basic Law   2, 3, 4, 13, 14, 17, 22, 23, 28, 34, 40, 42, 43, 46, 47, 50, 52, 56, 57, 58, 59, 60, 61, 62, 65, 73, 76, 81, 82, 83, 84, 85, 86, 87, 88, 89, 90, 91, 92, 93, 94, 95, 97, 98, 99, 100, 101, 102, 103, 104, 105, 106, 107, 108, 113, 114, 115, 116, 118, 121, 122, 123, 124, 126, 130, 131, 134, 135, 136, 137, 138, 139, 140, 141, 143, 144, 145, 146, 147, 148, 149, 151, 152, 154, 155, 156, 157, 161, 163, 164, 169, 170, 171, 173, 178, 181, 202, 203, 205, 209, 211, 213, 216, 217, 225, 233, 234, 238, 239, 245, 247, 248, 249, 250, 252, 266, 268, 269, 271, 273, 274, 277, 278, 279, 280, 281, 283, 284,

285, 287, 290, 291, 292, 293, 294, 300, 307, 308, 311, 313, 318, 321
Basic Law Committee   59, 90, 93, 95, 107, 108, 113, 135, 137, 144, 171, 178, 280, 281
Basic Law Committee member   95, 107, 171, 178
Basic Law interpretation   13, 14, 43, 52, 57, 59, 60, 62, 73, 82, 83, 84, 86, 87, 88, 90, 91, 92, 93, 95, 98, 99, 100, 101, 102, 104, 105, 106, 107, 113, 115, 130, 134, 144, 146, 147, 268, 274, 278, 284, 307
Beijing   1, 2, 3, 4, 6, 7, 8, 9, 10, 11, 12, 13, 14, 15, 16, 17, 18, 19, 20, 21, 22, 23, 24, 25, 26, 27, 28, 29, 30, 31, 32, 33, 34, 35, 36, 37, 38, 39, 40, 42, 43, 44, 45, 46, 47, 48, 49, 50, 51, 52, 53, 54, 55, 56, 57, 58, 59, 60, 61, 62, 63, 64, 65, 66, 67, 68, 69, 70, 72, 73, 74, 75, 76, 77, 78, 80, 82, 84, 86, 89, 90, 91, 92, 93, 94, 96, 98, 99, 100, 101, 102, 104, 106, 108, 110, 112, 113, 114, 115, 116, 118, 120, 122, 123, 124, 126, 128, 129, 130, 131, 132, 133, 134, 135, 136, 137, 138, 139, 140, 141, 142, 143, 144, 145, 146, 147, 148, 149, 150, 152, 153, 154, 155, 156, 157, 158, 159, 160, 162, 164, 165, 166, 167, 168, 169, 170, 177, 178, 179, 180, 181, 182, 183, 184, 186, 187, 188, 189, 190, 192, 193, 194, 195, 196, 197, 198, 199, 200, 201, 202, 203, 204, 205, 206, 208, 209, 210, 212, 213, 214, 215, 216, 217, 218, 220, 221, 222, 223, 224, 225, 226, 228, 229, 230, 231, 232, 234, 235, 236, 238, 239, 240, 241, 242, 243, 244, 246, 247, 248, 249, 250, 251, 252, 253, 254, 255, 256, 257, 258, 259, 260, 261, 262, 263, 265, 266, 268, 269, 271, 272, 273, 276, 289, 291, 293, 294, 295, 297, 300, 301, 305, 306, 311, 312, 316, 317, 318
Beijing-Taipei relations   37, 149, 182, 198, 225, 228, 234, 240, 242, 234, 248, 252, 257
Beijing's fear of Taiwanization   13, 37, 256
Bird-cage type of democracy   258
Britain   1, 8, 21, 39, 70, 111, 174, 227, 231, 236, 237, 240, 241, 251, 254, 255, 259
Bureaucratic politics   7, 21, 22, 34, 37
Business   11, 12, 13, 15, 18, 21, 25, 29, 32, 45, 47, 49, 53, 54, 58, 59, 65, 66, 67, 68, 70, 71, 73, 74, 75, 76, 87, 121, 140, 153, 155, 156, 160, 162, 168, 179, 187, 192, 195, 198, 204, 206, 208, 209, 212, 213, 214, 215, 218, 276
   business elites   11, 12, 13, 32, 49, 68, 74, 75, 76, 168, 208, 212
   business interest   58
   business party   75
   business profession   204, 206
   business sector   75, 153, 179, 214, 218
   business tycoons   12, 29, 140, 160

Cable TV   176, 182, 276, 283, 296, 309
Canada   91, 175
Capitalism   34, 248, 232, 233, 235
Capitalist   9, 10, 12, 15, 16, 30, 35, 37, 54, 68, 70, 78, 132, 134, 135, 158, 161, 233, 234, 254, 262, 292, 294, 318
Cardinal Zen   50, 51, 62, 179, 180, 268, 302
CCTV   177, 178, 179, 182, 261, 296
Censorship (also see self-censorship)   3, 32, 42, 70, 138, 151, 175, 176, 177, 181, 182, 218, 222, 239, 255, 263, 277, 296

Index **325**

Central government 7, 14, 16, 17, 20, 21, 22, 25, 26, 28, 29, 30, 35, 36, 45, 48, 49, 50, 52, 53, 56, 57, 68, 73, 85, 88, 89, 92, 96, 101, 104, 114, 123, 124, 130, 135, 136, 137, 138, 139, 140, 141, 142, 143, 144, 148, 149, 157, 158, 159, 165, 166, 167, 168, 169, 181, 188, 189, 190, 193, 199, 200, 201, 205, 209, 210, 213, 215, 216, 217, 221, 223, 225, 232, 236, 251, 253, 255, 256, 258, 266, 273, 278, 281, 282, 284, 294
Central-local relations 16, 92
Central Policy Unit 31, 166,
CEPA 3, 11, 23, 25, 35, 40, 52, 65, 70, 167, 215
Chan, Anson 25, 26, 46, 47, 51, 66, 97, 98, 99, 100, 101, 180, 189, 200, 205, 216, 276, 301, 302, 310
Chan, Margaret 126
Chan, Tat-ching 262
Chen, Albert Hong-yi 91, 178, 272, 294
Chen, Shui-bian 13, 56, 169, 172, 228, 229, 230, 234, 239, 246
Chen, Zuo'er 23, 176, 216, 271
Cheng, Albert 40, 52, 56, 57, 165, 206, 303
Cheng, Joseph 203, 213, 265, 303, 306
Cheng, Yiu-tong 19, 122, 155, 157, 187, 191, 193, 215, 293
Cheung, Anthony 42, 185, 186, 188, 190, 277, 295
Cheung, Chi-kong 177
Chiang, Ching-kuo 228
Chief executive 1, 2, 4, 9, 11, 12, 13, 14, 16, 17, 18, 19, 20, 21, 22, 23, 26, 30, 31, 32, 33, 34, 35, 36, 39, 40, 4, 47, 49, 51, 52, 53, 54, 56, 57, 59, 60, 61, 67, 68, 69, 73, 74, 83, 94, 99, 104, 114, 115, 116, 118, 119, 120, 122, 124, 125, 126, 127, 128, 129, 130, 131, 132, 134, 136, 137, 130, 140, 141, 142, 148, 153, 155, 156, 165, 166, 169, 170, 178, 179, 181, 185, 189, 192, 193, 199, 200, 201, 202, 203, 204, 205, 206, 208, 209, 210, 211, 212, 213, 214, 215, 216, 217, 218, 219, 220, 221, 222, 223, 224, 225, 234, 255, 256, 257, 258, 259, 264, 265, 268, 270, 271, 272, 273, 274, 277, 283, 287, 288, 289, 290, 294, 297, 300, 301, 302, 303, 307, 308, 314, 315
chief executive election 4, 9, 17, 18, 44, 47, 69, 74, 136, 193, 199, 200, 201, 202, 203, 204, 205, 206, 211, 212, 215, 216, 217, 218, 219, 220, 221, 222, 223, 224, 225, 256, 258, 264, 271, 294, 297, 300, 301, 303, 314, 315
chief executive election bill 297, 315
chief executive election campaign 74, 205, 209, 214, 224
Chief Executive Office 33, 125, 289, 307
replacement chief executive 49, 268, 270
China's annexation of Hong Kong 8, 10, 34, 37
Chinese civilization 15, 16, 34, 36, 43, 51, 174, 238, 253
Chinese Communist Party 9, 10, 11, 16, 17, 18, 19, 20, 21, 22, 27, 33, 34, 36, 37, 41, 43, 46, 49, 51, 68, 73, 76, 140, 141, 142, 145, 148, 168, 169, 170, 171, 181, 182, 198, 201, 230, 234, 250, 251, 262, 264, 295, 298, 301, 315, 317
Chinese Foreign Ministry 22, 143, 216
Chinese nationalism (also see nationalism) 73, 138, 181, 270, 321
Chow, Selina 33, 156, 223, 303
Chu, Pui-hing 129
Chung, Robert 125, 177, 268, 291

Civic Party 4, 161, 164, 213, 215, 218, 224, 262
Civil liberties 1, 4, 42, 43, 50, 58, 62, 67, 73, 75, 76, 77, 148, 151, 159, 160, 165, 236, 239, 253, 254, 255, 271, 293, 310, 318
Civil service 20, 30, 33, 40, 42, 45, 47, 129, 160, 179, 268, 287, 288, 289, 293, 310, 311, 319, 321
Civil service party 20
Clash of civilization 7, 15, 7, 34, 43, 263, 313
Colonial mentality 255
Commercial Radio 52, 266
Common law 14, 42, 62, 67, 91, 99, 113, 132, 144, 145, 146
Consensus 17, 26, 89, 93, 116, 121, 123, 141, 152, 171, 214, 218, 238, 245, 246, 252, 258, 259, 260
Constitutional conventions 3, 108, 109, 111, 112, 113, 115, 117, 119, 121, 122, 123, 125, 127, 129, 131, 132, 133, 137, 144, 146, 147, 148, 285, 286, 288, 313, 315, 317, 321
Convention of self-restraint 81, 90, 92, 93, 107, 108, 113, 132, 136, 141
Convergence 2, 3, 4, 39, 41, 42, 43, 44, 45, 47, 48, 49, 50, 51, 53, 54, 59, 62, 63, 68, 70, 71, 72, 73, 74, 75, 76, 77, 78, 79, 233, 234, 253, 260, 266, 267, 268, 312, 313, 314, 317
Convergence theory 41, 73
Cooptation 32, 37, 263, 321
Coordination 7, 24, 25, 26, 30, 36, 40, 46, 47, 52, 66, 124, 167, 276, 288, 321
Corruption 8, 32, 34, 94, 126, 128, 259, 261, 265, 319
Court of Final Appeal 59, 76, 81, 84, 113, 147, 277, 287, 315, 321
CPPCC 130, 168, 196, 198
Crime 27, 265
Cross-border prostitution 26

DeGolyer, Michael 177, 203, 261, 302
Democratic Alliance for Betterment of Hong Kong 10, 18, 30, 33, 40, 45, 46, 47, 48, 54, 56, 58, 62, 63, 74, 108, 118, 119, 122, 123, 125, 134, 142, 148, 154, 155, 156, 158, 160, 166, 172, 173, 178, 179, 188, 189, 191, 192, 193, 196, 204, 205, 215, 222, 223, 252, 270, 271, 281, 289, 294, 297, 320
Democratic Party 42, 58, 68, 118, 119, 140, 171, 172, 173, 185, 187, 215, 222, 262, 281, 285, 297, 298, 299, 301, 320
Democratic Progressive Party 13, 16, 37, 56, 140, 169, 172, 228, 230, 241
Democratization 11, 15, 16, 17, 23, 36, 52, 54, 56, 57, 60, 68, 69, 75, 76, 78, 115, 132, 134, 140, 148, 162, 163, 168, 169, 170, 172, 173, 174, 176, 199, 200, 209, 214, 217, 221, 222, 224, 225, 234, 255, 256, 257, 258, 262, 264, 267, 277, 288, 289, 292, 301, 305, 313, 315, 318, 319, 321
Democrats 11, 12, 13, 16, 23, 31, 32, 44, 45, 46, 51, 53, 54, 55, 56, 57, 58, 67, 68, 69, 73, 74, 75, 77, 78, 119, 125, 138, 140, 141, 147, 155, 157, 162, 164, 168, 169, 170, 171, 172, 173, 174, 175, 176, 180, 186, 187, 188, 195, 196, 197, 199, 200, 201, 202, 203, 208, 209, 211, 213, 214, 218, 221, 222, 257, 258, 259, 262, 268, 272, 299, 303
 mainstream 202, 203, 213
 pan-democrats 74, 203, 213, 214
 radical 74, 78
 social 138, 164, 202, 213, 218
Deng, Xiaoping 1, 10, 14, 16, 20, 33, 40, 77, 135, 140, 145, 171, 176, 232, 238, 253, 262, 292, 293, 294, 302, 312, 313

Dependence 12, 15, 65, 70, 74, 78, 233, 267, 313
De-Sinification 79
Direct elections 11, 12, 13, 19, 20, 51, 53, 54, 55, 56, 57, 59, 60, 67, 69, 114, 117, 134, 137, 140, 142, 148, 163, 169, 170, 181, 186, 199, 205, 210, 211, 213, 214, 215, 216, 217, 222, 224, 255, 256, 257, 258, 272, 277, 288, 290, 294, 304
District Councils 10, 19, 31, 44, 46, 137, 142, 186, 202, 207, 214, 262, 293, 298, 316
Distrust 34, 47, 55, 148, 171, 200, 202, 257
Divergence 2, 39, 43, 52, 53, 54, 62, 67, 68, 76, 77, 78, 79, 111, 267, 306, 312, 315

Eu, Audrey 60, 174, 291, 303
Executive Council 4, 19, 30, 31, 32, 44, 46, 47, 48, 84, 100, 101, 104, 112, 119, 121, 122, 123, 130, 134, 136, 152, 153, 155, 156, 157, 205, 211, 292

Face 35, 44, 52, 82, 103, 168, 174, 189, 245
Factional politics 34, 195, 201, 301, 313
Factionalism 195, 201, 301, 313
Factions 202, 242
Fan, Rita 118, 187, 191, 196, 208, 281, 303
Federalism 231, 232, 238, 258
Federation of Trade Unions 30, 58, 155, 160, 164, 188, 192, 193, 215, 293
Fiscal relations 7, 28, 35
Fujian 15, 29, 24, 44, 58, 196, 233
Functional constituencies 52, 53, 55, 57, 114, 115, 202, 210, 214, 257

Gao, Siren 49, 166, 167, 194, 266
Germany 145, 154, 290
Ghai, Yash 93, 103, 104, 111, 144, 277, 278, 281, 285, 287, 294, 321
Groups opposing Article 23 of the Basic Law 161, 162, 163, 164, 165
Guangdong 15, 24, 25, 26, 32, 65, 71, 143, 195, 196, 262, 265, 273, 276, 308, 319
Guanxi 4, 8, 9, 18, 22

H shares 11
Hardline 36, 57
Hard-liners 155, 274
Harmony 16, 51, 52, 68, 69, 117, 144, 163, 209, 211, 216, 221, 260, 268, 296
HKSAR 1, 2, 3, 4, 7, 8, 9, 10, 11, 12, 13, 14, 15, 16, 17, 18, 19, 20, 21, 22, 23, 24, 25, 26, 27, 28, 29, 30, 32, 33, 34, 35, 36, 37, 39, 40, 41, 42, 43, 44, 45, 46, 48, 49, 50, 51, 52, 53, 54, 55, 56, 57, 58, 59, 60, 61, 62, 63, 64, 65, 66, 67, 68, 69, 70, 71, 72, 73, 74, 75, 76, 77, 78, 79, 81, 82, 83, 84, 86, 88, 89, 90, 91, 92, 93, 94, 95, 96, 97, 98, 99, 100, 101, 102, 103, 104, 105, 107, 108, 111, 113, 114, 115, 116, 118, 119, 120, 121, 122, 123, 124, 125, 126, 127, 128, 130, 131, 132, 133, 134, 135, 136, 137, 138, 139, 140, 141, 142, 143, 144, 145, 146, 147, 148, 149, 151, 152, 153, 154, 156, 157, 158, 159, 160, 161, 165, 166, 167, 168, 169, 170, 171, 172, 173, 174, 175, 176, 177, 178, 179, 180, 181, 182, 183, 185, 186, 193, 196, 197, 199, 200, 201, 202, 203, 205, 206, 208, 209, 210, 211, 212, 214, 215, 216, 217, 218, 219, 221, 222, 223, 224, 225, 227, 231, 232, 233, 234, 235, 236, 238, 239, 240, 251,

252, 253, 254, 255, 256, 257, 258, 259, 260, 261, 262, 263, 266, 267, 269, 274, 275, 276, 278, 280, 282, 283, 286, 289, 290, 291, 293, 295, 296, 297, 298, 301, 303, 306, 307, 308, 315, 316

HKSAR tenth anniversary 2, 21, 28, 45, 67, 119, 136, 151, 154, 166, 175, 176, 177, 178, 179, 180, 182, 238, 240, 253, 254, 256, 259, 261, 263, 276, 296

Ho, Albert Chun-yan 140, 141, 185, 186, 188, 222, 262, 293

Ho, Cyd 222

Ho, Edmund 26, 141, 236, 265, 306

Ho, Stanley 29, 213

Hong Kong Alliance in Support of the Patriotic and Democratic Movement in China 9, 11, 141, 185

Hong Kong and Macao Work Committee 22, 49

Hong Kong external relations 22, 147, 148

Hong Kong identity 51, 63, 64, 73, 76, 151, 155, 156, 157, 160, 165, 174, 176, 177, 181, 182, 214, 236, 254, 255, 256, 265, 275, 294, 311, 317

Hong Kong Macao Affairs Office 21, 22, 23, 24, 49, 155, 157, 158, 166, 167, 168, 176, 255, 271

Hong Kong Transition Project 12, 64, 177, 202, 263, 302, 312

Hong Kong's relations with China 147, 148

Hong Kong-Zhuhai-Macao bridge 25, 27, 35, 51, 66, 143

Hongkongers 1, 2, 8, 9, 10, 15, 32, 43, 52, 62, 63, 67, 68, 72, 90, 133, 134, 145, 148, 151, 155, 158, 165, 171, 176, 180, 181, 199, 202, 224, 241, 256

Hongkongization of mainland China 8, 10

Hu, Jintao 2, 22, 39, 49, 165, 230, 247, 262, 273, 290

Huntington, Samuel 15, 43, 174, 263, 313

Identity change 151, 153, 155, 157, 159, 163, 165, 167, 169, 171, 173, 175, 177, 179, 181, 182, 183, 294

Independent Commission Against Corruption 8, 32, 126, 128, 169, 291

Infrastructure 27, 28, 66, 67, 214

Integration 3, 9, 26, 37, 66, 77
   economic 25, 37, 66, 67, 69, 75, 76, 276, 319
   political 37, 77, 266, 320

Intermarriage 9, 276

Internationalization of Taiwan's future 249, 252

Ip, Regina 12, 44, 59, 97, 98, 99, 122, 126, 152, 153, 154, 159, 160, 206, 263, 269, 290

Japan 228, 229

Japanese 63, 145, 228

Jennings, Sir Ivor 109, 286

Jia Qinglin 216

Jiang, Enzhu 49, 101, 281

Jiang, Zemin 10, 17, 22, 40, 49, 98, 101, 151, 167, 215, 216, 230, 238

Judges 84, 85, 86, 87, 90, 105, 113, 139, 278, 279, 284, 285

Judicial activism 86

Judicial autonomy 14, 59, 60, 61, 67, 73, 76, 81, 83, 85, 87, 89, 91, 93, 95, 97, 99, 100, 101, 103, 105, 107, 108, 113, 146, 277, 287

Judicial politics 254

Judicial review 92

Kuan, Hsin-chi, 44, 203, 213, 272, 273, 298, 300, 314,

Kuomintang 37, 79, 240, 241, 251, 259

Lam, Woon-kwong 128
Lau, Siu-kai 166, 268, 272, 273, 293, 298, 310, 311, 314, 315
Law, Fanny 128
Law Society 101
League of Social Democrats 138, 164, 202, 213, 218
Lee, Allen Peng-fei 40, 56, 57, 94, 95, 156, 187, 189, 190, 192, 195, 206, 208, 222, 266, 271, 281, 282, 300
Lee, Martin Chu-ming 23, 42, 44, 104, 119, 157, 171, 172, 173, 174, 180, 187, 193, 268, 276, 283, 285, 294, 303
Lee, Teng-hui 228, 229
Legislative Council 16, 19, 33, 44, 51, 52, 53, 54, 55, 57, 58, 59, 60, 68, 69, 75, 86, 91, 94, 97, 98, 104, 112, 114, 115, 121, 130, 142, 148, 170, 172, 173, 175, 186, 193, 202, 204, 205, 208, 214, 115, 216, 217, 257, 264, 265, 272, 273, 277, 281, 283, 287, 288, 289, 293, 295, 296, 298, 307, 308, 311, 313, 314, 315, 316, 321
   members 130, 289, 308
   Secretariat 265, 289, 307
Legislative Yuan 198, 242, 248
Legitimacy 239, 263, 268, 275, 288, 289, 291, 295, 301, 305, 306, 311, 315, 316, 319
Leong, Alan Kah-kit 4, 60, 136, 174, 202, 203, 207, 215, 216, 217, 220, 223, 224, 225, 299, 302, 304
Leong, Chi-hung 120, 128
Leung, Antony 50, 59, 122, 123, 124, 126, 127, 131, 132, 142, 159, 269, 271, 289, 290
Leung, Chun-ying 19, 100, 122, 134, 211, 298
Leung, Elsie 44, 60, 61, 84, 91, 97, 99, 100, 102, 114, 119, 122, 125, 130, 154, 169, 179, 291

Leung, Kwok-hung 32, 69, 206, 208, 214, 303
Li, Andrew Kwok-nang 85, 86, 95, 97, 278
Li, Gang 216
Li, Ka-shing 29, 49, 213, 298
Li, Richard 49, 213
Liaison Office 10, 18, 21, 22, 24, 36, 40, 49, 57, 58, 124, 137, 148, 157, 158, 166, 167, 168, 172, 186, 188, 189, 190, 191, 193, 194, 195, 196, 197, 216, 255, 258, 264, 266, 269, 271, 273, 293, 300
Liao, Hui 23, 32, 49, 50, 98, 153, 155, 167, 270
Liberal Party 9, 31, 32, 33, 47, 54, 59, 74, 75, 118, 119, 123, 125, 153, 155, 156, 157, 158, 189, 190, 192, 193, 194, 204, 205, 215, 223, 304
Lien, Chan 240
Lo, Vincent 67
Loh, Christine 44, 120, 269, 270, 272, 290, 312
Loyal opposition 201, 202, 203, 224, 225, 302
Loyalty 10, 19, 31, 32, 33, 47, 49, 51, 69, 76, 139, 181, 197, 198, 201, 289
Lu, Ping 21, 49, 140, 167, 176, 240, 306
Lu, Xinhua 22, 216

Ma, Lik 46, 58, 94, 95, 187, 189, 190, 191, 205, 215, 222, 297
Ma, Ying-jeou 252
Macao 5, 16, 20, 21, 22, 24, 25, 26, 27, 28, 29, 35, 40, 49, 51, 57, 66, 71, 85, 98, 114, 124, 138, 140, 141, 143, 216, 227, 230, 232, 233, 234, 235, 236, 237, 238, 246, 247, 248, 250, 251, 252, 253, 259, 260, 265, 266, 275, 292, 294, 296, 305, 306, 311, 315, 316, 318, 320

Mainlandization of Hong Kong 10, 39, 41, 42, 43, 44, 45, 47, 49, 50, 51, 52, 53, 55, 57, 59, 61, 63, 65, 67, 69, 70, 71, 72, 73, 74, 75, 76, 77, 78, 79, 175, 239, 252, 255, 258, 260, 266
Mao, Zedong 170, 295, 317
Mass media 2, 3, 17, 32, 42, 43, 58, 69, 97, 104, 125, 127, 129, 132, 138, 151, 154, 157, 165, 169, 170, 171, 175, 181, 183, 188, 194, 211, 212, 217, 223, 242, 252, 253, 256
  Political correctness 177, 178, 179, 180, 182, 212, 263, 303
Material benefits 32
Migration 72, 93
Military 9, 40, 71, 72, 135, 228, 229, 230, 232, 240, 245, 246, 247, 248, 250, 260, 261, 301, 312
Military Affairs Commission 230
Ming Pao 180, 181, 182, 194, 217, 219
Ministerial resignation 3, 124, 126, 127, 128, 131, 132
Moriarty, Francis 177, 296, 317

National People's Congress 4, 23, 24, 27, 81, 82, 83, 84, 85, 86, 87, 88, 89, 90, 91, 92, 93, 94, 95, 96, 97, 98, 99, 100, 101, 102, 103, 104, 105, 106, 107, 108, 134, 135, 136, 137, 144, 147, 171, 185, 186, 187, 188, 189, 190, 193, 194, 195, 196, 197, 198, 204, 206, 209, 213, 216, 217, 222, 250, 277, 278, 279, 280, 281, 282, 283, 284, 285, 294, 297, 299, 300, 306, 307
  elections 186, 194, 195, 196, 198, 297, 300
  Legislative Affairs Commission 61, 98, 102, 114
  members 4, 27, 84, 92, 93, 94, 95, 96, 101, 107, 108, 197, 217, 281, 282, 297

National security 73, 134, 136, 151, 153, 155, 159, 161, 163, 165, 167, 169, 171, 173, 175, 177, 179, 181, 183, 211, 318
  agents 138, 273
  bill 4, 60, 62, 142, 152, 154, 155, 156, 157, 159, 160, 164, 165, 167, 181, 182, 295
  national security law 211
  National Security (Legislative Provisions) 42, 48, 50, 119, 151, 152, 295
Nationalism 73, 138, 181, 270, 321
Ng, Margaret 23, 60, 92, 97, 104, 120, 123, 174, 213, 262, 268, 271, 274, 278, 283, 289, 290, 294
Nomenklatura 18, 19, 20, 34, 36, 263
Non-material benefits 32
North American Free Trade Agreement 24

Olympics 9, 63, 73
One country, one system 17, 235, 254
One country, three systems 238
One country, two systems 1, 2, 3, 4, 5, 7, 10, 16, 29, 3, 35, 36, 40, 44, 45, 52, 53, 54, 65, 68, 70, 71, 76, 77, 78, 79, 89, 92, 97, 100, 130, 132, 135, 148, 167, 178, 180, 227, 229, 231, 232, 233, 234, 235, 236, 237, 238, 239, 241, 243, 245, 247, 249, 251, 25 253, 254, 255, 258, 259, 260, 262, 273, 284, 292, 305, 306, 307, 310, 312, 318, 320, 321
One Country Two Systems Economic Institute 66, 177

Partyization 20
Patrimonialism 200, 201, 224, 261, 264, 301, 312, 320
Patriotism 10, 12, 15, 20, 45, 48, 58, 63, 74, 140, 151, 170, 171, 172, 173,

178, 179, 181, 255, 256, 274, 275, 295, 317
  blind 255
  rational 15
Patron-client pluralism 7, 9, 11, 13, 15, 17, 19, 21, 23, 25, 27, 29, 31, 33, 35, 37, 258, 261
Patron-clientelism 7, 32, 33, 34, 74, 236, 254, 255, 258
Patron-clientelist exclusionism 151, 170
Patronage 32, 34, 44, 46, 47, 223, 265, 268, 320
Patten, Christopher 47, 49, 54, 115, 123, 158, 180, 272, 288, 297, 312
Peace Accord or Pact 245, 248, 249
Pearl River Delta 24, 26, 276, 321
People's Liberation Army 135, 136, 178, 292
People's Republic of China 1, 2, 3, 4, 7, 8, 9, 10, 11, 12, 13, 14, 15, 16, 17, 18, 19, 21, 22, 23, 25, 26, 28, 29, 34, 35, 36, 37, 39, 40, 41, 42, 43, 44, 45, 46, 47, 48, 49, 51, 52, 53, 54, 56, 57, 59, 63, 65, 67, 68, 70, 71, 72, 73, 74, 75, 76, 78, 79, 81, 82, 84, 88, 92, 97, 98, 100, 101, 102, 104, 107, 108, 111, 114, 115, 116, 117, 123, 124, 129, 130, 133, 134, 135, 138, 139, 140, 141, 146, 148, 151, 152, 164, 165, 167, 168, 170, 172, 173, 174, 175, 176, 179, 180, 181, 182, 183, 185, 189, 197, 198, 199, 201, 206, 213, 215, 216, 218, 223, 224, 225, 227, 228, 229, 230, 231, 232, 233, 234, 235, 237, 238, 239, 240, 241, 242, 243, 244, 245, 246, 247, 248, 249, 250, 251, 252, 253, 254, 255, 256, 257, 259, 260, 262, 264, 265, 267, 268, 270, 271, 272, 276, 278, 281, 287, 288, 290, 301, 306, 308, 318
Phoenix 2, 179, 180, 182, 261, 296, 297

Police 26, 30, 41, 45, 136, 153, 156, 157, 159, 173, 180, 214, 236, 247, 292, 305, 316
Political bias 179, 217, 218
Political correctness 21, 43, 45, 177, 178, 179, 180, 182, 212, 254, 260, 263, 303
Political culture 4, 36, 71, 170, 199, 200, 223
  Hong Kong's 4, 17, 71, 199, 200, 201, 203, 204, 205, 207, 209, 211, 213, 215, 217, 219, 221, 223, 225, 256, 300
  mainland's political culture, 11, 145, 171, 200, 201, 223, 224, 225, 245, 258, 264, 267, 275, 311
Political parties 11, 57, 118, 148, 196, 210, 213, 265, 320
Political reform 3, 14, 16, 17, 23, 49, 54, 56, 57, 67, 68, 75, 77, 114, 115, 118, 119, 120, 124, 133, 134, 141, 142, 154, 158, 162, 169, 170, 171, 181, 200, 202, 214, 216, 222, 225, 256, 257, 258, 268, 270, 272, 273, 288, 297, 302, 313, 314, 316
Portugal 236, 237, 259
Prevention of Bribery Ordinance 34
Principal Officials Accountability System 3, 4, 30, 33, 34, 47, 50, 51, 115, 116, 119, 122, 123, 124, 129, 132, 271, 289
Pro-democracy 2, 10, 20, 31, 57, 62, 67, 68, 123, 125, 133, 136, 139, 145, 153, 160, 172, 173, 180, 181, 197, 199, 200, 202, 204, 206, 212, 213, 217, 218, 222, 224, 236
  activists 54, 58, 73
  elites 11, 16, 17, 23, 30, 36, 48, 68, 133, 141, 146, 148, 170, 253, 254
  movement 78, 214, 300, 314
  parties 56, 142, 213
Pro-independence 1, 13, 16, 37, 172, 182, 198, 240, 242, 246, 247, 248, 259

Protests   8, 15, 24, 27, 33, 40, 41, 46, 48, 52, 56, 63, 69, 73, 74, 114, 124, 126, 127, 131, 136, 139, 141, 153, 155, 156, 158, 161, 165, 166, 172, 174, 176, 179, 180, 202, 236, 247, 262, 264, 271, 276, 287, 291, 292, 293, 296, 315, 316
Public opinion   21, 35, 36, 104, 105, 106, 117, 122, 132, 155, 157, 158, 168, 177, 203, 217, 219, 240, 241, 242, 243, 248, 252
Public Security Bureau   58, 91, 173, 273

Qian, Qichen   22, 98
Qiao, Xiaoyang   23, 61, 84, 98, 102, 213, 216, 257, 278
Qing dynasty   90, 145, 181

Radio Television Hong Kong   129, 177, 268, 291, 303, 315
Rao, Geping   17, 135, 292, 318, 319
Reunification   1, 37, 40, 65, 79, 148, 151, 182, 233, 234, 235, 238, 240, 247, 248, 250, 251, 252, 253, 259, 260, 301, 306, 312
Right of abode   3, 13, 14, 50, 59, 60, 81, 82, 83, 84, 85, 86, 87, 89, 90, 91, 92, 93, 95, 96, 97, 98, 101, 102, 104, 105, 107, 113, 130, 134, 281, 283, 285
Rule by law   201
Rule of law   3, 10, 16, 34, 36, 42, 43, 65, 70, 76, 87, 90, 100, 103, 104, 105, 106, 159, 160, 161, 163, 201, 239, 253, 254, 268, 274, 277, 279, 280, 282, 284, 285, 293, 310, 317, 321

SCNPC   13, 14, 15, 27, 56, 57, 59, 60, 61, 62, 65, 73, 75, 76, 81, 82, 83, 84, 86, 87, 88, 90, 91, 92, 93, 94, 95, 96, 98, 99, 100, 101, 102, 103, 104, 105, 106, 107, 108, 113, 114, 115, 130, 134, 136, 144, 145, 146, 147, 148, 161, 250, 257, 258, 274
Scott, James   29, 34, 261
Sedition   2, 40, 50, 122, 138, 161, 202, 234
Self-censorship   3, 32, 42, 70, 138, 151, 175, 176, 177, 181, 182, 218, 222, 239, 255, 263, 277, 296
Separate voting mechanism   115
Severe Acute Respiratory Syndrome   2, 23, 28, 40, 45, 46, 66, 122, 126, 127, 128, 131, 159, 160, 165, 215, 236, 269, 290, 312, 316
Shanghai   12, 22, 51, 67, 71, 233, 273
Shenzhen   8, 12, 14, 25, 26, 27, 28, 50, 61, 65, 66, 143, 153, 166, 261, 315
Shiu, Sin-por   66, 86
Sing Tao Daily   218, 219
Singapore   12, 231, 243, 244, 245, 246, 249, 252, 263, 270, 305, 310
Sino-British Joint Declaration   117, 239, 241, 259
Sino-British negotiation   5, 231, 237, 240, 241, 242, 249, 260
Sino-Portuguese negotiation   237, 247, 251
Sit, Victor   85, 94, 187, 192
Socialism   10, 34, 135, 232, 233, 262
Soft power   71, 72, 277, 317
Soong, James   240
South China Morning Post   105, 224
Sovereignty   1, 3, 8, 16, 17, 39, 54, 56, 111, 133, 134, 136, 140, 151, 199, 233, 235, 236, 237, 240, 246, 249, 252, 253, 266, 267, 276, 287, 300, 301, 313, 314, 320, 321
Spirit of compromise   200
 of concessions   239, 240, 246, 258, 260
 of consensus   238, 245, 246, 252, 258, 259, 260

Spy   21
State Council   22, 22, 39, 40, 49, 57, 82, 98, 99, 101, 114, 129, 167, 216, 274, 283, 307, 308
Stock market   11, 12, 15, 18, 28, 29, 35, 65, 143
Strategic Development Commission   44, 68, 69
Subversion   2, 40, 50, 122, 138, 161, 202, 234
Surveillance   138, 139, 148, 236, 293, 313, 314
Szeto, Wah   171, 172, 297

Taiwan   1, 4, 5, 13, 16, 17, 36, 37, 40, 52, 54, 56, 57, 65, 72, 78, 79, 107, 108, 131, 132, 135, 140, 148, 149, 167, 169, 170, 171, 172, 174, 181, 182, 183, 186, 198, 218, 224, 225, 226, 227, 228, 229, 230, 231, 232, 233, 234, 235, 237, 238, 239, 240, 241, 242, 243, 244, 245, 246, 247, 248, 249, 250, 251, 252, 253, 254, 256, 257, 258, 259, 260, 275, 276, 296, 297, 301, 305, 306, 311, 314, 315, 316, 319, 321
Taiwan Basic Law   248, 249, 250 (also see Basic Law)
Taiwan corruption   259
Taiwan democracy   174, 229, 235, 260
Taiwan's political future   260
Taiwan's referendum   239, 240, 248, 249, 252
Taiwan's self-determination   241, 252
Taiwanization of Hong Kong   13, 256
of the PRC   37
Tam, Maria   90, 92, 95, 171, 187, 191, 280, 281
Tam, Yiu-chung   100, 169
Tang, Henry   122, 208
Tang, King-shing   136

Thatcher, Margaret   236
Tiananmen Incident   8, 11, 19, 21, 36, 148, 170, 276
Tong, Ronny   60, 174, 218, 291
Treason   2, 40, 50, 122, 138, 161, 202, 234
Triad   262
Tsang, Donald   1, 2, 3, 4, 9, 11, 13, 19, 20, 23, 26, 28, 30, 32, 33, 39, 43, 44, 47, 49, 53, 61, 68, 70, 77, 114, 119, 128, 130, 132, 139, 140, 141, 154, 169, 178, 179, 202, 204, 206, 207, 216, 218, 220, 223, 225, 253, 256, 258, 270, 296, 304
Tsang, Hin-chi   95, 171, 187, 209
Tsang, Jasper Yok-sing   2, 19, 46, 118, 154, 155, 157, 178, 179, 193, 222, 223, 303
Tsang, Tak-sing   19, 187, 189, 191
Trust   5, 45, 52, 140, 155, 158, 171, 215, 225, 227, 228, 231, 236, 237, 239, 242, 243, 244, 252, 259, 260
Tung, Chee-hwa   1, 2, 3, 4, 11, 13, 14, 17, 18, 21, 22, 23, 25, 26, 30, 32, 33, 35, 36, 39, 41, 42, 43, 44, 45, 46, 47, 48, 49, 50, 51, 52, 53, 54, 55, 56, 57, 58, 59, 60, 61, 62, 63, 65, 66, 68, 70, 72, 73, 74, 75, 76, 77, 83, 95, 97, 98, 99, 102, 114, 115, 116, 118, 119, 122, 124, 125, 126, 127, 128, 129, 130, 131, 134, 136, 139, 140, 143, 152, 153, 154, 155, 156, 157, 158, 159, 160, 165, 166, 167, 168, 169, 179, 189, 196, 199, 202, 205, 215, 216, 223, 236, 253, 255, 258, 264, 266, 268, 269, 270, 271, 279, 285, 286, 288, 289, 290, 291, 293, 298, 299, 307, 310, 315, 316
TVB   2, 175, 176, 177, 182

Underground Chinese Communist Party   18, 19, 20, 33, 141, 142

United front   4, 18, 19, 30, 32, 40, 44, 49, 52, 124, 142, 148, 157, 158, 161, 164, 169, 170, 171, 172, 173, 174, 175, 181, 182, 183, 195, 196, 197, 203, 263, 264, 270, 272, 274, 293, 295, 316, 318
   united front cadre   272
   united front campaign   172, 173, 175
   united front organization   19, 44, 142
   united front strategy   44, 197, 263, 270, 318
   united front tactics   32, 169, 170, 181, 182
   united front work   4, 18, 49, 52, 148, 171, 174, 181, 182, 183, 263, 264, 270, 274, 293, 295, 316
United States   21, 61, 71, 160, 171, 172, 174, 229, 244, 247, 252, 254, 255
Universal suffrage   12, 13, 56, 57, 114, 115, 132, 134, 137, 140, 141, 148, 154, 162, 170, 171, 172, 174, 176, 180, 181, 186, 199, 211, 212, 217, 221, 223, 225, 234, 255, 257, 258, 259, 301, 305, 310, 320

Wang, Zhenmin   17, 60, 135, 178, 292, 294, 320
Washington   229, 267
Wen Jiabao   39, 50, 153, 165, 216, 223

Wen Wei Po   24, 122
Western civilization   16, 18, 36, 43, 174, 181
Western-style democracy   12, 13, 16, 37, 41, 51, 132, 174, 234, 252
Women trafficking   26
Wong, Andrew   116, 118, 288
Wong, Raymond   32, 40, 52, 56, 57, 162, 165, 218, 263, 266, 293
Wu, Bangguo   22, 23, 217
Wu, Gordon   25, 66, 75
Wu, Raymond   90, 171, 187, 191, 269, 280, 281

Xenophobic sentiment   174, 181, 234
Xiao, Weiyun   17, 89, 123, 170, 271, 277, 321
Xinhua   57, 84, 171, 297
Xu, Chongde   17, 60, 88, 130, 140, 141, 171
Xu, Jiatun   21, 264, 321

Yang, Ti-Liang   216
Ye, Jianying   250, 258
Yeoh, Eng-kiong   123, 126, 269, 290

Zeng, Qinghong   22, 40, 124
Zhao, Ziyang   236
Zhou, Nan   21, 176, 179
Zhu, Yucheng   20, 22, 23
Zhuhai   25, 26, 27, 28, 35, 51, 66, 88, 143